P9-DMI-273

'Le pur-sang des automobiles'

Fourth Edition

H.G. Conway

B U G

Le pur-sang d

T T I

es automobiles

BUGATTI

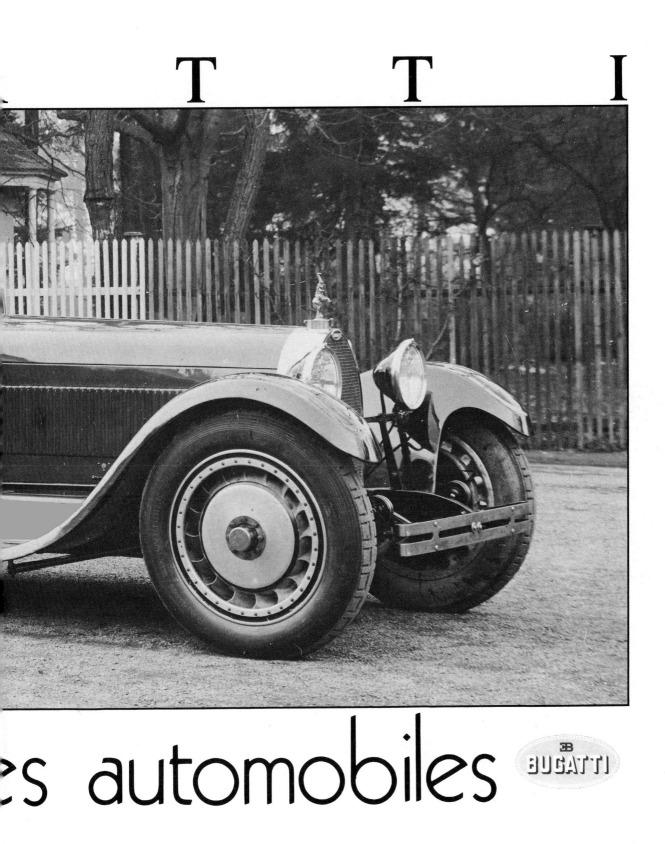

ISBN 0 85429 538 0

A FOULIS Motoring Book

First edition 1963
Reprinted October 1964
Reprinted October 1965
Second edition 1968
Third edition 1974
Reprinted April 1975
Reprinted September 1979
Fourth edition published 1987

Published by:
Haynes Publishing Group
Sparkford, Near Yeovil, Somerset BA22 7JJ

Haynes Publications Inc.
861 Lawrence Drive, Newbury Park, California 91320, USA

British Library Cataloguing in Publication Data
Conway, Hugh
Bugatti: le pur-sang des automobiles.—4th ed.
1. Bugatti automobile—History
I. Title
629.2′222 TL215.B82
ISBN 0–85429–538–0

Library of Congress catalog card number 86-82635

Editor: Mansur Darlington,
Layout design: Mike King
Printed in England, by: J.H. Haynes & Co. Ltd.

Ettore Bugatti, 1881–1947

Contents

PART II – HISTORICAL INFORMATION

PART III – BUGATTI MISCELLANY

PART IV – THE BUGATTI CLUBS

APPENDICES

Foreword to the Fourth Edition

THIS BOOK was originally written almost twenty five years ago and seems to have met with a certain approval from those interested all over the world in the Bugatti automobile, and indeed in the personality of Ettore Bugatti himself. Interest has grown, too, in the remarkable works in other fields of the father Carlo, the brother Rembrandt and, as we identify his special talents, the son Jean. The book set out – successfully, one hopes – to record an accurate description of the cars, and as new editions were issued the level of detailed accuracy could be improved as more knowledge came to light.

This new, fourth, edition has been considerably revised without changing the original format, which relied to a considerable degree on contemporary descriptions of new models as they appeared, many of the texts having a particular charm, helping to preserve the impact of the vehicles on the culture of the period. Few of us can comprehend life without the modern road network and the cheap and reliable motor car, whose performance can exceed easily the best of sports cars of 50 or 60 years ago. It does us good in more ways than one to have a chance of a drive in the older ones!

Some technical material on the racing Bugattis has been omitted as it is available in more detail elsewhere. Nor has an attempt been made to make more than passing reference to the furniture or animal sculpture of the other Bugattis, also available in other works. The layout of the book, concentrating first on the Molsheim built 'real' Bugattis, and adding later information of early pre-Molsheim activity, remains.

Since work was first started around 1961 many friendships have been made providing invaluable information. The enormous help of the elder daughter L'Ebé has always been acknowledged, but she and her sister Lidia, Countess de Boigne are no longer with us. Elizabeth Junek has been another willing helper with personal knowledge of Bugatti and racing in the 1920s. Noel Domboy, who designed into practice much of Bugatti's ideas from 1932 has opened wide a remarkable memory. Finally, among those not directly associated with Bugatti and Molsheim must be put first Uwe Hucke, who acquired much of the family records on the death of Roland Bugatti, and who has generously allowed access to documents invaluable in providing accuracy, and who shared many a day of stimulating debate on conclusions to be drawn from the evidence.

'Every day you learn something' is an old adage and true indeed in Bugatti matters. None of us was there at the time and thus conclusions may sometimes be wrong, or perhaps right for the wrong reasons. But we are getting more accurate as time and study pass!

Foreword to the original Edition

THE ORIGINAL Bugatti Book, Published in 1954, was the outcome of a great deal of hard work on the text and illustrations by C.W.P. Hampton. Hampton was, at the time, Editor of *Bugantics*, the journal of the Bugatti Owners' Club of England, a weekend labour of love if ever there was one. While the Book, no doubt, had a few editorial faults, it was packed with information and is probably the principal reason for the resurgence of interest in the marque Bugatti. It has been bedside reading all over the world.

In this revised or new Bugatti Book another Author has been roped in with the full support of the previous ones, and some effort has been made to eliminate editorial faults, and to correct a few errors which have come to light. The main change has been to separate information on each model or type, so that data can be found more quickly. The bulk of the text on the various cars is thus new and wherever possible more contemporary comment has been added from appropriate motor journals. Additional historical data have been included on early cars and Bugatti aero-engines, and a selection of extracts from folklore is included for interest and, perhaps, enjoyment.

The Register of Bugatti cars, now totalling about 1,100 cars, has been published by the Bugatti Owners' Club and makes an excellent companion to this volume.

Special thanks must be made to a number of people who have contributed: to Mr C.W.P. Hampton for much help with many things; to him and Mr J. Lemon Burton for checking the technical data on each model; to (Mr F. Seyfried) at Molsheim; Mr Tim Cree; (Mr J. de Dobbeleer); Mr S. Falise and Mr E.J. de Flines; Mr O.A. Phillips in Los Angeles; Mr D. Park in Chicago and others in the United States. To (Mr W.F. Bradley) in Roquebrune who discussed Ettore at length; and to (Mr Jules Goux, Dr Espanet and Mr Maurice Phillipe) who corresponded freely. And finally Mr T.A.S.O. Mathieson in Portugal has been an unfailing source of historical detail.*

Acknowledgements must be gratefully made to the Editors of the *Autocar, The Motor* and *Motor Sport* for permission to reproduce text and illustrations from early copies of these two journals. As far as possible the source of illustrations and short extracts has been given, as well as the authorship of various contributions.

*We have shown in brackets those no longer with us in 1986.

Introduction

THE CASUAL reader or the idly curious may well ask – what is there about a Bugatti that makes so many people dream of owning one, and a surprising number actually succeeding in doing so? There are many cars offering far better performance than a Type 57, many vintage racing cars that can outdo the normal GP Bugatti, and perhaps other more sensible playthings than a 1923 Brescia for the impecunious enthusiast; but once 'bitten with the Bug.' the Bugattiste regards his car beyond all others, and even after selling it (usually in a fit of irritation) remains faithful to its memory until the end!

The success of the original Bugatti Book and the appearance of a new one result from the widespread interest in the car, its creator Ettore Bugatti and all aspects of its 'folklore'. Mystique is perhaps the word for the Bugatti atmosphere which Ettore Bugatti managed to create not latterly, not even during his successful racing period in the 1920s, but even before the First World War in his first years at Molsheim, 1910–14.

There are keen Bugatti Clubs in Britain, USA, Australia, Germany, Holland, Switzerland, and two in France: one in Alsace, the other based on Paris. There are groups of enthusiasts in Spain, Japan, South Africa, New Zealand and Argentina.

A major stimulus taking the recognition of Bugatti beyond the cars has been the growth of interest (and thus value) in the works of Carlo and Rembrandt Bugatti, culminating in the memorable Amazing Bugatti Exhibition at the Royal College of Art in London in 1979. This exhibition brought together the creative works of this unique family by displaying furniture, silversmithing, animal sculpture, engine and chassis work, and superb coachwork, even leather harness items, under one integrated roof; it was followed by similar exhibitions in Paris and Hamburg.

This broadening of the artistic base of the name Bugatti seems to have heightened the interest in the cars. The reasons are perhaps not difficult to understand. Many men, and a few women, love cars, particularly sports cars; many would enjoy owning a vintage car in

this day when cars are built (admittedly well) for driving and not to tinker with. And again many would enjoy searching for, buying, cheaply and restoring more or less completely an old quality car. And a Bugatti is a good choice for a variety of reasons. Almost all models have a good or at least interesting performance – they are enjoyable to drive. Indeed there is a wide variety of models to choose from and a remaining population of at least 1,800 cars. Spare parts can be obtained, either new or second hand, from several sources; advice is freely obtainable from the Clubs or from other owners; technical data, some in considerable detail, have been published on most models; the construction of the cars while complicated in some respects is surprisingly straightforward in most; accessibility is good. The car was made and finished well when it was new and calls for craftsmanship and care now – it is thus satisfying to work on. And if you think your car is well restored there is always another chap (perhaps with more money to spend than you) with a better one, to keep you humble.

Most countries tolerate old cars on the road, if in good mechanical condition, and many do not expect modern improvements such as seat-belts and flashing indicators; several have reduced-rate licence fees. Old cars on the road add to the colour of the scene, give pleasure to the viewing public, and are indeed part of a heritage not to be forgotten. And a Bugatti is always interesting, often beautiful, and most of them produce a sound that delights the ear!

BUGATTI

BUGATTI

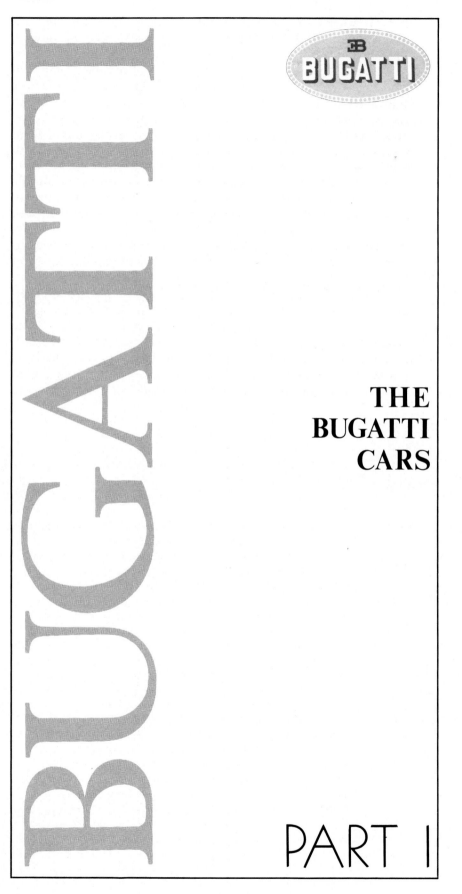

THE BUGATTI CARS

PART I

Bugatti types

ETTORE BUGATTI'S life as an automobile designer can conveniently be divided into three eras: the period during which he acted as a consulting designer (1898–1909); the main period at Molsheim* when he became a manufacturer in his own right (1910–39), interrupted during the first world war by a period of activity on aero-engines in Paris, and a final phase during and after the Second World War when a variety of products and a few unsuccessful cars were produced. In this book we are concerned mainly with the Molsheim-produced cars (Types 13 to 59), but we include some information on the later, twilight era cars (T60 to T102); pre-Molsheim cars and aero-engines are dealt with later in the book.

The cars are described under type numbers, but a few preliminary remarks are appropriate for the benefit of those who are not familiar with Bugatti cars or not well versed in the jargon of the Bugatti enthusiast. All Molsheim cars had either 4, 8 or 16 cylinders; no 6 cylinder Bugatti car was ever produced. All Molsheim-sold cars had overhead camshafts and, from 1912–13, the characteristic reversed quarter-elliptic rear springs. Although the front suspension of the FWD Type 53 was independent, all other models had conventional fore-and-aft laminated front springs. Light alloy castings were used extensively in the cars from the earliest model. Even to the inexperienced eye a similarity between the earliest and the latest model can be seen, particularly in the detail design of the rear axle or the gearboxes. Other items such as the steering box or clutch were used on several models over a period of twenty years. The predominant nut up to about 1924 was 6 mm, thereafter until 1939 (and later) a 7 mm nut with a milled hexagon to give an integral washer, a simple enough detail but one which epitomizes Bugatti's approach to automobile design – quality as he judged it (and he often judged wrongly), uncompromised by manufacturing costs.

The type numbers of Bugatti cars continued to interest many people, particularly as some numbers are missing or their identification is in dispute. The tabulation lists the correct identifications with all the authority that Bugatti Works catalogues and research by the author in the drawing office library at Molsheim can justify.† The existing drawing

* Pronounced 'Moltz-heim', rhyming with 'waltz-time'.

† The factory originally used the designation 607 for the 8 valve cars, 617 for the first series 16 valve and 619 for the early Brescia type, although the usual numbering system was used in catalogues. We also have contemporary evidence that the factory used the prefix 6 on most of the models, e.g. 635, 639 etc, for T35, T39. It has not been possible to find the reasons for this alternative system.

office records are incomplete, the official records having suffered during the Occupation and memories are faulty, so a few gaps are still present; one thing is clear however, that Bugatti used type numbers as much to identify chassis length as anything else in early days.

Bugatti Type Numbers

Pre-Molsheim cars

Type	*Model*	*Year*
1	Prinetti & Stucchi Tricycle	1899
2	4-cylinder car, 90 × 120 mm	1900
3	16 hp de Dietrich, 114 × 130 mm	1901
4	24 hp de Dietrich, 124 × 130 mm	1902
5	50 hp de Dietrich, 160 × 160 mm (Paris-Madrid)	1903
6	Mathis	1904
7	Mathis	1904–5
8	Deutz, chain drive	1907
9	Deutz, shaft drive	1908–9
10	'Pur-Sang', 62 × 100 mm	1909
11	–	
12	–	

Molsheim-built cars

13	8 valve, 4 cylinder, 2 m wheelbase	1910–20
	16 valve, 4 cylinder, 2 m wheelbase	1914, 1920 on
14	–	
15	8 valve, 4 cylinder, 2·4 m wheelbase	1911–13
16	(100 × 160 mm engine for Prince Henri Cup, probably engine in 471)	
17	8 valve, 4 cylinder, 2·55 m wheelbase	1911–13
18	Production 5 litre 'Garros' model	1913–14
19	Baby Peugeot licence car	1912
20	Larger Peugeot licence car	1912–13
21	–	
22	8 valve, 4 cylinder, 2·4 m wheelbase	1914–20
	16 valve, 4 cylinder, 2·4 m wheelbase	1921 on
23	8 valve, 4 cylinder, 2·55 m wheelbase	1914–20
	16 valve, 4 cylinder, 2·55 m wheelbase (a few with 8 cylinder engines)	1921 on
24	–	
25	As T22 with 8 valve 68 × 108 mm engine	1914
26	As T23 with 8 valve 68 × 108 mm engine	1914
27	Strictly engine only, 69 × 100 mm, 16 valve, but this designation used in France for 16 valve chassis	1914, 1920 on
28	Prototype 3 litre car, 69 × 100 mm, 8 cylinder	1921
29	Probably 1½ litre version of T30	1922
30/30A	2 litre, 60 × 100 mm, 8 cylinders, passenger car; 30A reinforced frame	1922–5
31	–	

Type	Model	Year
32	2 litre 'Tank' racer	1923
33	2 litre passenger car, gear box in rear axle, not produced	1923
34	2 bank, 16 cylinder, geared aero-engine	1923
35	8 cylinder GP (versions A, B, C, T)	1924 on
36	8 cylinder single seat racer, initially without rear springs	1925
37	4 cylinder 1·5 litre GP (37A with compressor, 1927)	1926
38	8 cylinder passenger car, 60 × 100 mm (38A with compressor, 1927)	1926
39	8 cylinder GP, 1½ litre, version of T35 (39A with compressor)	1926
40	4 cylinder 1½ litre passenger car with T37 engine (40A, 1·6 litre, 1929)	1926
41	8 cylinder Royale luxury car, 12·8 litres	1927
42	Marine engine	
43	8 cylinder, 2·3 litre, supercharged Grand Sport car (43A roadster, 1929)	1927
44	3 litre passenger car, 69 × 100 mm	1927
45	16 cylinder, 3·8 litre racer, supercharged	1928
46	5 litre passenger car (46S with compressor)	1929
47	Grand Sport version of T45	1928
48	Engine for Peugeot 201 X	1930–1
49	3·3 litre passenger car, 72 × 100 mm	1930
50	4·9 litre supercharged sports car (50T, Tourisme version)	1930
50B	Racing engine: B1, 4·7 litres, compressor, 84 × 107 mm B2, 4·5 litres, no compressor B3, 3·0 litres, compressor, 78 × 78 mm	1935–9
51	8 cylinder GP, twin cams, (51A = 1·5 litres)	1931
52	Baby electric	1927–31
53	4-wheel-drive racer	1932
54	4·9 litre GP racer	1931
55	8 cylinder, 2·3 litre, supercharged super-sports	1932
56	Electric runabout	
57	3·3 litre Touring car (57S sports, 57C and 57SC with compressors)	1934–9
57G	Tank racing car	1936
57S45	Tank racer, not proceeded with	1937
58	Diesel engine, conversion of T41 engine, for railcar	1934
59	3·3 litre GP racer	1933
60	4·1 litre, 4 valve 86 × 88 mm aero-engine, not made	
61	Railcar gear box and bevel drive	
62	Gear box for T59 with dry sump and pump	
63	Chassis with T50S (S = sport) engine	
64	3·3 litre T57 replacement, alloy frame, prototype only	1938–9

Type	*Model*	*Year*
65	Single cylinder, study only	1940
66	Aero-engine, 50B Type	1938
67	Aero-engine project, Vee, 4 valves, not made	1938–9
68	350 cc baby car, 48·5 × 50 mm., 4 valve	1942
69	–	
70	Hydraulic coupling of 4 engines	
71	Marine engine, 8 cylinders 140 × 150, 18·5 litres	
72	Cycle motor, 24 × 28 mm., 13 cc.	
73A	4 cylinder passenger car, 70 × 95 mm, 1·462 cc, compressor	1944–5
73C	4 cylinder racer, twin cam, 76 × 82 mm, 1488 cc, compressor	1945
74	Steam engine, 4 cylinders	
75	Single cylinder marine engine (for You-You), 60 × 60 mm, 3 valve	
76	Truck engine, 8 cylinder 65 × 90 mm	
77	Marine reverse gear, 100 hp	
78	8 cylinder touring engine 80 × 106 mm	
79	–	
80	Marine reverse gear for 12 cylinder Licorne engine	1949

(*Note: Many of the projects 60 to 80 were paper studies only*)

Projects after the death of Ettore Bugatti

101	Post-war version of T57	1951
102	4 cylinder sports car project	
251	8 cylinder racing car (designer: Colombo)	1956
252	4 cylinder sports car project	
451	16 cylinder project, not completed (designer: Noel Domboy)	1957

There are thus a few unidentified Type numbers, which may not indeed have been issued. It was only in the 1930s that the general public came to use these numbers, which were originally intended as reference numbers to appear on drawings. Later the convenience of using the Type numbers in Molsheim catalogues and price lists became obvious.

The drawings themselves sometimes have other suffix letters for convenience, for example 39D for a version of the T39, or 57bis for later Type 57 parts.

Note regarding car serial numbers

With few recorded exceptions, the Molsheim factory made use of a consistent series of chassis numbers, in numerical sequence for early cars, and with the type number followed by the car number from about 1928 onwards.

Eight valve cars were numbered from 361 in 1910 to 843 in 1920 with a few gaps. The 16 valve plain bearing cars were from 900 to 1611 although the Crossley-Bugattis were in the overlapping series 1600 to 1625; the 16 valve ball bearing Brescia cars started at 1612 up to about 2900. The engine number in all these cases rarely appears as a separate entry, although invariably found stampd on many engine parts, and on the front face of the crankcase.

Eight cylinder chassis (Types 30, 35 and 39) began at No. 4000 and finished before 5000, but engine numbers were stamped on the crankcase, generally a 1, 2 or 3 figure number. The earliest T35 is number 4323, and there is a small batch of T39 cars in the 4800 series. The cars as they left the factory often had the engine number repeated on gearbox and axles or a number close to it.

Types 37, 38, 40 and later have chassis numbers beginning with the type number, e.g. 37204. In the case of rare cars, the numbers do not necessarily start with 100, e.g. 47155 and 47156. These are one or two obscure numbers such as 222570 which cannot be explained, and 27150 which was a 'misprint'. After much research work, it can be said that no authentic case of duplicate numbers has been found, most anomalies being explained by restamping for special reasons. Many countries in Europe had been bedevilled during the war with fuel rationing, customs barriers and triptyques; at least several of the number anomalies encountered are known to have resulted from efforts to overcome these difficulties. At least one car entered a country as a Type 43 and left as a Type 44!

A persistent problem, much intensified in recent years with the increasing value of the cars, has been the restamping of numbers for fraudulent purposes, often to allow a car to be offered as a more worthy and valuable product - a 'genuine racing 35B' etc. The warning 'caveat emptor' can be repeated, pointing out that the main Bugatti Clubs, especially the Bugatti Owners Club, have access to authentic factory record data, and their experts can usually identify false number stamping.

Bugatti name plates

Before the first world war, when Molsheim was part of Germany, the car name plate read:

Ettore Bugatti
Molsheim i/Els (for Elsass)
Wagon No., Motor P.S., Gew kg

In the immediate post war period the name plates read:

Ettore Bugatti
Molsheim Alsace
Chassis, Moteur, Poids

In at least one case the engine power is quoted as 'hp'.

Finally the plates read:

Ettore Bugatti
Molsheim, Bas-Rhin
Chassis, Moteur, Poids,

the motor horsepower being given in the normal French 'cv'.

A rarity is a genuine car plate reading 'Ettore Bugatti, Paris' but under what circumstances these plates were issued is not known.

The 1913 engine had a new oil pump at the front of the camshaft.

valves and valve mechanism, the shape of the combustion chambers and the unrestricted flow of the intake and exhaust gases. But whatever the reason may be, the one fact stands out beyond question that the power is there, and this coupled with the efficient transmission and light total weight gives the car a speed which is only comparable with that usually associated with those of at least three times its nominal power.

Power and speed, however, are not the only, nor perhaps the most important, attributes of a car intended for use on the road. To find favour with the *cognoscenti*, it must also possess a sense of liveliness, a delicacy in responding to control movement, as ease of gear change, powerful and smooth brakes – in short, it must possess 'refinement'. It is in the possession of this complex quality that the Bugatti ceases to be a light car. Though light in weight and running expenses, no steps whatever have been taken to simplify the design with the aim of keeping down first cost; in fact, it is an automobile of the highest grade, *en miniature*.

Both the steering and suspension were everything to be desired. In respect to the first of these, we need only say that we have never handled a steering wheel that called for less physical exertion. The rear suspension is somewhat uncommon in form, its peculiar design perhaps accounting for its undoubted excellence.

The 8 valve car established Bugatti in the front rank of light-car manufacturers. The competition successes helped, especially a 'cheeky' entry in the 1911 Grand Prix de France at Le Mans, where Friderich came in second to Heméry on a large Fiat (being the only other car running at the end). But it was the light weight and excellent handling of the little car which were really the basis for its reputation.

Black Bess

4 cylinder 5 litre

IN 1912 BUGATTI began to build a batch of 4 cylinder, 5 litre chain driven cars for competition work. Many years later he claimed to have built the first of the model in 1908, no doubt referring to a Bugatti-designed Deutz car he drove in the Prince Henry trials in 1909 and 1910. Today we ascribe his Type 18 to the production batch. In January 1913 he wrote to his friend Dr Espanet: 'I have under construction several cars of 100 mm bore and 160 stroke. I would wish to have you as a customer for one of these cars if that would interest you and I would make you very special terms.... I would like very much to have you visit and I hope that you will profit from the trip of Mr Garros to come with him.'

Roland Garros was a well-known pioneer French aviator who was killed on operations at the end of the First World War. The car that Garros himself bought has had a remarkable history and seems today as good as ever; in 1935 Ettore wrote to Colonel Giles who had just bought the car, saying 'I only built a few cars of this type, which was one of the best models of the period. The first one was built in 1908 and the first sale was in 1912. The car which you have was delivered 18 September 1913 to my late regretted friend Garros, the airman of whom you have doubtless heard. This car has therefore an historical interest'.

This car was chassis 474, Bugatti himself using 471 in a few hill-climbs, including Mont Ventoux. It seems likely that 471 had a Deutz-related chassis with a new Molsheim built engine (Type 16). This engine had five plain crankshaft bearings although the later ones had three, and a very ineffective drip lubrication system. When Col. Giles acquired the Garros car he found the remains of 471 in Switzerland and bought if for spares. In the 1970s the car was rebuilt to completion and now performs well.

The Garros car came to Britain in the early 1920s and was much raced at Brooklands and elsewhere, being named 'Black Bess' by its driver Ivy Cummings, after the black horse of the infamous highwayman Dick Turpin.

Apart from 471 and 474, 715 remains unused and now in the National Museum in Mulhouse, 472 and 473 having disappeared; 716

Roland Garros with his car, bodywork by Labourdette.

Later the car came to England where it became known as Black Bess, and has been owned and maintained in fine condition by Mr C. W. P. Hampton; it is the only Molsheim model with chain-drive.

The engine of Black Bess, 5 litres, 3 valves per cylinder; the camshaft is built up and the rockers have rollers on their ends. There are three main bearings, but there is not yet a proper oil pump.

A pair of chassis at Molsheim in 1913 or 1914. The chassis has the reversed quarter-elliptic springs at the rear and chain drive. The additional oil tank on the crankcase at the front can be seen.

Right: *A Bugatti 'fiacre' style body, this time evidently on the shaft drive car which went to Indianapolis.*

An intriguing front view of the car and its honeycomb radiator.

may have been the Indianapolis car, making a total production of six.

The 5 litre car had a bore and stroke of 100 mm × 160 mm, a single overhead camshaft and, unlike the 8 and 16 valve cars (and earlier Deutz designs), had rockers between cams and valves. The general layout, however, is similar to the smaller engine, with a vertical bevel shaft driving the camshaft and a cross-shaft driving the pump and magneto. Bugatti now introduced the 3 valve arrangement (two inlet valves and one exhaust) which he was to use on the aero-engine and all 8 cylinder designs until the Type 50, almost twenty years later. A distinguishing feature on this model was the use of chain drive for the rear wheels. It seems likely that the assemblies used were at least similar to those of the Deutz car, which Bugatti had designed a year or two previously.

Bugatti, as Friderich recounts later in this book, drove one of these cars in various races, winning his class at Mont Ventoux in 1912. Ernest Friderich himself drove one of the cars in the 1914 Indianapolis race, although the car had the chain drive replaced with a normal rear axle and the stroke increased to 180 mm. A bearing failure in this unit eliminated the car.

Another chain driven car went to the USA for the 1915 race, entered under the nationality of Germany (America not being at war at that time), and now with a stroke of 150 mm to bring the engine capacity below the 300 cu in. limits specified. The standard dimension 100 × 160 mm would give 306 cu in. (These dimensions are from *Automotive Industries*, 6 May 1915, which quotes 3·9 in. × 5·9 in.; it is assumed

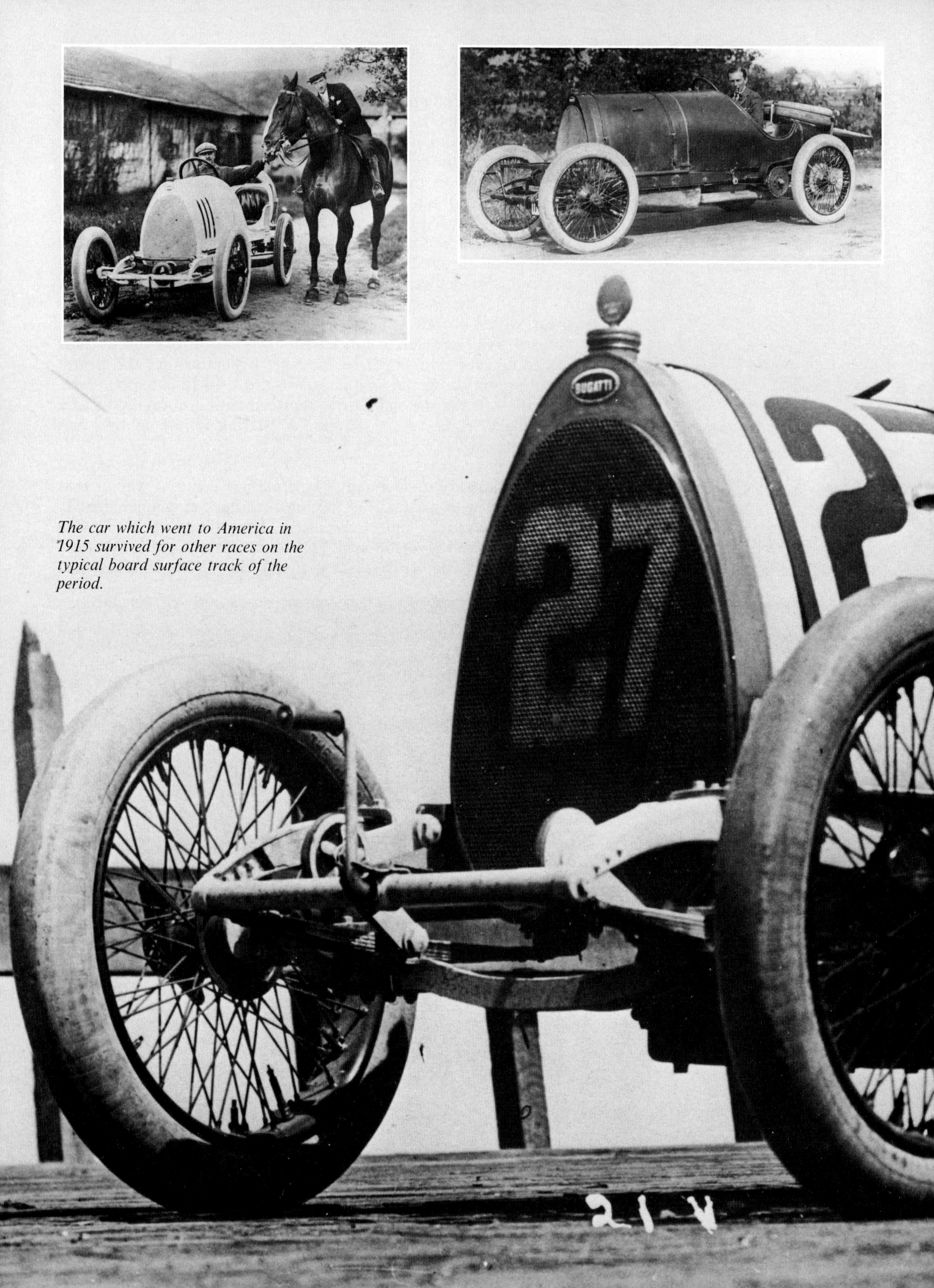

The car which went to America in 1915 survived for other races on the typical board surface track of the period.

Far left: *Friderich and Ettore before departure to America, in the shaft drive car.*

Left: *Duke Ludwig Wilhelm, known as the Prince of Bavaria, in Bayern. He was a personal friend of Bugatti and spent much time with him at Molsheim until separated by the War in August 1914.*

Above: *Bugatti turned up in the 5 litre car at Mont Ventoux, in 1912 with a cowl at the front and a tail at the rear, but seems to have left the cowl off for the event!*

Car 471 survived and has been rebuilt. It runs as well as it looks.

that 3·9 was really 3·94 or 100 mm.) The car was entered by C.W. Fuller of Pawtucket, Rhode Island, with B. Oldfield as the nominated driver. He did not like the car, not being able to better 81·5 mph in the timed trials, and threw a rod. Somehow the car seems to have been repaired as Mr J.R. Hill drove in the race, but the car was eliminated after twenty laps. The same car was then in that year driven by Johnny Marquis in the Vanderbilt Cup and the 400 mile Grand Prix of America without success, but managed a 4th place in the Grand Prix of California again in 1915. What happened then to the car is not known.

In 1919, Bugatti announced his intention to market the model alongside the 16 valve car but evidently did not do so.

He had taken chassis 715 with him to Italy when he left Molsheim when war began in August 1914, and must have contemplated using this car for racing.

The engine of 471.

J. R. Hill at Indianapolis in 1915. The car had problems.

16 valve 4 cylinder car

IF THE 8 valve pre-war cars established Bugatti as an independent manufacturer of consequence and one to be reckoned with in voiturette racing, it was the improved model with a 16 valve block, originally 66 mm × 100 mm, and then 68 × 100 and finally 69 × 100, which began Bugatti's decade of remarkable success in motor racing. In mid-1914 Bugatti produced a design for a new engine for his Type 13, to be designated Type 27, with 4 valves per cylinder operated as before by curved sliding tappets. The bore was increased to 66 mm which, with the existing 100 mm stroke crankshaft, gave a displacement of 1368 cc. The car was intended for the Grand Prix des Voitures Legères due to be run at Clermont-Ferrand on 23 August 1914. The race cancelled by events, the new blocks and camboxes were wrapped up and buried safely at Molsheim, when Ettore left, to be dug up after the war. Three T13s with the new 'Seize Soupapes' engines performed sensationally in the 1920 Coupe des Voiturettes at Le Mans, winning at a record speed of 57·6 mph over 256 miles. Other early successes were in the 1921 Brescia race, good runs in the 1921 200 mile race at Brooklands and the team prize in the 1922 TT. Raymond Mays took delivery of his first car in early 1922 (the famous Cordon Rouge) and began an unparalleled succession of seasons of wins at hill-climbs. Many famous drivers used the model.

The way the 16 valve engine could be tuned was astonishing. In touring trim, with plain bearings, it might rotate at 3,000 rpm and do about 70 mph, which coupled with typical Bugatti steering and road holding made it a most attractive sports car by contemporary standards. But the same engine, with ball crank bearings, was made to rotate at over 5,000 rpm by several drivers – Mays claims 6,700 – and could lap Brooklands at over 100 mph. Mays claims 6,900 rpm for his second ball bearing car (Cordon Bleu)! It is little wonder that various drivers fitted front wheel brakes for hill-climbs.

Not only successful in the sporting world, the 16 valve car created sufficient impression in the motoring world to enable Bugatti to sell licences to Rabag in Germany, Diatto in Italy and Crossley in England immediately after the first world war. None of these licences could have been particularly profitable to Bugatti, except in the short term enabling

him to expand his own Molsheim production, since only twenty-five or so cars were, in fact, produced under each licence. But licencing of the 16 valve car in three foreign countries undoubtedly did much to enhance Ettore's prestige abroad and must have helped Molsheim sales considerably. Further details of the licence-produced cars are given later.

What is now commonly called a Brescia started as a Type 13 with bolster tank at the rear and the minimum of bodywork, and, in its 1920 Le Mans form, is strictly a '16-valve'. Here is Pierre de Viscaya before the race. The engine was 66 × 100 mm for this race, but was soon enlarged. The first models had a single magneto, but later for the 1921 race at Brescia, where it swept all before it, it had twin magnetos mounted in the dash, and a ball bearing crankshaft.

Left: *The 1920–22 cars had a pear-drop radiator.*

The typical 16 valve and Brescia chassis, in this case a long wheel-base touring version.

Terminology

The 16 valve cars should be described as Types 13, 22 or 23 depending on the wheelbase which should be respectively 2, 2·4 or 2·55 metres. Type 13 was used exclusively for racing, originally with a plain bearing crankshaft, later with ball bearings (after the 1921 Brescia race success, when the model became known as the Brescia), and sometimes with twin, dash-mounted magnetos. The other two cars had proper coachwork, but continued to use the plain bearing crank, until for the last three years or so of production they were fitted with the ball bearing engine (and in 1926 front wheel brakes), and became known as the 'Modified Brescia' model; a 'Brescia' is strictly a short wheelbase car, but sometimes called a 'Full Brescia' although a few 'Full Brescia' standard cars were raced on the Type 22 frame, the longer wheelbase perhaps helping road holding.

The model develops

The car shown at the 1919 Olympia Show was 66 mm × 100 mm, fitted with a snappy three-seat clover-leaf body. The cars which won the 1920

Le Mans 1920, de Viscaya and the 16 year old Emil Mischall, who later was sent to open the Brixton Road Depot in London.

Le Mans were 16 valve, 66 mm × 100 mm models, at least one having 8 plugs, 4 each side (not 8 in line on one side). This is clearly illustrated in the 1921 catalogue. The two-spark single magneto used was at the front, as on the 8 valve engine, not with the double dash-mounting used on the later Brescia racing model. A contemporary account states that the other two cars had single ignition.

One of the 1920 Le Mans cars was sent to England and, registered as XE 6132, became the property of H.O.D. Segrave. It was fully described in the *Autocar* of 26 February 1921 in an article entitled 'The Racing Bugatti'. According to this article the car was standard, except that the bore was 65·64 mm, additional main bearing oil feeds were provided, the block had plugs on each side, a weird hot air inlet pipe led from exhaust manifold to carburettor across the back of the engine, and the front axle was up-swept rather more than usual to lower the car. The engine is stated to have developed 29·5 hp at 2,750 rpm.

At Brescia (8 September 1921), however, the cars were enlarged to 68 mm × 100 mm, and the crankshaft was mounted on ball bearings. The design of the front of the engine and the closeness of the vertical shaft driving the camshaft precluded fitting a ball race to the front bearing, and the plain bush was retained. However, the crank was split in the centre to allow use of a large double-row ball race, another being used at the rear. For Brescia the rods also had rollers, the caps being split, but as far as is known all similar models sold reverted to plain 'squirt lubricated' bronze big ends. Apparently on test the engines gave no increase in power, and the modification, introduced to avoid the disappointing bearing failure which had been experienced the previous year at Le Mans (see page 329), was removed after the race. Perhaps this accounts for the non-appearance of the team at the 1921 Le Mans race on 18 September although the cars did perform well at Brooklands in the JCC 200 mile race on 22 October. Meanwhile, the entry at Le Mans and in the 200 mile race showed the cars as 69 mm × 100 mm, not the 68 mm × 100 mm used at Brescia, giving the full 1·5 litres.

Right: *Friderich at the start of the 1920 race. Behind him is Charles Faroux, the doyen of French automobile journalists of the period.*

A GN and de Viscaya at the start; note the track surface.

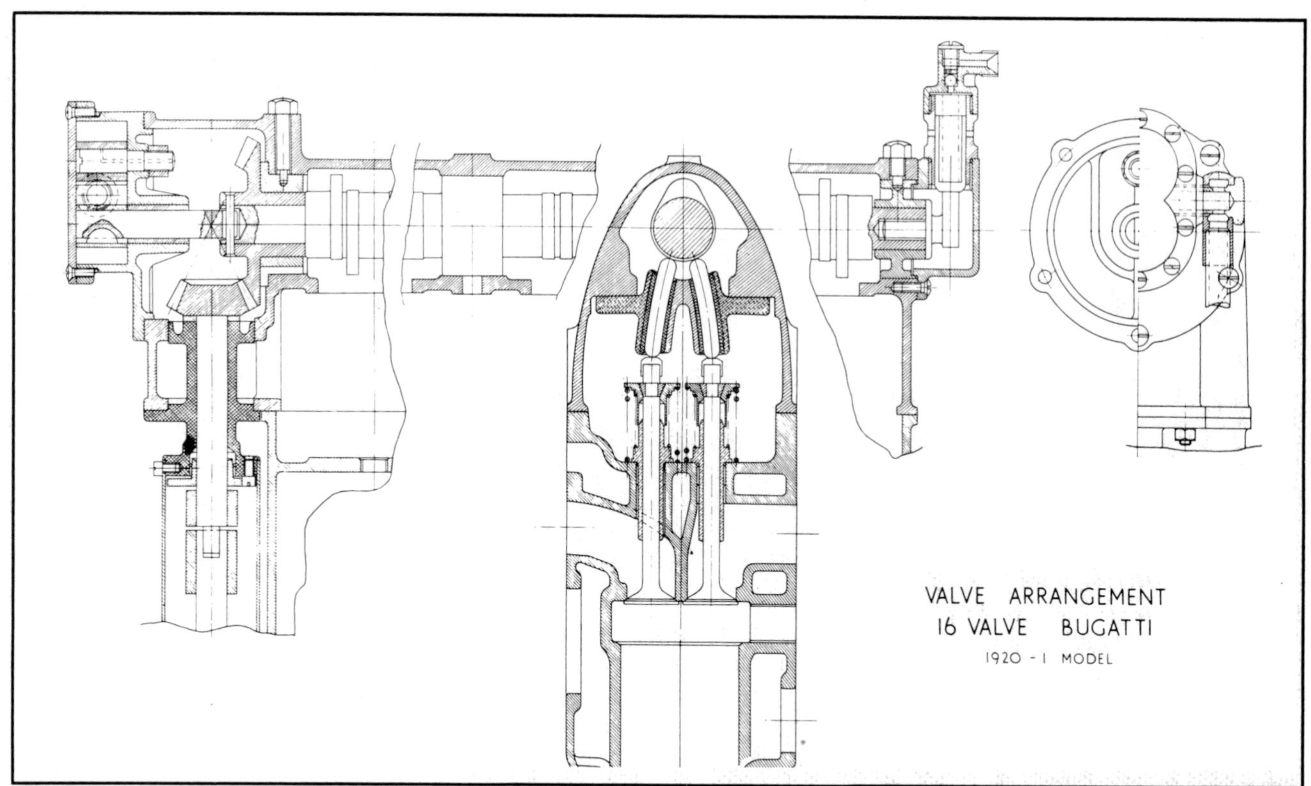

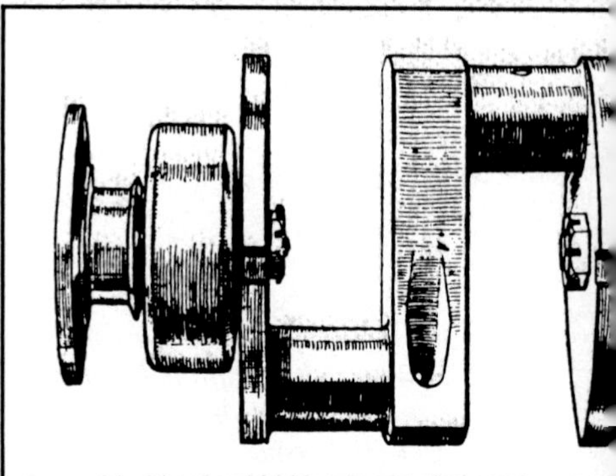

The original ball bearing crank used on the Brescia had scoops on the webs to receive oil; the crank was in two halves to allow assembly of the centre bearing.

A Max Millar drawing of the tappet block.

Valve operation was by curved tappets sliding in white-metal blocks; the oil pump is at the front, the air pump for pressurizing the fuel tank at the rear.

1921 Catalogue. This makes no mention of a short wheelbase Type 13. Some contemporary race references however give the wheelbase of the Brescia cars as 6 ft 5 in., which is 1·95 m (see below), and the 1920 Le Mans cars were certainly the same.

Summarized Data

	Type 22	*Type 23*
Engine, mm	68 × 100	68 × 100
Track, metres	1·15	1·15
Wheelbase, metres	2·4	2·55
Tyre size, mm	710 × 90	710 × 90

The 16 valve engine described in the catalogue has plain lead-bronze bearings and the cambox now uses a gear pump for lubrication, an improvement over the 8 valve engine. As compared with the earlier engine the carburettor and exhaust connections are reversed, the inlet being on the left-hand side with the water pump. The steering box is mounted directly on the chassis, and rear wheel brakes plus a transmission brake are used as in 1911. The radiator is now slightly higher with an aspect ratio of 10:7, still with a starting handle cut-out at the bottom.

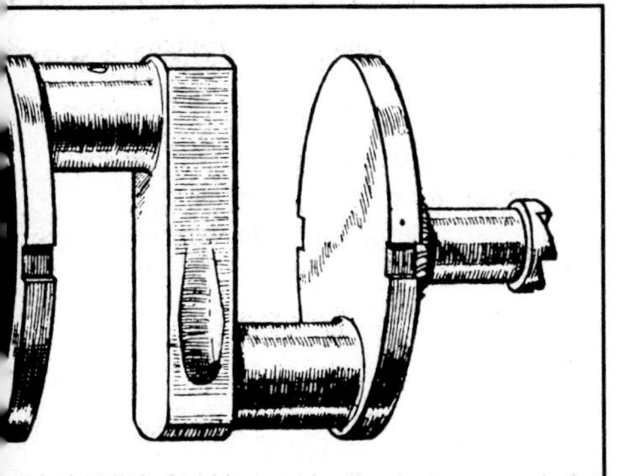

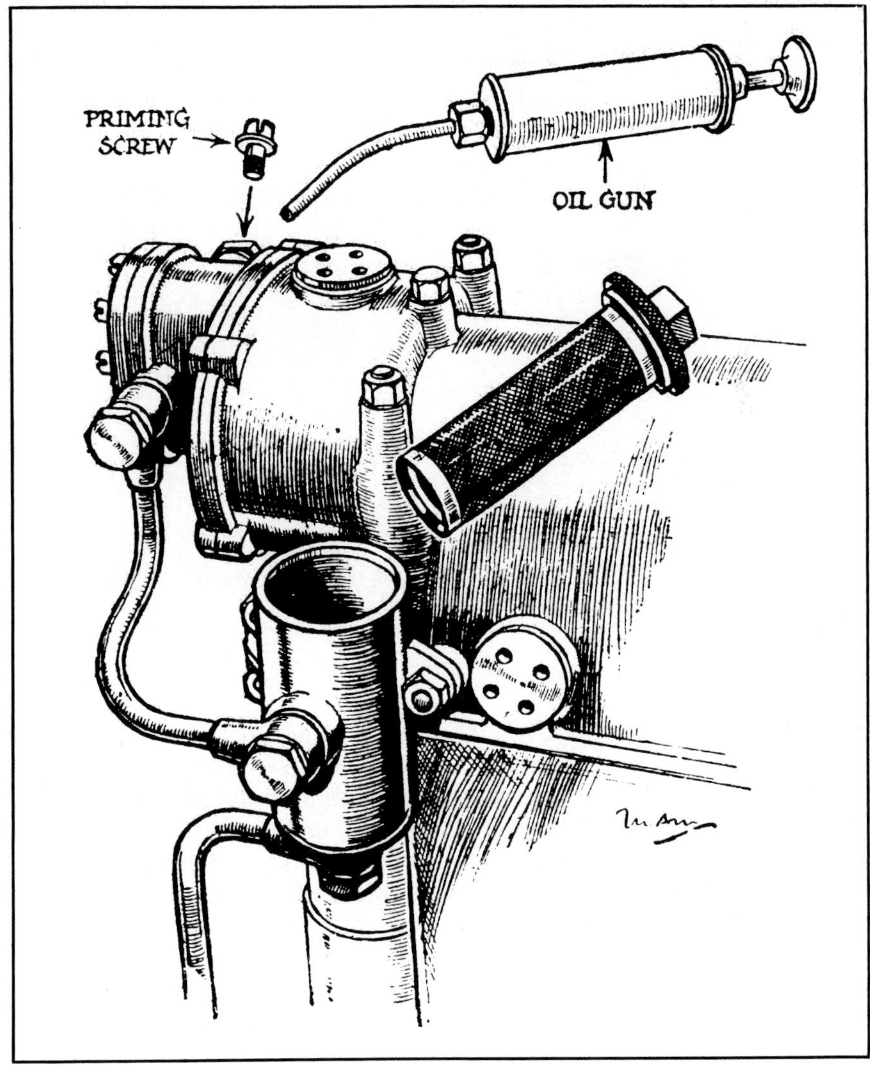

Oil filter and a very necessary priming screw for the pump.

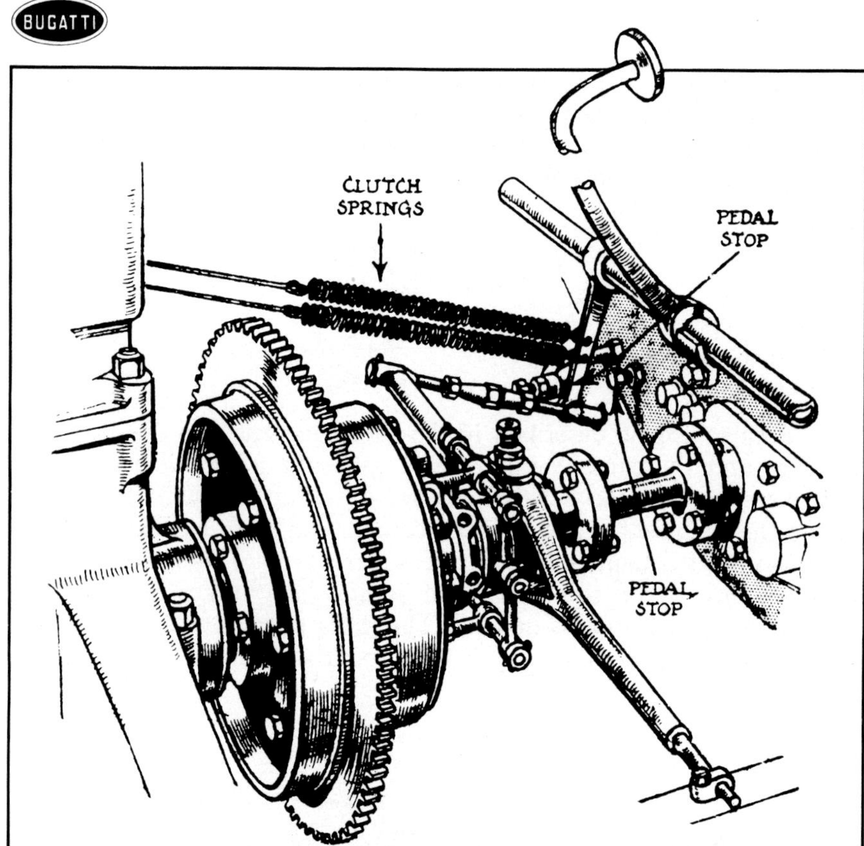

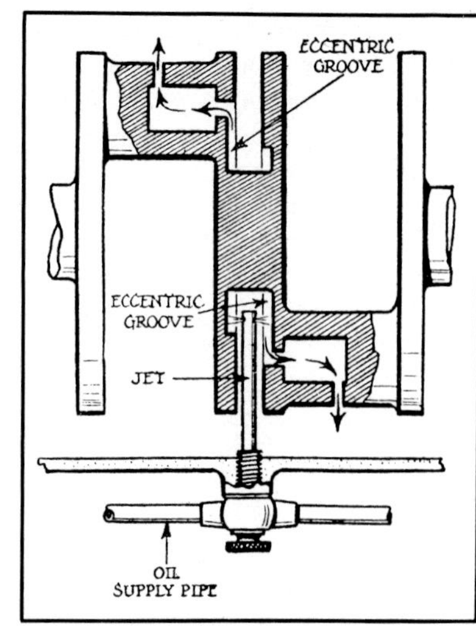

Later cranks had circular webs and oil fed sideways into grooves.

Clutch withdrawal mechanism. (Autocar, *2 and 9 July 1926*)

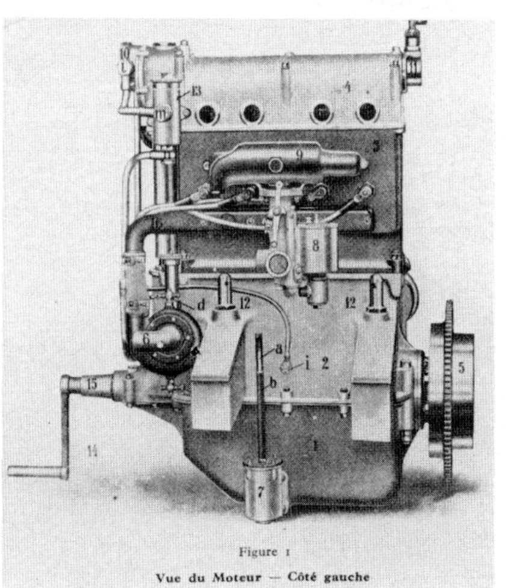

Figure 1
Vue du Moteur — Côté gauche

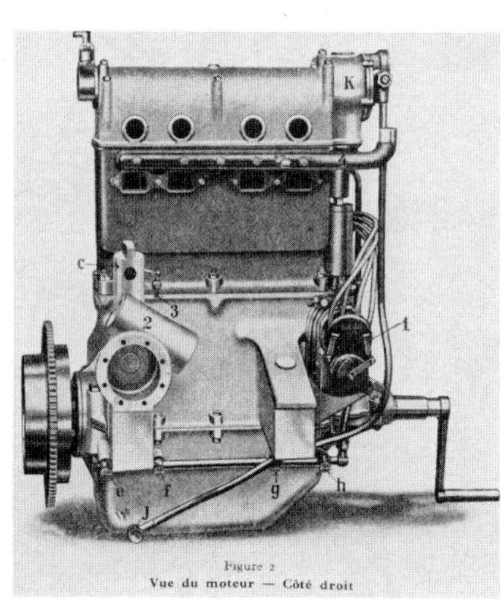

Figure 2
Vue du moteur — Côté droit

Far left: *The late Brescia engine as illustrated in the Works Instruction book. The oil feed to the centre main bearing is at 'i', and '13' is the oil filter. The flywheel has teeth for a starter motor.*

The steering box casing is part of the upper crankcase casting. The long oil pump suction pipe from 'j' to 'k' is a weakness, the pump often not priming. The big-end bearings get oil from jets at 'f' and 'g'.

1922–23 Catalogue. This contains the 1922 race results, but not the October Gaillon result, so no doubt was printed in October or November 1922. It states clearly that the 'firm of Bugatti manufactures three types of chassis (13, 22 and 23), that differ only in their "coachworkable" length'. The three main bearings are in lead-bronze as before. Bore and stroke are of 68 mm × 100 mm. The lubrication system consists of a gallery pipe in the crankcase with jets which project oil directly into scoops in the crank webs. Brakes are as before, the rear wheels having cast iron brake shoes, unlined, while the transmission brake is fitted with 'ferrodo'. The radiator seems to be the same as on the previous year. The cars shown at the 1922 Olympia Show conformed to this description.

Later cars had a dash-mounted dynamo, belt driven from the camshaft. Note the cast bulkhead.

The twin magneto drive with 2:1 step-up drive gears

Summarized Data

	Type 22	*Type 23*
Engine, mm	68 × 100	68 × 100
Track, metres	1·15	1·15
Wheelbase, metres	2·4	2·55
Tyre size, mm	710 × 90	710 × 90

There is still no catalogue information on Type 13.

At the Olympia Show in 1923, the 68 × 100 touring model was shown alongside the 69 × 100 'Modified Brescia' car, the latter being more expensive. In the *Automotor Journal* of 15 November, Mr E. Duffield wrote:

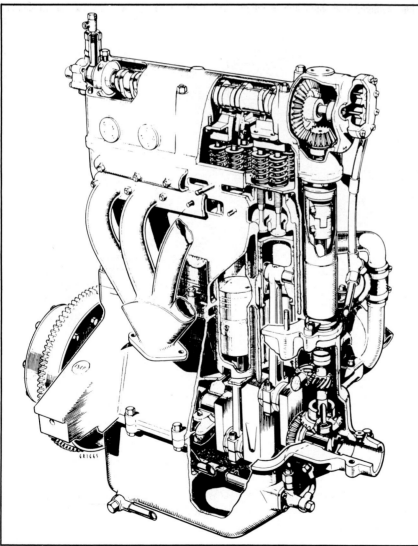

The early cars had a gearbox with narrow gears, and a drum brake.

The later gearbox, with strengthened gears and helical constant-mesh gears. The gear change is a delight, explained by the layshaft being 'high-speed' – the constant mesh gears at the rear, and not accelerated when gears are changed.

The plain bearing 16 valve engine in section. In 1920 the oil feed pipe in the sump had 4 jets feeding scoops in the big-ends; later in 1922 two jets feed the crank webs. It will be noted how difficult it would be to fit a ball bearing at the front of the engine without a major redesign, hence the retention of a plain front bearing when the centre and rear ones were changed to ball races.

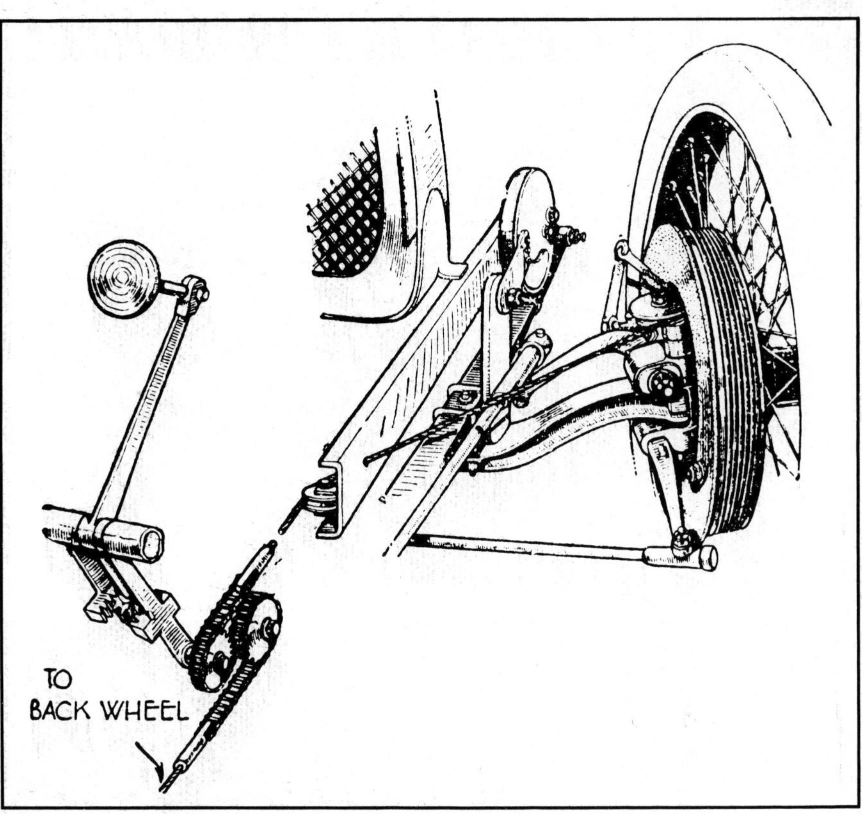

Brescia type front wheel brakes.
(The Motor)

The Bugatti exhibit at Olympia was very impressive, in a restrained sort of fashion. To judge by the demeanour of our inscrutable young friend Lefrère, he might have been in charge of a display of Dunkley motor-perambulators. Although he would agree that 'who sells fat oxen should himself be fat', I suppose, he has never allowed himself to betray his enthusiasm in a noticeable manner, and to hear him reeling-off the car-speeds, engine-revolutions, and so forth of the 1924 chassis (received just in time to wheel it into place on his stand), as though he were saying what jolly weather we were having, struck me as most impressive, because of the entire absence of any intention to make an impression!

I gather that the new model is our old friend the Brescia – so nicknamed after its galvanic performance in the Italian Grand Prix of 1921 – minus only the duplicated ignition. It has an engine-starter and dynamo lighting-set in its 1924 development, and is obtainable in two or three lengths of wheelbase. There is still a super-sports model, with duplex ignition, but anybody who wants one of that type stamps himself as a really desperate person.

1923 Instruction Book. Dated September 1923, this describes the 69 mm × 100 mm car and illustrates and describes the ball bearing construction with steering box integral with the crankcase. A works drawing, showing the modification to the crankcase to include the box, is dated April 1923 so it seems certain that this change was made in the autumn of that year. Another change is that the connecting rod bronzes are now white metal lined. This book, however, quotes the wheelbase of the T13 as 1·95 not 2·0 metres. It thus seems reasonable to conclude that the ball race crank and the integral steering box came in at the same time in 1923, in production cars if perhaps earlier in special race versions. The genuine Brescia racing type of 1921 is known to have had a separate steering box and a small series was made and sold in this ball-bearing construction.

Cars similar to the Le Mans cars were soon being sold: E. Charavel, who raced under the pseudonym of 'Sabipa', in a car with even less bodywork than the Works cars.

After the race, the team poses in front of the Bugatti tent, with a proud Bugatti behind.

Five cars were prepared for the Voiturette race at Brescia in Italy in September 1921, and conquered all with a sensational average of 72mph for the 200 miles; the first four places went to Friderich, de Viscaya, Baccoli and Marco.

1924–25 Catalogue. The car is now labelled 'Brescia Modifié'; the catalogue contains 1924 race results so no doubt was printed in October or November 1924. There is still no reference to Type 13 in the text. The crankshaft, as before, is split and carried on two ball races and a plain front bearing. Lubrication is by jets squirting axially into the crankwebs, where the oil is distributed by centrifugal force, and the steering is now stated to be lubricated from the engine, although it is doubtful if this feature persisted. Apart from the bore, other relevant data are as quoted in the 1922–23 Catalogue. The radiator is fatter again with an aspect ratio of 4:3, and has no starting handle cut out.

1925 (November) Catalogue. This refers again to the 'Brescia Modifié' and states that three types of chassis (13, 22 and 23) are produced. T13 was probably produced to special order; its wheelbase is again quoted

One of the Le Mans cars came to England, and was bought by Henry Segrave for use at Brooklands. It was supposed to be the winning Friderich car, but the repair to the honeycomb (shown in a front view of the car) suggests that it may have been the Baccoli one.

Mays in his car known now as Cordon Rouge.

A pair of true Brescia type cars came to England in 1922, one being sold to Raymond Mays. This Autocar *picture shows a convenient way of photographing a chassis in full length! Note the separate steering box, the twin magnetos and the enormous exhaust pipe. On the original print it is possible to read the chassis number on the crankcase arm as either 1317 or 1318, a pair of chassis which were recorded in factory records as delivered to 'Jarrott & Letts, London 28 March 1922'.*

as 2 metres and an available drawing describes this later version as the 13A. The only important change seems to be the addition of four-wheel brakes 'as on the Grand Prix cars', but the radiator is now lower and similar to that on T30 (see below).

1926 (November) Catalogue. This makes no reference to Brescia or Type 30 models. Types 38 touring, 35A 'Course Imitation', 35 GP, 37 Sports, 39 GP and Type 40 are illustrated, all but the Type 35 being mentioned for the first time. Thus the 16 valve car went out of production in mid-1926 after the production of over 2000 cars – the greatest model production Bugatti was to achieve.

Above: *Another very successful Brescia driver at Brooklands was Leon Cushman, here with mechanic Payne, in the 1922 JCC 200 mile race. He had trouble in the event and finished 7th at 76·5 mph, but the year following managed 2nd place in the same event at an incredible 91·1 mph, on alcohol fuel.*

Top left: *Raymond Mays with Amherst Villiers making notes; he was responsible for many improvements to the engine which raised its maximum engine speed to over 6,500 rpm, and gave Mays many wins in hill climbs.*

Contemporary road test impressions

The following article by 'Omega', E. Duffield, in the *Automotor Journal*, 14 April 1921, entitled '200 miles on the 10 hp Bugatti' is worth reproducing:

The Bugatti, being quite an exceptional car, the Editor of *The Auto* has permitted me to stray over the confines of my usual stamping-ground, in recounting my

For the 1923 200 mile race the Bugattis had cowled fronts and long tails, to reduce drag; this is Blackstock who was unplaced.

Top right: *The long wheelbase Brescias often carried pretty touring bodies of this typical Lavocat & Marsaud type.*

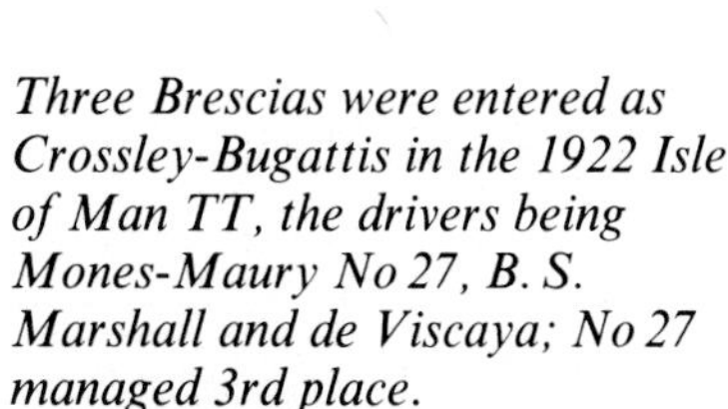

Three Brescias were entered as Crossley-Bugattis in the 1922 Isle of Man TT, the drivers being Mones-Maury No 27, B. S. Marshall and de Viscaya; No 27 managed 3rd place.

impressions of a road-test. To come to the kernel of things at once, I regard the Bugatti as a car of a thousand, and the voiturette of the entire world's automotor industry. Unless [Germany] has a super Bugatti up [their] sleeve – something in the way of possibilities which I doubt, because the Bugatti is an essentially sporting proposition – there is nothing like it. England, France, Italy, America, have nothing to offer which can match it.

Mr W.M. Letts having asked me to try the car, and Major Lefrère, the manager of Chas. Jarrott and Letts, Ltd, having arranged for me to do so, I took over a chassis with a couple of aeroplane seats bolted to it, on the Saturday morning. On the first day I did a matter of 100 miles, by the time I had picked up my moorings; and on the second I again totalled 100 miles by dead reckoning, although no meter was fitted. The mechanical detail of the new Bugatti has been very faithfully described in *The Auto*, but all mention of its behaviour has up to now been of the second-hand, hearsay order. Having been shown the run of its four-speed-and-reverse 'gate', I got aboard, and set forth. In town the Bugatti is decidedly a chassis to know, because of its beautiful responsiveness to the accelerator-pedal, and the surprisingly small difference in gear-ratio between the fourth and third speeds. Once out on *la route libre*, however, one loses the finger-on-lip feeling, and revels in its absolutely galvanic acceleration. Light cars as a class are surprising to those accustomed only to heavier boats; but the Bugatti holds revelations for those even well-accustomed to light cars in general.

An English bodied tourer was used as a demonstrator by Lefrère, the Sales Manager of Jarrott & Letts.

The suspension is uncannily perfect. The steering is a delight. The response to the spur makes one forget the lightness of the whole outfit; but the craft embodied in the complete make-up is such that a very tyro could come down off the banking on the forward side of the Members' Bridge at Brooklands well up in the 70s, and yet hit the railway straight without anything in the way of alarm. Tested by a trustworthy chronograph, this Bugatti chassis which I tried lapped Brooklands at 60 odd, which seemed to suggest that the manufacturer's guarantee of 80 mph on the level is quite safely offered. The chassis I had was milk-new, and there was a wicked breeze blowing dead in the radiator of this astonishing baby. I did not time the lower gears, but at a venture I should say that one can get 30 on first, 40 on second, and 60 mph on third gears. The pinions were frankly rough; they were plainly noisy; and if I bought a Bugatti – which, plainly speaking, means if I could afford a Bugatti – I should run it at least 500 miles before handing it to the body-builders. But the suspension, even in front, and still more so aft, is wonderful when running *ventre-à-terre*, and if a round half-dozen of avaricious Brooklands habitués had not already put themselves down for Bugatti chassis this Season I should hypothecate all the assets I have and buy one, looking to the 1921 Season's 'pots' to recoup me, even out of the silversmith's ladle.

On the road, the car is staggering. There was nothing abroad on my two days which it could not 'pip'. Even when hot stuff were sailing uphill, I had only to take a hundred yards of that wonderful 'third' to squeeze comfortably by them, on both Portsmouth and Brighton roads; and a car which will climb Reigate Hill (from the Brighton side, of course) on third speed at 25 mph is one

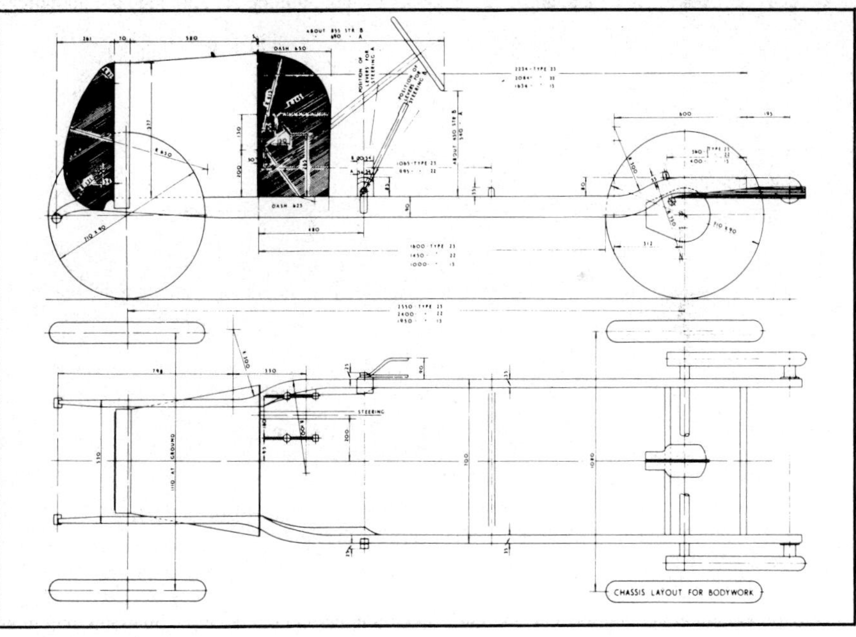

Right: *Chassis drawing of the T13, 22, 23 (traced from an original Molsheim drawing dated 11 October 1922).*

on which the unregenerate could have lots of fun, I should imagine, especially when the same machine will tick along at 5 mph on fourth, as smoothly as any 50 hp 'six'.

Whence the power comes, only M. Ettore Bugatti knows, up to now; but it is there. We know all about the performance of this car in the voiturette Grand Prix last summer, on the Sarthe circuit. Like most other folk, I had imagined that the team of cars used for the job were very, very special, and handled by supermen. I have now satisfied myself that they were not. I have further satisfied myself that, given a day's induction or initiation, the veriest Old Maid of Lee could trundle about on a Bugatti without causing the vicar's eyebrows to arch themselves – unless she happened indiscreetly to depress the accelerator-pedal!

A few Brescias carried closed bodywork; Friderich in the Monte Carlo Rally of 1924 or 1925.

The engine starts easily, decelerates smoothly. The brakes are sweet to astonishment. The suspension is incredibly even. The fore springing is like that of the 1921 Vauxhall. The rear suspension cannot be described so perfect is it. Can you 'corner' at 40 mph on any other car, of twice the weight? I trow not! the steering is excellent, and the chassis as a whole could be improved only by fitting some means of regulating the minimum throttle-setting from the driver's seat, for those meeting the car for the first time. I say this in my search for something to criticize, because I did by failing to keep it primed when I dropped from high speed to a standstill – forgetting that I had only the accelerator-pedal to keep a useful supply of gas going in to the cylinders. This, however, is nothing. The great point, the whole point, is that here is something so light that any fit man can, using both hands, lift the whole rear-half of the car jack-high, and yet is good for 80 mph on the flat, and further yet will tour the British Isles (at a 25 mph average) at over 30 miles per gallon of petrol! The standard tyres, on French Rudge-Whitworths, are 710 × 90 mm. Those on this chassis were, to my mind, extravagantly inflated. But the wonderful springing (kept in check by the amortisseurs fitted fore and aft) neutralized the effect of this circumstance and I have never completed a couple of days' driving of a strange machine – particularly of a very fast little machine – with less fatigue or more regret.

A French-bodied early car with front brakes added.

A very pretty cloverleaf-bodied early 16 valve car.

Another 16 valver with Swiss body outside the factory at Molsheim a few years ago.

A recreated T13 based on many of the parts from Raymond Mays' car.

Modern road impressions

Several thousands of miles experience with an early 16-valve car have enabled a modern driver to confirm the charm and performance of this model. Steering and road holding are excellent and if the absence of front brakes requires the car to be manoeuvred rather than stopped – especially as the foot operated transmission brake makes alarming noises when used at any speed – the whole car gives a surprising feeling of safety. Gear noise is considerable and it is difficult to tell the difference in performance between 3rd and 4th gears! Above 60 mph the engine is very rough and 70 mph seems fast!

It is easy today to see why the car evoked such enthusiasm sixty years ago.

16 valve licence cars

THE IMMEDIATE post-war market for cars was a hungry one and many new designs sprang up all over the world. Industrialists realized the advantage in manufacturing well-known foreign cars in their particular country under licence. And the 16 valve Bugatti car had the unusual distinction of being produced in three countries other than France, namely Italy, Germany and England, although probably not more than twenty-five cars were produced in each country.

Italy

Diatto had had a licence arrangement with Bugatti during the first world war for his 8 cylinder aero-engine (see page 330). In 1919 at the Paris Automobile Salon, Diatto showed a sample of their 16 valve chassis fitted with a substantial saloon body and known as the Diatto model 30. This appears to have been a Type 23 chassis, although it had a Diatto rather than a Bugatti radiator. How successful this model was is not known. Factory records list two complete 16 valve chassis as being delivered to Diatto in March 1921 (902, 903, well out of sequence), and a third (930) earlier in May 1920 but the significance is also not known.

Germany

In the *Autocar* of 20 August 1921 was an announcement that the Rhenian Motor Building Company (Rheinische Automobilbau AG) had concluded an agreement with Bugatti to manufacture the 4 cylinder car at Mannheim and Berlin. This company (from whose initials derives the adopted name Rabag) seems to have been more successful than Diatto. The car was shown at the 1923 Berlin Auto Show, in a specification conforming with the 68 mm × 100 mm, Type 23.

Mr W. Schmarbeck writes:

The Rheinische Automobile – A.G., Düsseldorf, Deutsche Gesellschaft for the licence Ettore Bugatti, was established by the Funke Brothers on 3 December

1920 with a capital of 13 million marks. The head office was in Düsseldorf and the manager was B.A. Gelderblom. Bodies were made by Bendikt Rock, Nordstrasse, Düsseldorf, using about twenty men. A car was shown in the 1923 Berlin Show. In June 1925 the Firm merged with A.G. für Automobilbau (AGA) in Berlin-Lichtenberg, who already produced Stinns and Dinos cars. Bankruptcy proceedings, however, began in November 1925.

Rabag-Bugattis were well known in Germany as fast and economical cars and were often seen in rallies and races; a Rabag was a competitor in the Eifelrennen on the Nürburgring in 1930.

The cover of a Rabag catalogue.

England

The *Autocar*, 19 November 1921, contained an announcement to the effect that Crossley Motors Limited would make the 16 valve car under licence at Manchester. This had been arranged by Mr W.M. Letts,

Managing Director of Crossley Motors Limited, and also a partner in the British Bugatti Agents, Charles Jarrott & Letts Limited. The model was to be the 68 mm × 100 mm type, no doubt with plain bearings. The story of these cars (two of which are still extant) is best told in the words of Mr Edgar N. Duffield in the *Automotor Journal* of 6 December 1923.

I think it was during the 1920 [in fact 1921] Olympia Show that Sir William Letts, K.B.E., announced his intention of manufacturing in the Manchester Works of Crossley Motors, Ltd, a British edition of the Bugatti. At that date a Bugatti was a rather costly chassis. The price when I bought my first new one was £575, so that a complete car came out at about £700, with anything in the way of bodywork really worthy of such chassis quality. I indicated my interest in Sir William's announcement on the Bugatti Stand at Olympia, by immediately handing a five-pound note (all I had on me) to Mr Arthur Bray, as deposit on the first Manchester-built chassis ready for delivery; but I never got that chassis, because immediately after the announcement Crossley got so very busy upon the famous 19·6 that they could not get down to the Bugatti proposition. Then came the Fourteen Crossley, then the 20–70 sports model, and so the poor little Bugatti was left standing on one leg.

In default of the original programme, Sir William imported a number of sets of Bugatti components from Molsheim, in the rough, so to speak, and set

A Rabag with body by Gasteu, Mainz. (*H. von Fersen*)

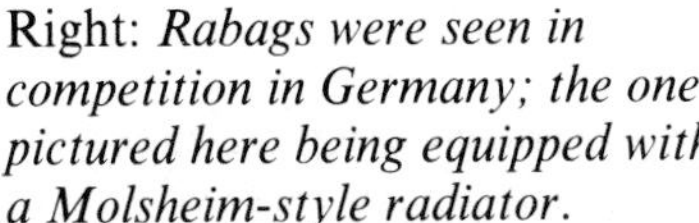
Right: *Rabags were seen in competition in Germany; the one pictured here being equipped with a Molsheim-style radiator.*

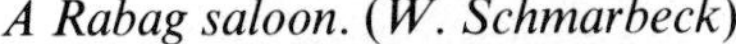
A Rabag saloon. (*W. Schmarbeck*)

aside a bay or two of his big works at Gorton for machining and assembling them, and I gather that the first batch of Manchester-built Bugattis have only just recently begun to come through.

Hearing of their availability, and having inspected a specimen at Olympia, just after the Show I borrowed one ..., and am now in a position to speak of its performance. Let it be clear that this chassis is constructed from original, genuine components, but that the machine-shop work is entirely British....

I would not for the worlds hurt the feelings of Mr Ettore Bugatti, especially while he is at work on the aircraft motor [Type 34?] to design which the French Government have given him *carte-blanche*, but at the risk of doing so I must say that the Manchester machine-shop work, and erection show quite a useful advance upon those of his own 'model' factory.

Of old the Bugatti was notable for a certain mild whine of gears. One could see nothing wrong, when one examined the transmission, but it was not remarkable for noiselessness, even on fourth speed, and my own little series of Bugattis were alike principally in the fact that their engines were very quiet and their gearboxes very noisy ... I always felt that if only Mr Bugatti would give us a little less pep, but a little more Englishness of workmanship, as it were, we should get chassis just as good as we wanted, from the point of power and therefore speed, but chassis much smoother in performance, especially as regards noise.

Well, here is the desirability consummated. The 1924 11·4 hp Bugatti built in Crossleys' shops, is a first-rate job selling at a very low price. The chassis is only £350 now....

I must at once say that the British-built Bug. seems to lack some of the sting of the Molsheim production. I should set it at about 8 to 10 miles per hour on fourth speed. That apart, I really regard it as a better car. It is capable of much smoother slow-running. It gearbox and final drive are almost incredibly less noisy. Its foot-brake is better. Its steering, suspension, clutch and gear-changing mechanism are every bit as good. The facing-up of engine joints, gearbox lid, and so forth, is quite as good. The only thing lacking is just that last ounce of vim – no loss, really, because it is very seldom that one can keep one's foot down for more than a few seconds on British roads....

Mere engine-efficiency was never a fetish of mine, for the reason just stated. I never fell down before motors which would do more than I wanted them to do, just because they were able to do it. My personal affection for the Bugatti was based primarily upon its beauty of suspension, steering and gear-changing....

Gear-noise is apparently unobjectionable to the Frenchman. He does not seem to mind it, in the least. Depending, as he does, very numerously upon a bulb-horn which cost five francs before the War, he may rely upon his gears to give audible warning of his approach! But whatever may underlie the fact, he would seem never to have worried about degrees of silence of gear-pinions, or bevels....

Although, as I have said, the Manchester-built chassis does not seem to have quite the 'fire' of the Molsheim product, it has very wonderful acceleration up to its limits on the various gears. It has, nevertheless, a greatly improved slow-running. Its lubrication seems better, because on a Molsheim Bug, it would be quite notable to do 200 miles without a single suspicion of a misfire, with anything, but Bosch three-pointed plugs, especially in the case of a new car, which any sensible person would be inclined rather to over-lubricate, keeping the level well up to the maximum.

One can get used to anything, and in appreciation of positive virtues can insensibly blind oneself to minor and negative demerits; but I must say that I do not known when I have spent a more pleasant 200 miles on a car other than of my own....

All the old flexibility, all the old charm of suspension and steering, of finger-only gear-changing, all the old acceleration. Not quite all the old genuine stingo, when the throttle is well opened and the spark-lever well forward; but then one

The Rabag engine differed considerably in detail from the Molsheim original but the family resemblance is clear enough.

could so very seldom get going all-out, or remain all-out for more than a couple of furlongs, that this really does not matter very much.

A very, very pleasant little car, Sir William, at a really wonderful price, and although I would not have you keep Crossley buyers waiting, I hope you will contrive to put-through an occasional batch of 25 or so, especially as nearly all the labour on them will be going into the breeches-pockets of British fitters!

In two respects the improvements on the cars from the Molsheim factory, may have accounted for the qualities noted by Mr Duffield; these were, first, that the width of the gears had been increased, resulting in longer life, and second, that the rear axle shaft was increased in diameter at the outer end and a much larger taper used to secure it to the hub; the latter was a big advantage and overcame the annoyance of losing one's wheels, a mishap which had occasionally happened with the earlier types. A considerable amount of trouble was experienced at first with oiled up plugs, but this was finally cured by fitting split collars to the valve stems with no gap at the split in conjunction with internally skirted valve spring collars and this too without cutting down the oil supply in any way. The performance was improved by milling one-sixteenth inch off the base of the cylinder block, thus raising the compression ratio.

D.B. Madeley, who made these observations, owned one of these cars for nearly eight years, and apart from the defects mentioned above, found it a very satisfactory vehicle. His car is still in existence (No. CM 1614). Threads on this car are BSF rather than metric, and there is a tie bar across the front spring eyes, instead of between the shock-absorbers as on normal Molsheim products.

Crossley Bugattis, no doubt using chassis numbers suggested or demanded by Molsheim, were numbered 1600–1625 with a prefix CM. Molsheim perhaps later overlooked this allocation, as they continued their own series, eventually changing over from the 'seize-soupapes' plain bearing, separate steering box number to the 'Brescia Modifié' right in the middle of the Crossley series, for the first of the ball bearing engines at chassis 1612 in February 1923. Only two Crossley versions are known to exist.

Type 28

The prototype 3 litre car of 1921

A SENSATIONAL new 8 cylinder car was shown at the Paris and London Automobile Shows in 1921, the first 8 cylinder passenger car Bugatti designed. The design stemmed in many details from the wartime aero-engine and the chassis as a whole was intended as a high quality product reflecting Ettore's preoccupation with the fabulous, which ultimately materialized in the Royale or Golden Bugatti. In the *Autocar* of 7 May 1921 W.F. Bradley wrote:

The person responsible for the present revival of the eight-cylinder-in-line is undoubtedly M. Ettore Bugatti. This statement must not be interpreted to mean that Bugatti designed or built the first modern car with an eight-cylinder-in-line engine, but he undoubtedly initiated the present movement. During 1913 Bugatti took up the question of eight-cylinder-in-line engines, and as an experiment built an eight-cylinder of 68 mm × 100 mm, bore and stroke with three overhead valves per cylinder, which was really two of his ordinary engines in tandem. This car was in use at the factory, until the declaration of war, and at the present time is in service in Paris. [In fact this prototype had two 8 valve engines coupled in tandem; its whereabouts in Paris in 1921 is an intriguing unsolved mystery.]

It was further pointed out that Monsieur Henry, who had designed the pre-war Peugeot racing cars, was responsible for production of the Bugatti aero-engine during the war; after the war he was engaged by Ballot to design racing models and his Bugatti experience 'doubtless influenced him to adopt 8 cylinders in line'. Further comment added 'in like manner adoption of the straight 8 for the Duesenberg racing cars is doubtless due to experience gained with Bugatti aero-engines'.

The 3 litre Type 28 car, one of the most interesting designs Bugatti produced, never got beyond the prototype stage (the original chassis is still in Alsace in the National Museum at Mulhouse), and the considerably altered design which eventually was produced in 1929 (Type 44) is not really related to it, although Bugatti persisted in so claiming in later years. A contemporary account continues:

It is a car bristling with original features and is on that account attracting much attention at the Salon. The engine, which has all the appearance of a monobloc, really has its cylinders in two castings, their dimensions being 69 mm × 100 mm,

Bugatti's interest in 8 cylinder engines seems to have started with the experimental coupling in tandem of two 8 valve engines in 1912 or 1913.

bore and stroke (2,991 cc). [Strangely enough all contemporary accounts give the bore as 69 mm, but the 1922 Bugatti catalogue quotes 70 mm.] Although it is a most compact group, there is a bearing between each cylinder, and a tenth bearing behind the clutch. A cast aluminium open housing is bolted to the rear face of the engine base chamber, and in the extremity of this is the tenth bearing.

The engine has three valves per cylinder, two inlet and one exhaust, mounted vertically in the head and operated by an overhead camshaft, the enclosed vertical drive shaft of which is in the centre. [The drive to the camshafts was via a pair of bevel-drives differing by one tooth, and held together by a friction clutch, so that the brake drag loaded the teeth and prevented tooth rattle – a device used on the Royale, and incidentally on some of the original electronic calculating machines.] A cross shaft at the base of the vertical drive shaft operates the high tension magneto on the right and the water pump on the left.

The magneto is hidden under a square aluminium box, corresponding in shape with the squared cylinder block. At 3,400 rpm the engine develops 90 hp. Plain bearings are used for the crankshaft and the connecting rod end, and the pistons are of aluminium. Lubrication is under pressure throughout. There are two carburettors of Bugatti's own design, bolted up directly to the right-hand side of the cylinder block. In addition to the main throttle control, there are separate hand adjustments for both the petrol and air.

There is not a feature of the car but has been treated in an original and masterly manner. There are only two speeds, and they are accommodated in

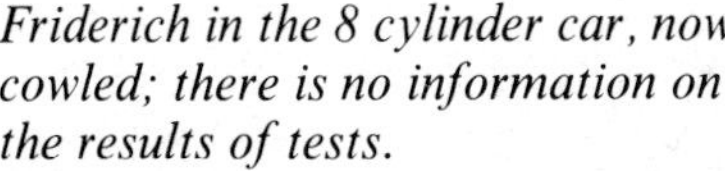

Friderich in the 8 cylinder car, now cowled; there is no information on the results of tests.

the rear axle housing, and operated by a hard wood lever. With an engine developing 90 hp and a chassis of exceptionally low weight, two ratios are considered amply sufficient. A central aluminum casing is used for the differential and the change-speed housing, while the axle tubes are machined out of the solid billets. On each side of the differential housing and bolted up to it as a light pressed steel torque member, with hardwood filling in the channel. These two are parallel with the propellor-shaft, and at the forward end attached to the extended crankcase housing in two pairs of compressed fabric links. [The 16 valve cars at that time used a ball and socket, but the flexible coupling was used on all models from then on. The material in fact was leather, as was the steering box joint mentioned below.] The change-speed and the brake lever are mounted on the front end of the torque member.

The steering column has a ball and socket mounting to the aluminium dashboard, and at its base is connected to the worm shaft in the steering gearbox by a fabric coupling, in the manner usually associated with propellor-shaft drives. This is quite a novel adaptation of the flexible fabric joint, worthy of further study. Above the steering column, and parallel with it, is a second column, also mounted in the dash carrying the carburettor and ignition controls. There are only two spokes on the steering wheel, and these are of such a shape and position that it is possible to pass the hand through the wheel to reach the carburettor controls. Furthermore, the wheel is clamped to the column on a key, and thus adjustable at will by the driver when seated.

The prototype Type 28 on show at Nice with Friderich.

Originality has been displayed in the attempt to obtain rigidity and longevity in the steering gear connections. The fore and aft connecting bar from the main steering lever to the steering arm is double and tubular. There is a star type universal joint to the main steering arm with hardened steel pins working in compressed leather bushings. The transverse tie rod has oval shaped ends formed

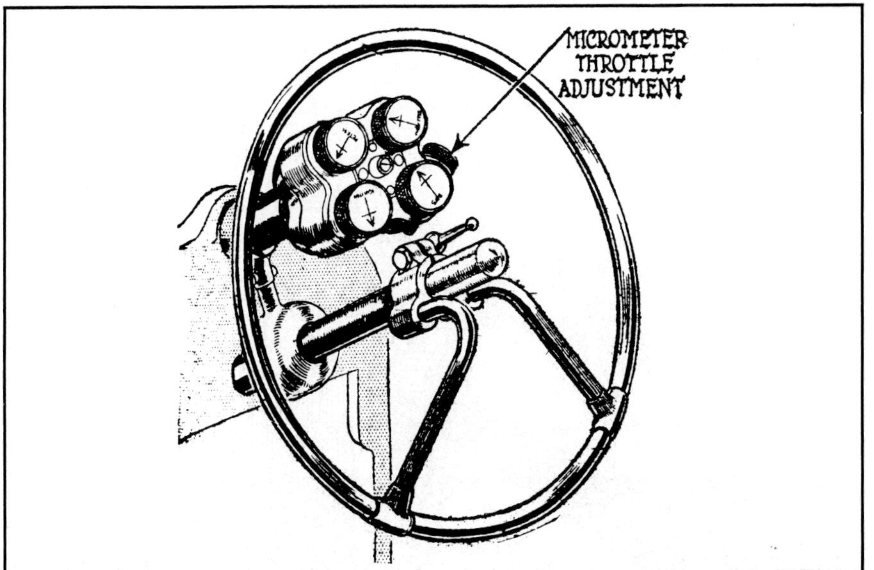

The remarkable steering wheel, adjustable for position and allowing sight of the [illegible] *carburettor adjustment knobs.* (Autocar).

T28 chassis as displayed at Olympia in 1921. (Autocar, *12 November 1921*)

The engine was incomplete and the carburettors were complicated Bugatti-designed units.

'Duplicated stub axle arm, tie rod and steering rod strike an unusual note. The front wheel brake drums are of a large size', stated the Autocar.

of compressed fabric held between a top and bottom steel plate. These parts cannot rattle, they are rigid and at the same time absorb shocks, and will require no lubrication. [A Coventry and Detroit novelty of the 1960s.]

The car is fitted with brakes on all the wheels, these eventually will be hydraulically operated, although at present they are applied manually. Quarter-elliptic springs with the thick ends rearwards are used at the rear and double semi-elliptics at the front, in accordance with Bugatti principles. At the rear a friction type shock-absorber is mounted inside the brake drums. At the front end there is a shock-absorber of the same type, the drum of which is mounted just ahead of the radiator, between the dumb irons. The petrol tank is at the rear, carried by the main frame, and has vacuum supply to the carburettors, whilst a reserve compartment of two gallons is provided in the main fuel tank. (*Autocar*, 15 October 1921 and undoubtedly written by W.F. Bradley.)

The car caught the eye of the celebrated Mr S.F. Edge who wrote in the *Automotor Journal* of 17 November 1921:

I suppose that the car with more new and striking ideas than any other in the Show was the eight-cylindered Bugatti. Original points obtruded, from whatever aspect one viewed it, and I expect that many of the designer's innovations will be standard practice in a few years from now; but for the time being it was rather 'ahead of the band', and as an exhibit I consider that it suffered greatly from the fact that certain details were not complete, for example, the connections of the front-wheel brakes, the ignition etc. To show such a chassis, absolutely alive with what in vulgar parlance are called 'brain-waves', in any but a perfectly completed state was rather unwise, I should imagine. But the look of what one could see made one wish to have a specimen on the road, so that one could see how much justification Mr Bugatti has for doing so many things in a way quite different from that followed by everybody else. He is a wonderful designer, and those who have met him recently tell me that he has developed a unique

personality. But the chassis gave me an idea in my own mind, of being the work of a man who cannot sit in a comfortable armchair, and read a book, for very long. The design was electrical, or rather galvanic. It was one succession of shocks to all our accustomed notions, and although I am all for progress, I must confess that I have also a respect for a certain type of conservatism. We shall see; we must wait to see. But it was quite easy to see that this new model has great capabilities, and no designer looking to the future could afford to miss a most thorough examination of it.

The left side of the engine resembled the later T44.

Right: *Gearbox in the rear axle, and two torque arms.*

The car was, in fact, ahead of its time, not only in the general sense but in the Molsheim context. Several years were to pass before a luxury car was a practicable proposition from that factory, until the esteem which racing successes brought made sales of such a car possible. Bugatti was clearly unable to finance the launching of the car, much more complex and under-developed than his 16-valver, into production. Some designs for coachwork were produced and an available photograph shows that the chassis was eventually bodied if not put into production.

From the purely historical point of view it is a pity that the technical novelty of the design much noted in 1921 has been smothered by a modern replica body on the Museum prototype, which has not managed to reproduce the interesting steering wheel.

Type 30

8 cylinder car

THE FIRST production 8 cylinder Bugatti was the 2 litre Type 30 introduced in 1922 and shown at automobile shows at the end of that year. No doubt Bugatti felt that the larger 3 litre Type 28 should be shelved in favour of a smaller, cheaper and more saleable model. Type 30 consisted of an entirely new 60 mm × 88 mm, 8 cylinder engine mounted in the Type 23 chassis and indeed offered in the short Type 22, 2·4 metre chassis, although probably only a few racing cars of this length were produced; later an even longer and reinforced chassis (2·85 m) was introduced.

The engine was the first production model to use the rectangular slab construction which was to become famous, and had 3 valves per cylinder, along the lines of the 1912, 5 litre racers, the aero-engines and the Type 28. The valves were small in diameter to allow them to be removed without disturbing the valve guides unlike the later T35 or T39 blocks. The crankcase had a detachable sump, the crank being carried on 3 large self-aligning ball bearings (plus 1 ball steady bearing) and being fed in from one end of the case. Big ends were plain with jet-feed from an oil gallery on the left side of the motor. A cross-shaft at the front drove a water-pump on the left and initially a gear oil pump at the right – probably Bugatti was tired of priming troubles with the high mounted Brescia pump; later the oil pump was lowered further to a drive off the crankshaft as on the T35. The blocks were in units of 4 cylinders with single plugs (a few had 8 plug blocks) and a cambox as on the later Type 35 design. Early cars had twin carburettors, but some later ones a single unit. Plug holes were tapped through to the cylinders, not recessed as on the later T35 cars.

The steering box was mounted on the rear engine crankcase bearer, the worm wheel rotating on an eccentric pin to enable backlash to be adjusted. The gearbox was Brescia 'with strengthened gears'. On early cars there was an outrigger bearing behind the clutch and contained in a housing carried off the rear of the crankcase, as on Type 28. The rear axle torque rod used a leather coupling at its forward end, as introduced on T28 the year previously, but the torque rod was not duplicated as on that model. Front wheel brakes were used for the first time on a pro-

Mr Peter Hampton owned this 'toast-rack' bodied T30 for many years.

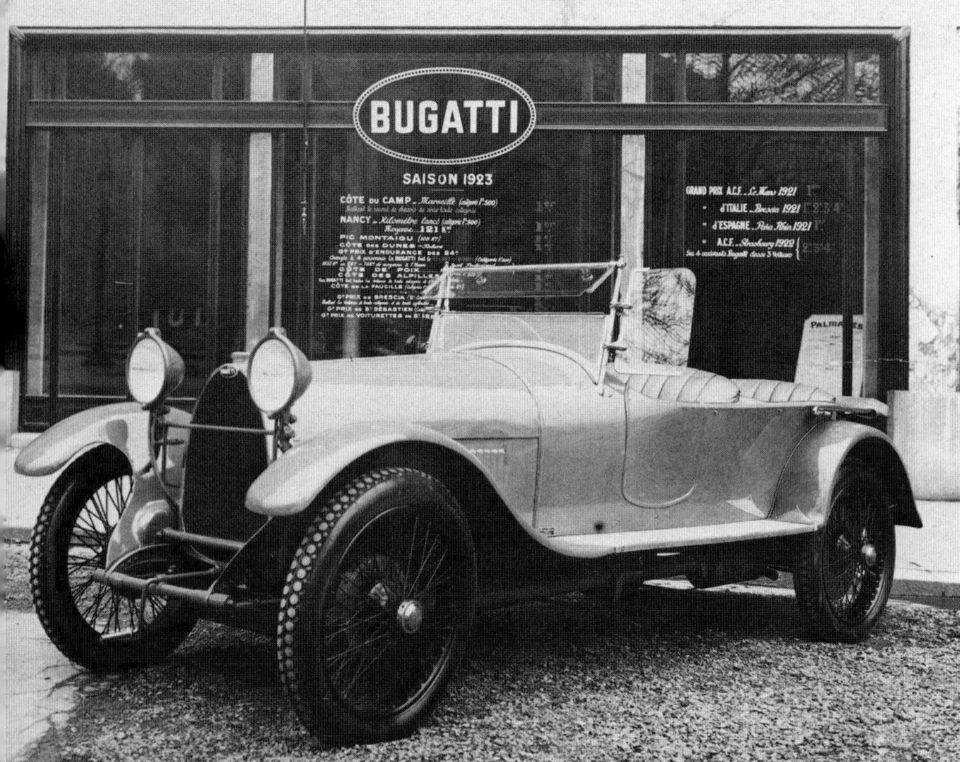

A new T30 on display outside the Bugatti showroom in Paris towards the end of 1923.

duction Bugatti and were hydraulically operated by a specially designed master cylinder, the rear brakes being cable operated. Bugatti's design of hydraulic brakes using a glycerine fluid and leather seals was defective, in that the master cylinder would not seal the system properly on brake application, and often required the pedal to be pumped. Nevertheless they seemed to work well enough until later, cable front brakes as on the last series Brescia and GP cars were used.

The quality and performance of later touring Bugattis has tended

A Type 30 owned by Member of Parliament Sir Robert Bird.

The standard of finish achieved by coachpainting and varnishing was exceptional; small hydraulic brakes at the front, large mechanical at the rear.

to exaggerate, in retrospect, the faults of this early 8-cylinder car, but at the time it created much interest. Charles Faroux wrote eulogistically to Ettore Bugatti in early 1924:

Whether one considers the engine, the steering, the road-holding qualities, or the suspension (from the point of view of either driver or passenger), you have sold me a motor-car which is absolutely unbeatable, which easily puts in the shade anything else which I have ever driven. I cannot imagine anything which could give me more joy than this experience with my two-litre Bugatti!

Strasbourg Grand Prix, 1922; de Viscaya at the pits.

I would prefer not to tell you the time in which I drove from Nancy to Paris, but I can tell you candidly, that – well as I know this particular road – I have never on any other chassis, of any power, approached the running-time of my trip of Sunday last. Quite apart from the great pleasure which this car has given me, as one with a reverence for beautiful mechanism, it has also given me profound joy as one of your most faithful admirers.

One feels that he must have bought the car on such favourable terms that he felt bound to be polite about it! The *Autocar*, 8 May 1925, was not so kind, disliking the noise of the engine and the poor brakes. Notwithstanding its faults the car could be made to go; Mr O.A. Phillips wrote in November 1960:

As a matter of fact my first Bugatti, No. 4006 in 1928, was an 8 cylinder bore 60 mm, stroke 88 mm, 2 plugs per cylinder, 2 Scintilla magnetos mounted on a steel firewall on a common aluminium casting, with step-up gearbox to bring the speed of magnetos from camshaft speed up to crankshaft speed.

This car was 95 inch wheelbase [Type 22] and had hydraulic brakes (approx. 11 inches diameter) on front, and mechanical (approx. 16 inches diameter) on the rear. They operated separately – foot on front, hand on rear. The complete car weighed only 1,250 pounds and was, supposedly, the Strasbourg winning car in 1923 [2nd in 1922].

One of the Strasbourg cars ran at Monza in September 1922, and then was displayed at the Salon, evidently Paris. The car behind seems to be a rare appearance of the Type 28 with a coach-style body.

The foot brake master cylinder was simply a direct acting plunger mounted on the firewall. The front axle was an 'I' beam and the ends of the 'tie rod' had leather couplings, similar to the one connecting the front of the torque arm to the gearbox. On the top of the right rear engine leg was mounted the steering box, while on the bottom of the left rear clutch housing was a Robert Bosch starter. There was no generator.

In 1929 I officially recorded 124 mph at Muroc Dry Lake, in full touring trim, but with two downdraft Winfield carburettors, instead of the original Zenith. In 1932 I sold the car to a friend of Eri Richardson in San Francisco, and have since lost all track of it. [The engine still exists.]

The first Type 30 cars were indeed the four cars (4001–4) built for the French Grand Prix at Strasbourg in 1922. Although Bugatti himself, at the time, argued that coachwork on a racing car was not worth its weight, and would have preferred a simple bolster-tank 'body' as on the racing 16 valve cars, he was persuaded by Pierre de Vizcaya to fit long tail 'cigar-shaped' bodies made locally in Strasbourg. The four cars were driven by de Vizcaya, Friderich, Mones-Maury and Pierre Marco, and the competition from Fiat, Sunbeam and the others was formidable. Nazarro and Fiat won, but de Vizcaya and Mones Maury kept going and finished 2nd and 3rd some way behind, all other cars failing. Mr W.F. Bradley wrote in *Automotive Industries*, 3 August 1922:

Insert: *Bugatti was proud of his 2nd and 3rd places in the Grand Prix.*

> Bugatti came to the start with four cars equipped with a new type eight cylinder engine. Friderich was the fastest of these drivers and succeeded in getting the lead for a few minutes on the third lap. On the 12th lap he went out by reason of the breakage of the gears in one of his two magnetos. These magnetos were mounted side by side on the dash and driven from the overhead camshaft by a universal joint shaft. When the magneto gears went they broke up the intermediaries. The three other Bugattis went to the end, but they were never at any time serious contestants for first place. They were very liberally lubricated and smoked freely throughout the race.

A few weeks later one car ran at Monza, there being some evidence that it was fitted with roller bearing big ends, using split connecting rods. The radiator cowling was removed for the race, the car running well but without result.

De Viscaya followed by a Ballot.

In May of 1923 a batch of five cars, two from the 1922 race and three others, was entered by the South American sportsman Alzaga for

the 500 mile race at Indianapolis, on a promise Bugatti made but did not keep of fitting the engine with roller bearing connecting rods. The cars had very pretty single-seat bodies.

The Indianapolis cars were described in detail by Mr Bradley in *Automotive Industries* of 24 May 1923:

The five Bugatti entries built by Ettore Bugatti, of Molsheim, Alsace, who specializes in a fast, sporting type of 122 cu in. chassis, are said to be stock models with only such detail modifications as are necessary for the special conditions of the Indianapolis track.

The single seater bodies for these cars are in the design of a French aviation engineer, Bechereau, who was responsible during the war for the design of Spad scout planes. As no changes of importance could be made in the chassis, the maximum width of the bodies is appreciably greater than that of the majority of American cars. The driver is placed centrally in the chassis, with his eyes just above the level of the scuttle and the top of his head flush with the top of the tail; this part is streamlined with the pilot's head, as in aviation practice.

One of the Strasbourg cars was sold to Vidal in Marseilles and much raced by him in events in Southern France.

The engine has a stroke of 88 mm, and its eight cylinders, cast in two blocks of four, are of 60 mm bore. They are mounted on an aluminium base-chamber which is carried directly on the chassis frame members. The cylinder blocks are rectangular, and the timing gear housing at the forward end is also squared off, giving a box-like appearance to the engine. The detachable cylinder head has a lapped face where it joins the cylinder blocks. [Oh Mr Bradley!] It carries three vertical valves (two admission and one exhaust) operated by a single overhead camshaft mounted in three ball bearings. [Surely wrong!] Light followers are interposed between the cams and the valves, the two shafts carrying these rockers being hollow and forming an oil duct through which lubricant is delivered directly to the cam faces. Maximum engine speed is 4,800 to 5,000 rpm and the power developed is declared to be 104 hp.

A two-piece assembled crankshaft, carried in three ball bearings, is employed. I-section white metal connecting rods and aluminium pistons having

four narrow steel compression rings are used. Normally the 122 in. Bugattis are fitted with two Zenith carburettors, but it is probable that they will be run at Indianapolis with four carburettors, and that benzol, or a mixture of benzol and gasoline will be used as fuel. Compression has been raised above normal with a view to the use of benzol. Normally ignition is by a high tension magneto mounted on the aluminium dashboard and driven off the tail end of the overhead camshaft by a fabric universal jointed shaft. In some races, however, use has been made of two magnetos, with external gears, and in others the Marelli combined generator and distributor has been employed. It probably will depend on track tests as to which type is definitely adopted for the race.

Engine lubrication is assured by means of a gear type pump driven off the right end of a cross shaft, the opposite end of which operates the water circulating pump. There is also a direct oil lead to the steering gearbox. All the oil is contained in an aluminium casting bolted to the basechamber and fitted with longitudinal copper tubes, open at both ends for cooling purposes.

De Viscaya in the single seater prepared for Indianapolis.

There is a rather unusual use in the Bugatti chassis of leather universals and links. Examples are the channel section pressed steel torque member, which is bolted at the rear to the differential housing and at the front end is attached by a double leather link and two pins to the rear face of the gearbox.

There is a somewhat similar use of leather for the transverse tie rod. This connection consists of two steel tubes with flattened ends attached by two bolts to oval-shaped blocks of compressed chrome leather having a top and bottom plate of steel. A socket is formed in the leather for the usual type of ball, the taper stem of which is mounted in the steering arm in the normal manner.

The race itself was disastrous for the Bugattis, whose engines especially in the bearing lubrication could not sustain the continuous high speeds allowed by the track. De Vizcaya had a good run but threw a rod towards the end, only de Cystria remaining at the tail end at the finish. Bugatti must now have realised that roller bearings must be introduced.

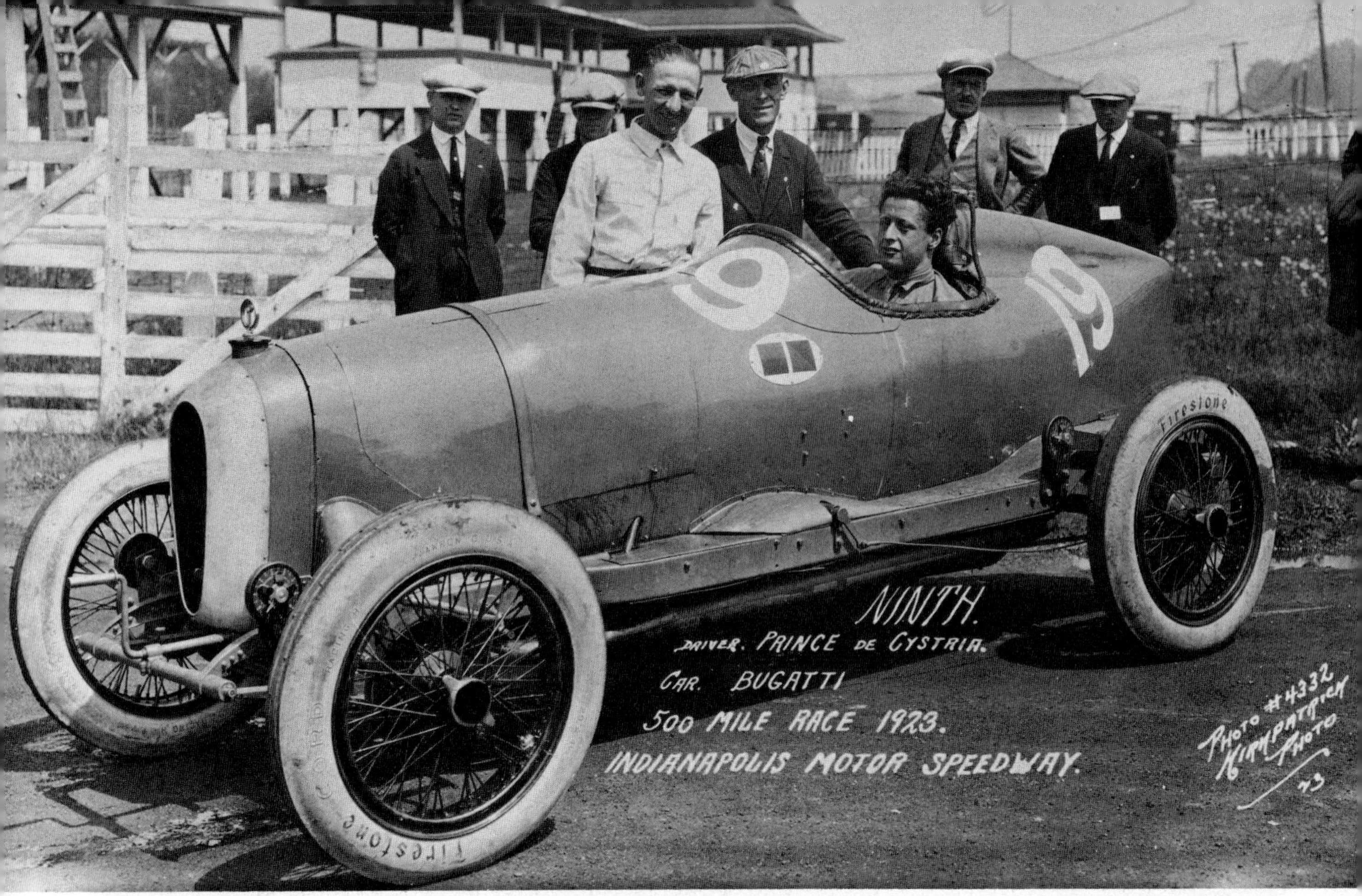

Prince de Cystria at Indianapolis 1923; he was the only Bugatti driver to finish.

Type 32. For the 1923 Grand Prix at Tours Bugatti did indeed turn up with a roller bearing engine but mounted in a strange new 'tank' car, with a 2 metre wheelbase and his idea of an aerodynamic body, of aerofoil section in side elevation and almost rectangular in front view. The axles were mounted on $\frac{1}{4}$-elliptic springs directed inwards at both ends of the frame, and the gear box was now contained in the rear axle, as on the 8-cylinder Type 28 touring car. Brakes were hydraulic, while the engine was more or less as before apart from the connecting rods, and a special crankcase to suit its mounting in the special frame.

For Indianapolis four carburettors were fitted.

An early T30 engine on the test bed. The early engines had high mounted oil pumps on the front right.

Once more the opposition from Sunbeam, Fiat, Voisin and others was formidable, seventeen cars starting. De Vizcaya crashed his Bugatti on the first lap, and Marco and de Cystria failed leaving Friderich to come home a belated third to the two Sunbeams of Segrave and Divo. The 'tanks' had far from good handling – aggravated no doubt by aerodynamic lift at high speed, and the short wheelbase – but later in 1924 Pierre de Vizcaya driving one of the 1923 unblown 'tank' cars at the speed trials at Arpajon near Paris broke the 2 litre class world record for the flying kilometre at 117·5 mph and the flying mile at 116 mph –

Another Strasbourg car went to Elizabeth Junek in Prague and was nicely rebodied.

Above: *The dynamo is driven from the rear of the camshaft by a belt.*

Top left: *A Type 30 in fine fettle today, with twin Winfield carburettors.*

not bad for what was basically a Type 30. At this meeting Eldridge on the monster 300 hp Fiat attained a hazardous 147 mph, 'Eldridge's approach was one of the most appalling sights which the writer has ever witnessed', wrote *The Motor*.

The results from racing showed the potential of the new 2 litre 8 cylinder engine, if reliability could be improved at high speed. Driven more modestly in touring form it performed well and sales of the standard T30 continued briskly. The chassis was strengthened and the wheelbase lengthened for 1924; production continued until January 1926, a total of 600 cars being produced.

Contemporary road impressions

Mr E.N. Duffield, after testing the car, wrote in the *Automotor Journal* of 26 March 1925 in his usual style but as a Bugatti fan:

Any little sounds which the engine may develop are lost in air-rush and the murmur of the gears. Bugattis are only relatively silent as to their transmission, but obviously the torque of the eight-cylindered motor tends to demonstrate the transmission at its best, and although it would be futile to speak of this car as dead silent, even on fourth, she is very markedly nearer being so than is any four-cylinder Bugatti which I have driven. She is easily good for 40 mph on second, on the flat, and running well within herself, she will do 65 mph, as registered by an A.T. speed indicator guaranteed dead correct, on fourth. She will probably do more, but that seems enough for two litres, on a very cold, windy day!

Her steering is delightful. I know how much of its charm to attribute to the suspension, but apart from that, the steering itself is wonderfully good. It is very high-geared; it has a gigantic worm-shaft and quite a large worm-wheel; it has the fabric-disc coupling at the base of the pillar to damp-out any little kick what comes through such pretty connections; and additionally it has the assistance of the very thin, very flexible spring-steel spokes of the wheel. Like every other

The remarkable single expanding shoe of the hydraulic brake, only working in a forward direction!

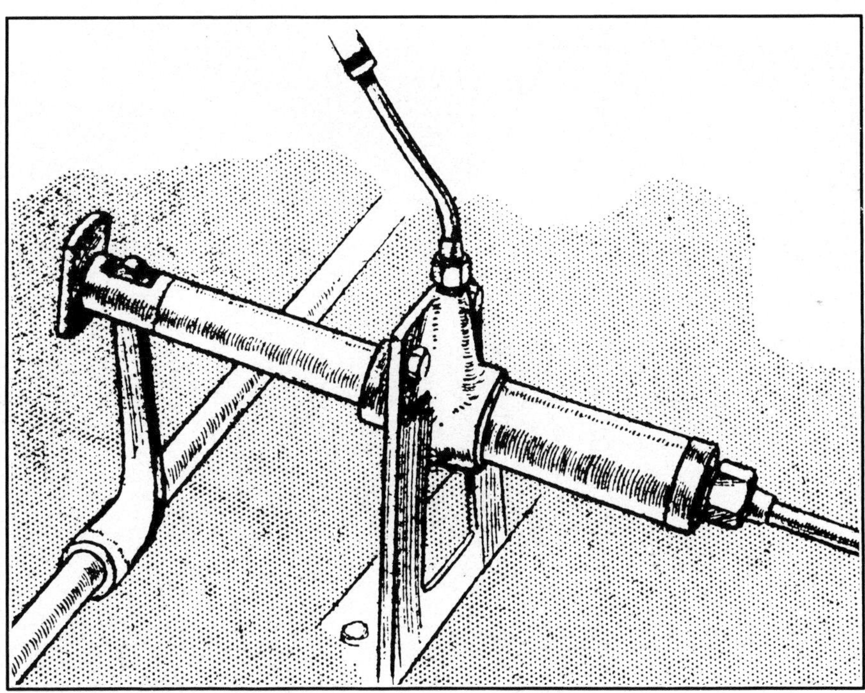

Top right: *The early cars had a hydraulic brake master cylinder, pushed directly, and coupled to the mechanical rear brakes.*

Bugatti, ever since the marque existed, this car can be put around any corner just as rapidly as the driver wishes, in perfect security.

Its gearbox is similarly true to type. In town one gets much practice in gear-changing, especially if one has the Bugatti habit, regarding a spell of third as quite a treat, and a stretch upon fourth as a positive revel; but I fear that I used the change-speed lever much more than I need have done, failing to make proper allowance for the superior torque of the eight-cylindered engine.

This particular car was tuned for power, and so would not run really sweetly upon fourth at less than something between 10 and 12 mph, but the feel of the engine suggested that it could be quite easily de-tuned without going farther than the carburettor, and – anyhow – anybody who buys a Bugatti, of any model, to crawl up and down Bond St and edify its principal or most numerous frequenters is not a really discerning person.

Later the hydraulic brakes were replaced by well-worked-out cable operated types, used afterwards on all models. Note the leather track rod end.

Top left: *The three Tank-bodied Type 32 Bugattis at the Grand Prix at Tours in 1923.*

Running freely, at from 25 to 40 mph, the engine is extremely pleasant. Tuned as this car's carburettor was, one had to be careful with one's toe. I should wonder, too, if a Bosch magneto might not give one finer ignition-gradation than could be got with the standard battery-and-coil set; but, again, one does not buy such a car exclusively for shopping.

I made no real use of the front-wheel brakes. They seemed to be there, and in business, but I use the hand-applied brakes of any and every car far more than those actuated by use of the pedal, and I am not a brake-driver, anyway.

The engine is wonderful, in its stream of power. The more one asks, the more one seems to get. The steering and suspension, the gear-changing, are if possible a little better than ever they were, and altogether this is a very wonderful machine. It is an 'outdoor' car, which begins to earn nuts and/or cigars only after Esher, or Staines or Watford. It can and will trickle through Regent's Park very demurely, but to use if for that kind of motoring is rather like using a Grand National winner to haul a cart-full of mangolds. It is a full-blooded, real man's motor-car, by intention and in performance.

Top right: *The 'cockpit' of the Tank, with the driver and mechanic well exposed to heat and oil leakage!*

Ettore showing the car to Charles Faroux, Costantini on the left.

BUGATT
RACER

Type 35 & 39

Famous racing models

IF BUGATTI established himself as a racing car manufacturer of consequence with his 4 cylinder 8 and 16 valve cars, it was the introduction of the 8 cylinder Type 35 which began the period of six or seven years when Bugatti dominated motor racing as no maker before nor indeed since has managed to do – although perhaps today Ferrari or Lotus as manufacturers of racing and touring cars are today in the same class. As a racing car the type had almost everything that could be desired in a car of that generation – everything that is except sheer power. It was available to anyone at a price that was within the compass of those who could afford to race. It was a car of considerable beauty – to many it was and is the most aesthetically satisfying car design ever produced – in notable contrast indeed to the ugliness of the earlier tank-on-the-tail designs. It was well finished, again in contrast to the earlier cars, making it highly desirable for purely visual reasons. It was small and light, handled superbly and therefore was a pleasure to own and drive to the second rank as well as the top rank of drivers. And above all it won races by the hundreds in the hands of romantic-sounding drivers of all types – capable Italians, titled dilettanti from several countries, mysterious Englishmen and flamboyant Frenchmen.

Bugatti himself claimed in 1927 to have won over 2,000 awards in sporting events. His catalogues of the era sometimes contained as many pages listing his awards of the previous season as on details of the cars he was selling! In one year alone (1926) he won 12 major Grand Prix, including:

GP of Rome 1: Maggi.
Targa Florio 1, 2, 3: Costantini, Minoia, Goux.
GP of Alsace 1, 2, 3: Dubonnet, Maggi, de Vizcaya.
GP of France, Miramas 1, 2: Goux, Costantini.
GP of Europe, San Sebastian 1: Goux.
GP of Spain 1, 2: Costantini, Goux.
GP of Boulogne 1: Eyston
GP of Italy, Monza 1, 2: 'Sabipa', Costantini.
GP of Milan 1, 2, 3: Costantini, Goux, Farinotti.

If any single design is responsible for the interest in the Marque Bugatti which exists today, for the founding of the Bugatti Owners' Club in 1929 and others later, and indeed for the existence of the many books dealing with Bugatti matters, it is the Type 35*.

Original factory pictures of the first Type 35 with the foreman of the construction shop. This first car had the front bonnet strap further back than normal, and the radiator shape is not yet quite perfect. It was driven by Ettore at Lyon but not in the race, and came to Olympia in October 1924 for sale.

*The model and its history are described in detail in the Author's book *Grand Prix Bugatti* – G. T. Foulis, 1968, 1983.

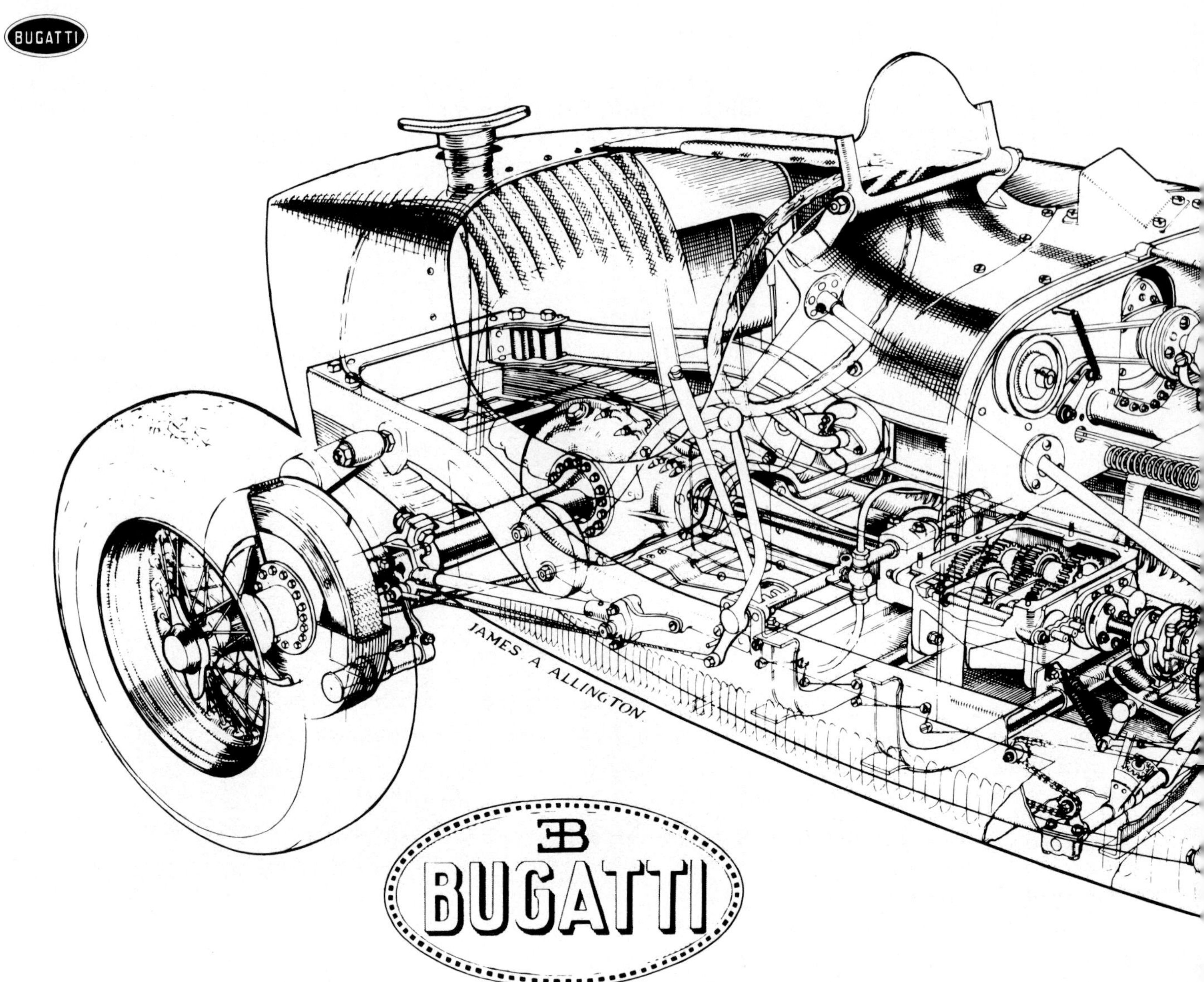

Evolution of the model

The 1923 Grand Prix had seen the rather unsuccessful tank-bodied Type 32, 8 cylinder cars and disastrous entries at Indianapolis. The defects of what was basically a good design were in the engine, which needed more than three crankshaft bearings and a proper means of lubricating the big ends of the connecting rods, in the chassis which needed better brakes, and in the body where a small two-seat layout of low frontal area more like the typical Fiat or Sunbeam of the epoch was obviously (even to the stubborn Ettore!) needed. So Bugatti evidently spent the winter of 1923–24 adding two main roller bearings to the crankshaft and, reluctant as he had shown himself since 1916 to face up to the problems of pressure-fed plain bearings, he designed a complicated, if effective enough roller bearing big end design for the connecting rods; improvements to the chassis and some excellent work on the brakes, and a wholly admirable improvement in the body work resulted in the brilliantly effective Type 35. First produced in 1924 in 2 litre unblown form, for the 1924 French Grand Prix at Lyon (the story is told below), it went through several stages of development culminating in the 35B, supercharged 2·3 litre car which continued until superseded by the Type 51, which had a 35B

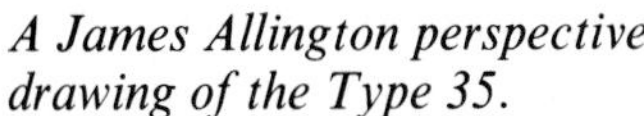
A James Allington perspective drawing of the Type 35.

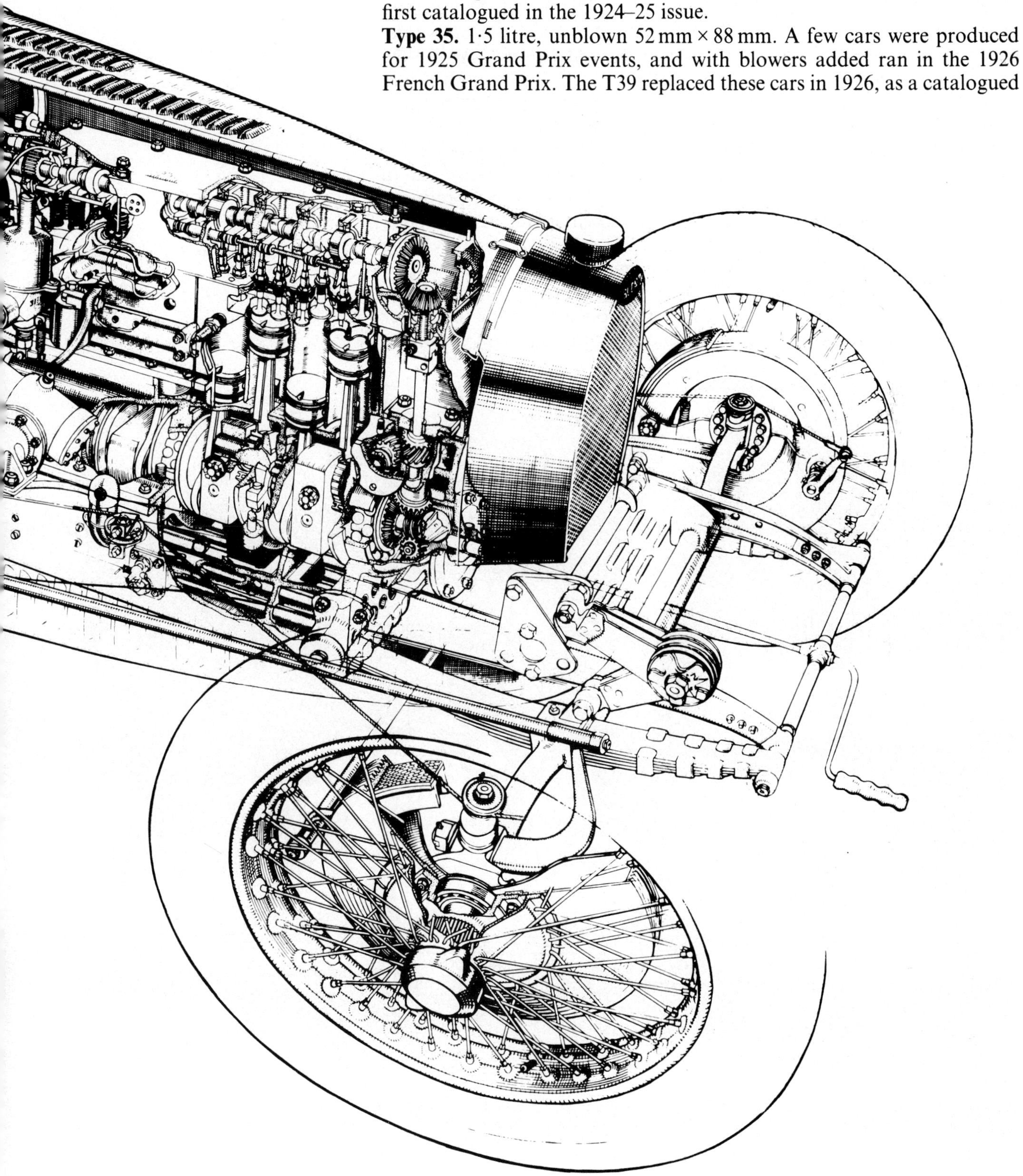

engine fitted with a twin camshaft block. All these models had basically the same 2 metre chassis and body. The various types produced were as follows:

Type 35. 2 litre, unblown 60 mm × 88 mm, small brake drums, cast alloy beaded-edge wheels with detachable rims, small narrow radiator, and first catalogued in the 1924–25 issue.

Type 35. 1·5 litre, unblown 52 mm × 88 mm. A few cars were produced for 1925 Grand Prix events, and with blowers added ran in the 1926 French Grand Prix. The T39 replaced these cars in 1926, as a catalogued

model. A few 54 mm × 81 mm cars were also produced in 1927.
Type 35. 1,100 cc. Three special supercharged cars were produced for the 1926 Alsatian Grand Prix, the engine being 51·3 mm × 66 mm. This was the first success that Bugatti had with a blown car. The single seat versions are strictly known as Type 36.
Type 35T. The 1926 Targa Florio saw the introduction of the unsupercharged 35T (T = Targa) model, an unblown car with longer stroke (100 mm), bringing it to 2,300 cc. Bradley in the *Autocar* of 21 April 1926 quotes the cars as 61 mm × 100 mm (2,350 cc), although 60 mm × 100 mm is normal. The October 1926 works catalogue refers to the T35 as being available with a 2·3 litre engine and blower on demand.
Type 35B. 2·3 litre, 60 mm × 100 mm, at last with a blower; to accommodate the drive for the blower the radiator was moved forward and in fact enlarged. This model, derived from the unblown car first produced for the 1926 Targa Florio, was thus often known as the Targa model; engine numbers generally have the suffix T, the car originally being known as the 35TC. The first blown car came out in early 1927, with a larger supercharger than that used earlier on the 2 litre car; the first cars retained the small brake drums, but were soon fitted with the larger drummed wheels with bigger tyres produced for the heavier Type 43.

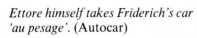

Ettore himself takes Friderich's car 'au pesage'. (Autocar)

The 5 competing cars at Lyon, the 6th being behind.

Garnier at the Esses in the race (Autocar)

Type 35C. A 2 litre version of Type 35B, with bore and stroke 60 mm × 88 mm, was produced in parallel with the longer stroke model from 1927, with the same blower and generally indistinguishable from it except by the absence of a compression plate about 6 mm in thickness as used on the larger model. Its first outing, fitted with a small blower was at Monza in September 1926, when it won the Milan GP.

Type 39. This was the catalogued (in the 1926 catalogue) 1·5 litre model, with a short stroke crank, resulting in a bore and stroke of 60 mm × 66 mm, more reasonable than the earlier modified 2 litre cars. The model first appeared in the Touring Grand Prix at Montlhéry on 19 July 1925, fitted with high-sided two seat bodies conforming with race regulations. Five cars were entered and they won the first four places! A few weeks later they repeated their success at Monza, now fitted with normal GP bodies. The model may originally have been intended as a sport car replacement for the Brescia but in the event the 35A and the 37 replaced it.

Type 39A. This is the normal designation of the supercharged version, using a small, narrow blower. Only a few were made for racing to the then standard 1½ litre formula. Some had a crankshaft 52 mm × 88 mm, but 60 mm × 66 mm was normal. The model established beyond doubt the success of the blown engine by winning the 1926 French Grand Prix (Goux). One of the 1926 works cars came to England and was driven in the 1926 British Grand Prix by Campbell.

Type 39D. The final 1½ litre version with a 60 mm × 66 mm crank, had a special block with enlarged exhaust valves and a modified cambox. A

Ferdinand de Viscaya at Montlhéry, 1925. Beaded-edge tyres are still used, small brake drums, and a mirror is fitted.

Bottom right: *One of the early cars came to Britain for Glen Kidson, here at Shelsley Walsh.*

batch of five cars was made for racing in 1927, competing in the Spanish and British Grand Prix that year.

Type 35A. An interesting version of the basic 2 litre model was produced in May 1925 under the catalogue description of 'Course Imitation' or unofficially the 'boy racer'; it was also known at Molsheim as the 'Tecla' model after the make of cultured pearls. This had an identical body and chassis to the GP car, but used the Type 38 touring engine. This differed from the racing car in having a 3 ball bearing crank, and plain big ends (indeed as on the Type 30) and although capable of speeds of 90 mph or so (at 4,500 rpm), it could not achieve the performance of the GP cars. However, sold at a substantially lower price it was very popular in sporting as opposed to Grand Prix circles; lucky was the young man whose father bought him a real Bugatti!

A typical scene from the Targa Florio: Costantini winner in 1926.

Lord Cholmondley had another early car in Britain, and Lady Cholmondley was enthusiastic at its performance.

Description of car

The chassis of the T35 followed the 16 valve car layout, but with a number of notable improvements; the rear springs were swept in at the rear to lie within the streamlined tail of the body, and the rear axle was given additional location by a pair of tubular side rods. The gearbox was similar to the Brescia box, but carried on cross tubes, and the gear shift lever was on the right. The clutch was normal Bugatti. Brakes were much improved; a simple mechanical cable layout, with chain compensation longitudinally and bevel gears laterally, was used. The front cables were so arranged as to give a servo action with axle twist by passing over the top of the horizontal wheel axis. Brake shoes were initially lined with

Three 1100cc cars in the 1926 Grand Prix d'Alsace, one with Dubonnet on the right with a standard chassis, the other two Type 36 springless versions.

Above: *Costantini in the winning 1500cc voiturette from the 1925 Voiturette Grand Prix at Montlhéry; the car is a T39.*

Malcolm Campbell and son Donald at Brooklands in one of the springless Type 36 cars. (Autocar)

Chiron at Molsheim testing the first T35B 2·3 litre supercharged model, now with big brakes.

cast iron segments at the rear, and Ferodo at the front, the brake cams having rollers in contact with the shoe ends. A new type of steering box, robust but simplified as compared with that on the T30, was fitted and indeed was used in various sizes on all subsequent models. The front axle was produced with a novel form, the centre being hollow and the ends solid. This was achieved by forging the axle straight, boring a central hole right across, slotting out two square holes for the springs to pass through, and then forging down the ends to the solid again and finally bending to shape for machining and polishing all over.

The Juneks from Prague followed their practice of buying interesting racing cars from Molsheim by having one of the 1925 voiturettes; here is Elizabeth at the Ecce-Homo hill-climb in 1926.

Cast light alloy wheels with detachable rims were fitted, the brake drums being integral with the wheel. This construction was very light and effective although the spokes were not very strong against side shock loads: the later Type 51 well-base wheel had not only an integral rim but stiffening ribs inside the spokes.

The engine was similar to the Type 30; the blocks, cambox and camshaft drive were almost identical, but the crankcase differed by being split on the centre line, the lower crankcase carrying the engine-to-chassis attachment arms. The crankshaft had five main roller or ball bearings, and was built up and had roller bearing rods lubricated by oil jets. On blown models, a gear train on the front of the engine drove the blower, a three bladed Roots-type drawing from a low mounted Zenith K type barrel throttle carburettor. To allow the blower drive to be fitted, the radiator of blown models was moved forward and enlarged; its size was progressively increased as engine power went up. Unblown models had twin carburettors, the manifolding being rather tortuous. Ignition was by magneto mounted on the dash and driven from the end of the camshaft.

A cross-shaft drove a water pump on the left, the early cars having a small Brescia type pump, later cars a larger unit. The oil pump was driven from a pair of helical gears off the crankshaft, and was mounted low in the front of the engine, instead of being driven off the water pump shaft as on the T30. Early cars had hand starting only, but later ones had a starter motor carried on top of the gearbox.

(For fuller details of the engine and chassis see *Grand Prix Bugatti* mentioned above.)

The appeal and racing success of the Type 35 resulted in a remarkable production run. Between its launch in August 1924 and the end of the decade over 200 of all racing versions, and 135 of the 35A models were produced. Peak production saw about one car being produced per working day!

Contemporary road impressions

The *Autocar* of 11 June 1926 had this to say on the car in an article headed 'The Enthusiast's Ideal';

If a year or two ago any firm had announced that it was prepared to offer to the public exact replicas of a car specially designed and built for the Grand Prix, it would probably have been deemed demented. Yet this is exactly what M. Bugatti has done with outstanding success. It is true that M. Bugatti is somewhat of a law unto himself, and that frequently he does things which no one would believe possible, and it is true, also, that the Brescia Bugatti was in some sort a racing car, though it now ranks as a sports model, but the 1924 Grand Prix Bugatti was something very different from every point of view.

When it first appeared for the race at Lyons, the little horizon-blue car

Left: *Jules Goux at San Sebastian in 1926, in a supercharged 1½ litre Type 39, still with small brakes.*

captured the imagination instantly. It was so well finished, with its nickelled axles and controls, its almost show-polished engine, and its shapely radiator, that it was the kind of toy which an enthusiast had only to see to desire. Yet, however much of the toy there was externally, it soon appeared that there was no lack of speed or power. The brakes also were really powerful. That there was a fly in the ointment was certain – with a racing car this is always the case – and this time it was the cast aluminium wheels, but this has now been reduced to the status of merely a minor defect, and the car is just as desirable from the sportsman's point of view.

The real Grand Prix car, which actually had been sold in considerable numbers, has, among other things, a roller bearing crankshaft, but along with it M. Bugatti introduced two other models, both with the same sleek, shapely body – one an eight-cylinder two-litre, the other a four-cylinder one-and-a-half-litre, with ordinary bearings, and incidentally, ordinary wire wheels. It is, however, with the genuine Grand Prix racing car that we now deal.

The average every-day motorist would probably recoil from such a mount not only because he would deem it fierce and intractable, but also because it has neither hood nor mudguards. But, fortunately for the romantic and sporting side of motoring, there is another section of the community to whom this car is its heart's desire, precisely because all these fitments are absent, and because it is fierce; but certainly it is not intractable.

Quite what it is that alters the feel and character of a car when the mudguards and hood are not in place, and the windscreen merely a minute segment, is difficult to define, but it is so insistent that it might be said that the stripped car has a soul that is lacking in the sober touring mount. The whole car seems different, and to an enthusiast a hundred times better. True, on muddy roads the state of driver and mechanic beggars description, yet somehow, even this seems good. Goggles and a sound waterproof are essential, yet there is something thrilling in the feel of rain against the face, and the freshness of the cold air.

Right: *Elizabeth Junek wins the Coupe des Dames at Montlhéry in 1927.*

Concerning tractability, this car, which can lap Brooklands at well over the 100 mph gait, and probably at 114 mph or more after a little attention, can be driven at 10 mph quite comfortably through say, Kingston, handled without trouble in London traffic, and is perfectly suitable for reasonable speeds on the road.

Once the engine is hot, starting is an easy matter, nor is it difficult from cold, save that the engine must be allowed to warm before the carburettors respond correctly. As a normal touring speed can be maintained with practically no throttle opening, the feel of the car is better than that of an ordinary touring machine, because the engine is extraordinarily smooth and gives that rare sensation of great reserve power. Care must be used to avoid making too much exhaust noise, yet once the trick is mastered this is quite easy. The steering, concerning the brakes would prove revelations, not unnaturally, to the average driver.

Lehoux leads the pack in the first Monaco Grand Prix in 1929, with the eventual winner behind on his left.

At full speed the car is indeed something worth having. It has its tricks, of course, and is rather bumpy though a slight modification of tyre pressure or some readjustment of the shock-absorbers might make much difference.

On the road in racing conditions is must be almost ideal. For anyone who

A T35A is indistinguishable from the 35 externally especially as in this case when specially ordered with alloy wheels. (Car 4875).

has to combine a racing machine with a touring car, the Grand Prix Bugatti cannot be beaten, and it has a most subtle way of gaining what can only be called one's affection, even after a short run, while it feels as though it would keep its tune.

During our test the car was taken on the track and lapped at over 100 mph without any preparation after its run on the road other than to change the plugs for a set of No. 268 KLGs, which suit the engine exactly for high speed. Deliberately, the tyres and shock-absorbers, number plates and spare wheel were left in position as ordinarily used.

Chiron raced his T35B successfully and dedicated this picture to his friend Jules Goux after winning at Rome, Marne, Spain and Monza in 1928.

An owner today could not describe the charms of the car better. Every word is still true!

Above: *A fine restoration of a T35B, showing the blower, manifolding and blower relief valve. The engine is as visually pleasing as the car as a whole.*

Top left: *The engine of the unsupercharged car is elegant and simple.*

The Grand Prix of Europe and of the ACF, Lyon 1924

Bugatti had made a considerable effort and was well prepared for the event with 5 cars to race, and the prototype as a spare. His drivers were experienced: Costantini, Chassagne, Pierre de Vizcaya, Friderich, and from Spain Garnier, less well-known but with ability. Sunbeam, Alfa Romeo and Delage were there in strength and there was a Miller and a Schmid. Bugatti had a large supply of Dunlop tyres sent over from England. The tyres soon gave trouble as he recounts, leaving Campari in the Alfa Romeo to win with Delage 2nd and 3rd.

A few weeks later Ettore sent this letter out to his agents and customers (translation):

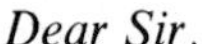

Dear Sir,
Very disturbed by the results of the European Grand Prix I had decided not to dwell on my defeat and not to draw the attention of my customers to the vicissitudes of the race.

Being daily consoled by people both friends and clients and wishing to do justice to those persons who have shown their loyalty by letter or article or who have made other personal gestures, I am obliged to explain as exactly as possible the circumstances of the event in order to demonstrate that the confidence which has been shown might easily have been justified.

First of all I would like to draw the attention of my friends and customers to a few extracts from testimonials which have been lavished on me:

M. Delage, the famous constructor, after himself driving the G.P. Bugatti sent me the following message on a visiting card:

'You have given me a great deal of pleasure in allowing me to try out your racing car and you ask my opinion. It is, with all the brilliant qualities of a racing car, the most perfect touring car that the amateur could dream of.

'I am happy to tell you this voluntarily. Cordially, Louis Delage.'

Mr Rapson, the celebrated English maker of racing car tyres, has written in an article published in the Autocar, *1 August 1924.*

'I supplied tyres only to the Sunbeams and the Miller of Count Zborowski, although I was warned that in not supplying Bugatti I probably missed the possible winner of the European Grand Prix.'

On 15 August last Mr Rapson wrote me a personal letter from which the following is an extract:

'I had like you many regrets for the bad luck that you had with your tyres in the European G.P. Without these misfortunes you car would have won or have finished in the first three. The tyre faults showed up the efficiency of your aluminium wheel which was very satisfactory. I was very favourably impressed by all the improvements that you have so judiciously made to your wheel, and I think that

Top right: *The original Lyon cars had a push-pull magneto advance lever in the dash.*

Below: *Later the magneto was raised and driven by step-up gearing from the camshaft, and a vertical advance level was fitted. A starter motor conversion was available.*

one of the large wheel makers in the U.S.A. would be ready to pay you substantial royalties for the manufacturing rights for that country.'

I made the greatest effort to produce, for the first European Grand Prix run in France, five cars and one reserve all identical, with irreproachable finish, fine appearance and perfectly developed. These six cars were ready well before the first practice on the circuit.

The six cars arrived the day before the first practice day with the circuit closed, no work was necessary and the drivers, out of pride, washed and polished their cars so that they could arrive at the start in impeccable condition. Next morning at 5 o'clock everyone was ready on the circuit and each had carried out the predetermined test programme on the lines of what he was expected to do on the day itself. No incident occured during practice and all tests were carried out similarly without even having to lift a bonnet either at the pits or on the circuit.

I had brought to Lyons a camping installation and to give an idea to those who have not seen it, it suffices for me to say that the transport of the camping equipment was made in three railway wagons and two road trucks with trailers. The racing cars went to Lyons under their own power and the supporting supply vehicles carried a total load of 30 tons.

Everything was provided: a wooden floor under a large tent, real beds for 45 people, a shower installation, running water in each cabin, plenty of electricity. Cooking was carried out in a solid wooden hut with everything necessary to feed the personnel properly for almost a month. At the side, ditches were dug for drainage. There were two ice-boxes, one of very large size, the other smaller. There was also a caravan for my own family.

The tyre shape I had adopted after making many tests, first of all on protected roads near my factory and then on the circuit itself, had given the best possible results. The construction of the cover itself and of the wheel allowed running with a deflated tyre, and I thought it better to risk loss of time due to a flat tyre than to carry a spare wheel which would certainly cause the loss of five minutes on the total time for the event.

Everything was thus prepared for the best.

Well prepared, more than satisfied with my drivers, happy with the choice of circuit, I believed my car the most suitable for this race. All the qualities of the 'thoroughbred' should come out in an event such as this: rapid starting, good acceleration, more than adequate speed on the straight, progressive and powerful brakes. Everything was well determined, well chosen and ready. Accordingly I arrived proudly at the start. I drove the reserve car and my five drivers followed with their handsome 'thoroughbreds'. The starting flag fell. The car driven by Mr Chassagne, carrying Number 7, lay third at Broken Bridge. The first ten laps were expected to be completed calmly and when I heard this news I thought to myself that I might be hopeful of the outcome of this race.

The first arrivals on completing the first lap included Mr de Viscaya with a deflated tyre, after completing part of the lap on the flat tyre. I wasn't worried; I was very pleased to see that my specially built wheels complied with one of the first conditions I imposed in their design, namely to operate without air pressure.

All went well, but then on the third lap Mr de Viscaya came in again with a tread off a tyre. Not a bit of rubber. The adhesive that joined the carcase to the tread was soft and could be rolled into balls, which confirmed the bad state of vulcanization of these two.

At this moment I realized that the race was lost as far as I was concerned. In succession Mr Chassagne on the fourth lap and then two cars at the same time came in to change rear wheels. I reminded my drivers that they should be careful, since in certain tests made previously with other tyres, the throwing of a tread had endangered the life of the driver. If a tyre lost a tread, pieces could wrap around the steering gear (this had happened to Mr Chassagne) and cause a serious accident. Happily no front tyre lost a tread during the Grand Prix and all drivers drove in the race without trouble due to this.

Car No. 22 driven by Mr Costantini had its gear change lever torn by a tread from a right-hand tyre. He had to complete several laps with the gear lever completely bent and unable to select 2nd and 4th, damaging the gears in the box also as they could not engage over their full width. He had therefore to retire. I might remark that this car came into the pits, and completed its last lap sufficiently fast, which shows that no other accident occurred to the car, which was driven in front of the Stand and left under its own power at the end of the race for our encampment.

Mr de Viscaya's car was put out of action due to tyres. Taking a corner, a tread failed, the car skidded unforseenly and demolished a barrier, running into the front of a house on the first corner at Givors. Heartbroken, the driver had to abandon the car which had the rear axle completely bent back and the chassis broken.

Once again I told my drivers to be careful, explaining why the two cars had been eliminated. It is for all these reasons that it was not possible to demonstrate what the cars could really do.

My greatest regret is that I could not demonstrate my new wheel, nor could I show the real speed of my cars.

The features of the new wheel are as follows:

a) good cooling of the tyre, due to the rim in aluminium, which has a much greater thermal conductivity than steel;

b) fixation of the cover to the rim by a safety ring preventing the cover being detached and all relative movement of rim and cover;

c) perfect cooling of the wheel including the brake drum.

There are some who thought that my wheel was the cause of the tyre trouble. It is sufficient for me to say that the tyres on the front wheels never budged, so that it was not a question of the wheel, nor of heat, but only a lack of adhesion of the tread to the ply which caused the tread-throwing probably because the tyres were of too recent manufacture.

Some said also: the cars are not fast. This I will demonstrate on another occasion, but it suffices to know that when Mr Chassagne was told that he did a lap in 20 seconds longer time than the car that made the record lap, he was astonished with the result, and if he had been advised during the event of this small difference he would have made an attempt at the record, for at no time had he pressed his car to the limit. On several occasions in the climb through the zig-zag up to Givors my cars had passed every other competitor. It must not be deduced that my cars were faster than my competitors, this would not be sportsmanlike, but what I can claim is that my cars were the fastest in the climb between Givors and Broken Bridge.

The public in the Stand were able to note the following: first of all the continual stops for tyre changing, the speed with which wheels were changed, the speed of refuelling, and the restart of the cars with a quarter turn of the starting handle. Everyone was surprised to see that my cars had no need to be pushed to start them. The mechanic had only to make a single twist and the engine started, which showed the good tune of the cars and the potentiality for normal use of these racing cars.

The built-up ball and roller bearing crankshaft used on the full Grand Prix models was a fine piece of precision engineering.

Right: *The front brake operation was by cable along the lines of the later Brescia and T30 cars.*

Ten of these cars have been built. They are almost all sold to customers. Some are already delivered and are a joy to their owners. One can use them as easily in town as in any race. I hope on the next occasion to make a better demonstration of the quality of my construction.

I will finish by saying that this car must not be considered a racing car. It has been built on the same principle as all the others, since I do not propose ever to race with a machine that is not strictly that that the customer can buy. The engine has only one change, namely roller bearings on the connecting rods and crankshaft, as well as a special extra light front axle, round and hollow. All other parts are similar to those of production cars.

The total weight of the car is only 1,450 lb. Great speed is obtained for the least weight, due to the good shape of the body and particularly by the road holding, since speed depends often on the way the car behaves on the road.

I would hope that after having studied the reasons which prevented me from confirming the confidence that has been accorded me in hoping for my success, you will be assured that although it will not be possible to make a new effort on this scale, I will always do my best to enter in a race with the maximum chance of showing my customers the excellence of my construction.

Yours truly

(Signed) Ettore Bugatti
MOLSHEIM

Type 37

4 cylinder racing model

In 1926 the 1·5 litre Brescia racing model was replaced with a new car which used the Type 35 chassis and body and was fitted with a 4 cylinder, 69 mm × 100 mm, 1,496 cc engine; this engine had a block and valve gear (three valves per cylinder) similar in detail to the 8 cylinder car, but the crankshaft was carried on five plain main bearings. The block and bearing arrangements came directly from the earlier Type 28 3 litre car which had not gone into production. Early models had jet lubrication but later a full pressure-fed crank was used. Wire wheels were fitted as standard in place of the light alloy GP wheels and ignition was by coil. A small blower (casing length 135 mm, compared with the T35B unit which was 185 mm long) was later added on the Type 37A; this model, usually referred to with the suffix CP by Molsheim, had a successful racing history, the late Chris Staniland lapping Brooklands at over 122 mph in one of them. These racing models had dash-mounted magneto

ignition and usually the detachable rim alloy wheels.

The unblown model first appeared at the end of 1925 and was first catalogued in the October 1926 catalogue, under the designation Grand Sport. The engine was also fitted to the Type 40 touring model described in the next chapter. A full contemporary description of the engine by Max Millar follows at the end of this chapter.

The simplicity of the four cylinder, plain bearing engine was, and indeed is, attractive to the would-be owner of a Grand Prix Bugatti, and the considerably lower price than the full racing Type 35, or even the cheaper T35A, created a new market for the model. Sales were good and production soon exceeded 10 per month in 1926, remaining at a good rate in 1927 and 1928, reaching a total of 270 by 1930. A substantial number of the later cars were the supercharged 37A model, much used by amateurs for sports car and racing events.

Bottom left: *The 4 cylinder T37 two seater from the original catalogue with road equipment and even a windscreen. This model replaced the Brescia in 1926 and was a very successful model for sporting use, or minor racing.*

The original version as sold in France, with beaded edge tyres and no mudguards. Later, improved lamp brackets were used.

Contemporary road impressions

In *Motor Sport*, September 1926, Richard Twelvetrees described a road test of an unblown Type 37:

One has only to glance at the 1,500 cc Grand Prix Bugatti, however, to observe that it is a distinct advance on any of its forerunners, and the manufacturers

The early version of the T37 engine from 1926, with small inlet manifold and a barrel-throttle Solex carburettor. (Autocar)

A young Jack Lemon Burton at a Bugatti Owners Club hill-climb in 1931.

have introduced a new era for the sporting motorist by placing a real production racing car in the hands of the public. That is to say one can purchase one of these machines, drive it away, and as delivered it will be fit to win races and competitions without any need of 'hotting up'. The actual car [tested] is that belonging to Captain J.C. Douglas and is used daily as a runabout by Mrs Douglas for shopping expeditions in the West End, which supports the maker's claim as to docility.

The stability of the Grand Prix Bugatti and its wonderful steadiness in cornering at speed is largely due to the very low centre of gravity, the chassis being very low without detracting too much from ground clearance. The suspension comprises semi-elliptic front springs, located outside the frame members and provided with rebound clips on the forward halves. The well-known and tried reversed quarter-elliptic springs carry the rear axle, shock-absorbers of the Bugatti design being employed for both sets of springs.

Though the seats are arranged very low the riding is quite comfortable and plenty of leg room is provided on either side of the clutch and gearbox, this part of the mechanism being covered by a readily removable leather flap.

When the bonnet was removed for examination of the engine, I was surprised at the amount of accessibility, for from the external appearance of the car one is apt to imagine that the mechanism must be somewhat cramped. There is, however, plenty of room to get at everything, and any of the normal running adjustments can be made with extraordinary facility. The four-cylinder engine ... revs up to well over 5,000 rpm almost as soon as the accelerator pedal is depressed. The overhead camshaft gear is enclosed in a neat square aluminium cover, which, conforming with the outline of the cylinder block, gives the engine a particularly neat appearance. Both the revolution counter and the Delco distributor take their drives from the rear end of the camshaft....

I was fortunate in being able to see the best of this attractive little sports model in really expert hands, for Captain J.C. Douglas is certainly amongst the top notchers of demonstrators. I had expected to be whirled along the main roads at lightning speed, having to keep my eyes well skinned in case a man in blue hove in sight. Instead of which the car was driven gently along at a comfortable touring pace, running with remarkable smoothness though some very pretty work with the gears produced something quite out of the way as regards acceleration. The body work gives a good position, but, as might be expected, fails to provide the luxurious comfort to be found in some of the more elaborate sports tourers, and one has to remember that the rear wheel is very close when tempted to put the elbow too far over the side.

Leaving the traffic, I was treated to a turn of speed along a good wide open road, and again by using the gears with fine judgment Captain Douglas made the little bus hum along merrily at over 85 mph, with plenty more movement left on the accelerator pedal. When going at over 70 mph, he shouted to me to hold tight and by applying the brakes brought the car to rest in an incredibly short distance, though I was expecting a skid, and said so ... I must say the Bugatti created a most favourable impression.

In 1933 a Type 37 road-equipped Grand Prix Bugatti was the subject of an article in *Autocar*, following Brian Twist's run in the car then owned by Mr R.J.W. Appleton. 'There is no car quite like a Bugatti to the enthusiast ...' observed the former. This particular car, a 1926 model, had been converted from the splash to pressure-fed big ends, as fitted from 1928 onwards; it also had two Solex carburettors instead of the normal one, a Scintilla megneto and special connecting rods. It had lapped Brooklands outer circuit at 96·8 mph, did 17–23 mpg on petrol-benzole, and 7–10 mpg on alcohol. Acceleration tests produced the following: 10–30 on the 9 to 1 bottom gear in 4·4 seconds, and 6 seconds on the 7 to 1 gear; 0–60 in 14·6 sec, and 0–80 in 30·2 sec, the former being accomplished in bottom gear, which is quite something and, incidentally,

6,000 rpm. It was pointed out that alcohol fuel was used and the carburation was unhappy on account of the cold weather during these tests. The brakes stopped the car in 30 feet from 30 mph, and approximately 85 yards from 70 mph which, as the author of the article comments, 'is pretty good'. He concludes: 'Finally, I drove the car back to the workshop and was fascinated by the ease of the steering, the smooth power of the brakes, the quite reasonable tractability in such towns as we passed through, and last, but not least, the wonderful Bugatti exhaust note.'

TYPE 37 ENGINE

(Under the heading 'Another Famous Engine', this illustrated article by Max Millar first appeared in the *Autocar* on 19 September 1952)

In the history of the car world during the years from 1911 to 1939, there were few names that could compete with that of Ettore Bugatti for his remarkable career and general attainments, and for his great success in the racing sphere; his name, moreover, is still regarded with as much respect and admiration among Bugatti enthusiasts as in the old days.

Top right: *The supercharged T37A versions appeared at the 1927 Coupe de la Commission Sportive at Montlhéry: Count Conelli before the event.*

Dubonnet at the Bugatti Grand Prix at Le Mans in 1928.

A biography of Bugatti by W.F. Bradley tells us that this great man (1881–1947) was a born artist as well as an engineer, and that for many years he not only designed his own cars but also made the drawings and supervised production in his shops at Molsheim. His cars were so outstandingly different from others that a mere superficial look at them at any time would be enough to excite great attention, but a closer examination reveals characteristics which indicate that Bugatti was an individualist in the field of design respecting almost every component, stud and nut in each of his creations.

By his personal ability to design, experiment and carry through the work to the production stage, Bugatti was able to do what he liked, and the long list of road and racing successes was ample proof of his capacity as a practical engineer; but the aforementioned abilities enabled him to design with such a superb sense of proportion and finesse that the contemporary efforts of other makers often seemed crude and wasteful by comparison, and, of course, he gained immeasurably in regard to weight reduction in his chassis.

In discussing Bugatti's achievements in engine design, it would be difficult to select any one power unit as being more interesting than others; they all

Top left: *T. P. Cholmondley-Tapper and Eileen Ellison successfully raced a T37A for several seasons in Europe in the 1930s. He wrote of his experiences in his book 'Amateur Racing Driver' (Foulis, 1954).*

A few T37s were fitted with closed coachwork, of special lightweight construction. Here is Miss Marie Dalbaicin at a 'Championnat Automobile des Artistes' in Paris around 1928.

exhibited remarkable features in one form or another; He produced many types of engine ranging from 4 to 16 cylinder units and from 1,327 cc up to the enormous Royale of 12,760 cc (although curiously a 6 cylinder engine was never listed), and a number were supercharged; but a 1925 Type 37 4 cylinder 1,496 cc engine may be taken as representative of Bugatti design some twenty-five years ago, and it exhibits many of those novel features that reveal the Bugatti mind as a designer and engineer.

In general, the Type 37 engine is remarkably simple as a unit, the cast iron cylinder block being a rectangular component, with the heads and valve ports cast in as one-piece job. Three valves per cylinder (one exhaust and two inlet) are fitted, and they are operated by an overhead camshaft bevel driven through a vertical shaft from the cranshaft, in the time-honoured system so frequently seen on sports or racing engines. The cylinder block is bolted to an aluminium alloy crankcase split across the crankshaft centre line, the lower half forming

The bare chassis is elegant and comparatively simple to maintain. This example was restored by R. Townsend. (Neill Bruce).

The supercharged engine has the steering box moved back to make room for the blower, and the magneto is now mounted on the dash as with the 8 cylinder car, but the unit is driven directly at camshaft speed, requiring a special 8/4 magneto.

the capacious alloy oil sump of 10 pints capacity, conventional in most respects except for one important point in that the four substantial bearer arms of the engine are attached to the lower and not to the upper half of the crankcase; the lower half, or sump, therefore, carries most of the dead weight of the engine.

The cylinder block of 69 mm × 100 mm bore and stroke has the four barrels cast together without interspace cooling, and they project into the crankcase for some distance. The block is machined all over externally and is flat sided, with the vertically disposed valves (inlets 26·5 mm, exhaust 36 mm) set to the maximum diameter available in the combustion chamber, with slight rebating of the cylinder walls to give clearance. The inlet valve ports are double siamesed; each group of four is connected with an intake from the induction manifold, and each exhaust valve is separately ducted in the cylinder head to individual exhaust pipes. The block, as a whole, is interesting in that Bugatti considerably simplified the coring and casting by not including the upper face of the head in

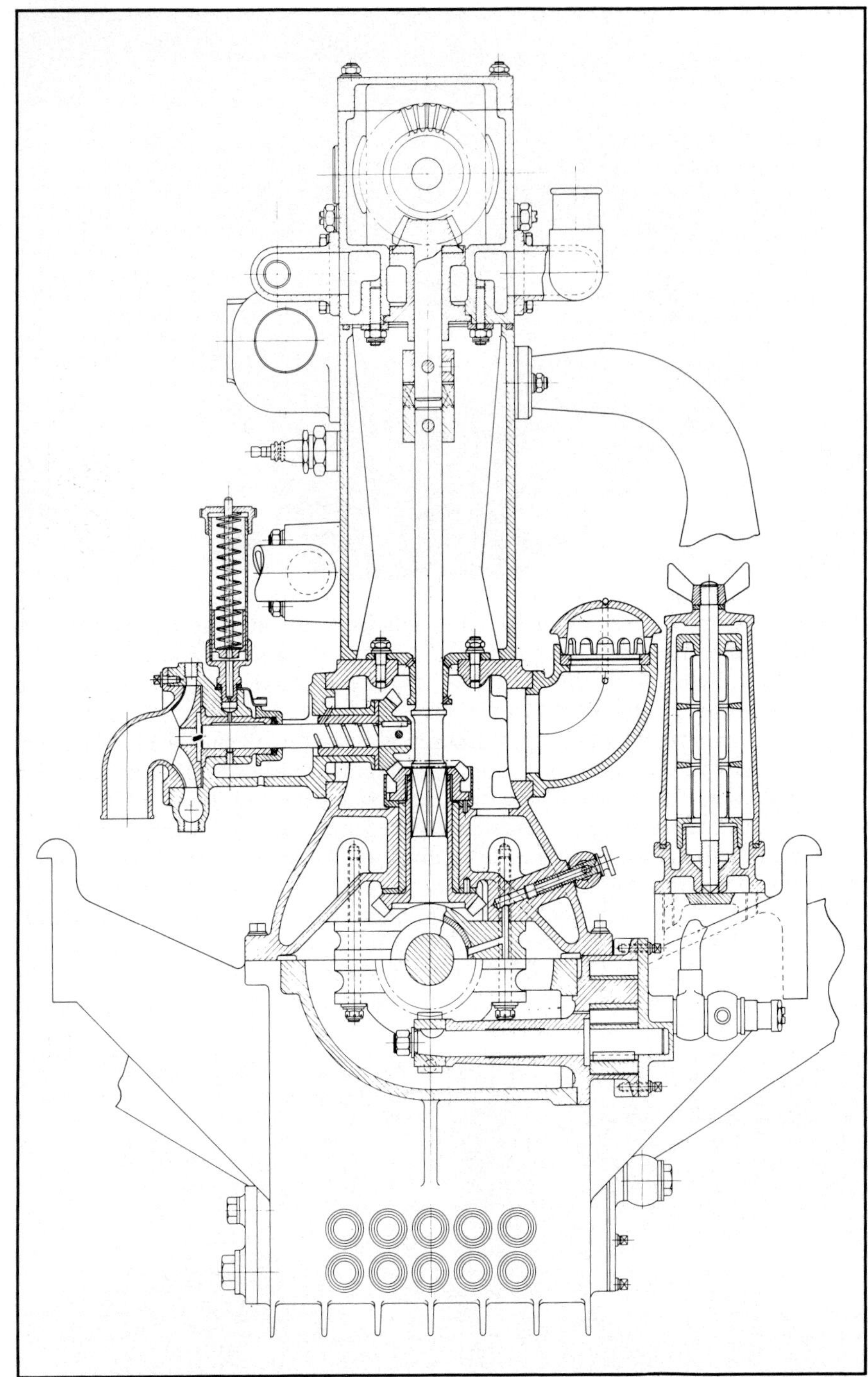

A vertical elevation of the narrow T37 engine.

the casting process, thereby leaving the ports and passages open to inspection before machining. After machining, a flat aluminium roof about $\frac{3}{32}$in. thick, drilled where necessary, was fitted on the top face of the head. This roof is held in place by the 12 threaded bronze valve guides, and by the six screw sockets that retain the overhead camshaft case in position. The firing order is 1, 2, 4, 3.

A study of the cross-section of the Bugatti engine reveals the extraordinary proportions and character of this power unit. Tall and narrow, the engine has a crankcase so tightly built around the circular webbed crankshaft that the minimum safe clearance has been given to the connecting rod big-ends; but the crankcase is more rigid in consequence, and there is a considerable saving in weight. The cylinder block is held to the crankcase by 10 small studs and nuts

on each side; the nuts lie in a machined slot, which is covered by an aluminium strip held in the slot by spring-loaded balls; thus the flat sided effect of the cylinder block is preserved.

In view of the fact that the close spacing of the cylinder bores involved an equivalent restriction on the lateral proportions of the crankshaft and its webs, it is not surprising that Bugatti made the webs circular in shape and very narrow in width (11 mm) to leave enough room for the three inter-crank bearings of the five bearing shaft. The webs are not balanced, and the crankshaft (weight 37 lb) is machined all over. In the early engines of the Type 37 the big-ends were lubricated by horizontal jets in the crankshaft main bearings – jets that fed oil into shallow circular grooves in the outer faces of the webs and thence by drilled passages to the crankpins. But at a later date the crankshaft was drilled for direct pressure lubrication as between each journal and crankpin. Splash lubrication of the cylinder bores is regulated by horizontal webs cast in the crankcase below the mouths of the bores; the webs further increase the rigidity of the crankcase in that area.

Four of the main bearings have four slender studs and nuts for retention of the bearing caps, in place of pairs of larger size, and the rear main bearing is held by six studs and nuts instead of a possible two or four as is usual practice. The flywheel, it it can be termed such, is only $8\frac{1}{2}$in. in diameter, but it is of considerable length (weight, 22 lb) to accommodate the multi-plate, semi-wet Bugatti clutch.

The connecting rods (weight 2 lb 1 oz) are of normal design, but have slender shanks for a fast engine, and are notable for the amount of extra metal

The longitudinal section of the engine shows the five main bearings carried on the upper half of the crankcase.

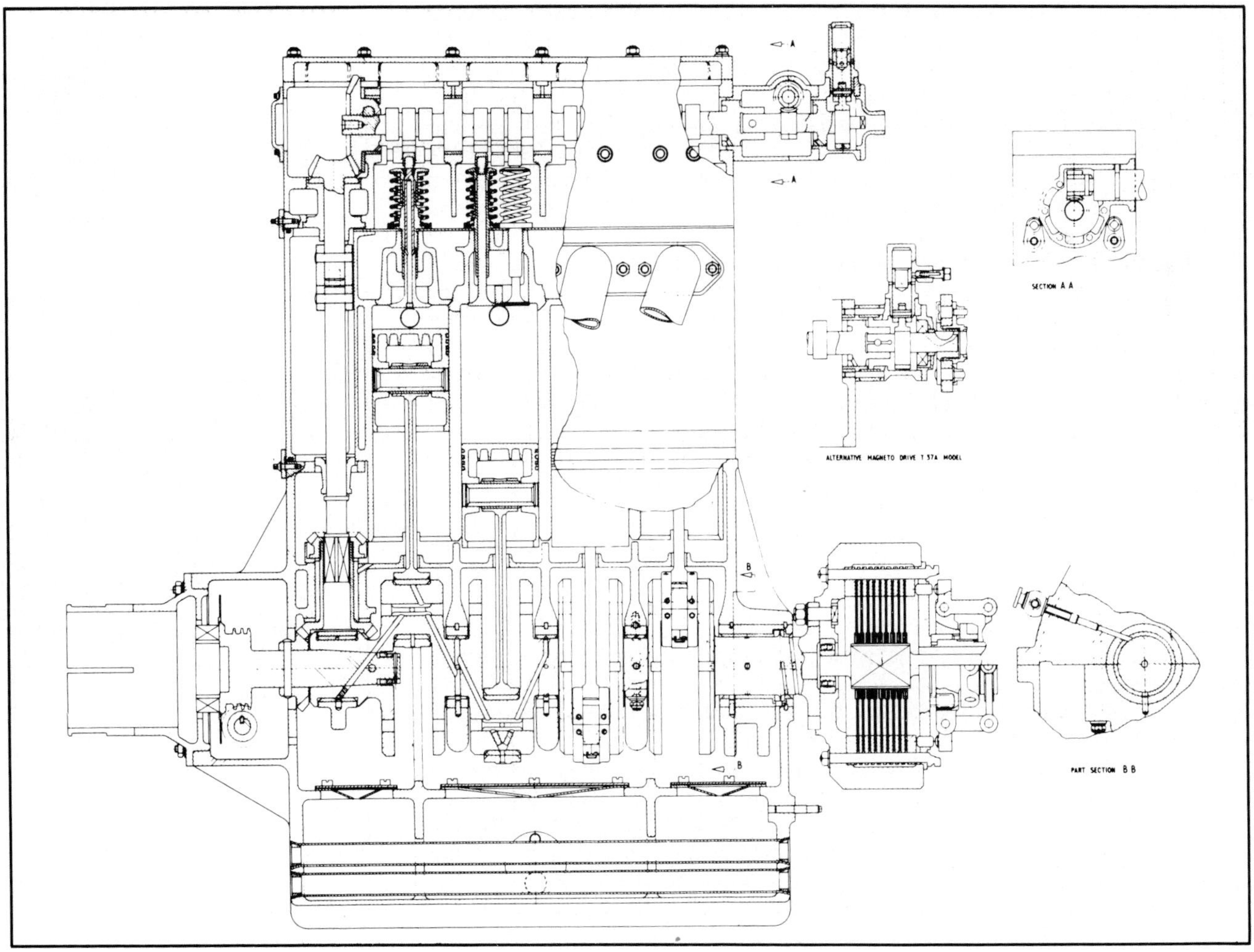

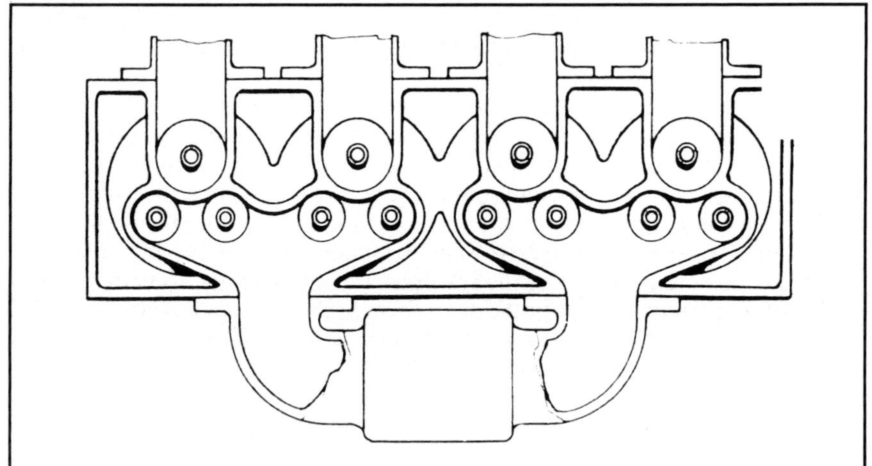

How Bugatti fed eight inlet valves with mixture from an internal induction manifold and single carburettor. The exhaust valves are ducted separately to a 'bunch of bananas' exhaust pipe.

in the big-end shells, and for the bronze white-metal-lined bearings, riveted to the shells to prevent rotation. Alloy pistons (weight, with gudgeon pins and rings, 14 oz) with three compression rings and one scraper, are of conventional design; the gudgeon pins are held in the piston by an interference fit and endwise locating rings. The 18 mm sparking plugs are fitted in the side of the combustion chambers, the electrodes shielded by shrouded recesses in the cylinder walls.

In this engine, Bugatti operated the inlet and exhaust valves from the single overhead camshaft through horizontal levers, two for each pair of inlet valves and a single one for each exhaust valve. The rockers butt against the hardened steel caps fitted on the valve stems and are each located laterally by an adjustable screwed peg in the side of the camshaft casing. The rocker spindles are drilled; oil fed through them from the oil pressure system lubricates the rockers, cams, and the camshaft bevel driving wheels and bearings; the four plain bush bearings supporting the camshaft are lubricated by splash oil caught in troughs above the bearings. The complete box-like camshaft casing, with flat-topped lid, is in shape just an upward extension of the cylinder block, and it heightens the general appearance of the tall, narrow engine.

Bugatti's penchant for tucking things in neatly, and for reducing weight and mass of metal in various places, is exemplified by his vertical drive to the camshaft and by the close association of the lower driving bevels with the front main bearing of the crankshaft. The vertical shaft is in two sections, linked together by a squared sliding joint, and at a midway level a further pair of bevels drive the horizontal spindle of the water pump. No ball or roller bearings are used in the drives; indeed, none is found in the engine anywhere. The upper portion of the vertical drive is enclosed at the side by an aluminium casting shaped to complete the box-like structure of the cylinder block and camshaft casing.

The oil pump, externally located on the nose of the crankcase, is driven transversely through a skew gear on a front extension of the crankshaft, which also carries the dog drive for the dynamo bolted to the front of the crankcase. the pump, drawing oil from the finned oil sump, feeds the main bearings through a high pressure filter and an external gallery pipe supplying the bearings through drilled passages in the crankcase webs. Two secondary pipes feed the hollow spindles of the overhead valve rockers, and the oil returns to the sump through passages in the cylinder block or downwards past the camshaft vertical drive. Cooling of oil in the sump is effected not only by external finning but also by horizontal air tubes, which greatly increase the total cooling area of the sump.

The simple, clean appearance of this Bugatti engine is enhanced by the layout of the water-circulation system, whereby the customary external piping is largely eliminated. Water from the pump is taken to the lower end of the cylinder jacket through an aluminium manifold which feeds coolant through a series of spaced holes in the jacket to provide a directional flow upwards past

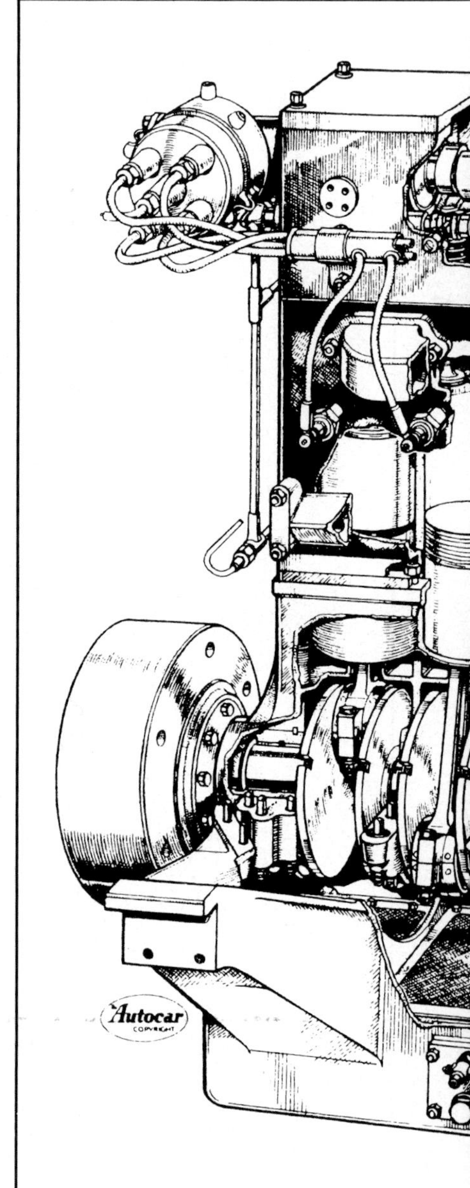

Section of cylinder head showing how valve guides are employed to assist holding down the cover plate on the top face of the head.

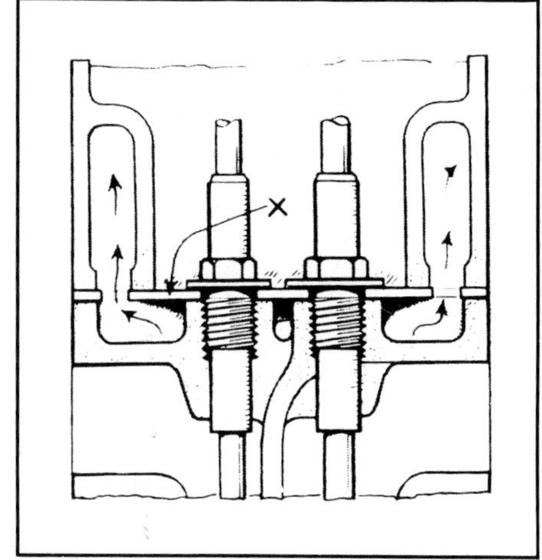

Below: *The disc-webbed, 5 bearing crankcase, compact cylinder block and overhead valve gear are special characteristics of the Type 37 engine. The worm drive to the oil pump is a source of trouble. It is inadequately lubricated and the high rubbing velocity of the worm causes the pinion on the gear pump to wear out fairly rapidly.*

the cylinder barrels. From the cylinder jackets the upward flow is further directed past the valve ports on each side and through another series of holes to the water manifolds cast in the sides of the camshaft casing; the return of water to the radiator is through two forward mounted elbows and hose pipes. Hot water for the induction pipe jackets is bled off at a central point from the cylinder block and is returned to the radiator via one of the elbows just mentioned.

Another feature indicative of the clean planning of the engine is the mounting of the coil ignition distributor (skew gear driven) at the rear end of the camshaft casing, and the neat rigging of the high tension leads. The water pump has an unusual feature in that it is equipped with a permanently-fitted grease gun for gland lubrication, and is fitted with a light external tell-tale spindle to indicate the quantity of grease remaining in the barrel. Throughout the engine are to be seen small square and hexagon-headed nuts of Bugatti design – many with special flanges, as in aircraft engine practice – and all external surfaces of the power unit are either machined or hand treated and polished.

With a weight of 15½ cwt, the Type 37 Bugatti Grand Prix two-seater model was capable of 95 mph at 5,000 rpm, with a rear axle ratio of approximately 4 to 1. Unquestionably, the fine road performance of this model, with an engine of only medium compression, was owed to the light weight of the chassis and ensemble, and to the fact that it could be handled and driven superbly by a competent driver. At the same time the conservative stressing of the engine gave a considerable degree of reliability, in terms of a sports car, and an unusual fuel economy of approximately 30 mpg, the engine having normally only a single Solex carburettor.

A later development from this engine was the Type 37A, which was fitted with a Roots-type supercharger; but not many – in comparison – of these units were produced, and the supercharged version never achieved the lasting fame of the Type 37. The Type 40 engine, also unsupercharged, was similar to the Type 37, but was a detuned version for a touring car, with a lower compression ratio.

The death of Ettore Bugatti in 1947 brought an end to an astonishing career, the details of which must be treasured by the many who knew him – a career that could not easily be emulated in the present world. The recent re-establishment of the Bugatti at Molsheim, nevertheless, offers good hope that some of the influence that Ettore so powerfully created will not be lost in future productions from the famous factory.

Type 38

8 cylinder

IN 1926 and 1927 an 8 cylinder 2 litre touring model was produced, using an engine based on the Type 35A; this model, Type 38, replaced Type 30 but was similar in most respects. The model was listed in the British 1928 catalogue, but only a few were produced in that year, production ceasing in November. It derived indeed from an earlier design, the T33 which had a gear box in the rear axle, but did not materialize. In fact, Type 44 replaced it as the 8 cylinder touring model and Type 38 more or less grew into Type 43 by the time the GP supercharged engine was fitted. The chassis (which is described in detail in the *Automotor Journal* of 21 July 1927) was rather longer than in Type 30, having the same wheelbase as the later T44, and the track was widened two inches from the earlier model. The front axle was of circular (but solid) section with the springs passing through the centre of the axle

The Type 38 replaced the T30 as the normal 8 cylinder touring model, still 2 litres. The engine was similar both to the T30 and the later T35A. The radiator is now flat based, and the gearbox was new, with a more conventional gear change, first gear being forward, and top back. It was successful enough with light coachwork, but really needed more power.

An elegant 'Fiacre' style coupé. (R. Jarraud).

as on the GP cars. The rear suspension and axle were normal Bugatti; wire wheels on Rudge hubs and large brake drums and cable brakes run on almost identical lines to the GP cars. Hartford type (Repusseau) friction shock-absorbers were used in place of the Bugatti model seen on earlier cars.

The engine was virtually a 35A unit, with a 3 ball bearing crank and plain connecting rod bearings, the crankshaft itself being the same unit as on Type 30. There were two Solex carburettors and coil ignition. The clutch was normal Bugatti, but used a Y-shaped vertical yoke for withdrawal in place of the transverse diamond shaped lever used on Type 30 and other earlier cars. A new gearbox was used, carried in a casting

An English bodied tourer by Compton.

A blower was added to make the T38A; this one had a body very much like the later T43.

straddling the frame as on the earlier cars, but the gear change was central, and the direction of change normal. Virtually all chassis details other than the engine were used on the later Type 40, 43, 44, 49 series cars.

Although the general design of the chassis and transmission was excellent, as its use on other models indicates, the engine lacked power and one of greater capacity was needed to make full use of the chassis. At the end of production Bugatti attempted to give the car a new lease of life by adding the small (Type 39) supercharger to the engine, with the same drive arrangements as on the racing model; although performance was improved, the 'bottom-end' of the engine was not up to the increased power and its weakness became apparent. About 50 of the supercharged models were produced from a total production of 380.

As has been said: 'there have been more successful models'.

Type 40

4 cylinder

TYPE 40 replaced the Brescia as the 1·5 litre, 4 cylinder touring car, a type of car indeed on which Bugatti had made his name. The type is sometimes rudely referred to as 'Ettore's Morris Cowley', but if its performance was a little pedestrian it still had all the good road manners of the earlier models coupled with sensible bodywork and a degree of simplicity which the 8 cylinder models could not offer, and finally was sold at a reasonable price.

The chassis, although of shorter wheelbase, was similar to Type 38, and the axles, gearbox and general layout were the same, although the track was 1·2 m as on the Type 35 and 37. The engine was that of the Type 37, already described, namely an unblown 4 cylinder 69 mm × 100 mm, 5 plain bearing crank, plain rods and three valves per cylinder in a cylinder block and cambox which were similar to half of the 8 cylinder GP engine and derived directly from the Type 28. As in the case of the Type 37 the jet lubricated connecting rod bearings on early engines were eventually replaced by a full pressure crank version. The crankcase casting itself had different attachment arms to suit the parallel front part of the frame. The standard Molsheim bodywork on Type 40 was a close-coupled 4-seat torpedo touring car with a single left-hand door and a hatch on the long tail to provide access to a luggage compartment, a style also used on the T43. But many proprietary coach builders fitted closed or convertible bodies to the model, the wheelbase of the car being lengthened during the production run to facilitate the fitment of closed bodywork.

Production of the Type 40 began in mid-1926 in the middle of Bugatti's 'hey-day' of racing success. Over 150 cars came out that year, 280 in 1927, with production continuing to a total of some 800 by 1932 – not as successful perhaps as the Brescia but still a worthy production for the period.

In 1930 a batch of about fifty Type 40A cars was produced, these having cylinder blocks from Type 49, with a 72 mm bore, dual ignition, and a ball change to the gear box, but otherwise similar to the standard model. Most had two seat roadster bodies with a folding rear seat, along classic American lines.

Contemporary road impressions

A road test of this model was published in *The Motor,* 10 December 1929, the car being a Molsheim bodied tourer with a single left-hand door. The front seat was 36 in. wide with a reasonable 9½ in. of rear leg room. The turning circle was commendably low at 36 ft to the right and 34 ft to the left.

Bugatti cars have always been famous for their successes in racing, but they have generally been considered just a little too expensive for the young man with sporting tastes but a limited bank balance. The Type 40 Bugatti, however, possesses many of the excellent features of the 1,500 cc Grand Prix model, but sells at the comparatively modest price of £365.

The maker's claims as regards maximum speed are by no means extravagant: 70 to 75 mph is the speed with which they credit the car, and we found that it would lap Brooklands at 70·64 mph, in thoroughly unsuitable weather, whilst its maximum speed attained on test with the wind behind was 76·8 mph. Moreover, the car is fast on its gears and will reach 62·5 mph on third, while the acceleration is distinctly good.

The Type 40 Bugatti is one of those cars which one appreciates to the full only after having driven it some considerable distance. At first one is apt to find

Bottom left: *A Molsheim picture of an early, probably the first, T40 with the shallow-section Brescia frame members, and small brakes. The chassis was supplied with dash, bonnet and side valances. Note the Bugatti door hinge behind!*

The T40 1½ litre 4 cylinder car was introduced in 1926 to replace the Brescia. It combined the road manners and driving charm of its larger and faster sisters, but at a surprisingly modest price, about a third of the racing model T35. The first series had a Brescia frame, but soon the chassis was lengthened and strengthened, and the standard factory body was this Grand Sport. Here is Maurice Phillipe, one of France's best known motor journalists of the period.

Bottom right: *The driving compartment, with central gear change.*

Below: *Geo Ham the motor and aircraft artist was another owner of a T40 Grand Sport.*

the gear change a little difficult. Indeed, the mechanically-minded Britisher rather shrinks from seizing the gear lever in a grip of iron and thrusting it without ceremony into whichever slot of the gate corresponds to the gear ratio required. Attempts to change gear as one does on the average British car – gently with two fingers – are seldom successful. As a matter of fact, the gear change is distinctly positive, and moreover very rapid. The higher the speeds at which the gears are changed the easier the manipulation of the gear lever becomes. On the intermediate gears the car is not quiet, but mechanical silence is never considered of great importance by the sports car enthusiast. On the other hand, the engine is quieter than most power units of its type, while the exhaust is by no means offensive.

The car is, above all, thoroughly roadworthy, and this surely is the greatest recommendation of all. One can swing round a bend or stamp on the brake pedal on a greasy stretch of road without experiencing the slightest qualm. Comfortable at low speeds, the springing becomes positively luxurious at a mile a minute or over; indeed, it is one of the best-sprung cars of its type which we have yet driven, and there is no need, for instance, to vary the shockabsorber adjustment even for wisely different conditions, such as low speeds in town and an all-out lap on Brooklands track.

The steering for the first few minutes seems a little stiff, but this impression soon fades, and once on the open road no car could be more easily controlled; one can steer to an inch at any speed.

The clutch, of the multi-plate type, is smooth and light to operate, while the back axle is fairly quiet.

Another good feature of the car is that it seems to delight in being driven hard. The accelerator pedal can be kept fully depressed for lap after lap of the track, and the car will, if anything, gain in speed. This partly due to very careful consideration having been given to keep the oil cool. The sump, besides being

deeply ribbed, is fitted with longitudinal tubes of large diameter, through which the air passes, thus cooling the oil very rapidly. The body-work is built on distinctly sporting lines and closely resembles that fitted to the famous 2,300 cc model which has done so well in races during the past year.

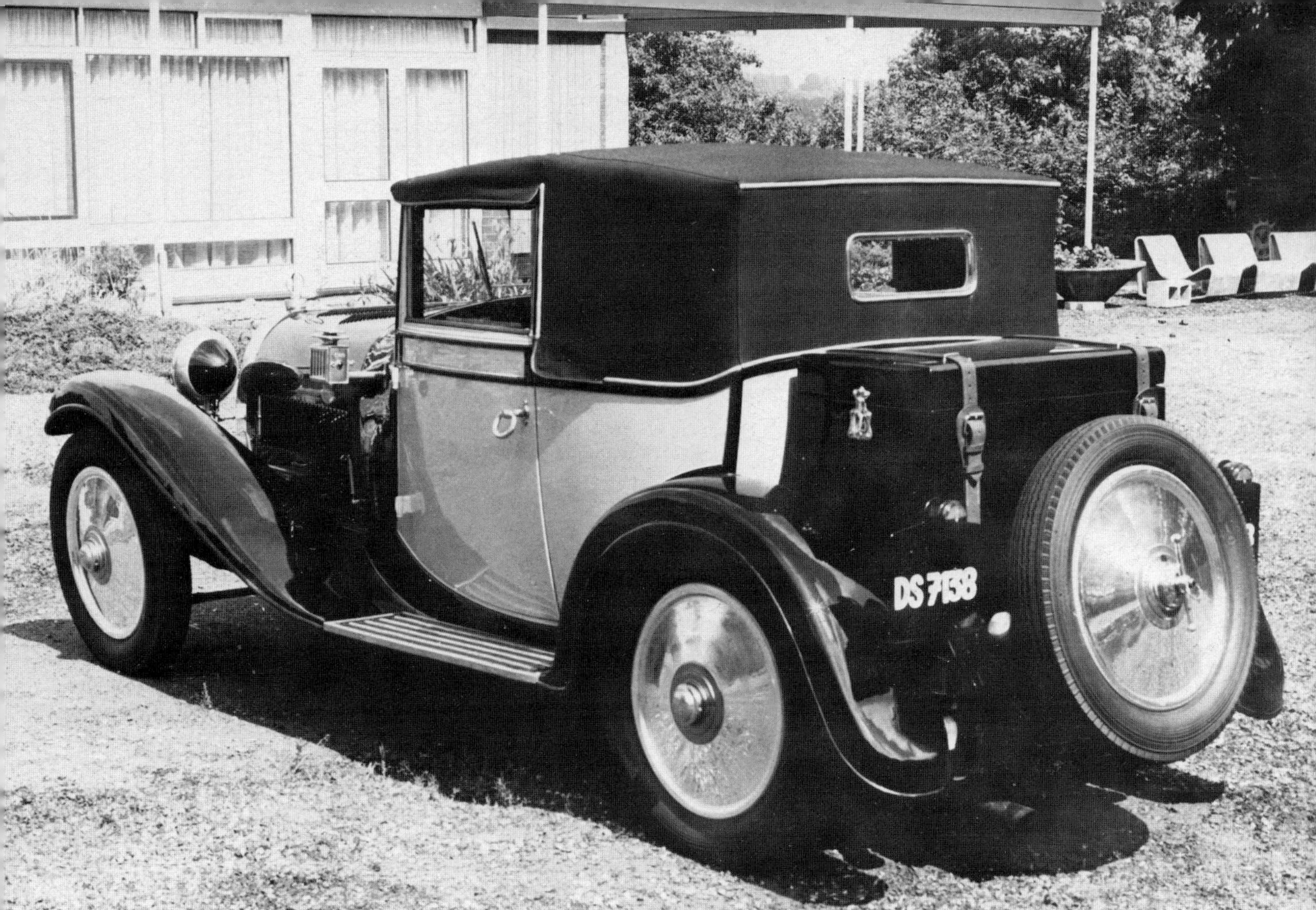

Lidia's car now restored superbly, and owned by Mrs Pat Preston.

Top left: *Many T40s were supplied as chassis for other coachwork, in this case an English boatdecked two seater.*

Jean Bugatti produced a special T40 with a 'fiacre' body for his sister Lidia, adding a supercharger from the T37A, and later the enormous brakes from the T46. It remained in Lidia's hands until the 1960s.

Mr Edgar N. Duffield also tested this Molsheim 'Morris-Cowley' for the *Automotor Journal* and reported in the June 1929 issue:

In 1913, using only eight valves with four cylinders, Ettore Bugatti astonished Europe. Later he added to his valve numbers. I have had four Bugattis – one 8-valve and three 16-valve; but to pretend that the £575 11·9 hp Bugatti chassis of 1923 was in the same class as this 1929 complete car at £365 is utterly impracticable.... Braking is now on all four wheels when one uses the pedal. The brakes are abundantly powerful, but also very quiet and smooth. Aforetime Bugatti brakes were at their best when used very inconsiderately, criminally so. Nobody wants, or is likely to get, better brakes than these. Repusseau shock-absorbers are standard equipment and lighting equipment by Marchal-Vaucanson. Wheelbase is 8 ft 11 in. The car was sent down to me by Colonel W. Sorel, the British representative of the Bugatti factory, in charge of a M. Mischall, a Molsheim-trained tester-demonstrator-service man.... I have never been to Brighton so quickly on any other car.

Mischall [see page 000] learned to drive on Bugattis, around the Bugatti works; learned to climb hills in the Vosges; learned the niceties of cornering and car-handling generally under the auspices of Bugatti stars. Never did he take any chances. He drove nicely, considerately, with beautiful judgment and every regard for his car; but quickly, you know, quickly! Bugatti gears are not sensationally quieter than they were; but the whole car runs with a solidity and onepieceness greater than ever; its suspension and steering are perfect. In those bad old days, dreadful stories ... were told about slow running in top gear. Today one really can drive through Crawley at 10 mph on fourth speed regularly, steadily, without any unevenness. One can also take surprising gradients on fourth, with the rev. counter showing only moderate engine-speeds. Our rev. counter showed 3,600, 3,700 rpm mile after mile; but its speed is only one of its

very real unquestionable merits because it is, all the while, in any circumstances, running on the level, up-hill or down-hill as joyously as one wishes, so thoroughly dependable, safe, trustworthy, a little Blue Devil!

The T40A was produced as an American-style roadster with its rumble seat, and a hatch for golf clubs. The engine was enlarged to 1·6 litres, and the gearbox now had a ball change.

A private owner's experience with a 1929 11·9 hp Type 40 shows a performance much above the average for a car of this size at that period. It reads:

At present I have a 1929 Type 40, and my previous car was a 1926 2 litre straight eight. I have driven these cars hard, but not carelessly, and have found that they are never 'sick or sorry'. There is no trouble whatever in starting. Maintenance cost is very small. Petrol consumption is 31 mpg, and speeds are as follows: Third, 65 mph, top, 82 mph. I have, however, made the following alterations which have definitely improved the performance: U type Zenith carburettor, Terry's valve springs, and slotted scraper rings. I have obtained a maximum of 4,300 rpm in top and can drive all day at 3,500 rpm without any strain. This is equivalent to about 60 mph. The old bogey of oiling up, which was evident in the very early models, is entirely absent in the later ones. The engine is noisy at low speeds, and the indirect gears are noisy.

The T40 engine had four cylinders, and a 5 bearing crank, but the layout was typically Bugatti. This is a T40A version externally identical to the T40, but with twin plugs per cylinder, requiring a twin spark distributor rather than this normal one. The carburettor was usually a Zenith

Type 41 ROYALE

The Golden Bug

IN 1913, three years after starting at Molsheim, Ettore Bugatti began to think of a large, luxury production. He wrote to his friend Espanet on 11 April 1913:

> As for the 8 cylinder, it is being designed, but not yet being made. The 8 cylinder car that I spoke to you about will have an engine with a bore of 100 mm, but the stroke is not yet settled.
>
> The car will be larger than the Hispano Suiza [this altered by Bugatti's own hand to 'Rolls-Royce'], but at the same time lighter; the speed of the closed car will reach 150 km/h, I hope to achieve perfect silence, when I have the first car on test I will make a long trip and I will not forget to come to see you to know your opinion on my new machine.
>
> There is no need to tell you that the production of these cars will be very limited and made with irreproachable care. All these cars will be delivered after tests of at least 1,000 km, and will have a guarantee of five years; the car will be extremely expensive, but will not be compared with any vehicle of this type.
>
> If I succeed in achieving what I am looking for it will certainly be a vehicle and a piece of machinery beyond any criticism.

We do not know what was 'being designed'. He had admittedly already produced large engines ten years earlier for de Dietrich and Mathis, and was producing a 100 mm bore 4-cylinder engine for the Type 18 'Garros' racing car. He had tried out an 8 cylinder car using two 8 valve engines in tandem (see page 000) and perhaps was now contemplating an 8 cylinder version of the 'Garros' engine. The war came shortly after, and his talents were soon put to the design of an 8 cylinder aero-engine; this, indeed, was followed by the double bank 16 cylinder version which was licenced to the USA (see page 000). When the war was over he experimented with a smaller 3 litre, 8 cylinder car (Type 28), but this did not go into production. In 1926, however, the project for a super-car was revived and the Golden Bug (so known because the prototype was much gilded) was born. This fantastic car, indeed probably the most fantastic car ever to be produced, turned out to be a straight eight of about 15 litre capacity (77·8 hp RAC rating the biggest ever to be put on the market), and naturally enough has been the subject of much Bugatti-lore, most of it untrue! It is said that Ettore designed the car after being

piqued by an English lady's reference to Rolls-Royce at a dinner party, but his letter of 1913 seems to put his dream of a super-car in a proper historical perspective. It has been said too, that the Golden Bug, or Royale as it was called in France, was a car of kings. But if a few kings may have seen the specification (no catalogue was ever produced), no king ever got as far as placing an order!

What helped Bugatti realize his dream during the period of peak activity and success at the factory in 1925–6 was the existence of a contract from the French Authorities to design and build (perhaps only a prototype) aero-engine Type 34, a 16 cylinder, double bank, engine of 125 mm × 150 mm. It had a sound, one piece block with the crankshaft carried on the main casting, and the 8 cylinder unit formed the basis of his new super-car engine.

Contemporary description

In the *Autocar* of 11 June 1926, Mr W. F. Bradley wrote, in an article headed 'The Golden Bug – Remarkable straight eight of nearly fifteen litres engine capacity which is being built in limited numbers of M. Bugatti at Molsheim':

While there is obviously but a limited market for a very costly high-grade car – a car which lays claim to be the best in the world – every motorist, rich or impecunious, is likely to have at least an academic interest in such a machine. Recently, during a visit to the Alsatian village of Molsheim, M. Ettore Bugatti gave us an opportunity of examining such a motor car, on which he has been at work for several years, and which will make its appearance at an early date.

It would be difficult to compare this new car with anything existing, for in the first place it has an engine of exceptional size, with eight cylinders of 125 × 150 mm, bore and stroke, giving a cubical capacity of 14,726 cc, and in building it no expense has been spared to attain perfection, so far as that is humanly possible. The size of the car is very much greater than that of any other private passenger vehicle, for it has a wheelbase of slightly more than 15 ft and a track of about 5 ft 6 in. It will carry a comfortable seven-passenger body, and as a model M. Bugatti has taken a body off an eight-cylinder Packard chassis and has placed it on the first of his own chassis with less rear overhang than usual.

There is no intention of producing this car in big series, but at the same time each one will not be a toolmaker's job with no interchangeable parts. Instead, most elaborate machinery is being laid down, and jigs and dies are being made so that the parts will be rigorously interchangeable, while the instructions accompanying the drawings permit no tolerance anywhere. The selling price of the car is not known, but it will be not less than that of a Rolls-Royce imported into France in the regular way. The 'Golden Bugatti', as it has been termed by those who have seen it, will be produced concurrently with the present models.

In full running order this Bugatti will weigh slightly less than 50 cwt, but to propel this weight it has an engine developing 300 hp at 1,700 revolutions, thus giving a ratio of less than 20 lb per horsepower. There are three gears, one being an emergency or starting gear, the second being the direct drive, and the third a geared-up ratio for very fast travel.

The engine weighs 770 lb, of which 238 lb are accounted for by the cast-iron cylinder block, and 220 lb represent the crankshaft, without the flywheel. Examined externally, it is difficult to understand how the engine is built, for it appears to be a huge block of aluminium, with carburettors added on one side and exhaust pipes on the opposite side.

The coachwork fitted to the Type 41.

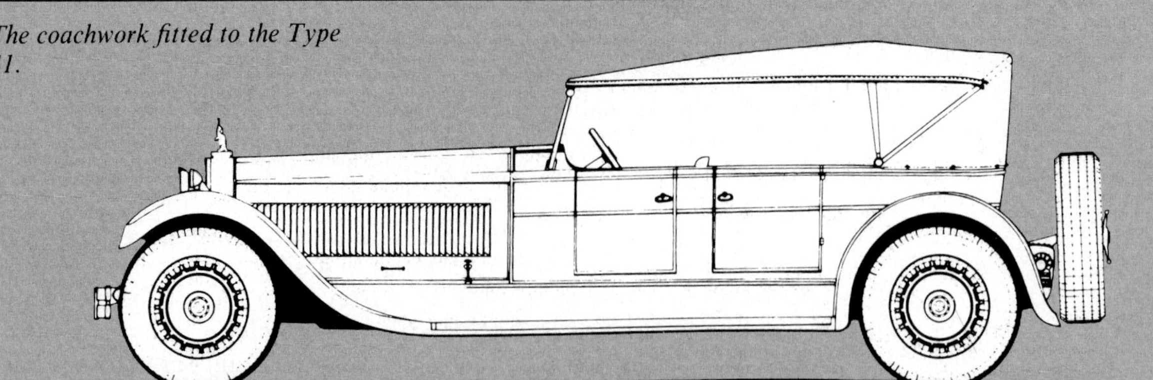

No. 1 *41100 The prototype chassis fitted with an American built body from a Packard.*

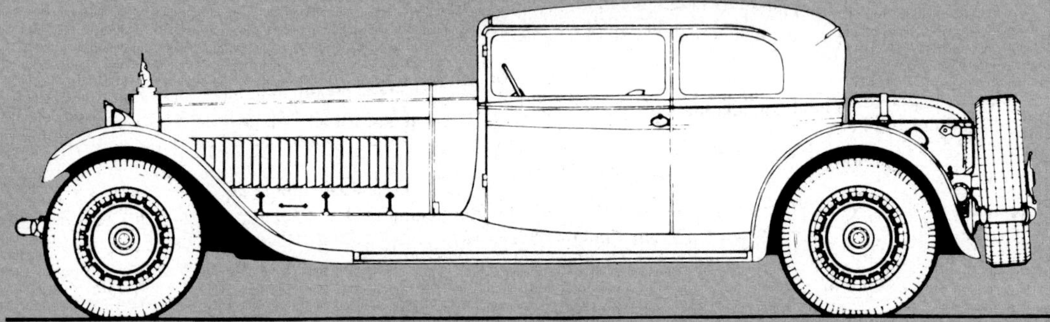

No. 1a *The fourth body on the prototype chassis was by Weymann of Paris.*

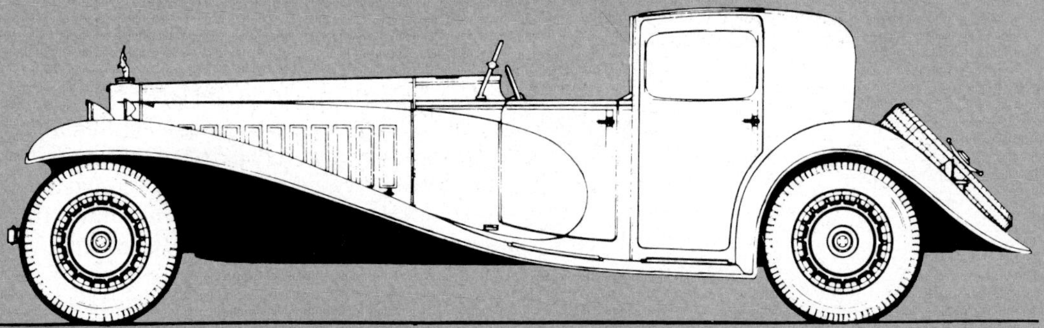

No. 1b *The so-called Coupé Napoleon designed and built at Molsheim, the fifth in fact to be fitted to the prototype chassis retained by the family.*

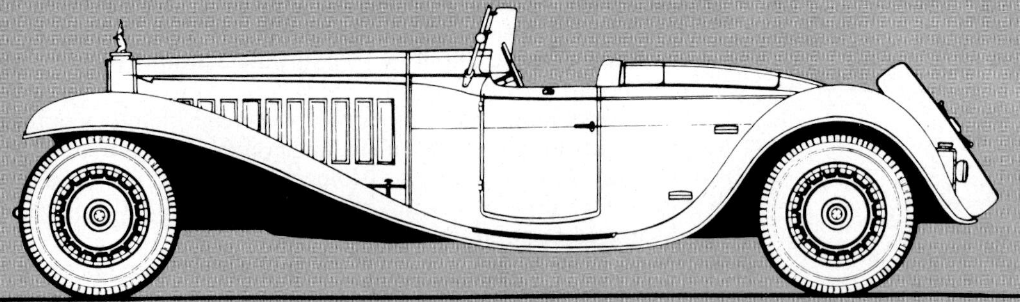

No. 2 *41111 The Roadster body designed and made at Molsheim for Mr. Esders.*

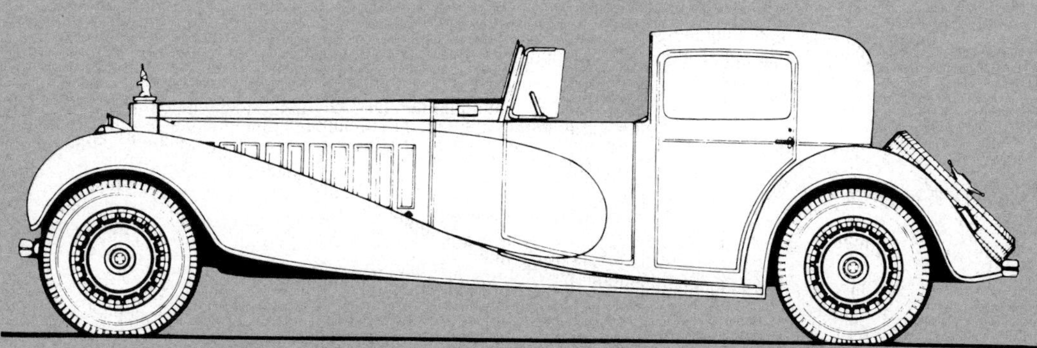

No. 2a *The second body fitted this chassis, 41111 was a Coupé de Ville by Henry Binder of Paris.*

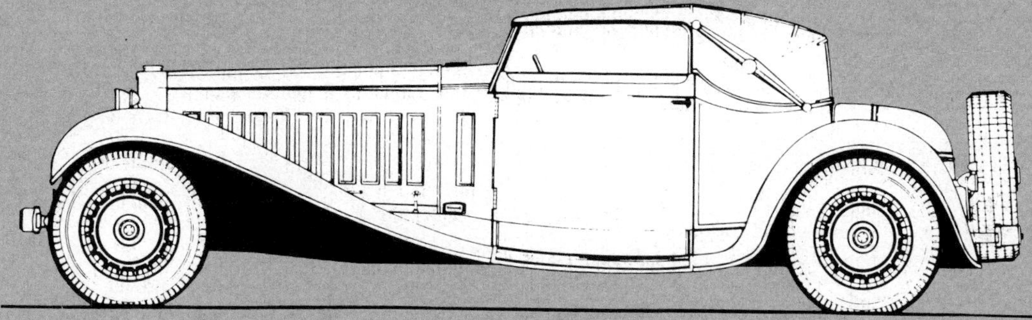

No. 3 *41121 Drophead Coupé by Weinberger of Munich.*

No. 4 *41131 Four door Limousine body by Park Ward of London.*

No. 5 *41141 Two door Coupé body by Kellner of Paris.*

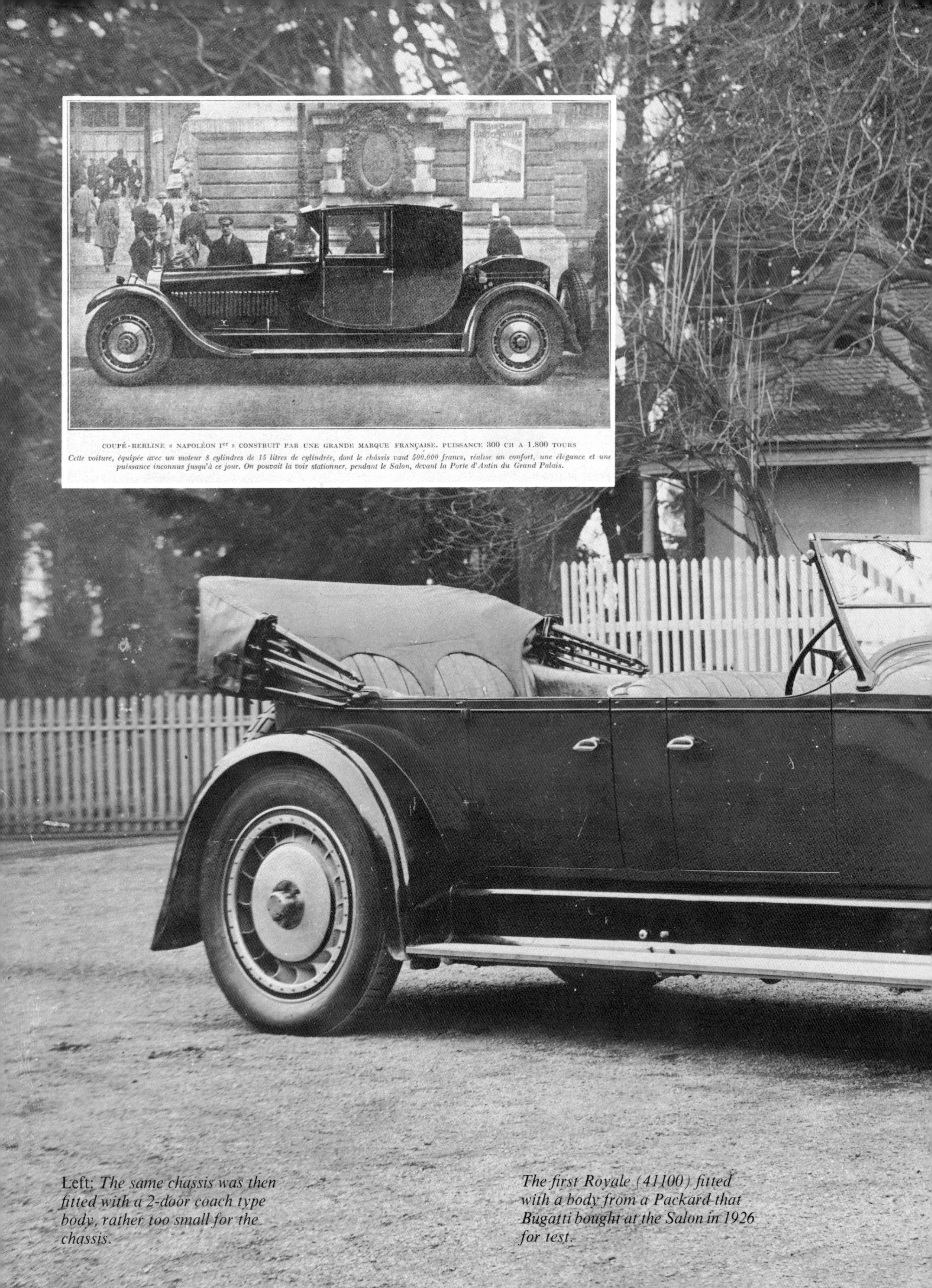

COUPÉ-BERLINE « NAPOLÉON Ier » CONSTRUIT PAR UNE GRANDE MARQUE FRANÇAISE. PUISSANCE 300 CH A 1.800 TOURS

Cette voiture, équipée avec un moteur 8 cylindres de 15 litres de cylindrée, dont le châssis vaut 500.000 francs, réalise un confort, une élégance et une puissance inconnus jusqu'à ce jour. On pouvait la voir stationner, pendant le Salon, devant la Porte d'Antin du Grand Palais.

Left: *The same chassis was then fitted with a 2-door coach type body, rather too small for the chassis.*

The first Royale (41100) fitted with a body from a Packard that Bugatti bought at the Salon in 1926 for test.

Right: *The third body on the prototype chassis was a 4-door coach but its lines probably pleased Bugatti more than his likely customers.*

The peculiarity lies in the casting, which is an extraordinary piece of work, for the eight cylinders, measuring 55 in, from end to end, form a single block with an integral head, having water spaces completely around each cylinder barrel, and the water-jacket extending right down to the nine crankshaft bearings. The mainshaft is carried, not in a separate crankcase, but in the cylinder itself. In other words, this casting, with its water-cooled main bearings, constitutes practically the complete engine; the light aluminium casings built around it act as dust excluders and oil and water retainers, and in no way add to the rigidity or solidity of the whole.

The crankshaft has circular webs; as already explained, it is carried in nine plain bearings, the pistons are a special aluminium alloy, the connecting rods are I-section, and the big-ends have white-metal bearings. By reason of the machinery installed and the processes employed, there is no hand scraping at all, and it is claimed that the rods and their bearings come off the machine rigorously exact to a thousandth of an inch, and any rod and piston can be changed for any other. The valve arrangement is similar to that of other Bugatti engines, there being two inlets and one exhaust, with overhead operating gear.

Three bronze hangers on each side attach the engine to the frame, but instead of the bolts being secured to the outer aluminium casing, as might be thought at first sight, they go right through the cast-iron cylinder block. Dry-sump lubrication is fitted, there being two scavenging pumps and one feed pump from a tank on the forward face of the dashboard. Double ignition is used, by magneto, and battery and coil of a special type.

Quite separate from the engine, immediately under the driver's seat, are a light flywheel and clutch contained in an aluminium housing. The gears are in the rear axle, which has a central housing of aluminium and two tubes containing the drive shafts. Straight bevels are used for the direct drive. The indirect gears consist of a reduction one for emergency work, such as starting on hills, and a high ratio for very fast travelling.

The frame members are special by reason of their dimensions, for they have a depth at the centre of 10 in. The front springs are semi-elliptics, having their rear extremities received between semi-circular bronze blocks. At the rear there are two sets of quarter-elliptic springs, one pair being behind the axle, outside the frame members, and the other set, which only come into play when a heavy load is carried, being ahead of the axle and beneath the frame members.

A front axle of the same general type as that used on the racing cars is employed. The construction of this is very unusual. It is a straight forging bored out from end to end, and having a greater thickness of metal outside the spring seats than is really necessary. After being bored out, the two extremities are hammered up until they are almost solid, the axle is heated and shaped, and the finished article is a one-piece axle, hollow in the centre and solid at the extremities.

The tyres for this car have had to be specially made Rapsons. They are straight-side balloons of 1,000 × 180 mm, mounted on special aluminium wheels forming a single casting with the brake drums.

There are innumerable details of construction which attract attention. All the brake rods are on roller bearings. The wearing parts of the universal joint can be changed in five minutes. The radiator filler cap is a bevel-faced valve with a hinge and a quick release catch. At the same time the entire filler cap can be lifted off and replaced by another if repair is required. Instead of an automatic oiling system for the chassis parts the design is such that attention has to be given only once every month or six weeks.

There is no intention of exhibiting this car at either the Paris or the London shows, for it is recognized that it will not appeal to the ordinary purchaser, and those who are likely to be interested in it will have other opportunities of examining it.

The fourth body on the chassis was this superb Weymann coach which won first prize at the Concours d'Elegance in Paris in 1929. Unfortunately Bugatti crashed the car, and the car was then rebuilt with a fine Molsheim designed 'Coupé Napoleon'.

The following year Bradley returned to Molsheim and tested the car, as reported in the *Autocar* 18 March 1927. He added a few technical details of the construction:

Double ignition is fitted, by magneto and by coil and accumulator, with two plugs per cylinder. There are two carburettors on the right-hand side, while the exhaust occupies the whole of the left-hand side, the pipes being dropped down at the centre of the engine and covered with an asbestos lined polished aluminium cover to deflect the heat from the bonnet.

The engine has no flywheel, and the clutch is mounted separately in a casing

under the forward seats. The change-speed mechanism is in the rear axle and consists of a geared-down indirect gear for starting and a geared-up indirect gear for fast running. On direct drive, through the spiral-bevel gears, the car has a speed of 95 mph at 2,000 rpm, while the geared-up indirect gives 125 mph, at the same engine speed.

There is a brake on the drive shaft to the rear of the clutch housing, and a foot-operated set on the four cast aluminium wheels. The wheels and the brake drums, it is interesting to note, are one casting, the spokes of the wheels being set so as to form a slight helice and thus direct a draught of air on the drums. The tyres, as already stated, have had to be built specially. They are four-ply Rapsons of 980 × 170 mm.

He went on to recount his experiences of a road test with Ettore at the wheel.

One might be excused for imagining that a car of this size and power would have to be employed entirely on main highways. Probably M. Bugatti divined that this suspicion was lurking on our mind, for, on taking the car out, he quickly turned off the national highway and entered narrow, twisty, hilly lanes with a particularly greasy surface. Further for a considerable portion of the time he handled the car in that dashing manner which so much appeals to young bloods.

This was done to prove the stability of the car on bends at high speeds, and it must be admitted, the demonstration was most convincing. Merely out of habit, the side of the car was gripped, but it was soon realized that even when cornering violently there was no tendency to be thrown sideways. To use a hackneyed expression, the car ran as on rails, with the difference that it was much more steady than anything on rails we have ever ridden in.

A considerable amount of traffic was met with, mostly consisting of farmers' wagons hauled by two horses, but no difficulty was experienced in passing them on the narrow roads. The same route had been covered earlier in the day on a sporting type Bugatti of normal dimensions, and the only disadvantage of the 300 hp model was that it needed reverse to get round a hairpin bend that the smaller car had taken on a single lock.

The final Coupé Napoleon, or perhaps Sedanca de Ville, on the car, now in the Mulhouse Museum. (J. M. Caron).

In view of the price of the car, we expected a high degree of flexibility and good, steady pulling at low engine speeds, and were not disappointed. The low emergency gear was used for starting, although it was quite possible to get away on direct drive, and the rest of the running was done on high. This included short, steep gradients with sharp bends on which the car was throttled down to 3 mph and then accelerated rapidly. Among the tests was the climbing of a short, steep hill on direct gear at the lowest possible speed and in a most silky manner. The same hill was taken on the indirect gear in order to show the terrific acceleration. On a straight road outside Strasbourg an opportunity was afforded of making use of the geared-up indirect gear, which was found to be just as silent as the direct drive.

A car of this price can obviously have but a small market, and probably some of the objections one would normally bring against it fall to the ground because of its special construction. The absence of a detachable head and the cylinder design make it impossible to change a valve, or even to grind in a valve, except by dismounting the engine, but the reply to this is that by reason of the construction, the high-class material, and the perfect workmanship, repairs are not necessary except at very long intervals, and the accessibility desirable on a normal car becomes unnecessary with this engine.

Royale sales technique

Bugatti seems to have adopted a sales technique as arrogant as the design of the car! In *Bugantics*, 13, 4 July 1950, Mr H. Dale tells the story of meeting Mr Ladopoulo in Cairo, and how Mr Ladopoulo had negotiated the sale of a car to Prince Mohamed Abdel Said: no sale took place on account of the price. Mr Paul wrote from Molsheim on 22 December 1933:

I thank you for advising me of your intention to acquaint His Highness Prince Mohamed Abdel Said with the 'Royale' Bugatti chassis.

I am, however, afraid it may not be possible to transact such a business without His Highness having been able to see and, the case arising, test the car.

The best way would be to take advantage of the forthcoming visit of His Highness to Paris in order to show him M. Bugatti's personal car, which is a small town coupé on the same chassis, and arrange an interview with him.

For such a special chassis I have never considered it necessary to publish a catalogue. There is, in fact, no need whatever of advertising such a model, the prospective buyers of which, who are essentially aristocratic, are inaccessible by the means adopted for standard cars.

To enable you to appreciate the main characteristic features of the chassis I am sending you herewith typewritten details thereof.

I am also sending you for handing to His Highness, photographs of the recent 'Royale' models delivered: Bugatti Roadster – to Mr Armand Esders, Paris; Park-Ward saloon car to Captain Foster (London).

Finally, a Grand Luxe Kellner Saloon which was made by those Coachbuilders for the Olympia Exhibition, London, and the preparation of which we are on the point of completing.

To give you an idea of the proportions of the Town Coupé designed by M. Bugatti, I enclose herewith a diagram, from which you will be able to appreciate the extremely elegant lines of this car.

The cost of the complete chassis supplied with five wheels fitted with tyres, accessories, tools etc., and covered by an unlimited guarantee, is fixed at 500,000 French francs.

I shall be pleased to furnish you with any additional information you may desire to have, and meanwhile remain,

Yours faithfully,
A. Paul, *for E. Bugatti*

Attached to the letter was a data sheet as follows:

CHARACTERISTIC FEATURES OF THE TYPE 41 'ROYALE' CHASSIS

The engine is an 8-cylinder monobloc type of up to 13 litres capacity.

The camshaft, as in all my designs in the last twenty years, is located above the cylinders.

Three valves are provided for each cylinder, two admission and one exhaust. The exhaust valve incorporates a special cooling device.

The Bugatti-made carburettor has been specially designed to ensure perfect delivery, both at extreme slow speed and at the highest speeds, that is to say in order to ensure homogenous combustion, unvarying whatever the speed. It is also possible with this carburettor to correct the proportions of air and fuel in such a manner as to obtain the highest efficiency both in hot and cold countries.

The fuel supply is looked after by electric pumps.

The gearbox is integral with the rear axle. It comprises only three combinations: a first speed for starting – a second direct mesh, which is utilized on all roads, and a third super-multiplied speed which can be utilized on long, straight runs.

The brakes act directly on the four wheels and incorporate a self-regulating device which permits automatically taking up wear on the linings. The braking stresses are extremely low.

The car can attain any speed desired by the designer.

It is characterized by remarkable road-holding qualities and unequalled ease and smoothness of drive. In a word, It possesses perfect docility and can easily be driven by a lady in spite of its size.

Moreover, it is strictly silent running at all speeds.

The dimensions of the chassis permit of providing extremely spacious coachwork affording 7 to 9 seats.

The production programme

Although a batch of 25 was hinted at (and probably hoped for) only six cars were built at Molsheim. The engine itself was later produced in some

The first car delivered to a customer was 41111, going to Armand Esders, who did not drive at night and needed no headlamps. The roadster bodywork was designed by Jean Bugatti and must surely be one of the most beautiful bodies ever fitted to an automobile, if not the ultimate!

249

numbers for the Bugatti railcar. Production cars had a stroke of 130 mm, unlike the prototype tested by Bradley, giving a capacity of 12,763 cc.

The six cars which were completed still exist and their history can be traced as follows:

The original body from the Esders roadster is rumoured to have survived, but the car was rebodied about 1938 with a Coupé de Ville by Binder. It is now in the Harrah Museum in the USA.

No. 1 (No. 41100) This car, the prototype, was built in 1926–7, and was originally fitted with a Packard touring car body from a 1925–6 model Bugatti had bought at the 1925 Paris Salon. It was next fitted with a curious 2-door coupé and then an ugly stagecoach body; then it was re-bodied once more with a magnificent Weymann body which won many prizes. This car crashed on a trip from Molsheim, Bugatti going to sleep at the wheel; the front of the car was badly damaged and the car was rebuilt retaining the original chassis number. A new Molsheim built body was fitted, a remarkable fixed head 'Napoleon' coupé, probably with the help of Jean Bugatti. This car survived the war at the family chateau at Ermenonville, until acquired by Fritz Schlumpf. It is now in the National Automobile Museum in Mulhouse.

No. 2 (No. 41111) This started life – the first Royale to be sold – to the order of Mr Armand Esders, a clothing manufacturer; he did not drive at night and needed no headlights. Jean Bugatti designed a two-seat roadster of superb lines, one of the most beautiful – and extravagant – cars ever to be built. Around 1937 or 1938 this body was removed and the chassis rebodied by Binder with another coupé de ville. It is now in the Harrah Museum at Reno.

No. 3 (No. 41121) This car was built to the order of Dr J. Fuchs of Germany in 1931 and fitted with a cabriolet body by Weinberger. Its story is told below by Mr C. A. Chayne and it is now in the Henry Ford Museum at Dearborn.

Mr C. A. Chayne formerly a Vice-President of the General Motors Corporation tells the story of his Royale, which now rests in the Henry Ford Auto Museum at Dearborn:*

* *Bugantics*, Vol 14, No 2, 1951.

THE STORY OF CAR 41121

This car was ordered by Dr A. Joseph Fuchs in 1930 and was delivered in 1931. The chassis was built in Molsheim, of course, and the body by Ludwig Weinberger in Munich. The original cost was equivalent to $43.000. The writer first saw the car during the practice days for the Vanderbilt Cup Race at Roosevelt Speedway, Long Island, in 1937. After this we lost track of the car, and it finally developed that the block had been frozen and cracked, apparently during the winter 1937–38, and, as Dr Fuchs was unable to have the car repaired in this country, it was left in his backyard on Long Island, covered with a sail, for a number of years.

I understand that the car was at one time taken to a shop in New York City for inspection, but they did no actual work on the car. Finally, in early June 1943, I received a telephone call from a friend in New York to the effect that the car had been sent to a junkyard in New York City and, if I wanted it, I had better move fast. I immediately telephoned Charles Stitch, who operates a foreign car shop in New York, had him buy the car and store it until I could make arrangements to have it brought to Flint. Because of the war and early post-war business obligations, I was unable to start serious restoration until the latter part of 1946. This work was completed in time to take the car east for the 1947 Glidden Tour of the Veteran Motor Car Club of America.

When we disassembled the engine, we found that the outer walls of the cylinder block had been badly cracked and bulged, both above and below the crankcase cover plates. Since the casting is very large and very complicated, it was decided not to attempt to weld the cracks, but instead to resort to the old reliable patching procedure. We knocked out the loose panels, milled the bulged panels flush with the sides of the case, and attached a plate of $\frac{5}{32}$ in. cold rolled steel on each side of the block. These plates, of course, had to be notched to clear the crank cheeks and the connecting rods, since the water jackets on this

Dr Fuchs had a coupé body built by Weinberger of Munich for his Royale (41121). The story of the car is related opposite; it is now in the Ford Museum.

engine extend around the upper halves of each of the nine main bearings. After screwing on the plates we filled the casting with salammoniac solution, flushed it thoroughly, allowed it to dry and then made sure of the seal by filling it with a resin type casting sealer under pressure which was then set permanently by baking the case for several days at a moderate temperature. While this procedure may have been more elaborate than was absolutely necessary, we accomplished the purpose of sealing the jackets and they have not leaked to this day.

We found that the freezing had squeezed the cylinders badly out of shape and it was necessary to rebore to about 0·03 in. oversize. I was fortunate enough to find aluminium piston castings that could be machined to fit. No work was necessary on the crankshaft or bearings. The crankshaft, by the way, is in two pieces, joined at the centre main bearing, and has circular cheeks to which the counter-weights are bolted. Connecting rods were magnafluxed and shotpeened. The engine has a full pressure lubricating system, except that the wrist pins are oiled by splash.

The water pump was badly corroded, consequently in the rebuild we modified it rather extensively, and fitted it with a modern 'permanent' type of seal. New valves and valve springs were made and installed, and it was necessary to make a new camshaft as the original one was very badly rusted, there being no ventilation provisions in the cam boxes. Fortunately, there were a few narrow areas on the original cams in good condition which permitted us to check the cam shapes and new master cams were made. The camshaft is also in two pieces joined at the centre bearings.

The camshaft drive is very unusual. At the top of the vertical shaft are two bevel pinions having opposite spiral angles. These mesh with two bevel gears, one of which is fixed to the camshaft. The second gear is concentric with the first, but drives through a friction clutch. As the second pair of gears is one tooth off from an even two to one ratio, the fiction clutch merely loads these gears so that the thrust on the vertical shaft is balanced by the opposing spiral angles. Just one more example of M. Bugatti's rugged individualism.

The major modification to the engine was made in the intake system. The original design consisted of a very large barrel-throttle air-valve carburettor, fitted to a single manifold with the four branches coming out of the bottom of the manifold. With the branches arranged in this manner it was obvious that all of the liquid in the manifold would drain into the centre four cylinders, and I could not develop any enthusiasm for spending time and money restoring the engine only to risk scoring one or more of the centre four cylinders on a cold morning start. I, therefore, designed short elbow connections and installed four single Stromberg carburettors with a ½ in. balance tube connecting the four elbows. Carburettors were balanced on a flow bench (including the idle settings) and no changes have been found necessary. The new intake system is completely satisfactory under all operating conditions. Since the water outlet manifold was originally cast as a jacket on the top of the intake manifold, the installation of the four single carburettors made it necessary to design and build a new water outlet manifold which was equipped with a large thermostat and by-pass leading to the intake side of the water pump.

The radiator was a honeycomb type, having square tubes which were badly corroded, and it was necessary to re-tube the core.

No work was done to the clutch, which is located under the driver's seat. The clutch is a typical Bugatti wet-plate design. The connection between the engine and the clutch is through two heavy fabric universal joints, there being no flywheel on the engine. Starter and generator are mounted on the clutch case.

The transmission is part of the rear axle, and is driven by a short shaft from the clutch. The transmission has two forward speeds and overdrive, and of course a reverse. Low speed is used solely for the purpose of starting the car and the shift to second which is direct drive, should be made at a fairly low car speed. All driving is normally done in direct. For high speed driving, the overdrive may be engaged at any speed above 75 mph. We did not find it necessary to open up the transmission or rear axle, and checked the ratios by

Transverse engine section of the T41 Royale engine.

BUGATTI

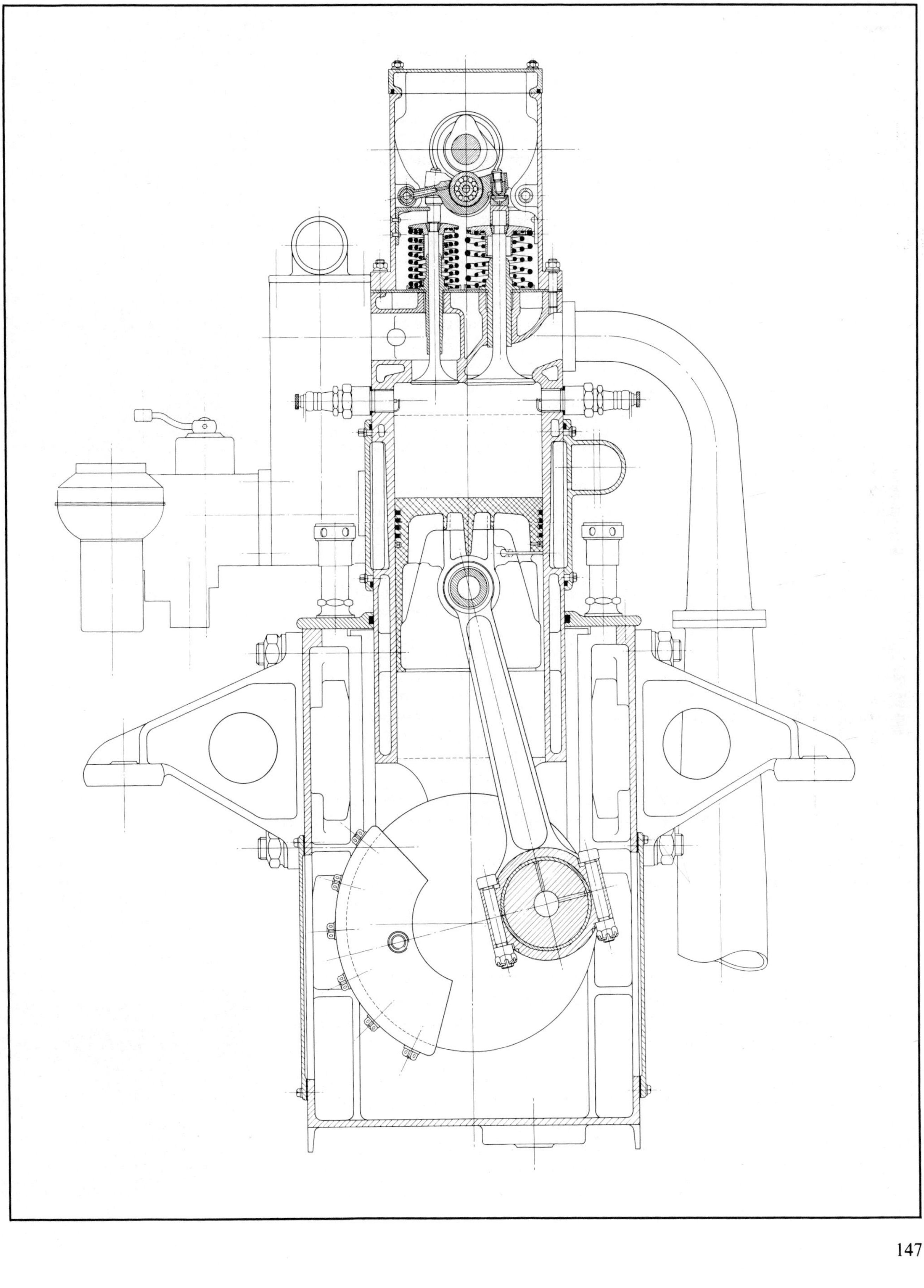

measuring the number of turns of the drive shaft necessary to rotate the rear wheels one turn.

Another major modification was made to the braking system. This was, of course, of the well-known Bugatti cable design. The chain and bevel gear equalizers were badly rusted and would have had to be completely replaced. I found, however, that one of the American brake manufacturers made a 'slave' cylinder which could be bolted to the outside of the backing plates, then by reversing the cams the operating levers could be made to apply the brakes with a push instead of a pull, and I ended up with about as nice a hydraulic brake system as anyone could desire. I heartily recommend the procedure to anyone trying to restore a car having old style mechanical brakes.

The tyres, of course, were a problem, but I succeeded in locating a 7·50–24 tractor tyre mould, having a ribbed tread and had tyres made in this mould with full rayon carcasses. The ribbed treads were 'siped' to give the necessary anti-skid characteristics. Hub-caps, with the well-known Bugatti monogram, and trim discs were added to the wheels to improve their appearance.

Paint and trim, of course, had deteriorated very badly during the 'weathering' years in a Long Island backyard. The car was originally fitted with beautiful pigskin upholstery, but this was so brittle that it was hopeless to attempt to restore it, and have it in keeping with the rest of the car. The original front seats had cushions that were luxuriously thick, but did not leave enough room between the cushion and the top of my 6 ft 3 in. I therefore installed front seats (new bucket type), and a new cushion and back in the rear seat, these being trimmed in dark green glove leather. The car is painted oyster white and dark green, matching the leather, and with a dark green top. The original leather covering on the trunk was also not usable, and while I had the body of the trunk restored, it is now fitted with a zipper cover, made of the same material as the top.

The electric wiring has been completely replaced and the car is fitted with legal sealed beam driving headlights. I kept the original Scintilla headlamps, but the beam they produce is highly illegal; and consequently they are never used for driving. The front fender lamps were converted to take two filament bulbs and new tail lamps fitted so that the car now has a direction signal system and back-up lights, in addition to the usual licence and stop lights. In order to have horns that are in keeping with the majesty of the car, I fitted a pair of Strombos air horns. The radiator cap ornament which shows in some of the pictures, is a design I developed for use on all of the cars in my collection.

The wood rim of the steering wheel had to be replaced and I used Tenite II in a colour to match the green upholstery. I might note in passing that the steering wheel is equipped with four horn buttons on the underside of the spokes, near the rim.

Originally the car had a very beautiful Jaeger chronometer stop watch mounted in the centre of the steering wheel but, as this was missing, I replaced it with a cap having a Tenite insert with the Bugatti ornament in silver letters.

No. 4 (No. 41131) Delivered in 1933 (orders were slow in coming) to Captain C. W. Foster in England; this car was fitted with an English Park-Ward 4-door limousine body and, after a sojourn in the USA, is back in France, in the museum at Mulhouse.

No. 5 (No. 41141) This car was fitted with a 2-door sedan body by Kellner and remained in the possession of the Bugatti family for some time, being used by L'Ebé Bugatti. It was exhibited at the Olympia Motor Show in 1932, and listed at £6,500 – more than double the finest Rolls-Royce at the Show! It survived the war in storage and was sold after it, with the sixth car, to the USA. It is now in the Briggs Cunningham Museum in California.

Chassis 41141 was fitted with a 2-door sedan by Kellner, but in spite of being exhibited at several Motor Shows, remained unsold in the hands of the family, and was sold to the USA after the war for a 'song'! It is now in the Cunningham Museum in California, still running well.

No. 6 (No. 41150) This car also remained in the Bugatti family for some time, fitted with a Bugatti designed and built coupé body, known as a Berline de Voyage. It is now in the USA.

Right: *The final car (41150) also remained unsold and went with the other to the USA after the war. This had a Molsheim-built 'berline de voyage'. In a museum for many years it was sold in 1986 for $6·5 million!*

The third car sold (41131) went to Capt Foster in England, and was fitted with a traditional but rather splendid saloon body by Park Ward. It is now in the Mulhouse Museum.

Few have had a chance to drive or test a Royale! A post-war account (The Autocar, 21 Oct 1949) gives some insight into the performance and handling of this extravagant machine, amusingly, told by Dennis May.

. . . it made merry monarchs merrier still, banished the blues of graver ones, and brought the delights of exclusive connoisseurship to a few – a very few – of the commonalty, including Jack Lemon Burton, the well-known London knotsmith who owns the only Royale currently resident in Britain, viz ALB2, the Park Ward Limousine whose likeness here appears.

It was thanks to Lemon Burton that I recently had an opportunity of motoring La Royale. . . .

For a start, let us take our place at the wheel and survey our surroundings. There is plenty to see and the functions of by no means all the instrumental and manipulative abracadabra are self-evident; in fact, even the owner frowns and goes let-me-see-now as he embarks on the course.

Of actual dials there are eight, as follows: (i) A superb Breguet [Jaeger?] stopwatch, mounted in the hub of the typically Bugatti steering wheel, wooden-rimmed and steel-spoked: this watch cost £85 and Le Patron threw it in as a cadeau, in common with the silver elephant mascot surmounting the radiator cap. (ii) Top left of a sixsome facia group, fuel contents gauge, the needle of which moves about as fast on the down-beat when motoring as on the up-beat during refills, because La Royale gives 8 mpg if driven economically, or if not, not. (iii) Top centre, ammeter. (iv) Top right, water thermometer. (v) Bottom left, clutch oil pressure gauge (the clutch divorced from the engine and also from

The engine of the Royale was by any standards a magnificent creation.

The one piece block casting, with integral cylinder head and main bearings, extending down to the crank centre line, and water cooled at that, was a tour-de-force of the Molsheim foundry.

Above: *The crankshaft and connecting rods, with balance weights on the webs.*

The typically Bugatti rear-axle and gearbox combined on the Royale, similar in conception to earlier and later Bugatti designs.

the three-speed gear box, which is mounted on the back axle, has an oil pump of its own). (vi) Bottom middle, 120 mph speedometer, which on ALB2, tyred as it is (more of that in its proper station) tells 6 per cent less than the truth. (vii) Way out of the group, at extreme port side, accumulator indicator serving the six 6-volt batteries, which are coupled to give 12-volt supply.

The rest of the facia furniture, which includes a total of thirteen switches, is far too numerous to detail *in toto,* but *en passant* one may mention the twin switches controlling one bank of plugs apiece (there are two plugs per cylinder and dual coils), a hand throttle lever matching an advance and retard ditto; three massive ivory-knobbed items for, severally, the throttle stop, a main-jet regulator and an extra air device on the Stromberg-type Bugatti carburettor . . . .

Type 41 dates from 1927 and, twenty-two years ago car designers, and Ettore Bugatti more than most, still expected the customer to enjoy getting the best out of a piece of machinery by doing the right things at the right moment . . . . Imagine what the 1949 customers would say – even the sports car customer – if confronted with four manual carburettor controls; and La Royale is a state carriage, which normally would imply the direct antithesis of 'Sports'. I say normally because, the steering and suspension arrangements being in the regular Bugatti sports and racing tradition ... the driver soon senses that this car could be handled much as one handles more portable examples of Molsheimware, if only one had a prairie to do it in.

Obviously, in a car 20 ft 6 in long ... it takes a mile or two before the unaccustomed crew member can reorientate his faculties to the Brobdingnagian scale of things. There are three speeds, of 4·5, 2·5 and 1·5 to 1, the last an overdrive for use mainly in uninhabited localities. On the middle ratio the speed range claimed was 3 to 90 mph with seven persons aboard and the radio playing. You get out of the 4·5 ratio the moment you are moving, and that isn't too soon. In overdrive, 120 mph and more will be there for the asking, though Jack L.B. has never asked it and personally I only visited the third notch for a matter of minutes.

The driving compartment of the Royale, in this case the Coupé Napoleon much used by Ettore (the odometer reads 27034 km), and thus no doubt authentic. Some cars had a Jaeger chronometer clock in the centre of the steering wheel.

A row of Royale engines as adapted for railcar use.

The gear positions are unusual. Up right for bottom, up left second, down left high. Engagement from neutral is easy by Bugatti standards but, owing to very slight clutch drag, cannot be achieved entirely without smalltalk, even by the owner. The character of the change itself – unaided, of course, by synchromesh – reminded me of the best class of truck; inside a couple of miles, by which time the left foot remembered, without prompting, to double de-clutch both up and down, one could lay wagers on making soundless shifts . . .

. . . [I] find consolation in the knowledge that Lemon Burton himself has never exceeded 90 on this car, and for a variety of reasons. One, it uses too much petrol at high speeds. Two, the tyres now fitted – Goodrich Silvertowns, 7·50 by 24 in, taken from a US Army mobile gun – are oversize and thought to have a deleterious effect on front wheel deportment under certain conditions. Three, the Bugatti brakes, cable-operated, lacking any form of servo and soon due for new linings, fall quite noticeably short of modern hydraulic standards of retardation.

But if 2¾ tons, travelling at say 80 mph, represents an awful lot of ertia, at least the Royale motorist has, as an alternative to arresting himself, adequate means of giving notice of his cataclysmic approach: there are two horns, one, with a dark brown note suitable to economic crises and such, being operated from the facia, while the other, less pompously pitched, has no fewer than four buttons, one under each wheel spoke.

Owing to its immense wheelbase, the Type 41 calls for quite a studied technique in negotiating right-angle corners in city streets. The wide sweep taken to avoid the deletion of corner-houses is naturally apt to land the operator over the white line, real or imaginary, and, in his haste to quit inhospitable territory, he tends to twirl the wheel so fast and so often that before he knows it his inside front wheel is taking a rubbing of the adjacent kerb.

Type 43

100 mph Grand Sport model

TYPE 43 probably shares the distinction with the Brescia, the Type 35 GP and Type 57 in being one of the four really great Bugatti models. Fast, exciting and fitted with a reasonable four-seat open body, this 100 mph model must have been a remarkable car in 1927 when it first appeared and certainly the first car to be offered with this speed capability. Even today a 43 has a performance which is pretty startling, a standing ¼ mile in 17 sec, a top speed over 100 mph, and a very 'long-legged' cruising performance. No matter that the modern mini-car might out run it! At a list price in 1927 of £1,200, however, the model was expensive.

Basically the car stems from Type 38, using a similar chassis but of slightly shorter wheelbase and waisted to follow the body lines in the centre, and with Type 38 axles, brakes, steering, radiator and gearbox, but with the T35B 2·3 litre supercharged GP engine, and detachable rim alloy wheels from the GP cars. The standard model had a Molsheim body of narrow, torpedo shape, with a single left-hand door, and a removable hatch in the tail giving access to a luggage compartment. This model was very suitable for sporting events such as the Alpine Trial, as well as long distance touring (across the national routes of France) and yet was also very suitable for hill-climbs and track racing. Many models were seen on the Brooklands mountain circuit, and teams were entered (with drivers such as Sir Malcolm Campbell, Earl Howe, Divo and Conelli) in the Ulster TT and long distance races in the late twenties and early thirties. In the early days of the Bugatti Owners' Club the car was often seen in rallies and sprint events.

It was the model to be aspired to in the period 1927–32 as a Ferrari may be today, as a road car with the qualities of its racing sister. Only later when mileages built up were the weaknesses of a roller-bearing crank evident, the need to warm up the oil to avoid roller skidding with thick oil, the habit of the oilways in the crankshaft becoming carboned up, stopping oil flow and making connecting rod failure likely. But if regular overhaul was accepted, the cars continued to give their owners – as they do today – much pleasure.

In 1930 the model became more respectable, sometimes being fitted

Supercharged 2300cc T43, a classic Bugatti model and the first sports car offered with a genuine 100 mph capability. This standard body was listed as a '3½ seater' as the room in the rear was modest. It is difficult to fault the body lines with the hood up.

The standard body has a fixed windscreen, and wipers were not fitted. The single door contributes to body stiffness.

with coupé bodywork; a special model known as the 43A was produced with an American-style roadster body with a rumble (or dickey) seat and even a small door for golf clubs. This was the period of North Atlantic influence rather unsuited to the type and it was soon out of production. The engine was too rough and noisy to be suitable for college-educated coach-work! The basic problems with the engine however did not go away and the 43A, like its spartan progenitor, was no car for the non-afficionado.

In December 1928, Bugatti prepared and may or may not have issued a data sheet labelled 'Super Grand Sport 1929, Type 43A', which was fitted with the 16 cylinder engine (60 mm × 84 mm, 3,850 cc) used on the Type 45 (see page 000). This car appears in the illustration to be identical with the normal Type 43 Torpedo bodied model except that the bonnet line is slightly raised; the axle ratio was 15:52, and the weight 100 kg up at 1,200 kg. The list price was a rather astronomical 400,000 francs or about £5,000! Fortunately, there is another Molsheim data sheet of about 1931 in date giving authority to the roadster model being Type 43A so the embarrassing intrusion of a 16 cylinder Type 43A will be ignored.

No less than 160 of these expensive cars were produced in the five year period from early 1927, with a peak production in 1928 of one per week. Some 60 still remain, for the mortality of the roller bearing engine, used for large mileages without the attention a racing car would get, was high.

Jean Bugatti at Molsheim in the first 'deux-litres-trois', with Roland in a Baby electric, and Rembrandt Bugatti sculptures behind.

Description of model

The *Autocar* of 18 March 1927 has this to say in announcing the new model:

There are indications, in France at any rate, that the supercharger, after being confined practically to racing cars, is to come into more general use. One of the most important steps in this direction is the introduction, by M. Bugatti, of an entirely new model fitted with a compressor.

The name of Bugatti is so clearly associated with racing and sporting type cars that one would almost naturally imagine a supercharged model from this factory to be the fastest and the raciest of the firm's products. It is surprising, therefore, to find that the new model, a straight-eight of 2,300 cc, has been designed for all-round work and is the most flexible car in the Bugatti series. As a proof of this, M. Ettore Bugatti, during a trial run we made with him in Alsace, stopped the engine, engaged top gear, and then started away by pressing on the starter button and rapidly accelerating without gear changes to a speed of 90 miles an hour.

The new model is a development of the cars which won the Targa Florio race, in Sicily last year. It appears to be the intention to deliver this car with a four-seater sporting-type open body. No attempt has been made to bring the body out beyond the frame members; there are no running boards; there are two doors [eventually one] on the left side only, and wells are provided for the passengers' feet. Protection is given by a fixed wide-screen, a very light folding hood is provided, and there is provision for baggage in the pointed tail. Briefly, the body is a sporting type, but one providing quite a reasonable amount of comfort for four persons.

Considered technically, the chassis has a close resemblance to other Bugatti types. The eight cylinders, cast in two blocks of four, but so close coupled that at first sight they appear to be one set, have a bore of 60 and a stroke of 100 mm. There are two inlet valves and one exhaust per cylinder, mounted vertically in

the fixed cylinder head and operated by an overhead camshaft.

The built-up crankshaft is carried in five bearings – two spherical ball bearings at the extremities and three intermediate roller bearings [in fact the centre bearing is also ball]. The connecting rods are I-section forgings in one piece, with roller bearings assembled on the shaft.

The distinctive feature of the engine resides in the compressor, which is a Roots type, mounted horizontally on the right side of the engine and driven from the timing gear crankshaft at engine speed by means of a horizontal shaft with fabric couplings. The carburettor is a Solex placed under the compressor, and not visible on raising the bonnet; indeed, it can only be reached by opening a trap in the sheet metal underpan.

The induction piping consists of a vertical branch flanged to the compressor and two horizontal arms, each one feeding four cylinders. There is a relief valve in the vertical arm to prevent damage to the blades in case of a blow back.

Separate lubrication is provided for the compressor from a small tank on the forward face of the dashboard, and a lead to each of the two ball bearings. As the quantity of oil required is very slight, the flow is connected up with the throttle, and is only opened at a given engine speed. While the carburettor is lacking accessibility, the rest of the engine is quite get-at-able, the water and oil pumps, plugs, oil filler, overhead camshaft etc., being easily reached.

The engine is separate from the gearbox, and has independent electric generator and starting motor. The clutch is of the multiple disc type; there are four speeds forward and a reverse, and the change-speed lever is in the centre, with right-hand steering. The rear axle has a final gear ratio of 4·15 to 1. Springing is by means of semi-elliptics in front, these passing through the hollow,

Friderich was an early competitor in the Nice area in a T43.

Mr and Mrs Williams and friends in a touring bodied T43 in the Monte Carlo Rally in 1929. He won a cup for the Mont des Mules Hill-climb.

forged and nickel-plated axle, and by quarter-elliptics, with their thin ends forward, at the rear of the car. Spoke-type, cast-aluminium detachable wheels are used, the spokes being designed to direct a current of air on to the brake drums which form an intergral part of the wheel.

During a test run made in the neighbourhood of Molsheim, it was fully realized that the car possessed a very high turn of speed. With a special gear ratio it is claimed that it can attain 125 mph on the level, while with the standard gear ratio it will run up to 112 mph. More impressive than the maximum speed, however, was the high average speed, due to the extremely rapid acceleration, the wonderful stability of the car on the road, and the high power-to-weight ratio.

Chiron in a 43, believed given to him by the works in lieu of payment for racing success. According to factory records this is the same car as illustrated above with its hood up.

Empty, the weight of the car does not exceed 20 cwt and, although figures regarding power output are withheld, it is known that the engine runs up to 6,000 revolutions, and it is not a difficult matter to estimate the power obtained. Most of the run was made on greasy winding lanes at the foot of the Vosges, with a certain portion consisting of an unmetalled track across country, and even under such conditions the suspension was good. Running at 80 mph, the stability of the car was really amazing, there being no tendency to slide on the greasy turns, and the brakes proved exceedingly powerful.

During the Targa Florio race the cars showed themselves perfect, and the new commercial model does not appear to be in any way inferior to the racing type. The compressor is silent at all speeds, and, judged from a sporting standpoint, the car is quiet.

The petrol tank has a capacity of nearly 16 gallons, and the fuel consumption is stated to be at the rate of between 17 and 18 miles to the gallon.

Contemporary road tests

The foregoing description of the car was sent in by Mr W. F. Bradley who was the *Autocar* European Correspondent at that time. He owned one of these cars himself and an account of his experiences was given in the *Autocar* of 26 July 1929:

On being introduced to the supercharged straight eight 2,300 cc Bugatti most motorists give expression to a feeling of fear. This model has all the characteristics of a racing car, and is indeed a racing car with a touring body; it looks fast, and it really is fast, but six months' experience with one on French highways has proved that it is one of the safest cars a motorist could handle.

Its maximum speed is about 112 mph: its gear ratio and the size of tyre used give 20½ mph per 1,000 rpm; thus at 5,500 rpm the road speed, ignoring slip, is 112 mph. I must confess that I have never driven the car at this speed, although there is no doubt that the Bugatti is capable of attaining it. I have, however, touched 5,000 rpm, or 102½ mph, and on good roads have held 4,500 rpm (92½ mph) for comparatively long periods. A very good cruising speed on Continental highways is 3,500 rpm, or about 70 mph. This engine speed is so much below the maximum that nothing is stressed: plugs stand up well to their work, oil consumption is low, and there is a very big margin for momentary acceleration when required.

One soon becomes satisfied with the knowledge that the car is one of the fastest on the road, and the greatest pleasure is obtained not in attempting to obtain the maximum from it (indeed, that is all but impossible except on a track), but in its wonderful acceleration, its high degree of flexibility, and its remarkable steadiness at all speeds, and particularly when one is negotiating winding hills.

The 2,300 cc Bugatti possesses a wonderful degree of flexibility; it is possible to engage top gear, move away by using the electric starter, and gain speed rapidly. To do this the engine should, of course, be warm and the road level. Starting in this abnormal manner a speed of 82 mph can be attained in 54 sec. There is no necessity to keep the engine reving fast to secure even running. It will glide along perfectly at 30 mph, and from this speed will jump into action, at the slightest touch of the accelerator, in a most impressive manner.

Using the four-speed gearbox the acceleration is really amazing. From a standing start the kilometre can be covered in 35 sec, and a speed of 70 mph is reached in 30 sec [probably a misprint for 90 mph]. To go from 1,000 rpm (equivalent to 20½ mph) to 3,000 rpm, or 61 mph, the period required is 34 sec, while 4,000 rpm, or 82 mph, are attained in 54 sec. These acceleration tests from 20 mph upwards were, of course, made without using the gears. It is evident that the power curve rises rapidly after about 1,400 rpm, for tests made from a standing start, with the use of the gears, showed that 82 mph could be attained in 54 sec, or in exactly the same time as required for running from 20 to 82 mph without the gears. [There is something wrong with these figures as the car would do 0 to 80 mph in about 25 seconds, not 54.]

This wonderful acceleration, combined with efficient brakes, makes it possible to put up amazingly high averages without excessive maximum speeds. A run from the gates of Paris to Le Touquet was accomplished in 2 h 25 min, or an average of 54·7 mph. The start being made at 5.00 pm, much traffic was encountered for the first half hour, and during that period the speed was not much higher than that of the average car. On some of the more deserted and well-surfaced French highways, distances of 60 miles have been covered in the hour, and averages of more than 50 mph for long distances have been maintained without at any time touching 80 mph. This Bugatti has been driven right across France without use of the gears, and it is very rarely indeed that a hill is encountered which calls for a third.

Racing experience is doubtless responsible for the extraordinary performance of this car. It sits on the road in such a manner and it steers so

A few 43s came to Britain in chassis form, this one having a touring body by Harrington.

Renée Friderich, Ernest's daughter, drove a T43 in the Paris-St Raphael Rallye Féminin in 1930–31.

wonderfully that never at any time during the 6,000 miles I drove it did I feel that it was being taken into a bend just a little too fast for safety. In other words, the margin of safety is so high that even on curves which previous experience with other cars had told me were ticklish there was a feeling of perfect security.

This does not contribute to recklessness. It has to be realized that the car is fast, and that consequently the driver has a much briefer period in which to act in case of danger. Keeping this fact in mind, the Bugatti is much safer than some cars having a decidedly lower speed. Of the many passengers carried in the car, some of them experienced motorists and some entire novices, all were impressed and apprehensive at first, but invariably they expressed unlimited confidence at the end of an hour.

The car was used for all kinds of work, varying from short runs in Paris to

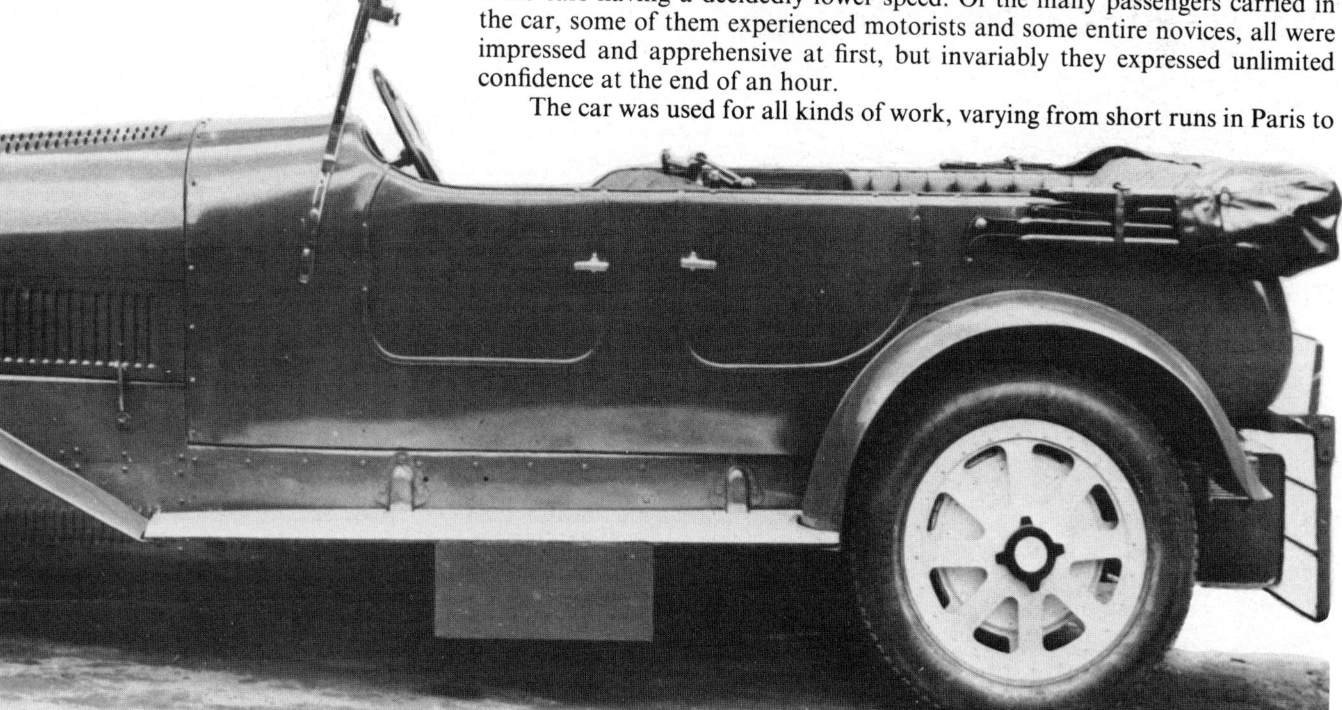

400-mile non-stop trips. Some country police objected to its racy appearance and signalled me to stop when following more silent and less speedy looking cars. The Paris police, however, were much better judges and never allowed themselves to be misled by the fast appearance of the car.

Petrol consumption depends largely on the manner in which the car is driven. If handled much as in a race, the consumption will be as high as 12 mpg, but if the driver is satisfied with less meteoric acceleration the figure can be improved to 16 or 17 mph. A petrol-benzole mixture was recommended, but the car was run entirely on pure petrol without any inconvenience. Oil consumption is low, but a good quality oil should be employed, Castrol R being recommended.

Malcolm Campbell's T43 had a disastrous fire in the pits during the 1928 Ulster TT.

In the same race later Dutilleux refuels while Campbell can only look on.

Compared with a normal car, the Bugatti calls for minor attentions, as distinct from repairs. As a matter of fact, the engine, being a racing type and never being run at anything like its maximum by the average owner, is very long lived; but it pays to keep it spotlessly clean so that loose nuts and connections, possible oil or water leaks, and other minor defects can be detected instantly. While the clearance is sufficient for the open road, it is not at all liberal, and

precautions have to be taken if lanes and tracks are traversed. In such cases the exhaust system is likely to suffer.

Fully equipped, with tanks filled and tools aboard, the weight of the car is 2,433 lb.

The T43 chassis without coachwork, unusual in that the frame is waisted to follow the body contour; this car has a ball change gear lever from a T49. (W. Granoff).

The Editor of *Motor Sport* also described his test of the car in May 1930 and confirmed Bradley's account of its attractions. In the issue of December 1932, the same journal tested a second-hand car (GU 17) belonging to Colonel Giles of the Bugatti Club and for sale at that time at £525.

A few strokes on the hand pressure pump, a touch on the starter-button and the engine fired. In a few moments we were threading our way through the West End traffic, the engine proving docile and flexible with the ignition half-retarded, third and top gears being used except where the traffic was very dense. The exhaust was inaudible, but the gears gave an occasional joyful shout as we trod on the accelerator.

Out in the country, driving the car was sheer joy. Light steering with adequate caster, almost unconscious cornering and terrific acceleration in the gears made it impossible not to put up a high average speed. Top gear acceleration was also surprisingly good, and from 50 mph the speed passed easily to 80. This top gear performance is very useful in populous areas, where the stirring howl of gears and supercharger gears is apt to be misunderstood.

10 to 30 mph took 3½ seconds, 10 to 40 mph, 8, and 10 to 80, 23 sec: this is a terrific performance and compares well with that of the double-camshaft model – 10 to 80 in 19 seconds. The engine revs happily up to 5,000 giving a limit in second and third gears of 60 and 80 mph. On two occasions on short sections of straight road we reached 99 mph and there was obviously 10 or more mph in hand if road conditions had allowed further accelerations. Colonel Giles, the owner of the car, has reached 110 on Salisbury Plain.

As is usual on Bugattis, the brakes require considerable effort in order to attain full stopping power, but from 40 mph, applied really hard, they brought the car to a standstill in well under 50 feet. This figure is the best we have ever encountered and was only possible on a road of abnormally good surface, the co-efficient of friction being well over 1, but even on a normal tarmac road not more than 54 feet should be needed.

A wartime reminiscence

Wartime nostalgia for racing and sports cars was partly satisfied by a series of articles entitled 'Talking of Sports Cars' in the *Autocar*. No. 164 of 6 August 1943 was the story of Mr A.C. Whincop and his Bugattis:

There is something about the combined surge of power, the complete feeling of mastery, the beautiful balance of the chassis and steering, the blend of supercharger whine, exhaust, gear and axle notes, and the smooth slice of the gear changes on the Grand Prix boxes which cannot be expressed on paper. It is just there and has to be experienced to be believed. ...

My car, like others of its type, had an engine almost identical with that of the Type 35B G.P. 2·3 litre, from which its power unit was copied. The maximum revs are between 5,000 and 5,500 rpm, at which bhp should be 140 in the Type 35B and 115 in the Type 43. These can be improved. ...

The engines are well balanced, and the optimum revolutions can be felt quite clearly by the sensitive hand; on my car it was quite clear – 5,100–5,200 rpm on the gears, and 5,300 rpm or what you could get on top gear, never exceeding 5,500 rpm in any circumstances, as it is quite pointless to do so from the power point of view, and has, of course, other possibilities. The extreme smoothness

The engine of the Type 43 is virtually identical to that of the T35B Grand Prix car, with a reduced compression ratio.

BUGATTI

right up to maximum revolutions makes it almost impossible to state any cruising speed, 2·3s just ask to be driven at full throttle where conditions permit, and usually are. If you want to cruise on English roads, well, try it, but you will usually find your speed mounting rapidly until you are holding your own strictly private Grand Prix. I have never met a car to equal the demand of the 2·3 Bugatti to be driven faster, and it is only really content when accelerating at full throttle in a rising crescendo of sound or is flat out on top gear at about 5,300 rpm, with the deep howl of the supercharger drowning everything in a perfectly tuned wavering top note of sound, as you blissfully watch the supercharger pressure – which is normally about + 7 lb per in^2 – gradually build up to about + 9.

My Type 43 (TR.4551) was amongst the first produced, being built in October 1927. Its life I know nothing of until 1935. . . .

I collected 'Two-three I' early in 1938, and used it as a general-purpose car throughout the year, covering ten thousand miles with no overhaul, and the sole replacement of one fabric universal joint. Only two speed trials were indulged in, so that my bank manager might have an opportunity of forgetting a blown-up 1½ litre, but those two hill-climbs showed some promise, returning a first and second for the sole trouble of changing the plugs and jets. I mention this as

A good T43 can still produce outstanding performance in Vintage Racing, over 100 mph and a standing 1/4 mile in 17 seconds.

rumour has spread it that Bugattis are not quite so reliable as they might be, and are apt to be difficult. Personally, I have found them extraordinarily reliable, with the exception of the four-cylinder models, provided they are carefully assembled by someone who is both interested and competent, and are thoroughly maintained, when little trouble should be encountered.

Plugs should not be a problem; my Type 43 would start, warm up, run in traffic and compete on Champion R.1s, never oiling in traffic, and only very occasionally when warming up, and only then when Castrol R has been used, as the engine was completely happy on Castrol XXL. For maximum performance sparking plugs should be scrupulously clean and gapped at 0·015 in.; also, if R.1s are used for much competition work their life is naturally short; in races of over three laps I used Champion R.11s, but then considerable care was needed before the start. For normal touring R.7s should be ideal, though never having had difficult with R.1s oiling I have not had the need to come down to a relatively soft plug. If trouble is experienced with the oiling of plugs in any of the single-camshaft Bugattis it will almost invariably be found to be the result of excessive wear in the inlet valve guides, where the clearance should be 0.003 in.; if it is as much as 0·008 in. the plugs will not unnaturally oil up, this condition being rectified by the straightforward task of unscrewing the old guides, carefully reaming and fitting new ones, and recutting new valve faces and seats if necessary before reassembly.

I mention this point as many Bugattis have run for ten years and more

without the owners thinking of the valve guides needing to be replaced, this probably being the root of the story that Bugattis oil their plugs. One must admit that the design of the heads of the single-camshaft cylinder blocks does involve operating at high sparking-plug temperatures, but this need cause no trouble.

My Type 43 in her present condition has a genuine maximum of 108 mph when stripped, this being represented by 5,300 rpm on a 13:54 axle ratio, using 5·25 by 19 in. tyres and making allowance for wheelspin. With road equipment the speed seems to be cut down to about 106 mph, with more, of course, under favourable conditions.

Modern road impressions

There is no doubt that the Type 43 is one of the most driveable models for today's owner who wants to use the car on the road. It has an excellent performance as already indicated and is surprisingly comfortable even on poor road surfaces. For long distance touring across France a regular pace of 65 mph (around 3000 rpm) seems an optimum, and on one occasion a trip of no less than 475 miles was accomplished returning from Molsheim to London in one day (in 1970). The main weakness from the practical point of view is a tendency to overheat in modern traffic conditions in towns and then to soot plugs – oiling up is not a problem if the bores and pistons are in good shape. With road use the crankshaft needs re-rollering every 6,000–8,000 miles. Fuel consumption is rarely better than 18 m per Imperial gallon, and oil consumption is mainly due to leakage and thus about 500 mpg! Fortunately Dunlop racing tyres, 5.00 × 19, which suit the car admirably are still being made.

The 43A roadster has a body significantly heavier than the standard Grand Sport model and its performance suffers accordingly. Whereas the earlier version can have its front seats adjusted to suit the driver, the seat on the roadster is fixed and only really suitable for Ettore himself or other average size drivers!

The T43A roadster came towards the end of the production run of the model; it was styled on the typical American roadster by Chrysler or Chevrolet with its rumble seat.

Type 44

8 cylinder refinement

AT THE end of 1927 Bugatti announced a new 8 cylinder production car of 3 litre capacity, derived from the prototype Type 28 exhibited in 1921, and replacing the 2 litre Type 38. In effect this new car was the combination of a new engine, with the single overhead camshaft driven from the centre of the crankshaft, and nine plain main bearings, and a chassis very similar to Type 38 or Type 43. The engine of the new car had the smooth torque of earlier models and a new degree of silence, which resulted from the elimination of the roller bearing crankshaft.

The general appearance of the engine is similar to – though noticeably larger than – that of Type 38, or other unblown 2 litre engines of the Type 35 family. The crankshaft is in two halves, with the camshaft drive bevel keyed to the centre. The shaft is carried completely in the upper crankcase which bolts to the lower case which itself is bolted to the chassis. A vertical shaft in the centre of the crankcase drives the camshaft through bevels and the usual dog coupling. A further pair of bevels drives a cross-shaft on the centre left-hand side of the crankcase; this drives the water pump, on the left between the exhaust manifolds, and through a further pair of skew gears and an extension shaft, a low mounted oil pump. Early models had the pump high mounted without the extension drive shaft. Early models, too, had 'Bugatti' lubrication by jets, but later engines were converted to full pressure feed. A relief valve was used on this oil system – a surprising innovation for Ettore! A long box-like inlet manifold was bolted across the two cylinder blocks and was fed from a single Schebler carburettor, an American unit Bugatti must have seen on some of the 8 cylinder American touring cars of the period.

The clutch, gearbox and back axle were virtually Type 40 or 43 units. The front axle was of the circular type with the springs passing through it, again as on Type 40 and 43. Brakes were of large diameter and similar to those on Type 43. In fact, the hubs and wire wheels of a Type 44 are often used as replacements of the alloy wheels on the 43.

The track was the same as the T38 or 43 but the wheel base with the new frame was the same length as the T38 and thus more able to carry heavier, closed coachwork. It was around this period that Bugatti

who was making open sports bodies for the T43, successfully extended the body shop at Molsheim to make splendidly designed and built closed coach bodies. Thus although many chassis were supplied bare for the owner to choose his own coach builder, an ever increasing proportion of the cars delivered were complete.

Contemporary comment

Edgar Duffield described the car in the *Automotor Journal* in 1928:

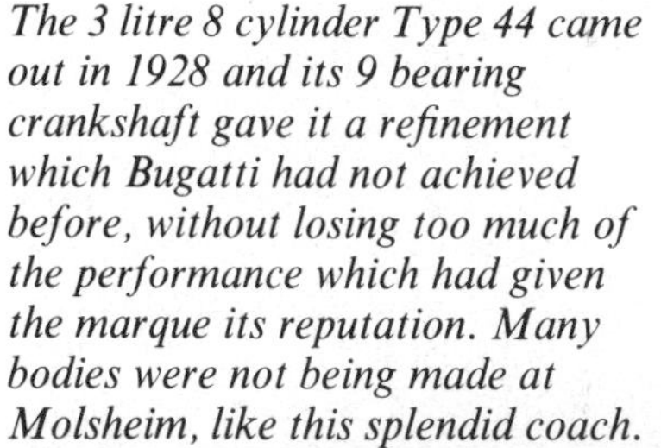
The 3 litre 8 cylinder Type 44 came out in 1928 and its 9 bearing crankshaft gave it a refinement which Bugatti had not achieved before, without losing too much of the performance which had given the marque its reputation. Many bodies were not being made at Molsheim, like this splendid coach.

Up to 1923 the Bugatti was still finding itself as a touring car. Maitre Bugatti would not agree, I know, but that was so, according to British ideas. But this new three-litre is really a very wonderful machine, and really a touring car, although it will bowl along the Cobham fair-mile at 75 to 80 mph with a lot of throttle opening to spare. And the notable thing is the refinement of this car's performance and its very marked engine flexibility.

The motor is an overhead and mushroom-valved straight eight with bore and stroke of 69 mm × 100 mm, giving a Treasury rating of 23·6 and a capacity of 2,992 cc. The camshaft is overhead and the crankcase has nine bearings. Cooling by pump; ignition is by battery and coil; a Schebler Automatic car-

BUGATTI

Another Molsheim body, with four doors and integral trunk.

burettor Autovac fed from a 13-gallon tank. Each cylinder has two inlet and one exhaute valves. The clutch employed is the Bugatti patented multiplate, running in oil, the discs being alternately of steel and cast iron. The complete car, with a genuine Weymann four-doored saloon, very elaborately finished and equipped, is priced at £850. In very many, if not all, details his design of today is almost as much ahead of its confrères as it was in 1914. Bugatti first showed the world what could be done with 1½ litres of gas before even he had begun to employ 16 valves on a four-cylindered motor.

This Bugatti is decidedly sporting; yet it is just as emphatically smooth and sweet, and the flexibility on fourth speed is remarkable. When I ran Bugattis, for 2½ years, I thought myself quite lucky if I got more than 400 or 500 yards of fourth speed in London. From my home, then alongside Hurlingham Club, to my office in Kingsway I travelled mainly on second. Occasionally I would get a few minutes of third. But to get more than a couple of furlongs on fourth was to have something about which to telephone home. This 3 litre straight

Right: *An elegant 'fiacre' style body, a style dear to Ettore.*

eight could be driven from 'The Bear' at Esher to Aldgate Pump on fourth speed, using third only for restarting after traffic lights. It is just as refined as it is fast; just as amusing a car in the hands as ever the little beggars were. But it is a gentlewoman's car, whereas up to even five years ago I regarded Bugattis as cars only for the strong, silent men. For what my judgment is worth, the 23·6 hp Bugatti is one of the five best, most interesting, most friendly, companionable and altogether delightful motorcars that can be bought in London today.

Contemporary road impressions

In July 1928, *Motor Sport* carried a short road test report on the car – a 4-door saloon model:

Lidia and L'Ebé in a T44 coupé at Molsheim.

At the last Olympia Motor Show, Ettore Bugatti departed from his previous practice of building only racing or sporting models, and surprised his many followers by introducing the first serious attempt at a Bugatti touring car.

BUGATTI

4578 RO

Above: *A pretty touring body with lifting half-deck at the rear and provision for a second windscreen.*

Top left: *Most T44 chassis were delivered bare to be fitted with coachwork to the purchaser's choice by the best coachbuilders: this is a typical English drop-head coupé.*

Top right: *O. A. Phillips in Los Angeles in a T44 in the early 1930s.*

Elizabeth Junek took this roadster T44 to India in 1929 and sold it there.

This was the new 3 litre, 8 cylinder model, which differs in size and in certain features of design from any other type of Bugatti. To begin with, excepting only the formidable 'Gold Bug' of some 15 litre capacity, this new car is the largest Bugatti (by some 700 cc) that has yet been produced.

Secondly, in view of the larger size of the engine, and in order to ensure the minimum of vibration, the designer has wisely used the maximum number of bearings to the crankcase, namely, nine, an interesting point when it is remembered that five bearings are considered sufficient for the 2,300 cc supercharged model.

In the past there have been many enthusiasts who were prepared to sacrifice docility and flexibility for the undisputed 'pep' common to all Bugatti models, but even the most enthusiastic could not claim that their cars were comfortable touring vehicles. The 3 litre model was introduced to remedy this state of affairs and, with a view to testing its success or failure in this direction, I was very pleased to accept the loan of Colonel Sorel's private car for a day's trial.

The car in question is fitted with a low built fabric saloon body of a type which is becoming increasingly popular among sportsmen who realize that the extra comfort more than outweighs the almost imperceptible sacrifice of performance.

Settling ourselves aboard in the heart of London, we, driver and crew, at once realized that a comfortable day was before us, for seating accommodation, suspension and ventilation seemed to be extremely adequate.

I was immediately impressed by the ridiculous lightness of the major controls and in particular of the clutch pedal. The latter was almost incredible and suggested those Olympia models in which a special (and quite useless) clutch spring is fitted to gull the unsuspecting buyer.

That the spring pressure was perfectly adequate we soon discovered on moving off.

In traffic, the car proved a delight to handle as either the top gear crawl or the second gear 'buzz and jump' method could be indulged in at will. It was soon realized that all the drawbacks of the more 'racing' Bugattis were absent, giving place to real docility, smoothness and silence at low speeds and at the same time not excluding such desirable traits as splendid acceleration and deceleration. Although it is hardly likely that a top gear fiend will ever drive one of these cars, yet if such should be the case, he would find that the engine would readily respond to his crude and lazy methods, in a manner surpassed only by the large and woolly American. On the other hand, once the rapid changes of engine speed have been mastered, the gearbox artist will find the

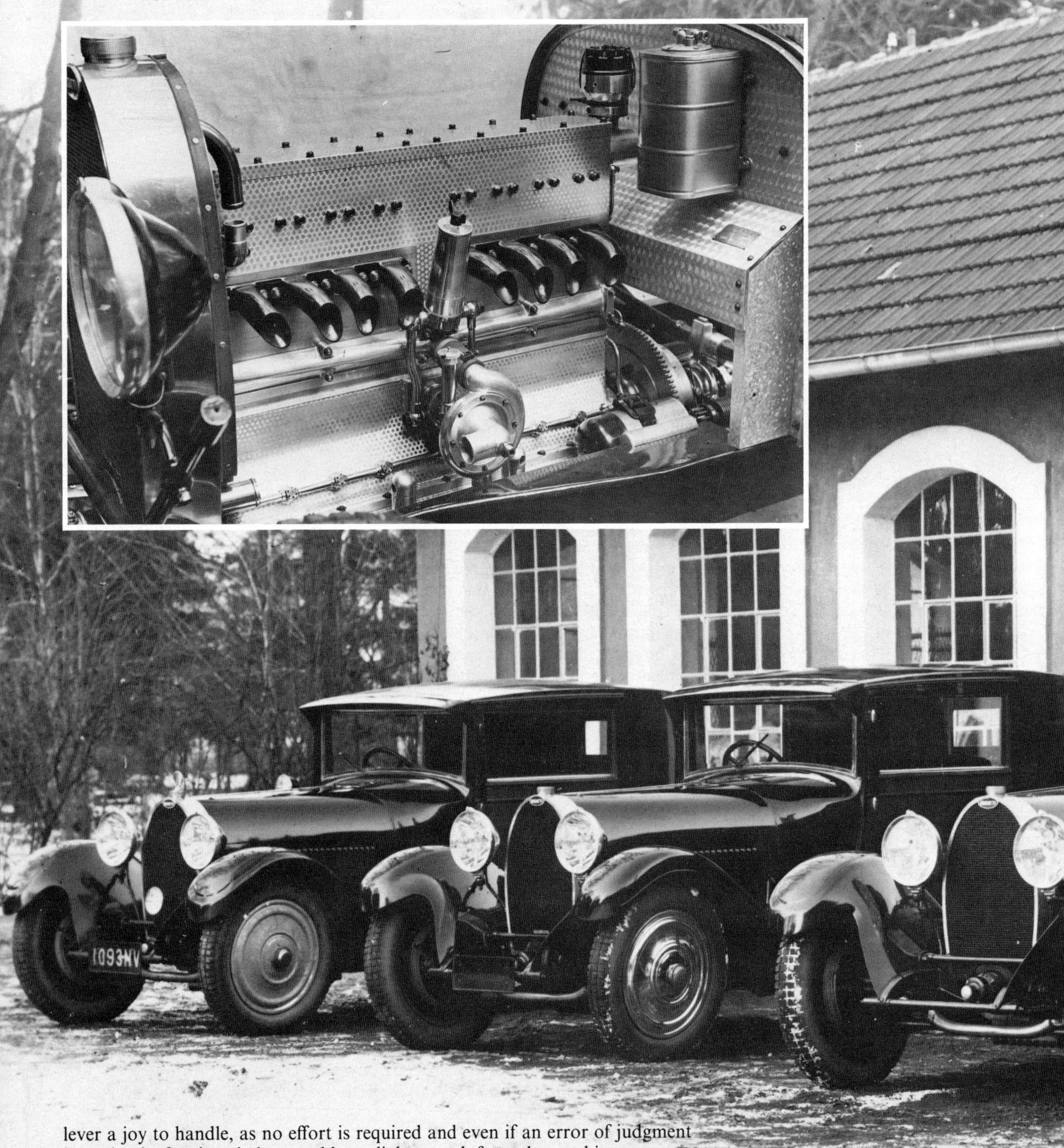

lever a joy to handle, as no effort is required and even if an error of judgment is made, the fact is only betrayed by a slight crunch from the machinery.

Tests showed that the corrected speeds on the various gears were approximately as follows: 1st gear, 30 mph; 2nd, 40 mph; 3rd, 60 mph. All these speeds were obtained with great rapidity and without fuss or vibration; when accelerating or decelerating a period lasting for about 1½ mph on the speedometer, is passed through at speeds corresponding to about 55 mph on top gear. This period was so short and withal so slight that it could not possibly be described as a fault, and seems to be an unavoidable feature of many high efficiency engines.

A collection of T44s and T46s at Molsheim, all with 'fiacre' or 'razor edge' coachwork.

The prototype show model T44 from the London Motor Show in 1928, not yet complete. (The Motor)

The engine has a single carburettor, normally a Schebler not a Solex, fitted to a large, one-piece water-fed manifold.

When we arrived at the track, we attempted a few speedy laps. All went well until half way round the Byfleet banking when the rear of the car swung from side to side in an alarming manner, indicating that the tyre pressures were more suited to road work than to high track speeds. After borrowing some of Mr Dunlop's potted air for our Michelin Balloons, we motored a fast lap to

The drive for the camshaft is in the centre and a bevel train drives the waterpump. On later engines the oil pump is low mounted on the crankcase and is driven by a vertical shaft from the water pump shaft.

test the behaviour of the car with the harder tyres. This time the steadiness was remarkable and the speedometer registered 95 mph for a considerable portion of the lap; unfortunately, the stopwatch *did* stop on this run so the speed was not checked. On attempting a second lap the rather touring plugs showed acute signs of distress and we were compelled to stop to allow them a respite. We then restarted and the stopwatch records recorded a lap speed of 77 mph, although the car was still suffering somewhat from tired plugs and failed to persuade its hopeful speedometer beyond the 90 mph mark.

There is little doubt that on the first lap over 80 mph was averaged, as the car was running infinitely better before the plugs 'cooked'; we were very sorry not to be able to attempt some all-out laps on a new set of 'Bougies'.

We then forsook the speedway for the public roads once more and I was again impressed with the delightful running of the car. The lightness of all controls, the liveliness of the engine and the really powerful brakes made traffic driving and cross-country spurts equally joyous and enabled high averages to be maintained with a complete absence of effort or danger.

Here we have a car with most of the virtues of a racing car, including an honest maximum speed of 85 mph, combined with economy (25 mpg) and tractability to satisfy the most fastidious owner.

Modern road impressions

The docility and smooth running of the Type 44 is still very apparent today. Engine tick over can be adjusted to almost steam-engine slow speed, and the car accelerated in third or top gear from a crawl. There is the ever present crankcase period at about 2500 rpm in spite of a vibration damping fly wheel on the front of the crankshaft (not a true 'Lanchester' damper however) but the driver learns to cruise above or below it! Brakes are excellent, and the steering exemplary. Ride comfort is surprisingly good and long distances can be covered without fatigue. 80 mph can easily be reached and indeed exceeded, but a comfortable cruising speed is around 65 mph.

Type 45 & 47

16 cylinder racing models

IN 1928 BUGATTI designed a pair of extraordinary 16 cylinder engines similar in conception to his aero-engines, and intended to be fitted in a GP racing car (Type 45) or a Le Mans regulation-bodied Grand Sport car (Type 47). The engines were identical, except that the GP engine was 60 mm × 84 mm, 3·8 litre, while the sports version was reduced in stroke to 66 mm, to bring it within the 3 litre class. The design consisted of two 8 cylinder engines somewhat similar to the Type 35 ones, geared together, each bank fitted with a rear mounted blower. The crank, however, differed notably from the T35 having roller main bearings, but plain big ends. The crank is in two halves, the centre main being plain to permit oil to be fed to each of the other main and big end bearings. The 8 main bearings have rollers carried in split steel housings themselves located on and bolted to the one-piece cylinder block. Thus Bugatti preserved the engine layout of the Royale T41, where the block with its solid head carries the crank directly, and the sump is merely an oil pan.

These cars, according to *Motor Sport,* March 1928, were originally intended for the 1928 French Grand Prix which was abandoned and, according to this journal, work on the cars was also abandoned. One car of each type was completed, and several spare engines; a batch of chassis frames was ordered and these were to come in useful later. The racing T45 had three outings in 1930 in hill-climbs making FTD on each occasion, but the crank gearing was defective. The model might be considered one of Bugatti's aberrations since so complex a design (there are 19 gears in the camshaft drive train!) was bound to need prolonged development, a process Ettore did not favour, expecting his designs to work first time! The two prototypes remained in the factory collection until bought by Fritz Schlumpf in the 1960s for his (now the National) Museum at Mulhouse.

Various spare engines and parts were sold after the war and now a third car has been built up and used for vintage racing.

The type was described in detail in the *Autocar* of 12 April 1929:

Sixteen cylinders, forty-eight valves, two crankshafts, two camshafts, a power output of 250 and a weight of roughly 500 lb, or 2 lb per horse-power, are the outstanding features of a most unusual engine produced by M. Bugatti. The

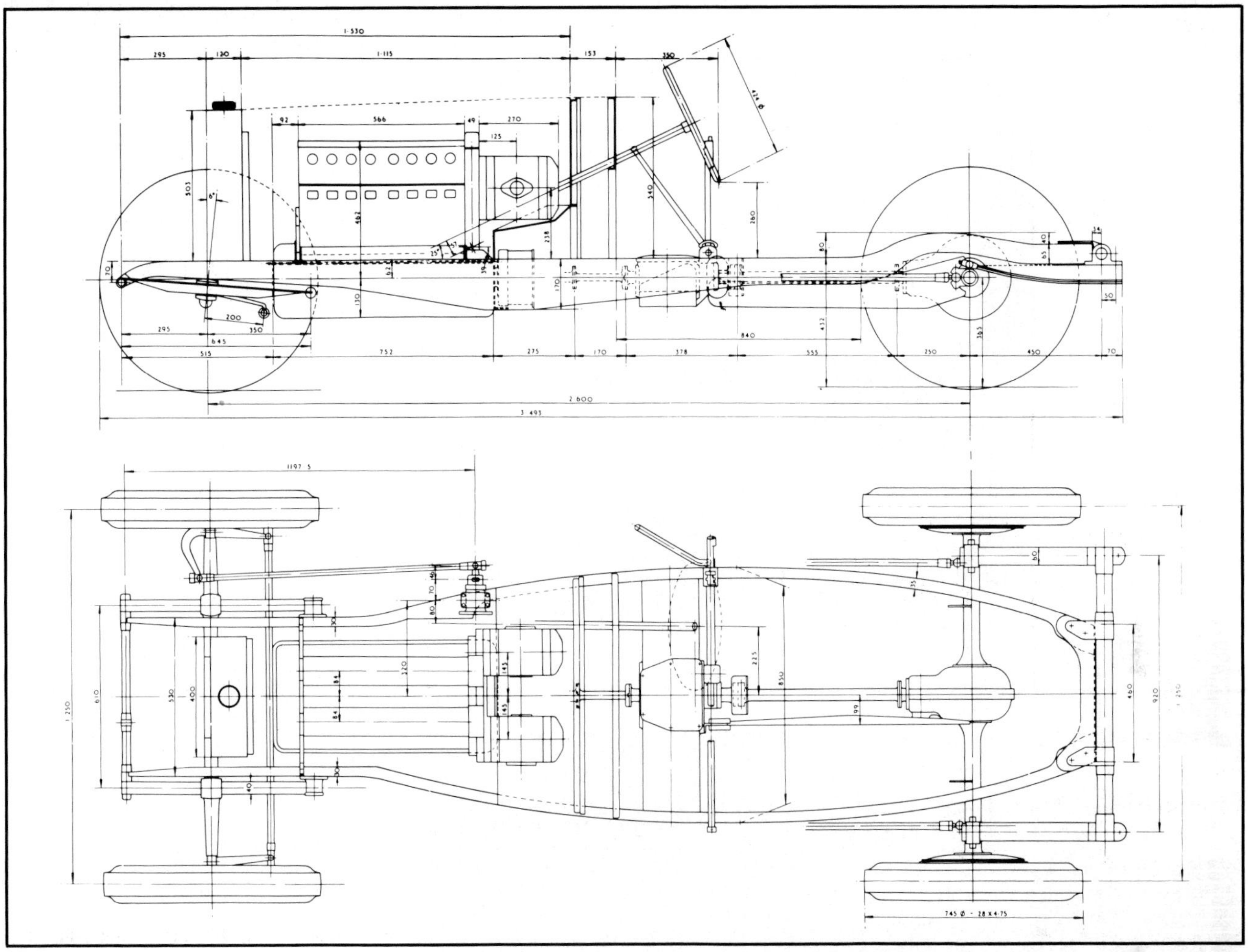

The Type 45 chassis arrangement (from an original Molsheim drawing dated 6 October 1930).

mere mention of sixteen cylinders suggests a bonnet of almost interminable length, but this Bugatti is shorter than the firm's eight-cylinder model of the same bore and stroke, for its cylinders are not in line, but in two banks of eight, each engine being complete in itself and the two being united by gearing.

It was during the war that Bugatti conceived the double eight engine for use on aeroplanes. A few were built, but for some reason or other the idea was not pushed, and now the dual power plant has been brought forth as a four-litre model, each engine having a capacity of two litres. It could be best described as a super-sports car, for it has been catalogued and plans have been laid for its production, but it is doubtful if many will get into the hands of the public before 1930. The intention is that it shall participate in races – the 24-hour event at Le Mans, records and hill-climbs – this year, and be openly offered for sale after it has proved its merits.

While, naturally, the number of motorists likely to be interested in the purchase of such a car is limited, for it is a costly model, it is such a distinct departure from anything that has yet been built that no motorist can fail to be attracted by it. The cylinders have a bore and stroke of 60 by 84 mm (3,800 cc). One of the features which immediately attracts attention is that the cylinder blocks are not designed to be bolted down to a crankcase, nor do they carry crankshaft bearings [not strictly correct]. They are rectangular cast-iron blocks, machined all over, having eight cylindrical borings, and, in accordance with the usual Bugatti design, three vertical valves in the head.

The overall length of an engine is determined first by the cylinder bores, secondly by the number and length of the main bearings. The Bugatti blocks

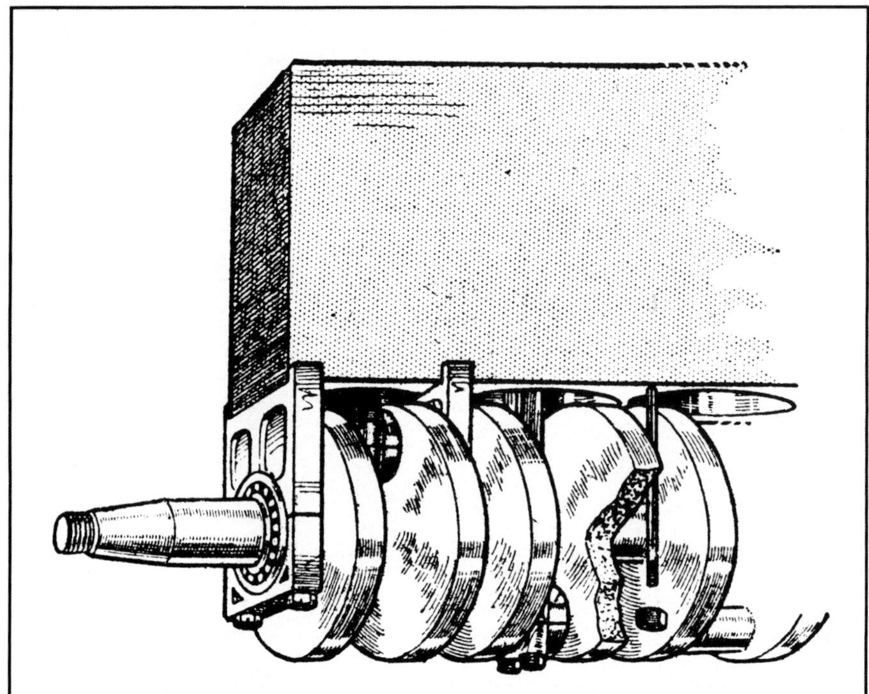

The crankshaft mounting. (The Autocar)

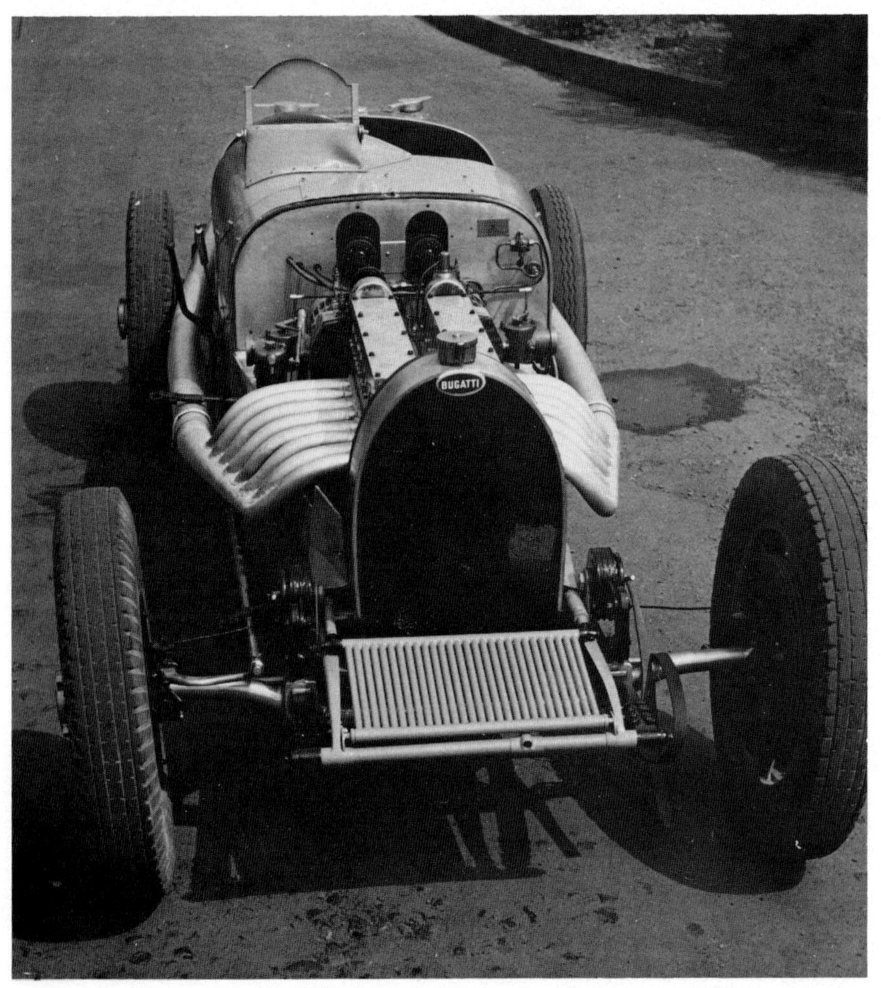

The 16 cylinder car, twin exhausts and an oil cooler in front.

Molsheim pictures of the original engine.

measure 22 in. from end to end, while the totalized diameters of the cylinders is just a fraction under 19 in., and yet in the remaining space of a little more than three inches it has been possible to lodge nine crankshaft bearings. This result has been obtained by having forged steel bearing supports fitted on to the bottom of the cylinder blocks and held to them by studs. Eight of these supports carry roller bearings; the central bearing is plain. The feature of the connecting rods is that the bronze caps are riveted and brazed to the rods and have an exceedingly thin white metal lining. If the white metal should melt, the resultant play in the big end would not be sufficient to prevent the running of the engine.

The two blocks of cylinders are united at the front by a steel plate, the outer ends of which are received in trunnions on the frame. At the rear there is

Chiron and Bouriat at a Hill-climb in Switzerland in 1930.

a steel housing, which unites the two blocks of cylinders, contains the timing gear, and also serves to carry the engine in the frame.

The crankcase is nothing more than an oil collector and a dust excluder. It is a light cast aluminium casing, with side pieces which can be lifted off so as completely to expose the crankshaft and the main and connecting rod bearings. Examined superficially, the engine is a complicated piece of mechanism, but in reality the design assures a high degree of accessibility. In addition to the rods and bearings, which can be seen and felt after lifting away a quickly detachable cover, the oil pumps are equally accessible, and, as the crankcase is only a shell, any main bearing or any piston and rod can be reached after five minutes' preliminary work.

Chiron at Klausen in 1930. (T.A.S.O. Mathieson).

The pair of cars built lay in this sorry state at Molsheim until 'rescued' by Fritz Schlumpf in the 1960s for what is now the National Museum at Mulhouse.

The Grand Sport version (T47) now in the Museum at Mulhouse without bodywork; it was never completed by the factory.

All the timing gear is at the rear. The mechanism consists of a spur pinion on each crankshaft, each one meshing with an intermediate pinion on the clutch shaft, from which the drive is taken in the usual way through the gearbox to the rear axle. There is a train of spur pinions up to the two overhead camshafts – one for each block of cylinders. These pinions are made use of to drive the two magnetos carried on the dashboard, with their distributors immediately in front of the driver, and also the two Roots-type compressors. The induction pipes are between the two banks of cylinders; the plugs are mounted horizontally on the outside, and the valves are placed vertically in the head and do not differ essentially from those of other Bugatti engines.

Three pumps are relied on to assure the lubrication of the engine, and they are driven off the front end of the crankshafts by worm gearing. One of the pumps scavenges the base chamber, another delivers oil at a pressure of more than 100 lb per square inch to the connecting rod bearings, while the third sends oil under low pressure to the overhead valve mechanism and other parts. It is because of the forced pressure feed to the connecting rod bearings that the central crankshaft bearing is plain. Oil is delivered direct to this bearing, then passes through oil ducts in the crankshaft to the connecting rod bearings. The oil supply is maintained in a tank within the chassis.

The water pump is on the front of the engine, but, like the other accessories, it is driven from the rear, use being made of a long shaft which passes between the two blocks of cylinders. There are two inlets from the radiator and two outlets, one going to the outside of each line of cylinders. A Zenith carburettor is bolted up direct to each Roots blower.

The engine develops its power at between 5,000 and 6,000 rpm, although it is claimed that it has been run under load up to 7,000 rpm. It weighs little more than the normal two-litre straight eight; it is shorter because of the special cylinder and crankshaft construction, and, as the width is only 14½ in., there is no difficulty in lodging it under an ordinary bonnet behind a narrow radiator.

There is nothing particularly distinctive in the chassis. As to the speed of the car the makers prefer to give no information, but with the power available and the low weight of the chassis it ought to be wonderfully fast and have extraordinary powers of acceleration.

Type 46

5 litre luxury model

IN THE autumn of 1929 a new, large chassis was announced, with an 8 cylinder, 5·3 litre engine and a wheelbase of nearly 12 feet. We may reasonably conjecture that Bugatti had realized that his chances of selling many of his large Royale chassis were slim, and if he wanted to have something larger than the 3 litre Type 44 it should fall well between the T44 and the monster. It was perhaps bad luck that if he had started in 1927–8 at a time of industrial boom he soon ran into a period of depression after the Wall Street problems towards the end of the decade.

So he chose an engine layout similar in conception to that of the Royale, using the same stroke of 130 mm, but drastically reduced the bore to 81 mm from 125, thus shortening and lightening the whole engine. In retrospect retention of the long stroke (stroke/bore ratio 1·6) seems odd, and he was later to reduce it on the Type 50.

He could now offer to those who could afford a luxury car, if not a Royale, a chassis on which the finest coachwork could be carried, and with the traditional flexibility and good road manners of a Bugatti. Two years later a blower was added to the 46S (Sport) model, giving it an even better performance than the standard coach. About 20 of these supercharged models were produced but they were soon replaced in production by the twin-cam Type 50. Type 46 was one of the best of the large Bugatti models. It was the forerunner of Type 50 which differed only in the engine, and was in many ways a small Royale. It was Ettore's favourite model; nearly 400 were produced well into the 1930s, although there was some difficulty in selling the last few, which accounts for the subsequent appearance of three or four brand new chassis.

A Freestone & Webb saloon.

Description of car

In the *Autocar* of 20 September 1929, we read:

The newcomer differs from its predecessors, however, in being far removed from the racing type and having all the qualities of silence, flexibility and comfort so much sought after by present-day motorists. M. Ettore Bugatti is generally looked upon as one of the chief exponents of the ultra-sports model, although

The Type 46 with its large 5·3 litre engine was a fine luxury car capable of carrying the finest coachwork, in this case a Molsheim-built coupé.

such types really constitute but 5 per cent of his production. In his new straight eight he has sought to meet the requirements of a larger class of owners.

The engine has a bore and stroke of 81 mm × 130 mm (5,227 cc) [5360!] and its overall length is 3 ft 1 in. In general design it is similar to the 'Golden Bug' – the 14 litre straight eight being built at Molsheim in limited numbers for the favoured few who can purchase the most expensive car in the world.

Rigidity is a most desirable feature in any engine, and it is secured by mounting all the auxiliaries direct on the cylinder casting. The crankcase serves

A Mulliner saloon.

Bugatti's favourite 'fiacre' style coupé.

only to collect oil and to exclude dust, and does not carry any moving component. It might be remarked that any engine with cylinders and crankcase in one casting falls into this category, but the feature of the Bugatti is that the cylinders are extended downwards, with suitable ribbing for rigidity, to allow the nine bearing crankshaft to be mounted directly upon it. These crankshaft supports are machined and ground to very fine limits; very thick bronze bearing caps with a minimum of white metal are fitted, and the lower cap is held in the usual way by studs. The crankshaft is a one-piece forging, with circular webs, and of very big diameter.

As in the case of other models of this marque there are three vertical valves per cylinder, operated by an overhead camshaft driven by bevel gearing from the front. The entire engine is assembled with its two oil pumps – one scavenger and one feed pump – its water pump at the front, its dynamo and the distributor, the last mentioned being driven from the rear end of the camshaft; it is only after completion that the single-piece aluminium crankcase is added.

The engine is carried in the chassis by means of four forged hangers bolted to the cylinder casting and having at their outer extremities a cup containing a rubber block to give an elastic attachment to the frame member. The entire crankcase can be dropped in a few minutes to give complete access to the main and connecting rod bearings, the oil pumps, and the front end drive for the camshaft and auxiliaries. In addition, there are big inspection plates on each side of the crankcase through which connecting rods, can be examined and withdrawn.

One of the patented features of the engine is the rubber-mounted flywheel. Instead of the flywheel being keyed directly on the crankshaft, a hub is fitted, and between this and the flywheel a thick rubber ring is interposed. This acts as a very efficient vibration damper and gives a slightly flexible drive. The clutch, a multiple-disc type with Ferodo facings, running dry, is in the flywheel. A multiple-jet Smith carburettor is fed with petrol from a rear tank by means of a couple of Autopulses. The whole of the lubricating oil is contained in a dashboard tank, connection between this and the oil-collecting base chamber being by means of flexible metal pipes. The oil filter projects from the tank, on the engine side, and can be dismounted immediately for cleaning without the use of tools.

The three-speed gearbox is a unit with the rear axle. A tubular cross-member carries the pedals and also receives an aluminium housing which

A roadster by Ottin.

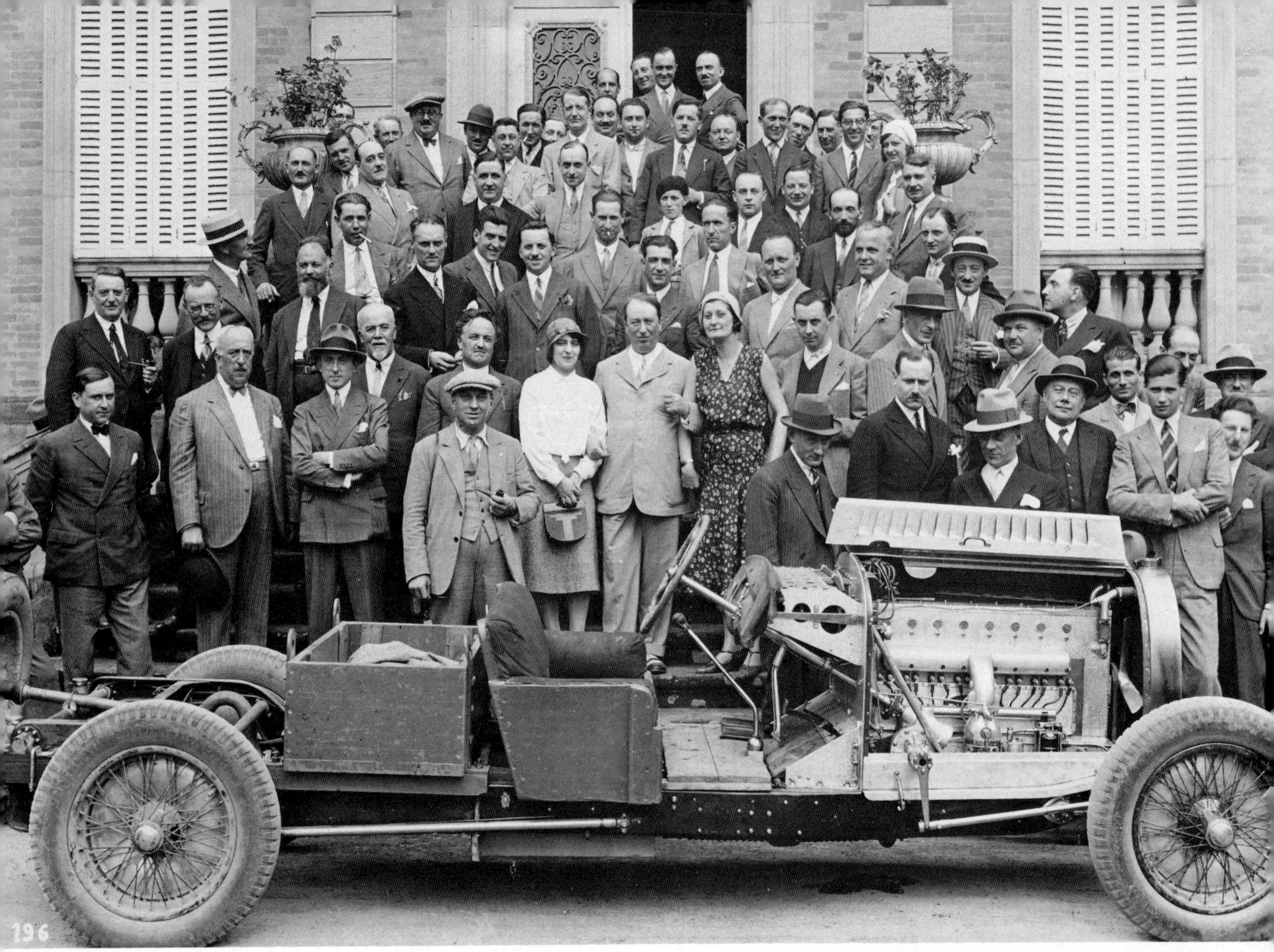

196

encircles the clutch and acts as a support for the starting motor. This aluminium housing is rigidly secured to the tubular cross-member, but merely fits over the rear of the engine crankcase, so as to allow relative movement to take place at times between the two units.

A vertically divided two-piece aluminium casing is used for the gearbox and the differential housing. The axle tubes are of chrome nickel heat-treated steel, the whole weighing only a couple of pounds more than the standard axle on the other models. The propellor-shaft is of the open type, with a fabric-type joint in front and a metal joint at the rear. The aluminium brake drums have an internal diameter of 15$\frac{3}{4}$in., and as the tyre size is 32 in. × 6 in., the brake drums are only a little less in diameter than the wheels. The position of the dynamo is somewhat unusual, it being under the floor-boards and secured by clips to the right-hand frame member. It is driven by means of a one-piece rubber belt from a pulley on the front end of the propellor-shaft.

Contemporary road impressions

There was a report of a road test of a Type 46 (No. 46219, still in existence) in *The Motor* of 1 April 1930:

A really solidly built, beautifully sprung, comfortable saloon car with exceptionally rapid acceleration throughout its speed range; that is the 32·5 hp or 'five-litre' Bugatti. It combines the luxury of a large limousine, the flexibility and top-gear performance of a thorough-bred town carriage with the perfect

A remarkable photograph of Ettore on the occasion of the completion of the 500th (sic) Type 46 chassis surrounded by his family, agents and drivers. Well-known personalities who can be identified include L'Ebé, Count and Countess Czaykowski, Chiron, Loiseau, Dreyfus, Friderich, Sabipa, Lamberjack the Paris agent, Docime and no doubt many others. This was probably chassis 46500 rather than the 500th.

A photograph of Fritz Schlumpf at the height of his Bugatti buying period, with an 'unused' T46S. He liked the photograph and asked for copies!

road-holding, the speed and acceleration of the best type of sports model.

Although in the appearance of the square-cut eight-cylinder engine, the shape of the radiator, the design of the rear springing and a certain lowness of build the new five-litre has a good deal in common with the famous racing cars from the Molsheim factory, the whole 'feel' of the car – its control and the manner in which it is driven – is different. Whereas with the sports models a lightning change-up is made after accelerating to the full on each of the intermediate gears, the driver of the five-litre is encouraged to get into top gear as soon as possible and to stay in top. The car then handles in a manner reminiscent of a large American car. It will creep through traffic at three or four miles an hour on top gear, will climb practically any main-road hill without there being any need to change down, and will accelerate, whenever the opportunity occurs, with surprising rapidity. Instead of the acceleration 'tailing-off' however, at high speeds, it continues almost the same until the maximum is reached.

The engine of the T46.

Of course, if one does change down to second speed – and the change is singularly easy – one can leave most other cars far behind. So the driver of one of these new, big Bugattis always has this second gear, as it were, 'up his sleeve', although to all intents and purposes his is a 'top-gear' car.

Possibly because of its low build and its admirable driving position, the Bugatti does not strike one as being a large car. Yet it is as wide and as long as most full-sized automobiles and, inside, it is as roomy, or roomier, than most. In traffic, however, it is handled with exceptional ease.

There seems always to be such an enormous amount of power in reserve that one drives the car instinctively in a very gentlemanly manner. What does it matter if anyone 'cuts in' ahead, or if exigencies of traffic compel one to slow to a crawl at the beginning of a steep ascent? The moment the accelerator is depressed the Bugatti leaps forward. The other cars fade into the background and the gradient seems to flatten as we devour it.

The suspension, by reversed quarter-elliptic springs at the rear and by half-elliptics in front, is all that can possibly be desired. Although all road shocks are completely damped out and one can take a culvert or hump-backed bridge at speed and scarcely feel it, there is a firm, secure feeling about the whole car that is most reassuring. There is no rolling on corners; one can swerve to the side of a steeply cambered road and yet feel completely at ease. Moreover, the springing is just as good at walking pace as it is at 90 mph.

Top left: *The supercharged T46S engine.*

Left: *The one-piece block casting was a fine piece of work even if the engine had to be completely dismantled to remove a valve.*

Above: *A photograph of the show model engine from* The Autocar *of 20 Sept 1929.*

The steering is absolutely accurate and pleasantly direct; it has a marked degree of self-centring action and, after rounding a bend, the steering-wheel spins back automatically to the 'straight-ahead' position. It is only at very low speeds that this caster action has the effect of making the steering just a shade heavy on sharp corners. At anything above 10 or 15 mph the steering is feather-light.

The clutch is very smooth in action and light to operate. The engine is most efficiently balanced and is delightfully smooth-running in consequence. It is quite inaudible at low speeds.

We put the Bugatti through our usual brake and acceleration tests at Brooklands and were particularly impressed with the liveliness of the car. As it was new we did not wish to overstress the engine. For this reason we made no attempt to exceed 50 mph on second gear although at that speed the power-unit was so quiet and there was so much throttle in hand that we could quite easily

Right: *A dismantled back axle, a unit common to the T50.*

Top right: *The 3 speed gearbox is in the back axle.*

have exceeded by a large margin the figure mentioned. In the same way we were contented with a flying half-mile at 82 mph on top gear and a lap at slightly over 79 mph and did not keep the car fully extended long enough to reach the ultimate maximum. We were assured by the concessionaires, however, that by using an alternative back-axle ratio, a speed of 96 mph should be obtainable.

Even when driving off the home banking at nearly 90 mph the car was beautifully quiet mechanically, while the body was completely silent.

The brakes were singularly smooth in action and absolutely safe. Judging by the size of the drums, they should last for an indefinite period.

We found that the Brooklands test hill could be climbed on top gear if approached at 25 mph and the accelerator depressed only when the car was actually on the gradient. From a standing start on first gear the test-hill was climbed in 12⅗ seconds, equal to an average speed of 19·37 mph. This is quite exceptionally good, especially when the weight of the car – 35 cwt 3 qr 2 lb – is taken into account.

The car we tried had a very smart Weymann body of the sportsman's coupé type, but far more roomy than is usual. There was plenty of room for those in the rear compartment and ample headroom.

The five-litre Bugatti is undoubtedly a very fine car and one which, in our opinion, will meet with an excellent reception in this country.

Type 48

The Peugeot 201X

The Peugeot 201X fitted with a 1000cc Bugatti engine, Type 48, and basically half of a T35 engine.

Type 48 engine, with four cylinders from the GP engine, many of its other features, and the magneto driven from the camshaft, on a cambox bearing the name Peugeot rather than Bugatti.

BUGATTI HAD had many contacts with Robert Peugeot and the Peugeot company, having sold them a licence to produce his Baby car of 1912 (see page 000), and indeed one for a design of a larger car, which was not put into production. He had even been asked in 1912 by Peugeot to offer his chain driven Type 18 or 'Garros' model in competition with a Grand Prix car designed by Peugeot's own designer Henry, whose 7.6 litre car beat the smaller Bugatti, and thus won over Robert Peugeot's ailing confidence. Contacts were evidently maintained with that Company since years later (in 1931) he designed a supercharged 1,000 cc engine for use in a special series of Peugeot 201 cars, known as the 201X; about twenty of these cars were made, mostly with cabriolet bodywork. Peugeot were anxious to produce a high performance sports car and the choice of a Bugatti engine was no doubt appropriate.

The engine, known as Type 48, was virtually half of a Type 35 engine, 60 mm × 88 mm, capacity 996 cc, and used half of the normal roller bearing, GP crankshaft and a single cylinder block, although the cambox had a rounded top. Another Molsheim feature of the car was the reversed, Bugatti-style, quarter-elliptic springs at the rear, but the transverse front spring was Peugeot. The wheelbase was 2·47 m and the track 1·15 m.

The Peugeot 201X had an unhappy history: the famous race driver André Boillot was killed in one of these cars on 5 June 1932, while practising for the Côte d'Ars race. He had had a long period of success as a driver for Peugeot and had just completed a few days previously a 24 hour run in a Peugeot 301C averaging 68 mph without a relief driver.

One example of the T48 engine is known to exist today.

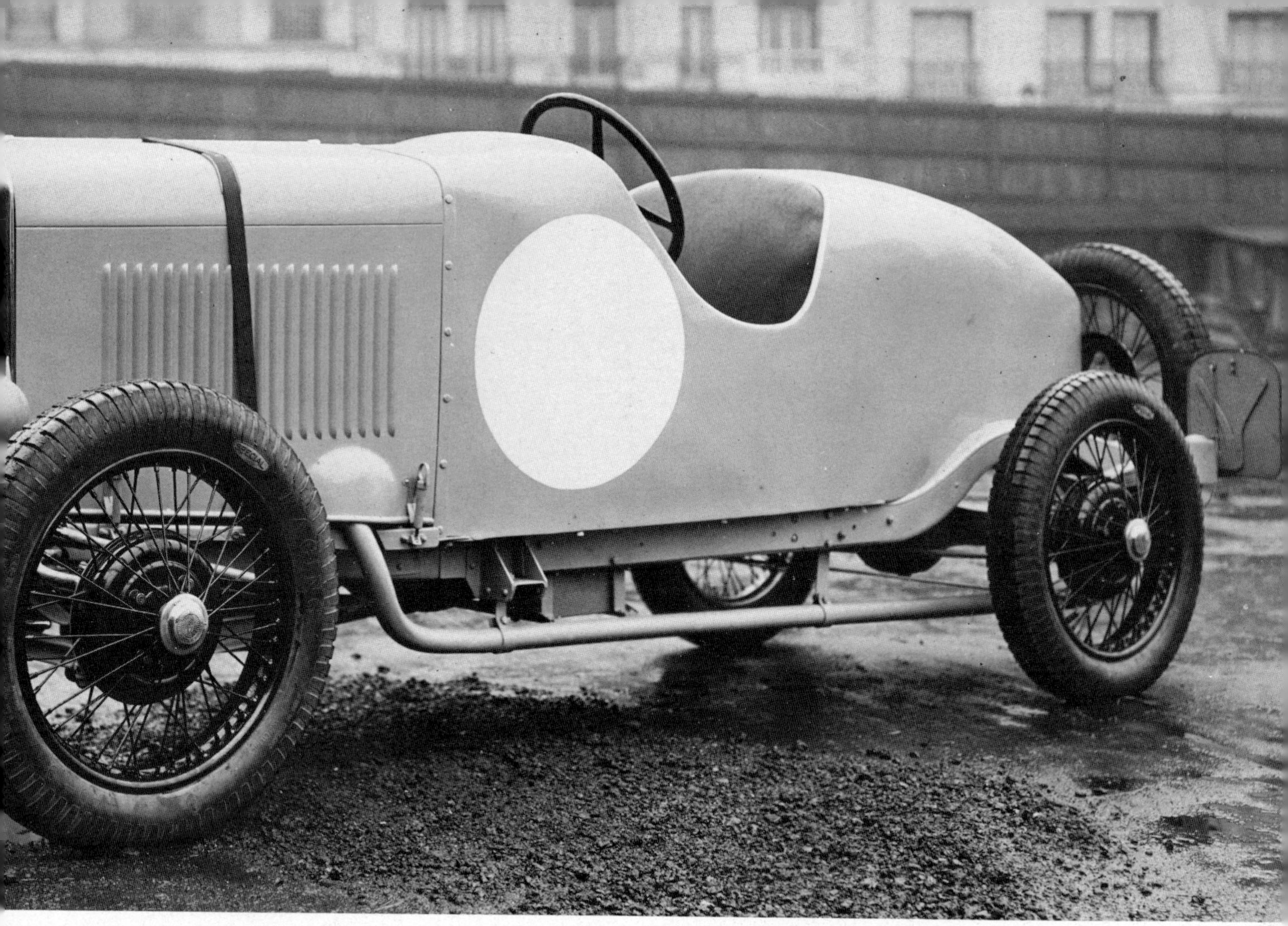

Type 49

The last single-cam car

MANY EXPERIENCED Bugattistes believe that the finest of all touring Bugatti cars was Type 49, which replaced Type 44 in July 1930 and continued in production for three years or so. It was the last single-cam engine produced and was virtually an enlarged Type 44, the bore being increased from 69 to 72 mm, a fan being added, the clutch being dry (except on a few early cars) and the gearbox having a ball change lever and the gears were now ground to try to silence them. The cylinder

A typical coach body.

The last single-cam Bugatti was the T49 replacing the T44 to which it was very similar.

blocks had two plugs per cylinder supplied from a dual Scintilla distributor. Bugatti alloy wheels were usually fitted and an enlarged radiator, but otherwise the car was very similar in all respects to the later series Type 44. A long chassis version was also available.

The front axle was of normal Bugatti design with the springs passing through the axle; the rear axle was also the same as on the 43–44 models but now had helical bevel gears, ratio 12 × 50, for silence. The brakes were operated by the normal compensated cables and on this model at any rate were excellent. Inside the car one could notice a speedometer in place of a tachometer and a neat cluster of instruments and switches in a solid walnut dash. The steering wheel had the simple steel centre with walnut rim as on earlier models and the racing cars – the larger touring cars (T46, T50 and later T57) had more complicated constructions.

The model was eventually replaced by Type 57, but had in comparison with it a 4 in. narrower track and 8 in. less wheelbase in standard form. These reduced dimensions and consequent weight saving gave it better handling than the later model. It did not have the performance of a Type 43, nor of the T57, but was an admirable touring Bugatti which compared very favourably indeed with any other car of the 1930 period.

Contemporary road impressions

The Motor, 1 November 1932, reported a road test of the car:

A FINE FRENCH CAR CAPABLE OF OVER 80 MPH, YET REMARKABLY FLEXIBLE AT LOW SPEEDS

The Type 49, or 3·3 litre tourer, combines all those qualities for which the Bugatti is famous, with an unexpected flexibility and silence at low speeds on top gear. It is, indeed, a car with a dual personality – a comfortable carriage and a lively sports model.

Lord Cholmondley had this 'canné' bodywork by Weymann.

It will lap Brooklands track at over 80 mph, and it will crawl through traffic and round street corners on top gear with never a sign of snatch. By means of dash-controlled, friction-type shock-absorbers the suspension can be instantly adjusted to give safe, bounce-free riding at any speeds from 10 to 80 miles an hour on any kind of surface.

So quickly and easily does the Type 49 reach a speed of a mile a minute that, on the average main road, it is possible to cover long distances in an astonishingly short space of time. So safe does the car feel that one has no hesitation about driving at the maximum whenever road conditions permit.

The car is, of course, beautifully finished. The engine is polished in a manner calculated to turn most enthusiasts green with envy. It is smooth running, too, except for a slight 'period', which could possibly be cured by adjusting the damper on the end of the crankshaft. The exhaust is quiet, as is the rear axle. Indeed, the only unit that lacks refinement is the gearbox. This is a four-speed

A smart Coupé de Ville for chauffeur drive.

A drophead coupé by Zuercher of Prague. 6

box of ordinary type, with no 'silent' gears. It is not easy to change gear with, and it is noisy on the lower ratios.

The gearbox has particularly well-chosen ratios, allowing, as it does, of a speed on top gear of over 80 mph with third and second gear maxima for 60 mph and 40 mph without over-revving the engine. The gear-change is exceptionally rapid, which probably accounts for the difficulty in gear-changing except at high road speeds, with the result that it is possible to make a remarkable get-away from a standstill. It only takes $20\frac{1}{5}$ sec to accelerate from a standstill to 60 mph using the gears, and changing up approximately at 25 mph, 40 mph and 60 mph. On second gear the car will accelerate from 10 mph to 30 mph in $4\frac{2}{5}$ sec, the top-gear acceleration between the same speeds being $8\frac{2}{5}$ sec.

In the course of our Brooklands tests, which were, of course, additional to our trial on the road, we lapped the track in 2 min $2\frac{4}{5}$ sec, which is equivalent to 81·11 mph. The half-mile was covered in $22\frac{4}{5}$ sec, which is equal to 78·95 mph. It may be considered by those unfamiliar with Brooklands track that this result is somewhat strange. All Brooklands *habitués* know, however, that with a certain direction of the wind it is possible to lap the track at a higher average speed than can be maintained over half a mile.

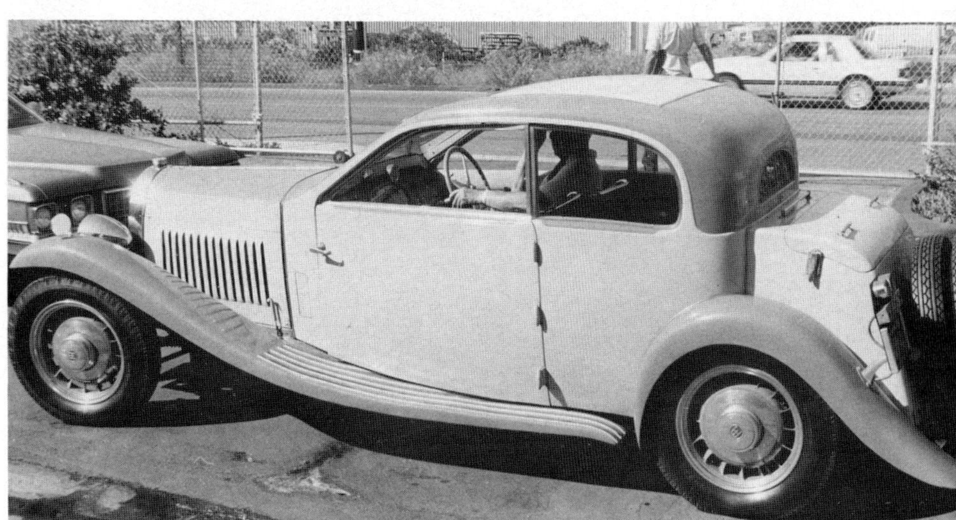

A style known at the factory as 'profilée' or streamlined, an effective style used on the later T57 'Ventoux' coach.

The T49 engine was distinguishable from the T44 by its dual ignition, and the use of a fan.

Elegant wheels with the bolts hidden by an 'enjoliveur' were normal on the T49.

The brakes, needless to say, proved to be exceptionally good, the pulling-up distances being better than is usually considered possible; at any rate, from low speeds. Several repetitions of the brake tests gave an average of 7 ft 6 in. from 20 mph , 23 ft from 30 mph , 50 ft from 40 mph and 78 ft 6 in. from 50 mph. It is to be assumed that the brake linings were well bedded down in the process, for the stopping distances, although very good, were not so remarkable at 60 mph and 70 mph, when they measured 131 ft 6 in. and 211 ft respectively. It was not considered worth while readjusting the brakes to get superlative results at these high speeds. The car pulled up dead straight on every occasion except one, when a rear wheel locked as the result of passing through a pool of water.

On the road the car handles delightfully. The steering is remarkably free from any reaction, is very light and fairly direct. Moreover, the amount of caster action given to the front wheels is not so great that it makes steering in reverse difficult.

Although carrying a really roomy four-seater body the Type 49 Bugatti is of handy dimensions, the wheelbase and track being 10 ft 7 in. and 4 ft 2 in. respectively. There are not many cars with engines this size which have such a narrow track, but the car is so steady on corners and the road-holding generally so good that one does not realize that the track is not the standard width of 4 ft 8 in.

Last winter we were able to make a long run on a similar model to that now described, covering some 320 miles in the day on a give-and-take road, including long straight stretches and a good deal of winding, hilly going, at a higher average speed than we have ever yet succeeded in maintaining for such a long distance.

We found that many main-road bends, which on the average car we would treat with the utmost respect, could be rounded on the Bugatti at such high speeds that it would be wiser not to quote them in this article. This run was accomplished without the slightest fatigue, which speaks well for the comfort which the suspension and bodywork afford and the freedom from worry engendered by the perfect road-holding and controllability.

As an instance of the remarkable hill-climbing properties of the Type 49, we may mention that the steep, winding roads leading out of Lyme Regis, in Dorset, in the direction of Exeter and Dorchester, were both climbed so fast on top gear that we were obliged to cut out for every bend. There are very, very few cars capable of equalling this performance.

For whatever purpose the car is used it invariably demonstrates itself to be a thoroughbred.

Type 50

Twin-cam, 5 litre luxury car

IN 1930 BUGATTI produced a new large luxury model replacing the 5·3 litre Type 46. It would perhaps be more accurate to say that it replaced the Type 46S, since it was supercharged and sold as a Grand Sport car. The chassis and transmission were identical with the earlier 5·3 litre car, but the engine was completely new. The wheelbase on the early models was shortened from the 3·5 m of the Type 46 to 3·1 m, but later a 'T' version (T = Tourisme) reverted to the longer frame. The bore and stroke were 86 and 107 mm, giving 4,972 cc (not 4,840 cc as given, unaccountably, by Brixton Road publicity, but not Molsheim, and repeated frequently). This now gave a more reasonable stroke/bore ratio of 1·25! The crankshaft was carried on nine plain bearings. The new and significant change in cylinder head layout was the abandonment by Ettore of vertical valves and the use of 90 degree inclined valves, two only per cylinder and operated directly by twin overhead camshafts.

The story has been told elsewhere that Bugatti saw and eventually acquired in exchange for three Type 43s, a pair of Miller racing cars that had been raced at Monza in 1929 by Leon Duray. Under pressure no doubt from his less-rigidly-minded son Jean he was persuaded that his vertical valve rectangular cylinder construction would allow for worse breathing than the hemispherical head with two 90 degree inclined valves of the Miller engine. Clearly too the Miller was producing more power than his racing Type 35B. So he was persuaded to follow the clearly established practices of others – after all Duesenberg had copied his engine ten years previously!

The new engine is a fine piece of engineering, with a massive cylinder block with fixed head. A vertical shaft at the front of the engine driven off the crankshaft by bevels, drives a pair of oil pumps through spur gears, the sump being of the dry type. An intermediate pair of bevels drives a short shaft lying across the front of the engine, then a further pair of bevels drives the longitudinal blower at twice engine speed. The top end of the vertical shaft drives the camshaft through five spur gears and idlers and a final pair of bevels. Twin Schebler carburettors were mounted below the blower. Ignition was by coil. The engine was reputed to develop 44 hp at 1,000 rpm, 113 hp at 2,000 rpm, 175 hp at 3,000 rpm

and 200 hp or more at 4,000 rpm. At peak revolutions the speeds on gears were 47 mph on 1st, 85 mph on 2nd and 110 on top, although so high a maximum speed was probably rarely achieved. The acceleration of the car was remarkable and the handling, steering and brakes excellent. Dash controlled shock-absorbers were used.

A car of this power is not one to be put in the hands of an inexperienced or impetuous driver. Col. Sorel, the manager of the British Bugatti Agency, evidently was reluctant to import such a formidable machine, and out of a production of 65 chassis, only one was sold to England, almost all the others remaining in France, where the open roads were more suitable.

An early Show exhibit was a 'profilée' body version.

The clutch, gearbox, chassis, axles and brakes on the Type 50 were identical with those of Type 46. Wheels were of the cast alloy type, with

Royale style hubs. Many magnificent bodies were mounted on the Type 50, a model which was at the peak of Bugatti's luxury cars, overlooked perhaps by the fantastic Royale. It was used occasionally for racing, a team of regulation-bodied touring cars being entered in the 1931 Le Mans 24 hour race. The car driven by Rost crashed, due to a burst tyre, and unfortunately killed a spectator; the team was then withdrawn, the other drivers being Conelli, Varzi/Chiron and Divo/Bouriat. The normal Type 50 engine, no doubt with increased power, was used in the Type 53 FWD car and the Type 54 GP car, although its weight was a fault.

The Type 50 introduced in 1930 was intended as a super-sport car with outstanding performance; it was the first Bugatti with twin overhead camshafts.

A special racing engine, with a light alloy crankcase and known as the 50B was later developed from the standard engine; details are given in the Section on the 1935–37 works racers.

A very elegant Molsheim body with pony-skin trunk covering.

A folding top two-seater coupé.

Later a longer wheelbase chassis was able to carry 4-door saloon coachwork.

A cabriolet with Czechoslovak coachwork. (Stan Marusak)

The supercharger is driven from the front of the engine by bevel gears. (*Stan Marusak*)

Left and right: *Factory pictures of the T50 engine. It was used also on the racing T54 and FWD T53 cars.*

Le Mans 1931, the Chiron/Varzi car.

Type 51

Twin-cam GP racing car

AS WE HAVE recounted in the last chapter Bugatti had at last agreed to adopt the hemispherical head, twin camshaft layout of the Miller for his engine. A Miller engine on test produced almost 50 more horse power than his equivalent engine had managed! So now a decision was made to update the 35B with a new cylinder block and camshaft drive, fortunately not difficult to achieve. The result was the Type 51, Bugatti's classic Grand Prix car at its zenith. It was announced at the Paris Salon in October 1930, but did not materialize until early 1931.* The engine consisted of a crankcase, roller-bearing crankshaft and blower with drive from the T35B, with a new block carrying 95 degree inclined valves, two per cylinder, and intermediate cups between the cams and valves as on Type 50. A single central 18 mm plug was used; manifolds were also new.

* A full description of the car and its successes is given in *Grand Prix Bugatti*.

The camshaft lubrication was by pressure pipe from the main oil gallery on the left-hand side of the crankcase, feeding the blower gears, the timing gears (four connections) and the camshafts.

Improved wheels with non-detachable rims were introduced, rather neater in appearance than the earlier GP type and with strengthening ribs inside each spoke. Tyre size remained dimensionally as before but using the new designation 5.00 × 19 in., in place of 28 × 4.95. Externally, however, the car was virtually indistinguishable from a T35B, although the experienced eye can notice the lower location of the blower relief hole in the bonnet, due to the difference in inlet manifolds, and the location of the magneto on the left-hand side of the dash, since it is driven by the left-hand, exhaust camshaft. A number of 1,500 cc, 60 mm × 66 mm, cars were produced under the designation T51A; a few 2 litre cars, 60 mm × 88 mm, were also produced, but there is some doubt that the designation T51C (by analogy with the T35C) is official. On test the 2,300 cc engine gave 187 hp at 5,200 rpm, and the 1,500 cc a surprising 158 hp.

Bottom left: *It is difficult to imagine a more beautiful classic racing car!*

Chiron, one of the most successful T51 drivers signs a picture for his friend, and former racing driver Jules Goux.

Of the 40 cars made some 26 have survived and many are regularly seen in vintage racing. To many they are the most beautiful and desirable of Bugattis.

Top left: *Williams in the 1931 Belgian Grand Prix, with his cap characteristically back to front. Crash helmets were rare in those days.*

Racing successes

The type made a good start to its racing career, Chiron winning the 1931 Monaco Grand Prix and Varzi the Tunis GP. He and Chiron jointly won the 10 hour French Grand Prix of that year at Montlhéry, covering 782 miles. From then on many examples were to be seen in races all over the world, and the car was very popular at Brooklands. It has been said that the car was no faster than a good single-cam version, but given an equal degree of tune it probably was. The exhaust valve seats probably cracked less often! Mr A. C. Whincop wrote in the *Autocar* of 13 August 1943:

Top: *Varzi in the 1931 French Grand Prix.*

Varzi in the same event. daylight showing under his inside front wheel.

The Type 51 was first built in 1931, it being half Ettore's answer to the Monoposto Alfa Romeo which was breaking down Bugatti's amazing run of European successes since 1926, if the brief reign of the 1½ litre Delage in 1927 is excepted. The other half of Ettore's answer was the double-camshaft 4·9 litre GP car, which in spite of its very much greater capacity and new chassis design was no faster on many circuits than the 2·3; and was definitely slower on the corners, through the 'magic' having failed on that one chassis. As a result of Ettore's two answers, the years 1931 and 1932 provided probably the most colourful racing we have ever seen with Monoposto Alfa Romeos, 2·3 and 4·9 Bugattis, Maseratis of various capacities, and an occasional short-chassis Mercedes-Benz, all fairly evenly matched in spite of all giving their performance in such different ways. The Monoposto, however, had that little extra power which enabled Alfa Romeo to depose Bugatti from the supreme position in motor racing. The Type 51 can well be content with its successes during this period, which earned it the reputation of being the most reliable and the most pleasant racing car of its vintage to handle.

The BOC car

At the Bugatti Owners' Club dinner in London in February 1939 Jean Bugatti made the astonishing announcement that his father and he were presenting the Club with a T51 GP car for use by those club members

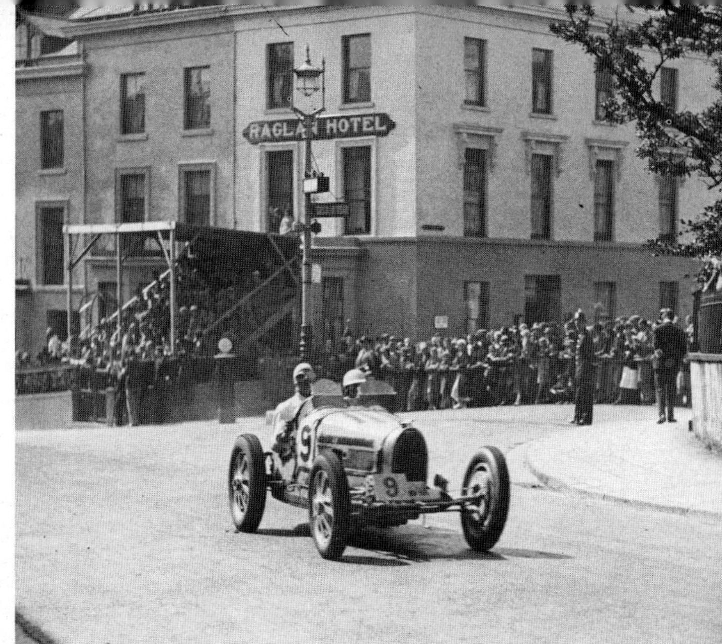

Top right: *Rose-Richards in the Isle of Man 1933.* (Autocar)

who could not afford a car. The car arrived a few months later and was tried out at Prescott successfully – rather too successfully by one member who disappeared off the course onto the trees below the last bend on the hill. The war came shortly afterwards; the subsequent story of the car has been communicated by Mr A. Rivers Fletcher:

Early in 1943 the BOC decided to sell the Type 51 Bugatti which had been presented to the Club by Ettore Bugatti in 1939. Although the car was a wonderful gift it proved to be rather a white elephant in that it was so difficult to decide who should drive it. Obviously, the people with the requisite amount of experience already had suitable cars of their own, and there were clear difficulties in handing over such a potent and expensive piece of machinery to an inexperienced person. No doubt, the BOC Council must have been very loath to part with the car but in retrospect it was a wise choice. The war was on and in any case there did not seem to be much prospect of any motor racing for a long time.

At that time I was working with my great friend, Peter Monkhouse, at the Monaco Motor and Engineering Company Limited at Watford. We were completely involved with war work of a fairly secret nature, but Peter was mad keen to get a suitable racing car organized for himself for post-war racing. He had always been very keen on Bugattis and was most enthusiastic at the prospect of buying the Club car. He did a deal with Eric Giles on behalf of the BOC and on Easter Monday in April 1943 Peter and I travelled down to the Giles' home in Surrey by railway train. We brought with us a pair of trade registration plates and a roll of four inch width canvas. Eric Giles had promised to fasten a batten across the radiator stone guard extending to the front wheels and another batten across the tail of the car so that we could stretch the canvas across from wheel to wheel making some sort of impromptu wings to comply with British law. We also brought with us a bulb horn from a child's fairy cycle! Thus equipped we set off in a very Grand Prix Type 51 Bugatti on a sixty mile detour round London – it was very nearly legal! Anyway, we certainly had a method of giving audible warning of approach! There was a rear view mirror on the scuttle, there were mudguards – at least we said they were mudguards – we were using trade plates, and maybe the requisite insurance was valid. The Type 51 had been filled with racing fuel on the outbreak of war, and although it had tended to separate out, we drained it out, shook it up and re-filled the tank before setting off. It was a fantastic journey. Peter drove nearly all the way though I had a short spell. We were cheered by numerous military convoys who were, no doubt, surprised to see and hear a Grand Prix car being driven in such a manner and in such a place. We came across several policemen but they obviously did not believe their eyes or ears, so we were well past them before anyone could do

anything about the situation. At one roundabout near Beaconsfield a military policeman gave us the thumbs up signal, and indicated to us to do just one more circuit of the roundabout for their delectation; Peter was driving and gave them the works – second gear with plenty of wheel spin and all the resultant tail wagging and pleasant odour!

The car was carefully stored at Monaco until racing cars could be got out again after the war. Peter drove the car at the Cockfosters Rally on the first occasion when racing cars were used in England in the new peacetime. He had offered to lend the car to our Patron, Lord Howe, to open the course, but Lord Howe declined the offer, wisely saying that something always happens if you borrow somebody else's car however carefully you drive it. Anyway he did use

The T51 given to the Bugatti Owners Club by Ettore Bugatti for use by members, just before the war.

The engine of the T51 in standard form.

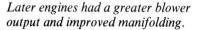

Later engines had a greater blower output and improved manifolding.

a Bugatti for the opening ceremony, as he used his own immaculate black and blue Type 57 SC coupé.

The first competition in which Monkhouse drove the Type 51 was in the VSCC sprint at Elstree in 1946 in which he made Fastest Time of the day, second place being taken by Roy Parnell driving Reg Parnell's Delage. This was on Easter Monday, just three years after the car had been collected from Eric Giles' home. Peter also got a second place in a short race at Gransden Lodge in June that same year, and of course he used the car at Prescott and in other sprints and hill-climbs during the next two years. Mrs Monkhouse won the prize for fastest lady driver driving the car in the Brighton Speed Trials, and in May 1947 Peter achieved 47·78 seconds at Prescott.

By that time the car had been modified by Peter's excellent mechanic Jack

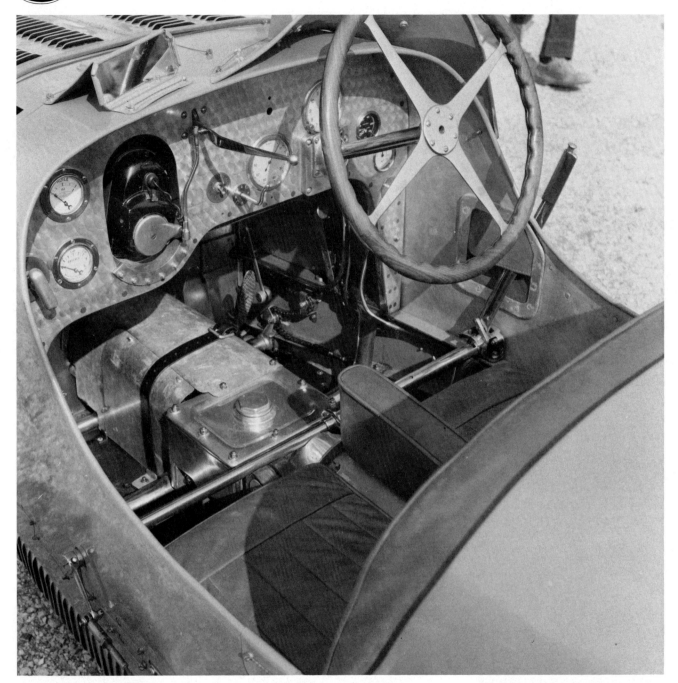

Jaguard, gearing up the supercharger to give more boost, and fitting a Wilson help-yourself gearbox instead of the original Bugatti clutch and gearbox.

Later in that year, in June, Peter in the Type 51 on the Holyhead Road near Dunstable was involved in a horrid shunt hitting a heavy lorry head on. The car was completely written off, but fortunately no one was seriously injured.

Monkhouse himself was tragically killed in April 1950 in the Mille Miglia in Italy. The car itself, 51155, had been one delivered new to Prince Leopold of Belgium (later King) and used by him as a sports car. The damaged car was eventually sold and rebuilt with a Ford engine finally being restored to more acceptable standards with a single cam engine; it is now in a Museum in England.

The driver's compartment was the same as in the T35 except that the magneto was on the left and the advance lever operated on the Scintilla unit directly.

Type 52 & 56

Electric vehicles and the Baby Bugatti

AT THE 1927 Milan Automobile Show, Bugatti showed an attractive miniature children's Grand Prix Bugatti; this was originally built for young Roland, the second son of Ettore, born in 1922. This children's car was later put on the market, the correct factory reference being Type 52. It was listed as the Type 'Baby' for children of six to eight years of age; it had a speed of 10 to 12 mph, driven by a 12 volt accumulator. It was six feet in length and weighed 150 lb, and had pneumatic tyres on detachable wheels, with brakes on all four wheels, the brake shoes consisting of a one piece expanding annulus of wood. Transmission was by a single-stage gear train from an electric motor mounted on the rear axle, the left-hand wheel being free on the axle. Reverse could be selected

The Prince of Morocco tests a Baby Bugatti on a visit to Molsheim.

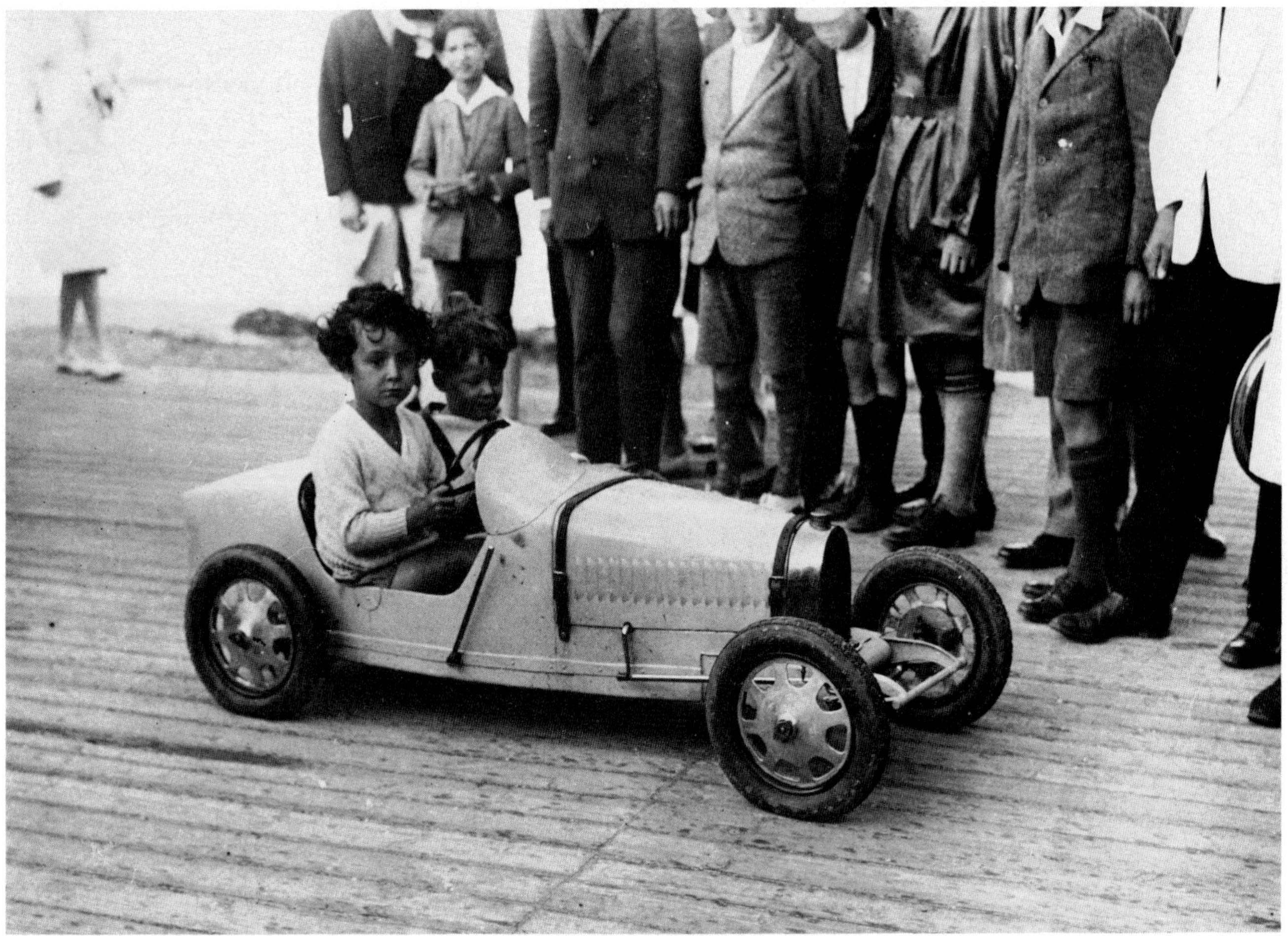

The Baby car was frequently seen in the hands of well-to-do youngsters at Deauville.

by a change-over switch in the motor field windings. A throttle-like lever operated a stepped resistance to vary speed. The prototype, had a wheelbase and track of 1·2 m × 0·6 m, exactly half of its full size parent; no doubt to increase leg room, the production models had the wheelbase lengthened at the expense of aesthetics to 1·3 m, the front of the frame being extended, and the bonnet (hood) having 21 not 16 louvres. Tyres were half scale 710 × 90 mm (355 × 45 mm) and specially made for the model, presenting a replacement problem today.

These Baby Bugattis were much sought after in France and were often seen on the promenades at Deauville and other smart resorts. Today they are collectors' pieces.

Type 56 was a two seat electric runabout built by Bugatti more or less as a personal transport. At least some consideration was given to marketing it since a data sheet was produced. The chassis frame was a combination of wood and steel, with full-elliptic springs, and steering tiller; the tyres were 26 in. × 3·50 in. Six 100 amp/hour 6 volt batteries in series provided the energy for a 36 volt 1 hp motor mounted on the axle and driving through gears by a mechanism very similar to that used in the Baby car. Speed control was by means of a right-hand lever. Foot and hand operated drum brakes were fitted. The total weight was under 800 lb, and a maximum speed of 16 to 18 mph was claimed.

A small batch of these electric vehicles was made and at least two survive, Bugatti's personal vehicle returning to Alsace to the Schlumpf collection (now Mulhouse Museum) via Illinois.

Today a T52 is much sought after and still much enjoyed by the young.

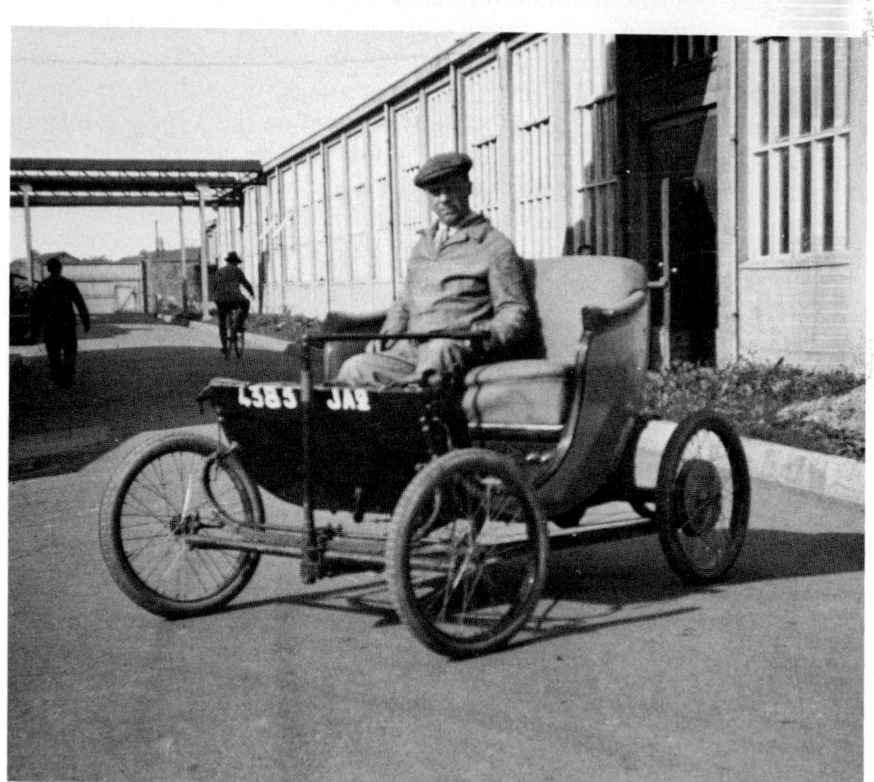

Ettore's electric vehicle – Type 56 – at Molsheim after rebuild postwar, prior to going to the museum at Mulhouse in the Schlumpf collection. The driver is Mr Fraehring, Chief Electrician.

Type 53

4-wheel drive car

IN 1932 BUGATTI announced a remarkable 4-wheel drive racing car, which apart from an experimental Christie car in the early 1900s, seems to have been the first time such a construction has been attempted in the racing field prior to the advent of the Ferguson car in 1961. If the chassis was completely new, the power plant was based on the Type 50, 4·9 litre engine, and was as used in the Type 54 GP car (see next Section). The original conception of the car was based on an Italian design which Jean Bugatti saw and persuaded his father to adopt, for development at Molsheim. The design was from a consulting designer G. C. Cappa, formerly of Fiat, who sent a colleague, Antoine Pichetto, to Molsheim to complete the design around the Bugatti engine.

J. A. Grégoire, the well-known designer of the Tracta, Hotchkiss and other front-wheel drive cars has written (*L'Aventure Automobile*, Flammarion, Paris 1953):

> About 1930, [Bugatti] met me one day, looking more red-faced and jovial than ever, and said, 'That won't work, that front drive car of yours'. I knew, of course, that he had designed and built a 4-wheel drive racing car which was causing him some trouble. And he added 'when you want to take a corner with this car, you can't hold the steering wheel and the car tries to leave the road'. Asking him how he managed the transmission to the front wheels, he explained to me that it was by normal universal joints. I tried hard to explain to him the causes of the trouble and the need for constant velocity joints, but he would not admit the clearly demonstrated facts. He condemned for always, as a result, front-wheel drive and regarded me with the benevolent sympathy accorded to a fanatic, until the decisive demonstration of Citroen.

One of the cars – only three being built – competed in a few hill-climbs in France, breaking the record at La Turbie, 1932, in the hands of Louis Chiron, and then being crashed by Jean Bugatti at Shelsley Walsh in that year. Dreyfus broke the La Turbie record again in 1934, exceeding 100 km/h for the 6·3 km course for the first time. He has confirmed from his experience how torque sensitive the steering was, exhausting him on this climb. What may be the remains of the prototype is in the National Museum at Mulhouse, and what is probably the remains of the car

Factory picture of the car.

crashed by Jean has been rebuilt, fitted with the correct type of engine, and survives in France. What happened to the other complete car is not known.

The car was of considerable technical interest and a more pliable Ettore might have seen better results. Today's limited slip differentials, torque balancing couplings and constant velocity joints have ensured the success of the several 'quatros' on the market.

Description of car

The *Autocar* of 25 March 1932 carried a comprehensive description of the car:

A four-wheel drive racing car with independently sprung front wheels has been produced by Bugatti and is expected to make its appearance in some of the leading Continental races this season. M. Ettore Bugatti does not claim to have invented four-wheel drive. But if many have thought of building a racing car having power delivered to each of its four wheels, it has remained for Bugatti to develop the idea and, after two years' labour, to produce an original and exceptionally efficient racing machine.

It is pointed out that, unlike other Bugatti models, this car is not intended for sale to the public. It is a special racing machine, designed for special conditions, under which it is almost unbelievably efficient. The advantage of four-wheel drive over rear-wheel drive is the absence of wheel slip and, consequently, vastly improved acceleration. The car, therefore, will show to greatest advantage on a hilly, winding course necessitating frequent braking and acceleration. On an easy, straight-away run there is no advantage in driving on four wheels – at any rate with engines of the size usually employed for road racing. There is, indeed, a disadvantage, for the more complicated transmission entails a power loss of about 4 per cent.

Any person who has handled a modern racing car, and particularly a machine such as the 4,900 cc supercharged Bugatti, is prepared for speedy acceleration. But the new Bugatti four-wheel drive is a revelation, even to the initiated. With an engine developing 300 hp wheel slip is inevitable if any attempt is made to transmit the whole of that power through two wheels to start away or to accelerate from low speed. But with only 75 hp going to each wheel the effect is amazing. Opportunities of appreciating this were given during a recent visit to the Bugatti works in Alsace, but as the car has not yet been seen in public it would be unfair to the maker to give any definite figures. It is sufficient to say that it is practically impossible to produce a skid; that for cornering on a rough or greasy surface the four-wheel driver is immensely better than the rear-wheel driver, and that its acceleration is so rapid as to be almost disconcerting to even experienced drivers..

The main interest lies in the method of transmitting the power to the four wheels. Behind the engine but connected to it by a universally jointed shaft, is a special gearbox, the housing of which extends right up to the chassis frame members, thus tending to stiffen the chassis. The gearbox contains three shafts (ignoring the reverse pinion shaft); the primary shaft, an intermediary shaft, and the driven shaft carrying a differential. Whatever the gear used, the power must go through the intermediary shaft, so that there is no direct drive. There are two sets of sliding pinions, one giving first and fourth speeds, and the other second and third. The reason for this is that for hill work second and third are the gears most frequently used, and quick changes from one to the other are essential. First is a starting-off gear, and fourth is only occasionally used [on the gate 2–4 are forward, 1–3 back. Reverse is engaged by lifting a knob].

As can be imagined, the gearbox is a very sturdy construction, with short stiff shafts and pinions well calculated for the immense stresses they have to

The chassis layout of the FWD T53. (Autocar) *1*

withstand. From the extremities of the differential shaft in the gearbox the power is carried forward by means of an open shaft alongside the engine to a pair of bevel gears in a front axle housing, and rearwards to what is practically a normal-type Bugatti rear axle housing, with the exception that the differential is considerably out of centre. The car thus has three differentials; one in the gearbox, one in the front axle, and one in the rear axle.

There is little to be said about the rear axle construction. It is a built-up type, with a vertically divided differential housing in aluminium and steel tubes which would appear fragile did they not have the proof of experience behind them. A truss-rod is used on the axle housing, and suspension is of the well-known Bugatti type, by quarter elliptics having their thick ends rearwards. A pressed-steel torque arm, with the usual elastic attachment at the front end, is made use of.

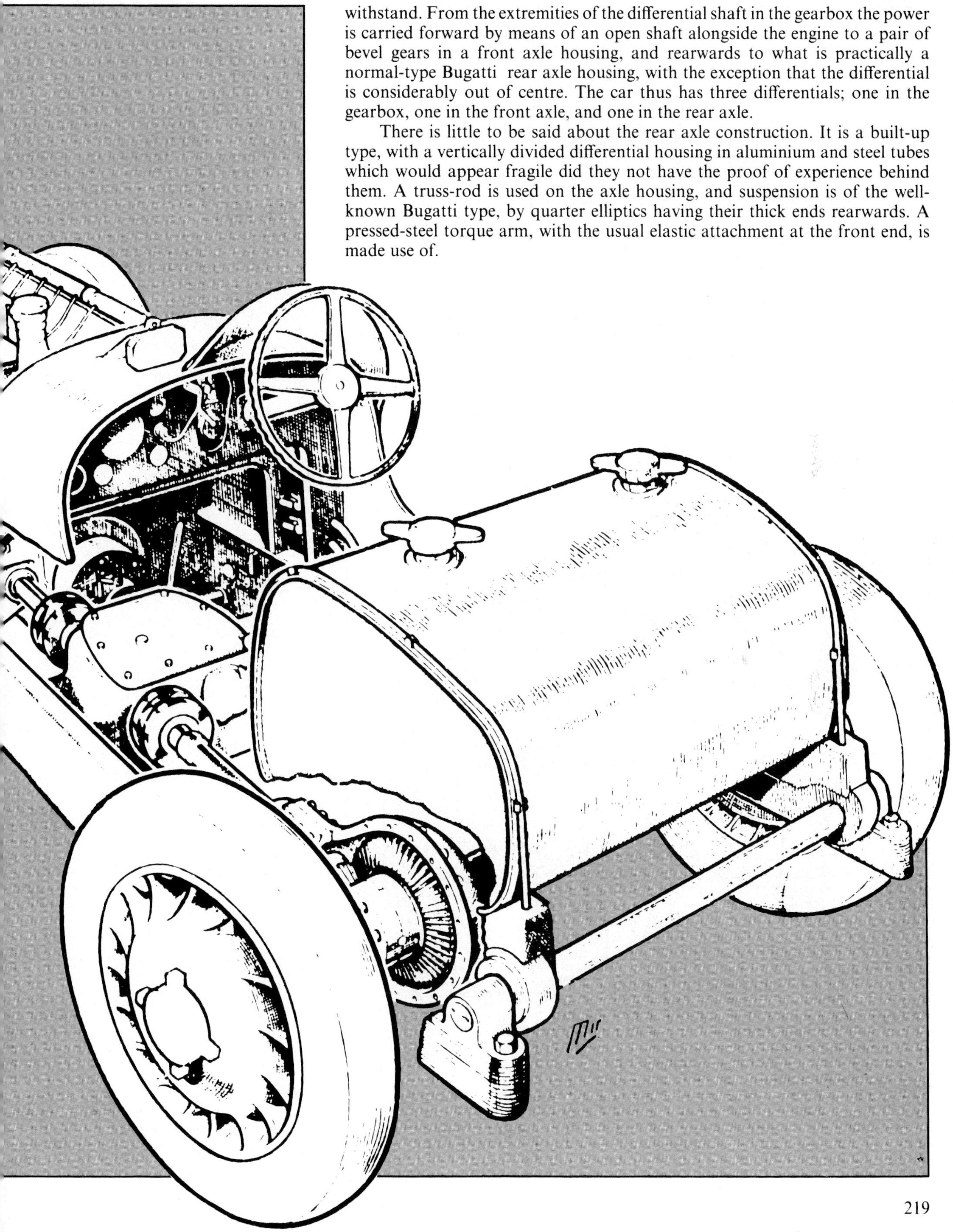

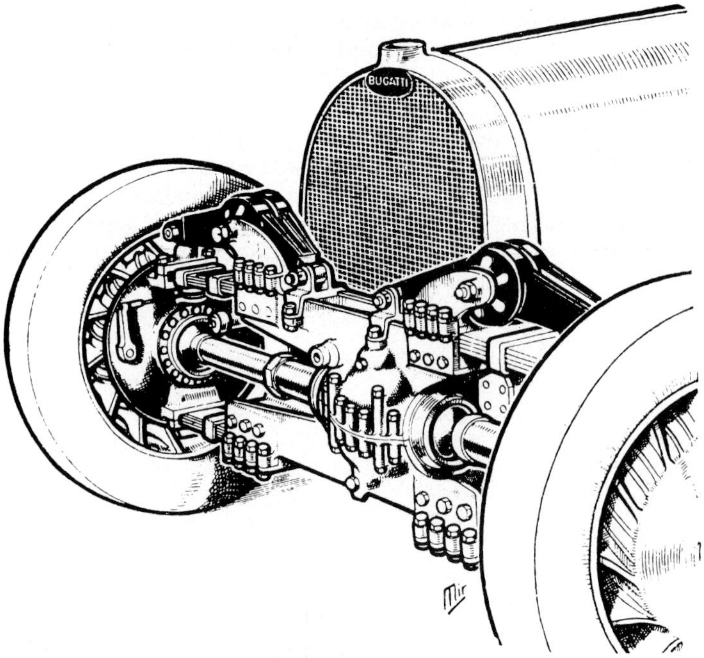

The front suspension with twin transverse springs. (Autocar)

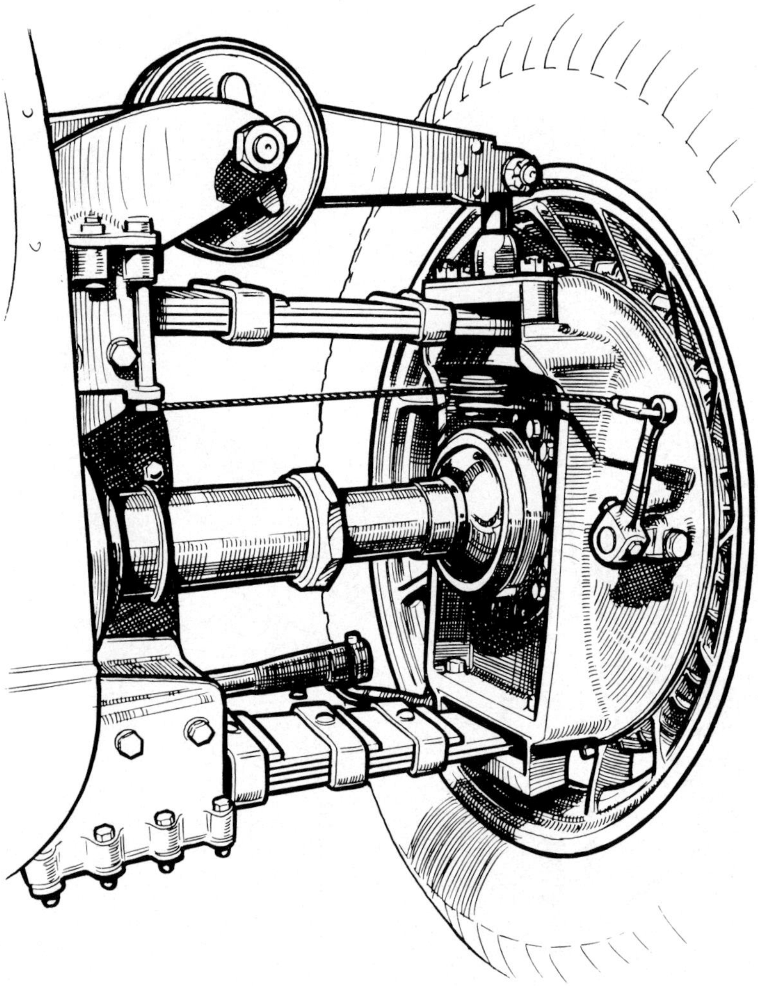

Detail of the universal jointed hubs; the design needed constant velocity joints. (Autocar)

At the front everything is new. From the gearbox the drive shaft is carried forward through the steel bulkhead through the left-hand rear engine hanger, in which it has a steady bearing, under the forward left-hand engine hanger, and has a metal universal joint connection to the bevel-pinion shaft. The method of transmitting the drive to the front wheels, and at the same time of assuring independent suspension of the steering wheels, is somewhat similar to other makes known to motorists, with the special advantages of lightness and extreme rigidity.

The two chassis frame members are united at the front by a two-piece aluminium casting not altogether symmetrical, each one consisting of a deep channel section rail and the half of a differential housing. The two are united by means of the differential housing, which, as can be judged, is out of centre, for the propellor-shaft runs by the side of the engine. Two very broad transverse springs, each one having five leaves, are carried in the upper and lower channels of the aluminium cross-member. Under load the springs are perfectly flat; their vertical movement is comparatively small, and they are so well guided in the channels in which they are housed that there can be no horizontal movement and no torsion under braking and driving stresses such as occur in racing.

Chiron and Varzi in the pair of cars at Klausen 1932.

There are no stub axles, but the four extremities of the springs are attached, by means of ball and socket connections, to flanges on a cast-aluminium circular plate which fills the functions of the usual steering knuckle and has the main steering levers bolted to it. Double-arm friction-type shockabsorbers, which also act as radius arms, are attached to this disc by means of ball and socket connections. The differential-drive shafts, which of course are of unequal length, have a metal universal joint at each extremity, the outer joint being in the vertical axis of the wheel. As in the case of other Bugatti cars, the wheel is a single aluminium casting, together with its brake drum, and has helical spokes to assist in cooling. Steering is on the right, most of the parts being the same as those used on the normal cars

As can be readily appreciated, the front of the car is entirely changed from the usual Bugatti design. Because of the front-wheel drive the radiator has reduced height, and, in consequence, has been made much wider than that of other cars. The head resistance has been increased, but an attempt has been made to nullify this by means of a cowling in front of the radiator which encloses all the central portion of the springs, the frame cross-member, and the differential housing. This gives the car a blunt bullet-shaped appearance when seen head on, with a very pronounced impression of power and speed.

The weight is carried equally on the two axles with petrol tank filled and in full racing trim. As the tank empties there is a slight excess of weight on the front axle.

The engine used on this car is much more familiar than is the chassis. It is the straight eight of 86 by 107 mm, bore and stroke, with the two overhead camshafts driven from the front, and a Roots-type blower placed fore and aft on the right-hand side and driven by means of bevel gearing from a cross-shaft. The most pronounced feature of this engine is the cylinder construction, the block of eight being a single casting, milled all over, with the nine bearings for the crankshaft direct on the casting, and the hangers secured to it direct.

This gives an exceedingly rigid construction to which the crankcase is merely an attached light housing to retain oil and exclude dust without in any way adding to the rigidity of the unit. There are two Zenith carburettors under the blower. Ignition is by magneto, driven off the end of the right-hand camshaft, with plugs placed vertically in the cylinder head. Dry sump lubrication is used, with the oil supply contained in a big tank on the left-hand side of the inclined dashboard, under the bonnet.

With a view to obtaining desirable rigidity and also as a precaution against fire, there is a stout sheet-steel bulkhead immediately behind the engine, and

Jean Bugatti brought a car to Shelsley Walsh for the hill-climb in 1932 but 'bent' it. Standing beside is Lord Howe. (*R. Chapman*).

What is probably the crashed car, or most of it, has been rebuilt by Uwe Hucke, who brought it to England again for its first hill-climb for over 50 years. The driver is A. B. Price and the photographer Bob Light.

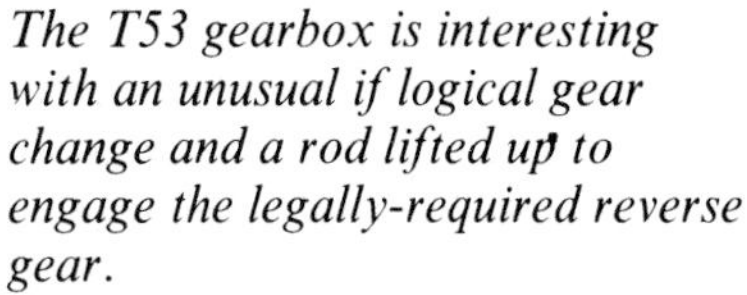

The T53 gearbox is interesting with an unusual if logical gear change and a rod lifted up to engage the legally-required reverse gear.

fitting closely around the clutch housing and having a hole cut through it just big enough for the drive shaft to pass through. Unlike the smaller racing models this engine has a one-piece crankshaft with plain bearings and split-end connecting-rods. It was used last year in several races, notably at Monza, but detail improvements made during the past winter have resulted in increased power, the output, it is claimed, being now slightly in excess of 300 bhp.

As an engineering production this car stands out as one of the most notable achievements of the past few years. Having been on the road, secretly, for the last six months, it is fully tuned up, and its public appearance will be watched with exceptional interest.

Type 54

The 4·9 litre Grand Prix car

ALTHOUGH BUGATTI had used the 4·9 litre engine for racing at Le Mans in 1931, with unhappy results, it was inevitable that he would seek to use it in a pure racing car, to match the large cars that Alfa Romeo and Maserati were fielding. The result was the Type 54 Grand Prix car. W. F. Bradley wrote in the *Autocar* of 11 September 1931:

The new racing Bugattis possess the distinction of having been designed, built and put on the road in 13 days. In view of the Italian models [12 cylinder Alfa Romeo and 16 cylinder Marerati] prepared for the Monza race it was realized that something faster than the twin-cam 2,300 cc racing machine would have to be prepared. . . .

The [engine] is attached to a frame cross-member in front, the rear attachment being to a steel bulkhead completely separating the engine compartment from the driver's compartment. The two axles are of the normal Bugatti type, but are of a wider track than for any other of the racing cars. [The engine power was quoted as 300 hp at 4,000 rpm.]

Kaye Don raced a 4·9 litre Type 54 at Brooklands, fitted with the compulsory silencer.

Brooklands Bank Holiday meeting, August 1933; Oliver Bertram tries to pass K. Don in the T54 inside in the Lightning Short Handicap; John Cobb ran through the field to win in the 24 litre Napier-Railton, but Don was second and did a lap at 129·36 mph. This superb track is no more.

In fact what Bugatti was able to do quickly (even if not in 13 days!) was to use the available frame and chassis components from the Type 45 16 cylinder car, which he now did not want to pursue. This frame, later used also on the Type 55, had wide-base rear springs and long locating radius rods for the rear axle. The initial layout of the car was similar to the T51, but on test it seemed front heavy due to the engine weight, and the radiator was moved backwards.

The T54 first appeared at the Monza Grand Prix in 1931, in the hands of Varzi and Chiron. Chiron retired after a tyre failure had cut a brake cable and left him with no brakes, although he tried to continue. Varzi finished 3rd also being delayed with tyre trouble. This was a race of giants, the other cars being 12 cylinder Alfas, or 16 cylinder Maseratis. For the next two years the T54 was raced by the Works, alongside the 2·3 litre Type 51, but it did not have a particularly successful career, being heavy and rather uncontrollable. Kaye Don and Czaykowski both drove 4·9 litre cars in the 1933 Brooklands Empire Trophy. Varzi won the 1933 Avus race at 138·48 mph, and in the same year Czaykowski, who had just gained the World's Hour Record at Avus at over 130 mph, met his death in the car in the final of the Monza Grand Prix, skidding on an oil patch. 10 September 1933 was a tragic day as he, Campari and Bozzacchini all died.

Only five or six of these cars were built.

Left: *The 1933 International Trophy at Brooklands; Kaye Don in the T54 leads Fotheringham Parker in a 2·3 litre T35B through the artificial chicanes.* (Autocar)

Another T54 went to the USA and was converted there for road work, even having a Hydromatic transmission fitted. It was used for suspension and road holding research by W. Milliken at Cornell Research Laboratory.

Middle right: *The engine of the T54 is similar to the T50 unit but seems even more magnificent in a GP frame.*

Bottom right: *The T54 gearbox has only three speeds to allow wider gears in a casing which straddles the frame.*

Lord Howe's T54 was converted for road use by L. G. Bachelier in 1936, and seen here driven in 1949 by J. M. James. (L. Klementaski).

Type 55

Twin-cam, Super Sport model

FOR 1932 BUGATTI introduced a new super sport model replacing the Type 43. This used the T51 twin-cam supercharged 2·3 litre engine in a T45 or 54 chassis, many of the chassis details being similar to the T43, but with a new hollow front axle with additional 'drop' in the centre to clear an enlarged Scintilla dynamo; the gear box was basically as on the Type 49 with a ball change. The engine crankcase had the same wide rear mounting as on the T51, to suit the GP frame. The car was fitted with a beautiful 2-seat roadster body, designed by Jean Bugatti himself. Certainly, with its long sweeping wings, GP wheels, rounded tail and rear mounted spare wheels, the car set a standard in appearance and purposefulness which has never been beaten and rarely equalled in the sports car world.

Its performance matched its appearance – 110 to 112 mph, and dazzling acceleration. The car was expensive, as had been the T43, and only 38 were made compared to 160 of the earlier model; the worsening economic situation must have made sales more difficult, but one may conjecture whether problems with the 'bottom end' of the T43 may have come to the ears of potential customers! A few cars had bodies from Paris coachbuilders although most had the superb Molsheim built roadster. Three or four had a similarly styled 2-seat fixed-head coupé, also made at Molsheim, very handsome but not very well ventilated inside.

No less than 28 of these 38 cars still exist, a very high fraction. A good one probably ranks second only to a Royale in value today.

Mr A. C. Whincop wrote of this car, as he had done of Types 43 and 51, in the *Autocar,* 13 August 1943, in the series 'Talking of Sports Cars':

The engine is almost identical with that of the Type 51 double camshaft supercharged 2·3 litre Grand Prix car, with all eight cylinders contained in the one block, and only two valves per cylinder operated by the twin overhead camshafts. The remainder of the engine is very similar to that of the Type 43, but the result of this improvement in design is to increase the bhp from the 115 of the earlier model to 135 bhp in the Type 55 at 5,500 rpm. There is also a very great increase in power low down in the engine speed range, which results in greatly increased acceleration. Maximum speed is not so noticeably improved, the same standard

The T55 engine was really a standard T51 Grand Prix engine with reduced compression ratio. (The Motor)

ratio of 13:54 being used, although, as with all 2·3 Bugattis, this can be altered at will, ratios of 12:54, 13:54, 14:54, 15:54 and 16:54, all being interchangeable on the Types 35B, 43, 51 and 55

Chassis details are, rather surprisingly, very similar to those of the Type 43, although the two cars look so totally different, and the actual chassis of the 55 is the same as that of the Grand Prix 4·9 litre. There are, of course, a number of small improvements, such as Tele-controls fitted to the Hartford shock-absorbers. The body fitted has such perfection of line that although designed in 1932 it will still be completely modern when this war finishes [it still is]. I feel

The standard Jean Bugatti roadster body. The detail of the mouldings on the body panels was most effective and facilitated two-tone painting.

that the appearance of the body in combination with the increased acceleration of the Type 55 is responsible for the impression that there is so much difference between it and the Type 43 which it replaced. In reality they both give almost exactly the same impression when driving, and, if anything, I prefer the handling of the earlier model, which, in spite of its 2 in. longer wheelbase, seems just a fraction lighter and more positive in control. They are both so perfect in this respect, however, that the impression was possibly caused by petrol rationing preventing me from becoming anything like as familiar with the 55 as I was with the 2·3, which seemed literally part of oneself when driving.

The lines of the roadster make it one of the most beautiful automobiles ever produced.

A number of companion coupé bodies was seen but the closed body showed up a basic lack of ventilation!

A T55 coupé at Kandersteg Hill-climb. (C. Renaud).

Some cars had coachwork by other than Molsheim, in this case Figoni, on a chassis which had run in the 24 hour race at Le Mans.

Unquestionably, the most spectacular feature of the later model is its acceleration, which is really terrific; when the first car was imported into this country and was road tested by a contemporary journal in 1932, figures were recorded of 10 to 80 mph in 18 seconds and 10 to 100 mph in 40 seconds; these figures can have been surpassed by very, very few standard sports cars ever produced, irrespective of engine capacity and price. Whilst V8 and V12 engines in specially lightened chassis show the most amazing acceleration up to 60, 70 and occasionally 80 mph, the graph is usually conveniently cut off before that extremely telling figure of 100 mph is reached, this acceleration of the upper end of the speed scale being all important for road racing, if not for sprint events

The brakes on the Types 43 and 55 are identical, being of straight-forward design, cable operated in 13 in. drums cast integral with the aluminium wheels; they are fully compensated so that equal pressure is provided on all four brake toggles, though slightly greater leverage is provided for the front wheels, this giving the maximum of controllability if on occasion late braking into a corner has to be indulged in. This advantage is such that it seems well worth sacrificing the slightly greater efficiency, on straight braking, of brakes operating very much more powerfully on the front wheels, since the arrangement in question gives complete confidence at all times. The hand brake operates on the rear wheels only and has a completely separate layout.

My [main] criticism of the Type 55 [is] the gearbox; again the touring version is very heavily built, resulting in great strength, and in this case a very quick gear change indeed, but the change is a rather heavy one with a tendency to drag when coming out of gear. To my mind, the very lightly built Grand Prix box is such a delight to handle, with its finger lightness that it is almost sacrilege not to fit it to a Bugatti, for it allows the most effortless tunes to be played on it up or down.

This criticism overlooks the advantage of the normal ball change box, from the Type 49, used on the T55, admittedly slower but more robust than the GP box, with its 'other-way-round' gear change. That box was really designed for a Brescia and does not last long handling the powers of the T51 engine. It is true however that the GP change is a delight

Contemporary description

The model was fully described and illustrated in *The Motor* of 14 June 1932:

Here is a really comfortable, well-sprung car with superlative road-holding characteristics and a performance that is altogether exceptional.

The power unit has eight cylinders in line, the bore and stroke being 60 mm and 100 mm respectively and the capacity 2,270 cc. There is one inlet and one exhaust valve to each cylinder, these being operated by two overhead camshafts, while the supercharger, of the Roots type, is fitted midway along the off-side of the crankcase with the carburettor underneath it and placed so low that it is reached by opening a trap-door in the undershield below the level of the chassis frame members. The supercharger is driven through a short flexibly jointed shaft from a train of gear wheels driven in turn from the forward end of the crankshaft.

Forced-feed lubrication is naturally employed, all oil pipes being external so that they can be readily dismantled and cleaned. Cooling is by pump, the centrifugal type waterpump being situated well forward on the near side of the crankcase. The ignition is by a single eight-cylinder magneto mounted in typical Bugatti fashion directly behind the facia board and accessible through an opening in the latter. It is driven through a short shaft with a flexible coupling at each end from the rearmost extremity of the nearside overhead camshaft. The other camshaft at its rearmost extremity drives the A.C. mechanical petrol pump and the revolution counter.

The dynamo is driven from the forward end of the crankshaft, while the starter motor is situated beneath the engine and behind the deeply ribbed base-chamber. The supercharger is lubricated separately from a small reservoir on the engine side of the scuttle dash. This tank is provided with a tap which can be operated from the driving seat and two other small cocks are connected to the accelerator pedal so that the flow of lubricant to the blower bearings starts immediately the accelerator is depressed

In order to ensure easy starting, an Atmos fuel injector similar in operation to the well-known Ki-Gass, is fitted on the dash and connected directly to the

double-T type induction manifold. While talking of dashboard controls, it is interesting to note that the advance and retard lever operates directly on the magneto contact breaker, while the two small levers that on earlier Bugatti models used to govern the ignition setting and throttle opening, are now used to open or close small ventilators in the top and at each side of the scuttle. The adjusting knobs for the frictional-type shock-absorbers, to which they are connected by Bowden wire, are also situated on the dash.

The 55 chassis used a T47 parallel type frame. (Y. Garnier).

A large petrol tank containing over 100 litres (22 gallons) of fuel is slung between the rear dumbirons, its contents being registered on a neat dial in the facia board. It is not necessary to use a strong 'dope' mixture for ordinary running, 25 per cent of benzole in the petrol being sufficient. Champion R.3 plugs are normally used and are placed centrally in the cylinder heads between the valves.

The exhaust manifolds are welded up from steel tubes, each group of four being welded into a collector manifold from which a large bore pipe conveys the exhaust to a flat oval-section silencer hidden beneath the near-side wings, which are extended to form graceful curved running boards. Between the exhaust manifolds are situated the oil filling orifice and a tap for draining the cooling system in frosty weather.

The transmission consists of a Bugatti patent multiple-disc clutch, a short shaft with a flexible coupling at each end connecting this to the separately mounted four-speed-and-reverse centrally controlled gearbox, whence a large-diameter open propellor shaft with a flexible joint at each end conveys the drive to the straight-bevel type rear axle, the direct drive ratio being 3·6 to 1 [generally lower].

The intermediate gear ratios, together with the compression ratio of the engine, the blower pressure and certain other facts about the car are not published by the makers, who consider it against their policy to issue such details. On top gear, however, 5,000 rpm – an engine speed which is said to be readily obtainable – is equivalent to 112 mph. The speedometer, incidentally, is calibrated up to 130 mph.

The well-known Bugatti patent cast aluminium alloy wheels are used, the flat thin spokes being stiffened by ribs cast at right angles on their reverse faces and the rims being made to take well-base tyres instead of the bolted-on type popular in Continental racing circles. This model is sold with Dunlop racing tyres. In this way, the purchaser is safely guarded against any risk of the tyres not standing up to really high speeds in hot weather. Another 'safety first' feature is that the axles, tie-rods, steering arms and all similar connections are left in the bright polished state, so that they may readily be inspected for fine cracks which might develop in the course of racing over very rough circuits.

Needless to say, a car capable of such high road speeds requires superlative brakes. Those on the Bugatti are unique because the steel-lined aluminium brake drums are cast integrally with the wheels [in fact pressed in], and the shoes, complete with linings, can be instantaneously renewed simply by removing a wheel which only means undoing its central lock-nut operating on the well-known Rudge–Whitworth system. The brakes are normally adjusted by a threaded turnbuckle conveniently situated at a suitable point on the brake-operating cables [not strictly correct].

One of the most interesting features about this car is the driving position, which is exactly similar to that provided on the Grand Prix racers. Instead of reclining in a semi-prone position with his feet on the same level as the seat, as in most sports cars, the driver sits upright, with the pedals situated low down in exceedingly deep floor wells.

The body on this new model is an exceedingly attractive streamlined two-seater, having a very large and properly carpeted luggage locker in the stern.

The gearbox straddled the frame, and was bolted to the webs perhaps to stiffen the frame a little. The gear lever had a ball-end.

On the model we inspected, a new and graceful colour scheme of black and red was arranged, the effect being one of more or less oval red panels, which added to the naturally fleeting appearance of the complete car.

It will be gathered from the foregoing that the new Type 55 supersports 2·3 litre supercharged Bugatti is an ideal car for travelling safely from point to point at really high speeds and in complete comfort. Considering its performance, it is really very reasonably priced at the figure of £1,350.

An article headed 'Stability Supreme' in the *Autocar* of 8 January 1937 described a test of a second-hand Type 55 which was first registered in October 1933, and had covered over 14,000 miles. This was the 1933 Olympia Show car, AUL 23, giving 10 to 30 mph acceleration in 7·9, 6·0 and 4·0 seconds in top, third and second gears respectively and from rest to 60 mph in 13 sec and 98·9 mph timed quarter-mile, still accelerating. The road-tester writes:

An engine of this kind is not expected to be quiet; while the exhaust note was distinctly moderate, there was considerable mechanical noise, also gear and probably axle noise from the straight teeth used, these all being principally noticeable at low and moderate speeds, but blending into efficient general 'scream' when travelling fast ... so excellent were the stability and general handling that the car was 'wished' round corners, rock-steady and feeling completely safe, yet the suspension was really comfortable for a machine of this kind ... it weighed 23$\frac{1}{2}$cwt ... the change needed knowing, but except that first and second gears would 'hang' if one revved up high on them it was a beautiful movement, quick and satisfying.

Modern road impressions

Apart from an appearance which to most Bugatti owners is unexcelled in sporting 2-seat cars, the T55 has a performance which also puts it at the front of all Bugatti road cars. It can out-perform a Type 43 in acceleration and top speed, and is very comfortable except for the tall driver who finds the leg room inadequate, but cannot adjust it. The gear change is slow and the flexible gear lever cannot be manhandled as quickly as a Type 43, but on balance is better than on the earlier model. The main advantage in practice is in the engine since the combustion characteristics of the twin cam engine allow a better mixture from the carburettor and the engine is not prone to sooting as in the case of the T43.

Accessibility is not so good on the T55, the body and mudguards being more enveloping but once the car is in good condition this is not particularly important.

A factory picture of the original T55 engine with Molsheim style show finish, scraping and mottling. The purist may note the irregularity of the circular mottling!

Type 57

Twin-cam 3·3 litre splendour

IN 1934 MOLSHEIM introduced what was to be the most celebrated non-racing car that Bugatti ever produced. It remained in relatively large scale production (a total of 680 of all models) until the end of 1939 or early 1940, and a few were even produced after the war. It was on this model that Ettore's son Jean exerted his influence to a considerable extent, refining the car and generally making it fit to compete on equal terms with the sophisticated automobiles of the middle thirties – Delahayes, Delages, Bentleys and so on. The days of semi-racing road cars were over and there was no market for extravagant Royales or 5 litre Types 46 and 50; but a reliable, high performance Bugatti could still sell when fitted with fine bodywork drawing on the best in French creative ability as to line and colour. The Ventoux, the Stelvio and the Atalante bodies catalogued and sold on these chassis were a credit to Jean Bugatti's imagination and the skill of French coach-workers.

The Type 57 was more or less new from stem to stern, except the bore and stroke which were the same as the Type 49, 72 mm by 100 mm. The engine had a 5-bearing (strictly 6-bearing) crank, and twin overhead cams with articulated rockers or fingers in place of cups, the cams being driven by a helical gear train from the rear of the crankshaft as opposed to the earlier front drive of the Type 50 and 51 constructions. The gearbox was mounted integrally with the engine and the classic Bugatti clutch was replaced by a single plate unit. The gears were of constant mesh, second, third and fourth engaged by dog-clutches. The rear axle started off with the existing standard touring axle but was soon strengthened with a heavier design drawn from the T46, with tapered roller bearings. Suspension was standard at the rear and front, except that the original few cars had a split articulated front axle, although this was not continued into production on this model, most of the earlier cars having the axles soldered up. Brakes were mechanical along normal Molsheim lines. Although as the model developed the angle of the front cables to the frame was brought nearer a right angle to reduce brake servo with axle twist, brake grab was a serious fault in the model.

Jean had first conceived a car with twin transverse front springs to give independent suspension, and two prototype chassis were so

A unique photograph taken by a young Robert Braunschweig on 23 August 1934 at Berne in front of the Bugatti team garage during practice for the 1st Swiss grand Prix, where Jean had arrived in the prototype car with independent front suspension, a novelty which Ettore, when he heard about it, instructed his son to remove! (Automobil Revue, *Berne*).

equipped. Ettore got to hear of the change and ordered at once reversion to a 'Bugatti' front axle!

A major change was made about 1936, the frame being stiffened and the engine mounted on rubber bushes. Then in 1938 the much needed hydraulic brakes were introduced.

A popular Molsheim body was the Ventoux coach.

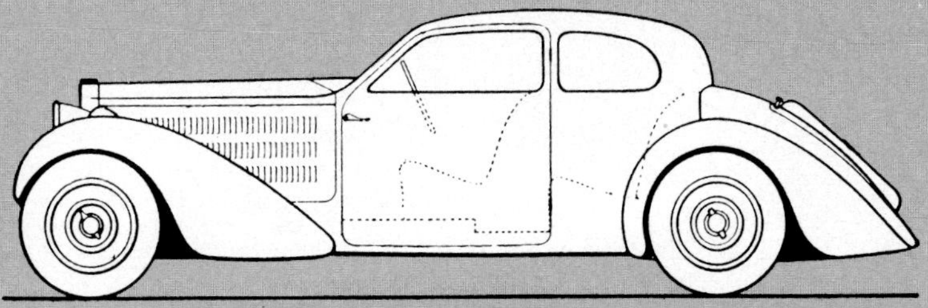

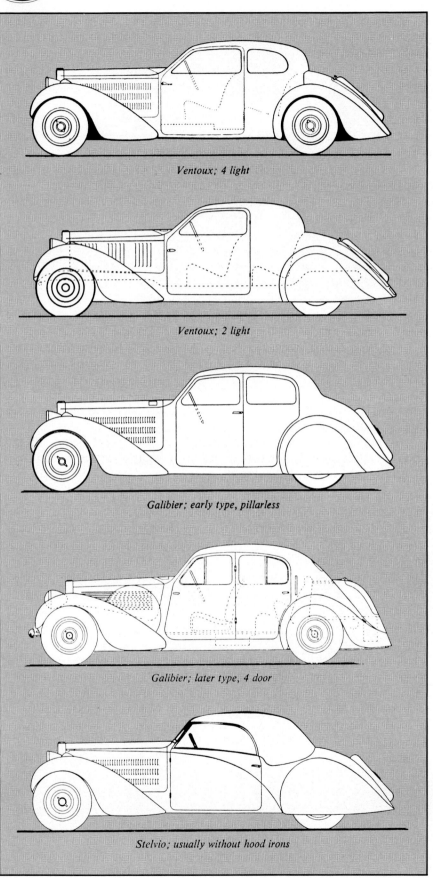

Ventoux; 4 light

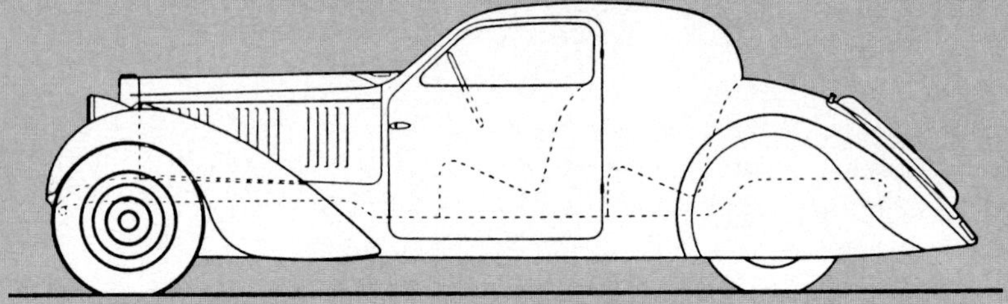

Ventoux; 2 light

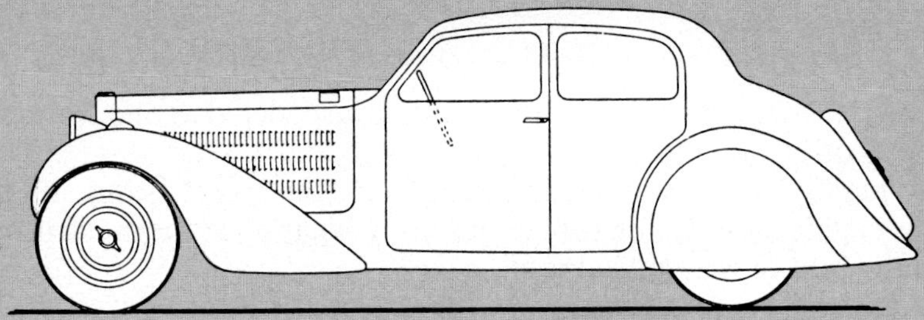

Galibier; early type, pillarless

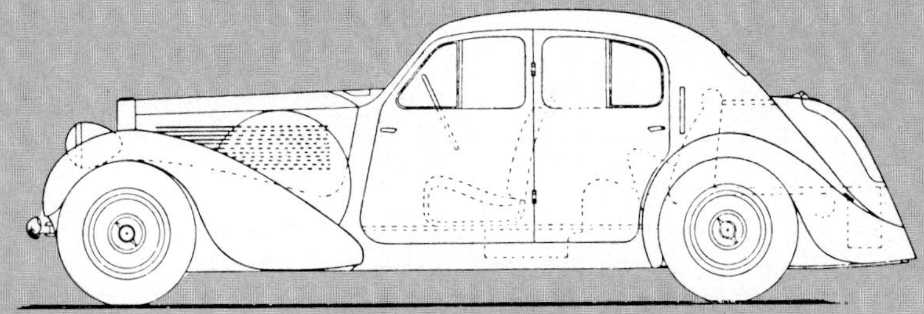

Galibier; later type, 4 door

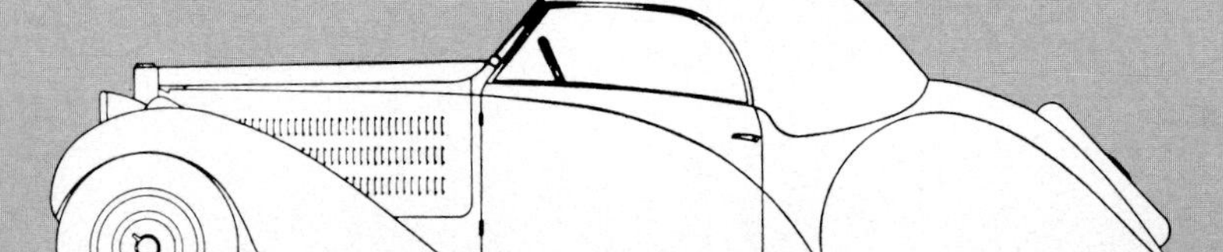

Stelvio; usually without hood irons

Bodies fitted to the Type 57.

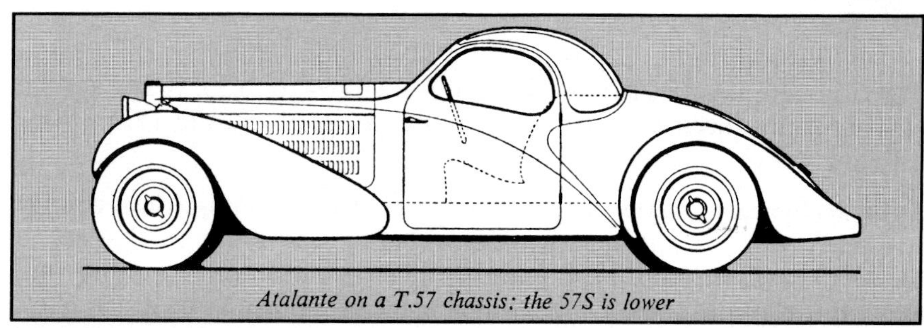
Atalante on a T.57 chassis: the 57S is lower

A pair of Ventoux at an exhibition in Nice.

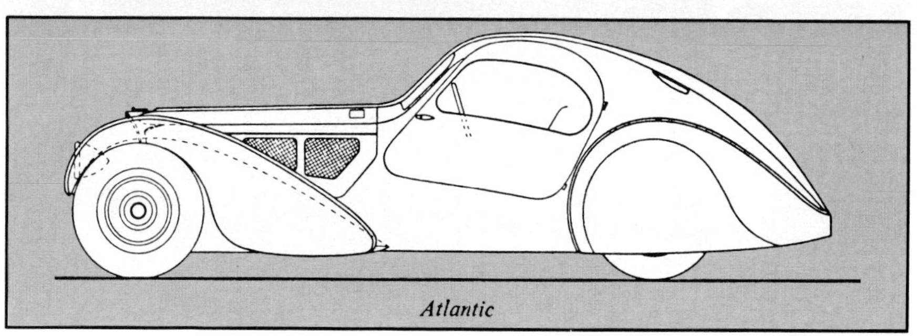
Atlantic

Development of the type

The original model was in production from 1934 to 1936. A few special cars were produced for sports car racing, for example the 1935 Ulster TT, the model sometimes being called 57T.

Type 57, Series 2. At the end of 1936 for the Salon an important change was made with the introduction of a rubber mounted engine, changes to camshafts and engine timing, a heavier chassis with more cross-bracing, and a different dashboard with twin in place of a single large instrument. The exhaust manifold was also changed, the down pipe being taken off centrally, instead of at the front. About this time too, the crankcase was modified to make provision for a blower drive, on the right side, the drive being blanked off on the normal car.

Type 57C. A compressor fitted to the standard model made the 57C; introduced also at the time of the 1936 Paris Salon. The Roots blower was driven by gears meshing with the camshaft train at the rear of the engine, an intermediate fibre gear being then replaced with a more robust steel one to drive the blower train. There are those who claim that the 57C is the best of the 'touring' 57 models, the supercharger enhancing performance and flexibility.

Type 57S. A short chassis, low slung sport version was introduced in time for the 1936 Paris Salon. This had a tuned engine with higher compression ratio (8·5 to 1) and a dry sump, a double-plate clutch to transmit the extra power, and a dash mounted Scintilla Vertex magneto driven from the left-hand camshaft. The front axle was articulated in halves with a rotating collar in the centre with appropriate brake torque radius rods, and de Ram shock-absorbers were used. The whole chassis was of lower build, the rear axle passing *through* the rear frame. The prototype had the normal flat radiator, but the production 57S cars have a handsome V and very low slung radiator.

Type 57SC. In mid-1937 a supercharger was added to the 57S to produce the sparkling 57SC, a car usually fitted with striking bodywork and certainly with a performance in speed and acceleration quite remarkable in 1937 and even today when other 125 mph cars are available. Both the 57S and 57SC were withdrawn after 1938, probably as they were too expensive to manufacture while the 57 and 57C were selling well enough.

The early 4-door Galibier saloon was of pillarless construction.

Type 57, Series 3. At the end of 1938 further improvements were made to the 57 to refine it. The most important was the introduction of hydraulic brakes of Bugatti-Lockheed design, with twin master cylinders, and the substitution of telescopic Allinquant shock-absorbers for the highly expensive de Rams, which in turn had replaced the cheaper, but less effective Telecontrol Hartfords of earlier cars. To allow the front shock-absorbers to be mounted vertically, the wings were swept up high alongside the radiator and usually were faired into the lamps. A final change made was to introduce a linkage device in the clutch mechanism to reduce the pedal load.

In 1938 hydraulic brakes and telescopic shock absorbers were introduced. (The Motor)

Bottom right: *The front right-hand front spring had a special 'kick' shackle to avoid shocks from the road being transmitted to the steering wheel.* (The Motor).

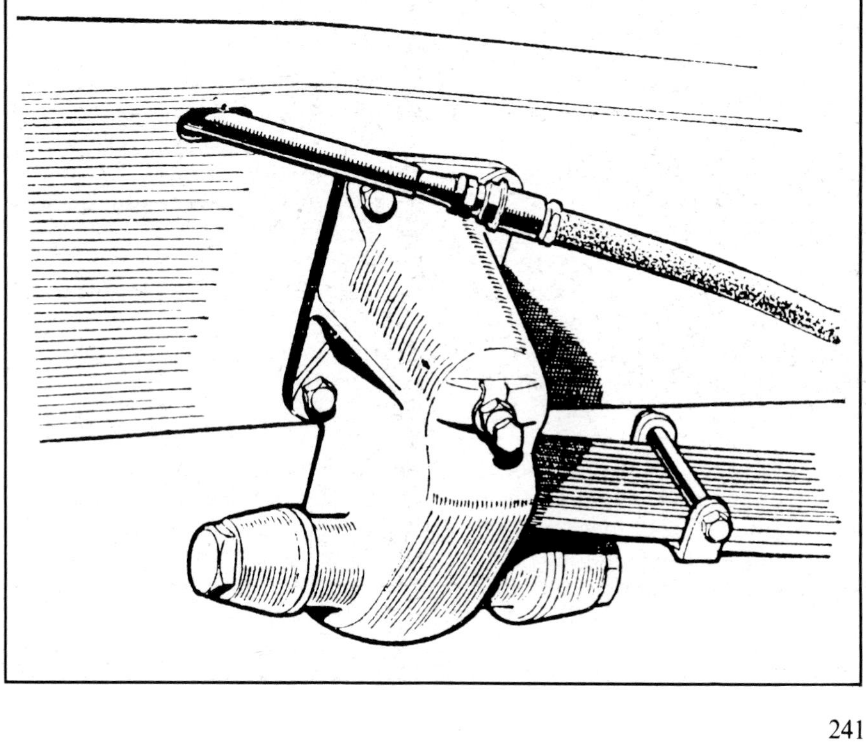

The rear end of the late series cars, with the traditional rear springs but with telescopic shock-absorbers added. The device below the spring serves as a guide for the jack.

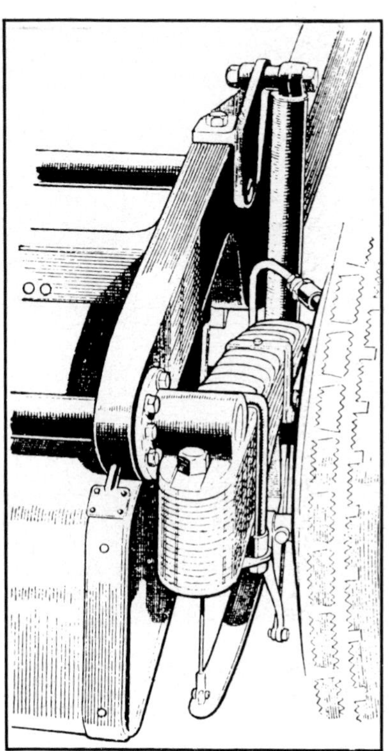

Later Galibiers had more normal door layout.

Contemporary descriptions

One of the early descriptions of Type 57 was given in the May 1934 issue of *Motor Sport*. This article is no doubt responsible for the error, since repeated, of ascribing nine bearings to the crankshaft instead of five, or six if the one behind the rear camshaft gear is counted.

Longitudinal section of the T57 engine.

The existence of a new Bugatti sports car, said to have almost the acceleration of the blown '2·3' up to 80 mph, has for some time been known in England, and a visit to Molsheim to try the new machine seemed indicated. When we did get there we found that the Type 57, as the new model is called, was already in good demand and a number of chassis were coming through. In fact, with two other widely differing activities, that is, preparing the racing teams and building the new rail-cars, the famous factory was very busy indeed.

In appearance the new car is not unlike the previous 3·3 litre model Type 49, except that it has shutters on the radiator and a built-up front axle. Rudge Whitworth wire wheels are used instead of the aluminium type.

The car we were to try was the one usually driven by Costantini, the first of its type and still used for testing purposes. Réné Dreyfus, for some years past one of the star performers in the Bugatti racing team, was at the wheel.

After three minutes of warming up we took our seats, and the car moved off smoothly. 'Delightful cars, these', said M. Dreyfus, and thereupon changed from bottom to top gear. In this ratio we burbled along perfectly smoothly to the factory gates, and so out on to the fine straight road between Molsheim and Strasbourg.

After a fast run up and down to get the oil circulating, Dreyfus pronounced himself satisfied. 'First of all notice the flexibility', he said, and ran down to 10 mph on top gear. 'Now the smooth pick-up', and proceeded to put his foot down hard. The speedometer needle swung round at an ever-increasing rate without any trace of hesitation. 'All-out speed', and we reached 95 mph. 'Finally the road holding', so we drove down a minor road at 75, slowed to 60 with a gentle application of the brakes, and took a 60 degree bend without any reduction in speed. The car neither rolled, slid nor gave any indication that the manoeuvre was at all unusual. '*Vraiment une voiture fantastique*', a remark with

A popular body was the Stelvio drop-head produced by Gangloff.

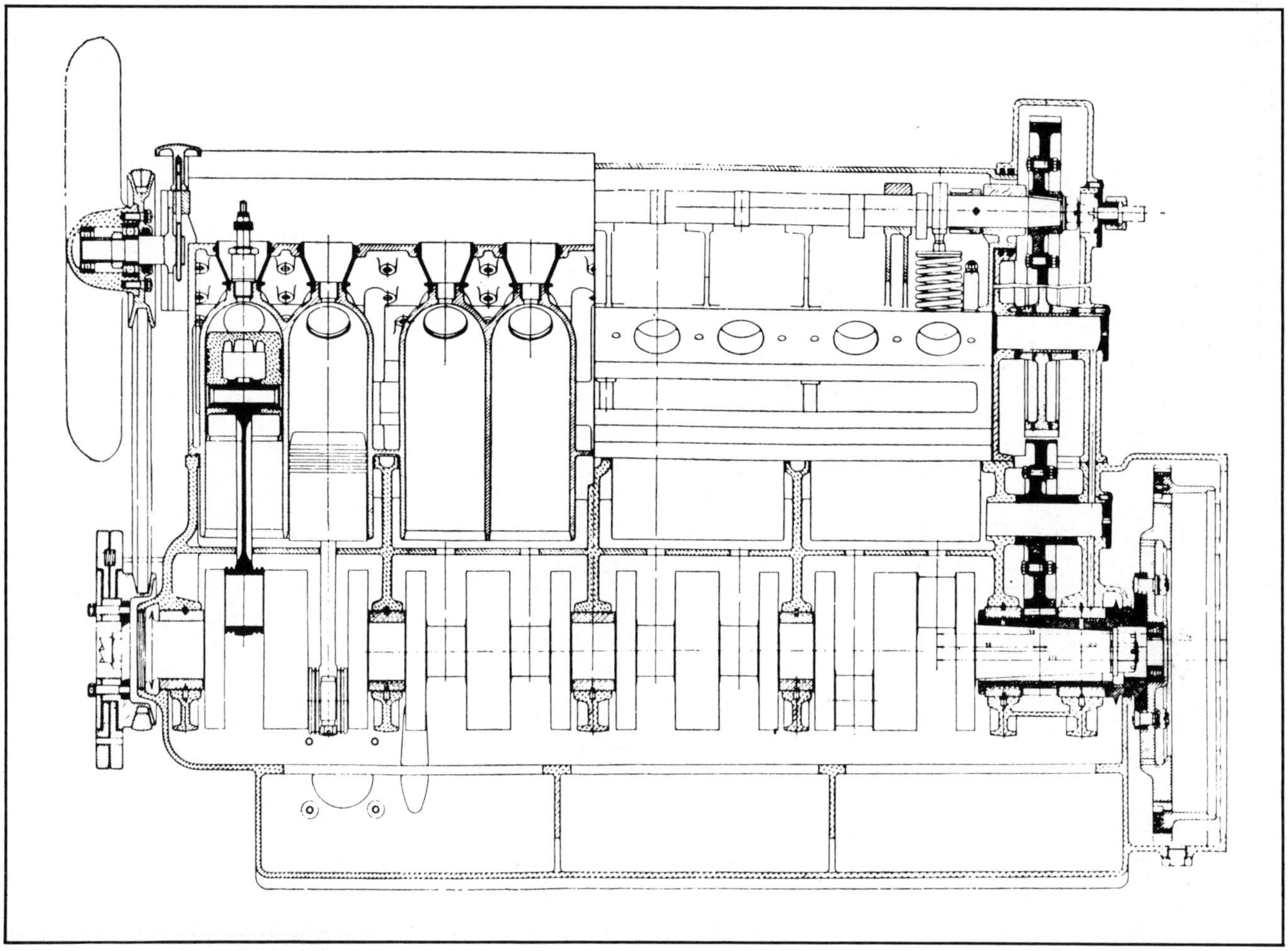

which we could not fail to agree as soon as we could think of an adequate reply.

The brakes were extremely efficient, and from a speed of 40 mph the car came to rest in approximately 53 feet, without any tendency to swing or for the wheels to lock. This test was, in fact, considered too tame, so we tried again, this time from 75 mph. The retardation was equally safe and sure, the distance being about 70 yards.

Instead of the shrill scream which usually comes from third gear on a Bugatti, on the '3·3' there is a complete absence of noise. Constant mesh gears are used for second and third gears, and the change is further simplified by having a single-plate clutch lined with Ferodo in place of the multiple-disc pattern which is usually fitted to Bugatti cars. The exhaust note is subdued and even when all out there is nothing more than a slight rumble.

Owing to the limitations of the Works insurance policy, we were not able to drive the car ourselves, but the ease with which it cornered and the accuracy of the steering could not be doubted from what we saw. The suspension was good throughout the range, aided by friction dampers controlled from the dashboard.

After lunch at the famous 'Hostellerie du Pur-Sang', that unique inn-cum-clubhouse which 'M. le Patron' has built to accommodate those who visit the factory, Jean Bugatti came with us instead of Dreyfus, and we went out on the high-road to obtain a series of acceleration figures.

Without doubt this latest product of the Molsheim factory is '*une voiture de pur-sang*', and no one can deny the benefits of racing when they experience the high performance and ease of handling which are directly derived from high-speed international competition.

BUGATTI

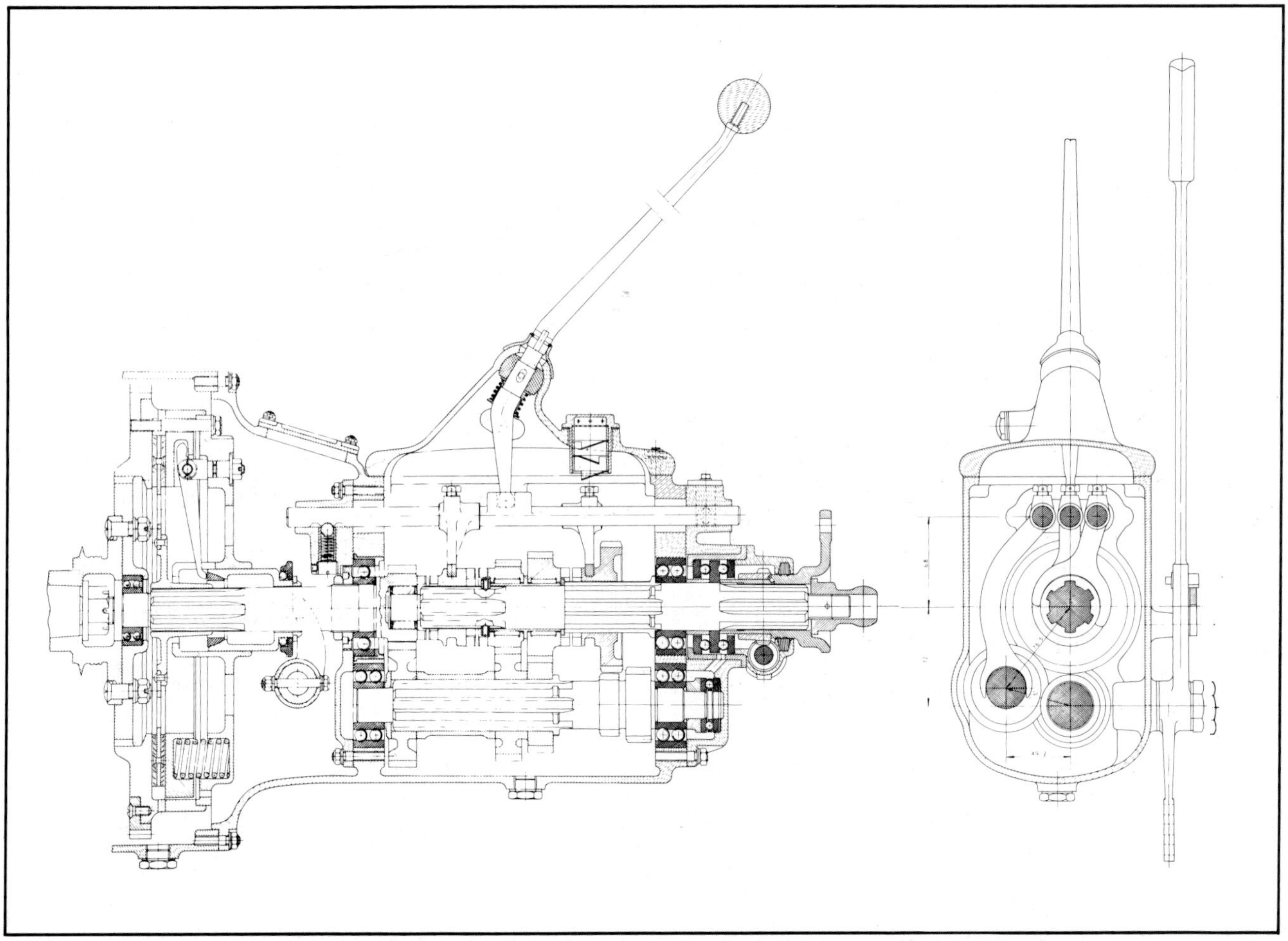

Left: *Section of the clutch and gearbox of the T57, traced from a Molsheim drawing dated 4 July 1934.*

Right: *Some early Stelvios had folding windscreens, an unusual feature for a drop head body.*

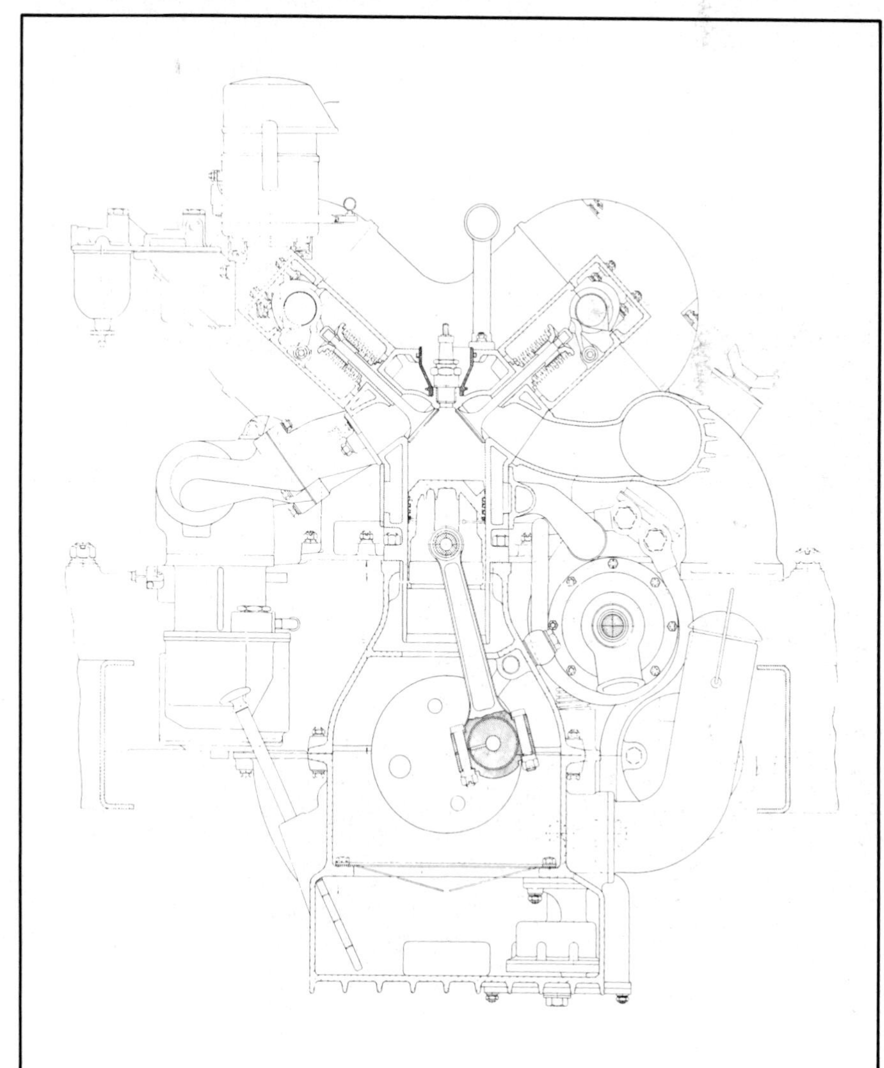

Right: *Front elevation in section of the T57 engine.*

The Atalante fixed-head coupé was very elegant; this is Lord Cholmondley's.

Top left: *The most elegant drop-head was the 1939 Aravis produced by Gangloff for the factory to list.*

Many other coachbuilders built bodies on the T57; this is a drop-head by Graber.

Top right: *A fixed head coupé by Van Vooren, in this case with the radiator moved forward a little.*

The maximum speed on the level is about 95 mph with closed bodywork, and would be comfortably over 100 in the case of an open car. 70 to 75 mph can be obtained in third gear, and 50 in second, and at 60 mph on top gear the engine is doing approximately 2,500 rpm. A rev-counter is not fitted as no harm results even if the engine speed reaches 5,500 rpm.

In the course of the timed tests the car several times reached 105 mph on slight down-hill slopes, and a flying kilometre was covered at over 100 mph. The standing kilometre was done in 39 seconds. All this was carried out with hardly a murmur from the engine, and Jean Bugatti finds that a fast average, even of over 60 mph, can be kept up with much less effort in a closed car than an open one.

After completing the tests we had occasion to go to Strasbourg, a drive which was performed with all the verve for which Jean Bugatti is famous. We arrived there too early of course, so the time was spent in driving through the crowded streets of the town at 7 to 10 mph on top gear. Another feature was shown on the return journey, when the driver suddenly executed a series of zig-zags at 60 to demonstrate the absence of rolling, but our new passenger, who had not yet become accustomed to Jean's virtuosity at the wheel, did not seem to appreciate it.

Turning to the technical side of the car, the engine is a straight-eight unit with two overhead camshafts, and gives 140 horse power at 4,800 rpm. The valves are inclined to one another at 90 degrees with the sparking plugs in the centre of the head, and the camshafts are diven by gears at the rear end of the engine. White metal is used in the nine [six] main bearings and for the big-ends.

Lady Cholmondley had her own car with body by Figoni.

This Corsica bodied roadster was very effective.

The cylinder head and block are in one unit and the cam-cases are made in that hand-polished aluminum which is the joy of every Bugatti owner.

The distributor and petrol pump are driven from the rear end of the offside camshaft, and two coils are mounted at the rear of the dashboard. A single vertical Zenith carburettor is fitted on the off-side. Water pump, starter and dynamo are all carried at the near side of the engine. The engine and gearbox unit has a rigid four-point suspension.

An open propellor shaft is used, and the back-axle reaction is taken by the usual long torque member.

The top line of the chassis runs straight as far as the back axle, where the side members are swept up, but from a depth of 10 inches at the rear engine mounting, the side members taper to the size of a normal dumbiron at the front of the chassis. The front axle is built up from two hollow sections with a shouldered shaft in the middle. A large nut with a right- and left-hand thread pulls the two sections up against the shoulder. [This feature was not perpetuated.] The front springs are half-elliptic, while the familiar reversed quarter-elliptic springs are used at the rear.

The brakes are of large diameter, cable-operated, with the cycle-chain compensators which have long been a feature of Bugattis. The engine sump holds 4 gallons of oil and the petrol tank 22 gallons of fuel.

A James Young saloon.

BUGATTI

Jean Bugatti has for some years been responsible for Bugatti coachwork, and has designed many striking closed bodies with ultra-sloping windscreens.

Jean produced this curious 'torpedo' roadster for the 1935 Paris Salon, and Veyron and mechanic Wurmser drove it in the 1935 Paris–Nice event.

Writing in the *Field*, 4 September 1937, Sir Malcolm Campbell, the famous racing driver, had this to say of his new T57S open two-seater:

If I was asked to give my opinion as to the best all-round super-sports car which is available on the market today, I should, without any hesitation whatever, say it was the 3·3 Bugatti. I grant that it is not the type of car that would necessarily appeal to the majority of drivers who merely indulge in a burst of speed from time to time, but it cannot fail to attract the connoisseur or those who know how to handle the thoroughbred. It is a car in a class by itself.

For many years it has been my privilege to be acquainted with Mr Ettore Bugatti, who, in addition to designing all the cars that bear his name, owns the factory where they are built. I can only say that no more brilliant brain than his exists in the motor industry today.

I have so far covered about 600 miles in my own car, as I have only recently taken delivery, but that brief mileage is sufficient to have made me enamoured with my new steed. It is an absolute joy to handle, and although designed for really fast touring, it is amazingly tractable in London traffic, which is unique for a car of this type. Its chief characteristics are superb road holding, really brilliant acceleration and very powerful brakes.

Bugatti cars have always been noted for their stability and this model certainly is no exception. It is probably the fastest standard sports car on the market today, and without doubt one of the very safest.

The radiator on the T57 had two interesting flutes or notches on the shoulders to correspond to a moulding on the bonnet panels. The honeycomb was replaced with a conventional core and thermostatically controlled shutters were added.

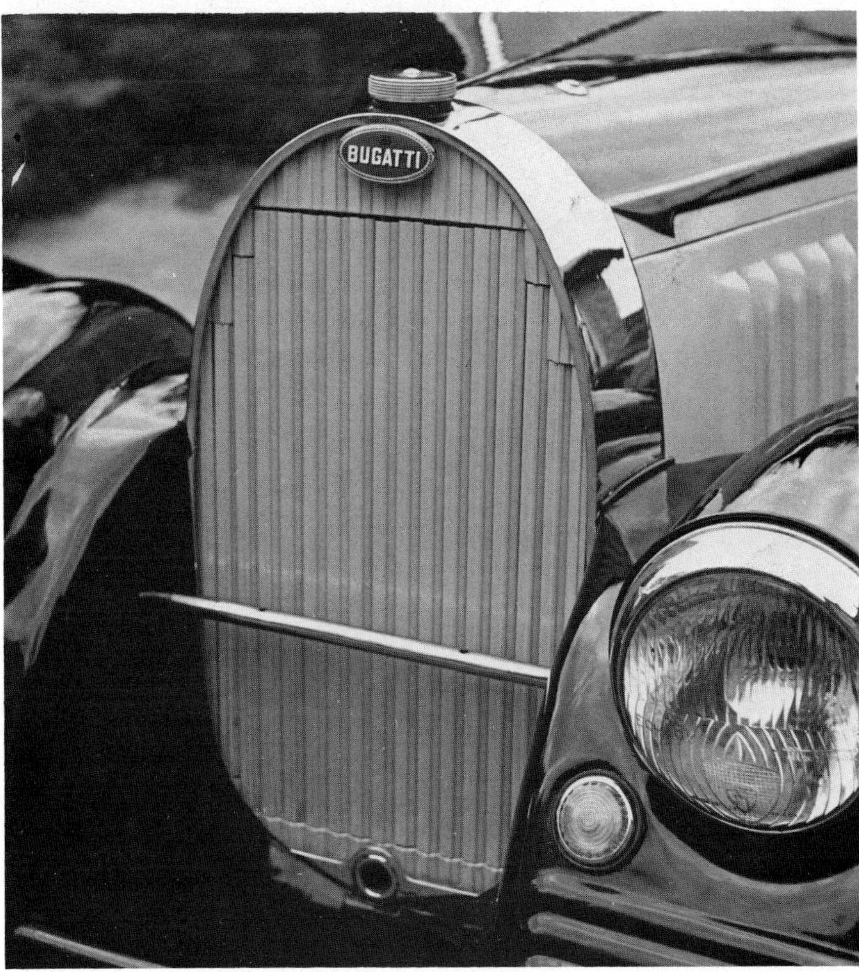

Although not really designed for racing, the so-called TT version was entered in the 1935 TT race in Ulster. Lord Howe drove this one, the Bugattis being the fastest cars in the race; he finished 3rd at an average speed of 79·72 mph.

Above: *The supercharged T57C engine, perhaps producing the finest model of all.*

Right: *The Type 57S cars were intended as sports versions of the standard T57, with a special frame, more power to the engine, a vee radiator and a lower build. Superchargers were added later to make the ultimate T57SC. Gangloff built the Atalante coupé in drophead form, Molsheim the fixed head.*

Modern road impressions

The Type 57 is perhaps the most popular model Bugatti today in France and in the USA, no doubt due to its suitability to the road systems in

these two countries and especially due to the fine coachwork seen on many models, often now kept in 'concours' condition. It is a car with comparatively 'long legs', better at cruising over long distances than pottering about, or being thrown about in competition. The engine is smooth and powerful, especially when blown, but feeling a little heavy on the throttle. The clutch is not light and the gear change slow, waiting for the dogs to engage. It is difficult to crash into mesh as on a GP or even the heavier Type 43–44. Road holding is quite good, steering excellent and the later hydraulic brakes first class. The earlier cable brakes have to be applied with care, as they have an unhappy tendency to grab.

On the rough roads the driver is rather conscious of the twisting of the chassis frame and the racking of the body, and it is probably for this reason that open body work seems the most desirable, if in practice less common.

Left and below far left: *Factory pictures of the original T57 engine. The rear engine mounting was not that which went into production.*

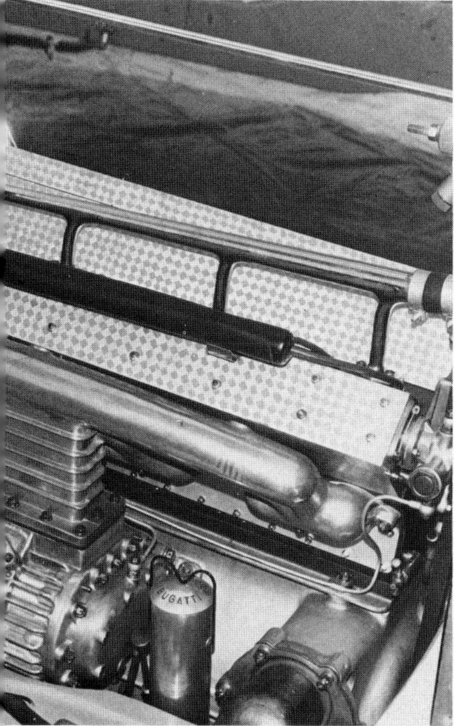

Below right: *A restored early type chassis in California.*

The splendid frontal aspect of the fixed head Atalante 57S.

Right: *The remarkable Atlantic coupé, with body panels riveted together, and doors cutting into the roof line; this first appeared on the normal T57 frame, with the standard radiator.*

Below right: *Col Giles, formerly Chairman of the Bugatti Owners Club, as a passenger in his T57S Corsica roadster.*

The three Atlantics built were all on T57S chassis. Here is Emil Mischall over from Brixton Road to collect Lord Rothschild's car.

BUGATTI

STANDARD
ROVER

BUGATTI

49
FYE 416

Far left: *T57S with coupé body by Van Vooren.*

Left: *This strange 2-seat body turned up at the Paris Salon in 1936; Jean arranged the wheel spats to turn with the wheels but soon abandoned the idea.*

Right: *The frame of the T57S allowed the rear axle tubes to pass through it.*

Below left: *Malcolm Campbell owned this Corsica 2-seater.*

The driving compartment of the T57S.

BUGATTI

BUGATTI
vous présente
Le Moteur au plus haut rendement
3L 300 8 Cylindres type 57 S.
Vainqueur en 1936
du Gd Prix de l'A.C.F.
du Gd Prix de la Marne
du Gd Prix du Comminges
en 1937
du Gd Prix de Pau.
Détenteur des Records
des 100k à la Vitesse de 216k543 heure
100 milles 217k537
200 K 217k835
Record de l'heure 218 K
Record des 24 heures
à la Vitesse de 199k445
31, rue BERLIOZ 82463
SPÉCIALITÉS ELECTRIQ
INSTALLATIONS
YACHTS DE PLAISANCE
DELCO-R
Fabrication BUGATTI
Record du Monde du Rail
196 Km. à l'heure
AUTO-RAIL RAPIDE
1.000 chevaux - 200 places
En Service Régulier PARIS le H

Friderich's stand at the Salon at Nice displayed an Atlantic and proclaimed Bugatti's 1936 successes.

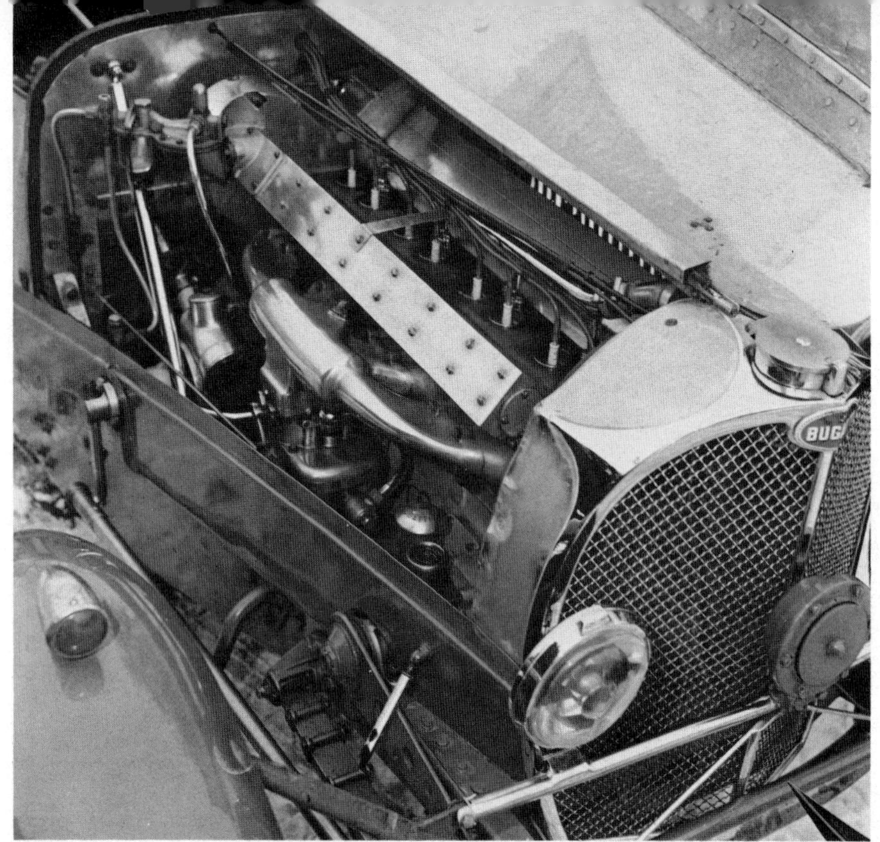

The T57S engine was very much like the normal T57; substitution of a camshaft-driven Vertex magneto for the normal distributor lowered the bonnet.

The front end of a T57S shows the special mounting of de Ram shock-absorbers, and the split front axle. (*S. MacMinn*).

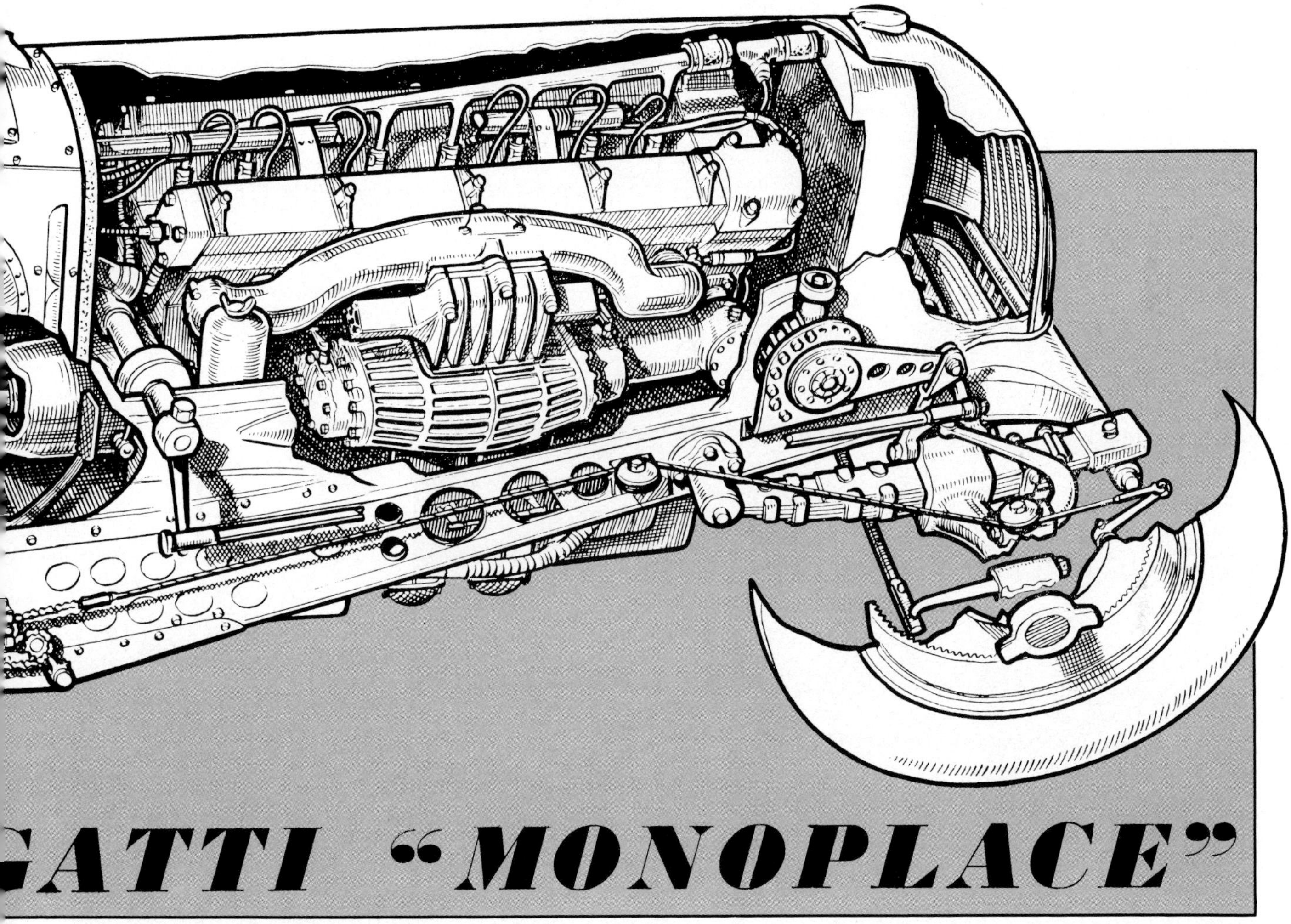

GATTI “MONOPLACE”

Benoist turned up at Monaco in 1936 in a car with a T50B engine but did not compete.

Wimille in the 3 litre single-seater at Cork, 1938. (The Motor)

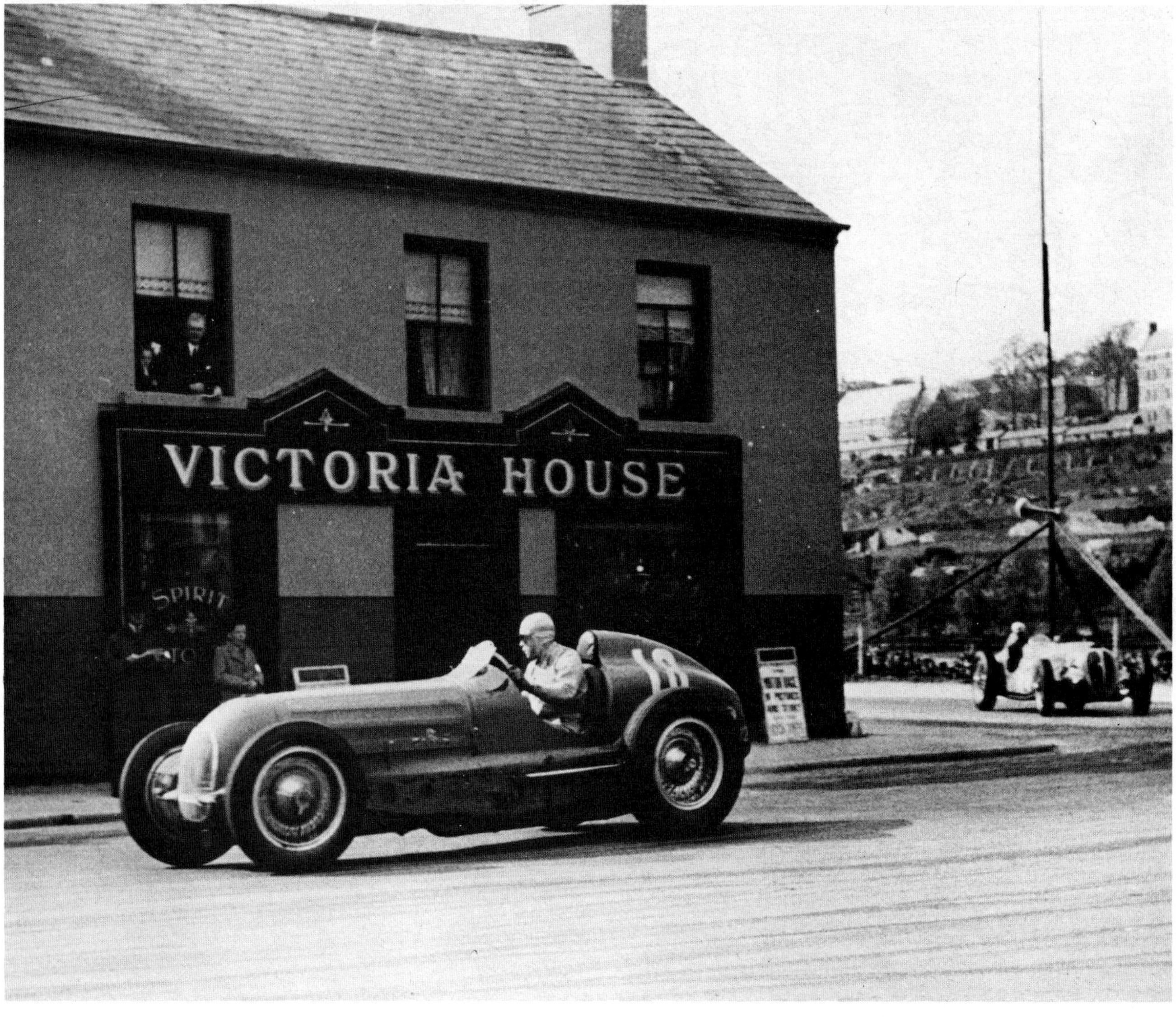

The 3 litre engine was clearly a T50B with front cam drive. (The Motor)

Top right: *Comminges 1939, the T50B-engined car driven by Wimille.*

The car without the oil cooler but a fairing behind the driver's head competed in the Vanderbilt Cup in the USA in 1937, Wimille driving and finishing second.

The car also was entered in the 'Million Franc Prize' at Montlhéry in that year, still with the fairing and the oil cooler on once more, but Wimille just failed to beat Dreyfus in a Delahaye.

(iv) A 3 litre single seater with 50 B111 engine seen at Rheims and Cork in 1938, now in pieces in the USA was first seen at the Cork race in April 1938, being timed over a kilometre at 147·2 mph, but was unplaced. The *Autocar* reported: 'Cork also marked the first appearance of the GP Formula Bugatti, which is not strikingly new in conception as far as one could ascertain. The engine is a twin-camshaft straight-eight with the supercharger and low-slung carburettor on the off side of the power unit. The chassis reminds one of that used on the 3·3 litre with deep drilled side-members, half-elliptic springs fore and reversed quarter-elliptics with de Ram shock-absorbers aft. The front axle is split. In appearance, however, Bugatti has followed the inevitable rounded contour of the modern racing car with a Mercedes-like radiator cowl and flowing tail. The mechanical braking arrangement and wheels integral with the drums are as before. The car was the fastest machine at Cork, and will no doubt make an excellent showing.' This car differed from the earlier one in having the radiator cowl elongated to lie forward of the front cross tube.

(v) In 1939 the final single seat car was produced, with faired-in sides to the body, hydraulic brakes and the supercharged 4·7 litre Type 50B engine. Wimille again was the driver, being 2nd fastest at the La Turbie Hill-Climb, then winning the Coupe de Paris at Montlhéry at 85·3 mph, and making 2nd Fastest Time at Prescott in July (the first and only appearance of a Molsheim entry at the Bugatti Owners' Club hill). The single-seater car was preserved during the war and is now in the National Museum at Mulhouse. Wimille also won the very first post-war race with it – the Coupe des Prisonniers in the Bois de Boulogne in Paris on 9 September 1945, averaging 71 mph. The serial number of the car is 50180.

(vi) The final event in which Wimille competed, winning, was the Grand Prix de Luxembourg in a 57–50B chassis 'equipée en sport', a much cowled car now in the National Museum at Mulhouse. This car is thought to be one of the 57S45 chassis from 1937, and used successfully against the Lago Talbots and Delahayes in sports car races.

Bottom: *Wimille at Prescott in the 4·9 litre single-seater, July 1939. The bridge has since been pulled down.*

The last works entry? Wimille in the single-seater, Bois de Boulogne, September 1945.

Twilight: 1939 and after

DURING THE mid-thirties Bugatti had survived with his railcar production (see page 348). By 1935 many more workmen were engaged on these rail contracts than on producing cars, and employment had reached a peak of about 1200. The industrial unrest throughout France had even extended to Molsheim, where workmen who had long enjoyed favourable pay and conditions joined the rest and downed tools. This saddened, sickened indeed, Ettore who now spent much more time in Paris, leaving Jean to run the works. By 1938 railcar orders were tailing off as the various railways became nationalized with a single SNCF. The fuel consumption of the non-diesel engined Bugatti railcar was against it.

In retrospect, too much must have been spent on racing even with its reduced programme but the argument must have been, understandably and, conceivably, rightly, that without racing performances Bugatti's touring car sales would drop. In truth they were doing so anyway; the annual output from 1934 to 1939 was between 100 and 120 cars, much less than the factory was capable of. There were many guarantee claims, too, as the car was more complex than before and the buying public less tolerant of Bugatti's idiosyncrasies.

By 1938 Ettore was spending much time in Paris seeking new railcar orders, and succeeded in obtaining a major contract for a high speed aeroplane (see page 343) from the French Air Ministry. The threat of another war, and another invasion of Alsace, hung always over them.

Type 64. Meanwhile Jean was working on the Type 64 as a replacement for the T57. He had already been experimenting with chain drive for the camshafts and a T57 engine so equipped had been well road tested. The chain drive required the retention of the gear on the rear of the crank, meshing with a first idler integral with a first sprocket, then up to the camshaft, their direction of rotation remaining unchanged. This engine was due to be installed in a new aluminium alloy (Duralumin) frame made into a box section by using two U-members, one inside the other and riveted in place, the flanges facing outwards. Now hydraulic brakes were used, the new components indeed being used on the last sales T57, and a Cotal electro-magnetic epicyclic gear box was specified (a box fitted as an extra to the normal model). A single car with a good looking

2-door saloon body and a Vee-radiator was completed, and is now in the National Museum at Mulhouse. A second chassis intended for display at the 1939 Paris Salon was also completed. Some study was made of the T64 with a new 4·5 litre engine but nothing materialized.

left: *A surviving T64 frame; double light alloy sections riveted together.* (*Uwe Hucke*)

A surviving T68 engine. (*L. Bezzola via E. Strebel*)

Tragedy overtook Bugatti, just before war came, with the death of Jean Bugatti on a road near Molsheim on 11 August 1939. He had been testing a 57C tank-bodied car prepared for the La Baule races, and ran off the road at high speed, when swerving to avoid 'a bloody-minded local on a bicycle who rode out of a side turning ignoring all caution on this stretch of a road which was "policed" by Molsheim mechanics'. Ettore moved to Paris and then Bordeaux during the war and, judging by his war-time patent specifications, was still designing cars, along with boats and machine tools.

The post-war programme, on which he was working at the time of his death at the age of 66 on 21 August 1947, included the Type 68 370 cc supercharged baby car and the Type 73 1·5 litre touring and racing cars. After his death the Type 101 (virtually a Type 57) was produced at Molsheim under the direction of M. Pierre Marco.

Type 68. Was a small two seater roadster with a 370 cc (48·5 mm × 50 mm) engine, with twin overhead camshafts and 16 valves. It was produced at a time when all France was clamouring for cheap motor transport with negligible fuel consumption; but no production materialized. A prototype was built but never adequately developed before Ettore's death; it is now in the National Museum at Mulhouse.

Type 73. The design of the 73 was under way in Paris towards the end of the war, Ettore having retained his two competent designers Noel Domboy and Antoine Pichetto. Production was slow, however, no doubt due to the prevailing conditions. The work was being carried out in the old factory of the La Licorne car at Levallois, a suburb of Paris, Bugatti owning this factory. A batch of twenty cars was reported at the time to

The Type 64 prototype.

T68 350cc baby car, produced at the end of the war.

Top left: *A T73 engine; the racing version had 16 valves, but was never properly developed.*

be under construction. A Type 73 chassis was shown a the 1947 Paris Salon a few weeks after the death of 'le Patron', together with the racing engine (T73C). A brief typewritten sheet handed out on the Bugatti Stand at the 1947 Show, stated that the bodywork would be a 2 door, 4 seat aerodynamic coach.

Type 73A. The chassis was conventional Bugatti with a solid front axle and usual reversed quarter-elliptic rear springs. The engine had 4 cylinders and a single overhead camshaft and blower driven off the front of the crankshft. The engine construction was slab-like with a detachable block and a cambox rather like a Type 40. The carburettor was a downdraught mounted on an elbow on the blower, which fed the manifold by a long pipe. The exhaust manifold, as Mr J.L. Burton put it, was 'no longer a bunch of bananas, but a product of cast iron'.

Oh dear! Large coverplates on the sides of the crankcase proclaim the name of the maker. So Ettore, who started at Molsheim with his signature on the valve cover of the 8 valve car, finished with his imprint in enormous lettering on the ill-fated T73 – an epitaph perhaps, poor man.

Many schemes were drawn for changes to the 73, the final version being a racing model, 73C, a single-seater with chain-driven twin cams and, as Mr J.L. Burton has put it, 'with detachable head - after forty years of success with the other sort. The blower is mounted on the nose, but is larger than the 73A, and the carburettor hangs below. The delivery pipe which is huge rises from the top of the blower and finds its way in a respectable swerve to the centre of the induction manifold. A technical note, possibly a sign of 1947, those expensive little nuts (so dear to us) are not so evident, but the ordinary hexagon type with separate washer were *de rigueur*.'

It seems that no 73C was completed and fitted with a body before the project was stopped. A number of engines and components were made, however, and later no less than four cars appeared, with bodies made later, using, in some cases, the lines of the body that had been designed in Paris for the car but not made. As far as is known although two cars have run, none has been properly tested.

These cars, if not to be ignored because of their parentage, are not

Type 73C with post-Bugatti bodywork.

'pur-sang'. Even the Master is allowed his mistakes.

Type 101. The factory at Molsheim, after the death of Bugatti, remained in the hands of the family – Roland and the two daughters – and managed by Pierre Marco. Eventually, in 1951, it was decided to resume production of the T57 chassis, using a few improvements, such as a downdraft Weber carburettor (the old Stromberg unit was not available anyway), and a Cotal gear box. Otherwise it was largely unchanged, although 17 in. wheels were used with 6·00 × 17 tyres. No attempt was made to modernize the suspension.

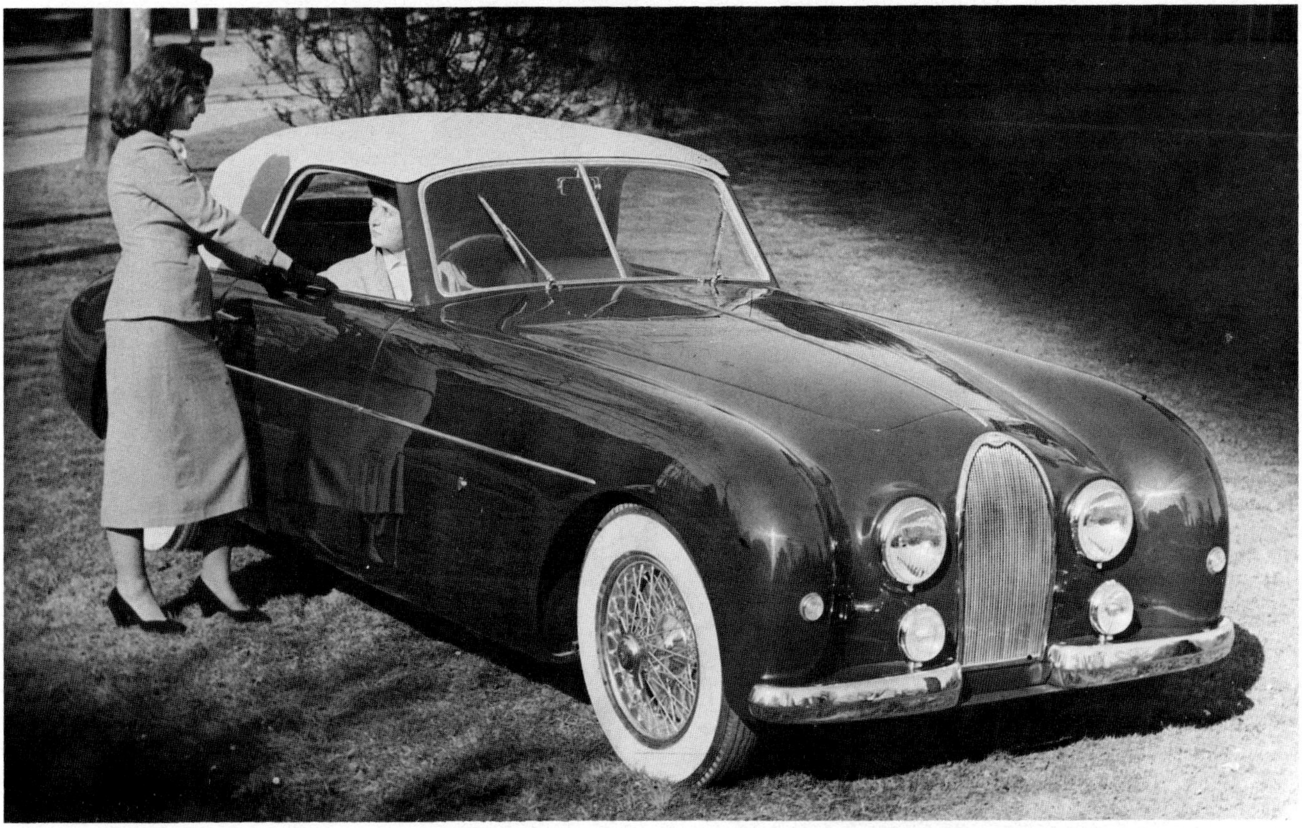

One of the batch of Type 101 models completed, body by Gangloff.

In the French motoring paper *L'Auto Journal*, 1 September 1951, there appeared front page headlines stating that 'The heir to the 57 will cost over three million francs', followed by an article describing the new model and illustrations of the complete car as it would appear at the Paris Salon in a few week's time. All this was, of course, most exciting as being the first solid confirmation of actual production activity since the many rumours and speculations of the previous few years.

The article started thus:

The famous iron curtain is being raised at Molsheim in Alsace and it is more likely to become a paper curtain capable of being torn aside by hand. Snow has given way to sunshine, silence to the noise of the machines and the air of sadness to smiles. Walls have been erected, roofs covered and machine tools installed. During the last six months the Bugatti Works have been rebuilt and a festive air pervades every brick, and every piece of metal plate, in fact, everything.

The General Manager, M. Marco, triumphantly announced that the Bugatti is at last ready to resume its place on the world automobile market. For the first time since the war, following a careful investigation, and with the will to continue, we shall be exhibiting the Works' latest offspring at the 1951 Salon.

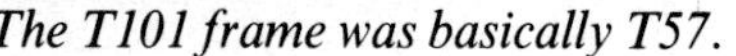

The T101 frame was basically T57.

The engine was a typical T57 straight eight with a double overhead camshaft, and had a cylinder capacity of 3,257 cc. Of monobloc construction, this engine had a non-detachable cylinder head with hemispherical head and central sparking plugs. There were still two valves per cylinder. Ignition was by Delco unit and a double Weber carburettor with pump was fitted. It was supplied with and without a supercharger, the engine, rated at 26 RAC hp, or 19 French CV, developing 135 hp at 5,500 rpm without the supercharger, and 188 hp at 5,200 with a 3 psi boost. With a 4½ psi supercharger pressure, more than 200 hp could be obtained. A 5-speed mechanical or Cotal gearbox was originally listed.

The T101 engine was a T57C with a few changes such as a downdraught carburettor.

It was claimed that this new gearbox, of Bugatti design, giving four speeds with a fifth overdrive speed, would be silent on all except first gear, but there is no evidence that a 5-speed box was in fact produced.

The Lockheed hydraulic brakes incorporated eight leading shoes, two on each wheel, each of these shoes being operated by an independent circuit. Accordingly, the risk of the car being without brakes in the event of a broken pipe were eliminated. Allinquant special telescopic shock-absorbers were used. Thus equipped, the weight of the chassis was in the neighbourhood of 2,300 lb and with coachwork it was expected not to exceed 3,200 lb. Coachwork was mainly by Gangloff of Colmar. The design of the cabriolet and of the coupé followed the contemporary line, being low and wide, and provided for four comfortably. Only six chassis were completed but the lukewarm reception that the car got, once sentiment had disappeared, and the weak finances of the Company, led to the project being abandoned.

Type 251. The factory struggled on on sub-contract machinery work after 1951 and then, surprisingly, in 1953, began to build a new racing car.

According to sources close to the project at the time the original idea of plunging the meagre finances of the company into a major racing car project was Roland's, although the management of the time, however, did not agree and thought the project unwise. Giocchino Colombo was engaged as the designer of the project at the end of 1953. He was well known for his work on the 153 Alfa Romeo, with 8 cylinders in line, the drive for the overhead camshaft being taken from the centre of the crankshaft between cylinders 4 and 5 – as indeed Bugatti had done

for his 3 litre Type 44. The new engine had a bore and stroke of 75 mm × 68·8 mm (2432 cc capacity), and was unusual in being in two 4 cylinder halves, as it were, joined in the middle; it ran for the first time on 29 July 1955; on test it performed well, although in the end always lacked 20 or 30 hp that the competition in Italy could find. More development should have put this right. The whole car ran for the first time at the aerodrome at Entzheim on 4 October 1955, with Marco at the wheel; a month later Trintignant tried it.

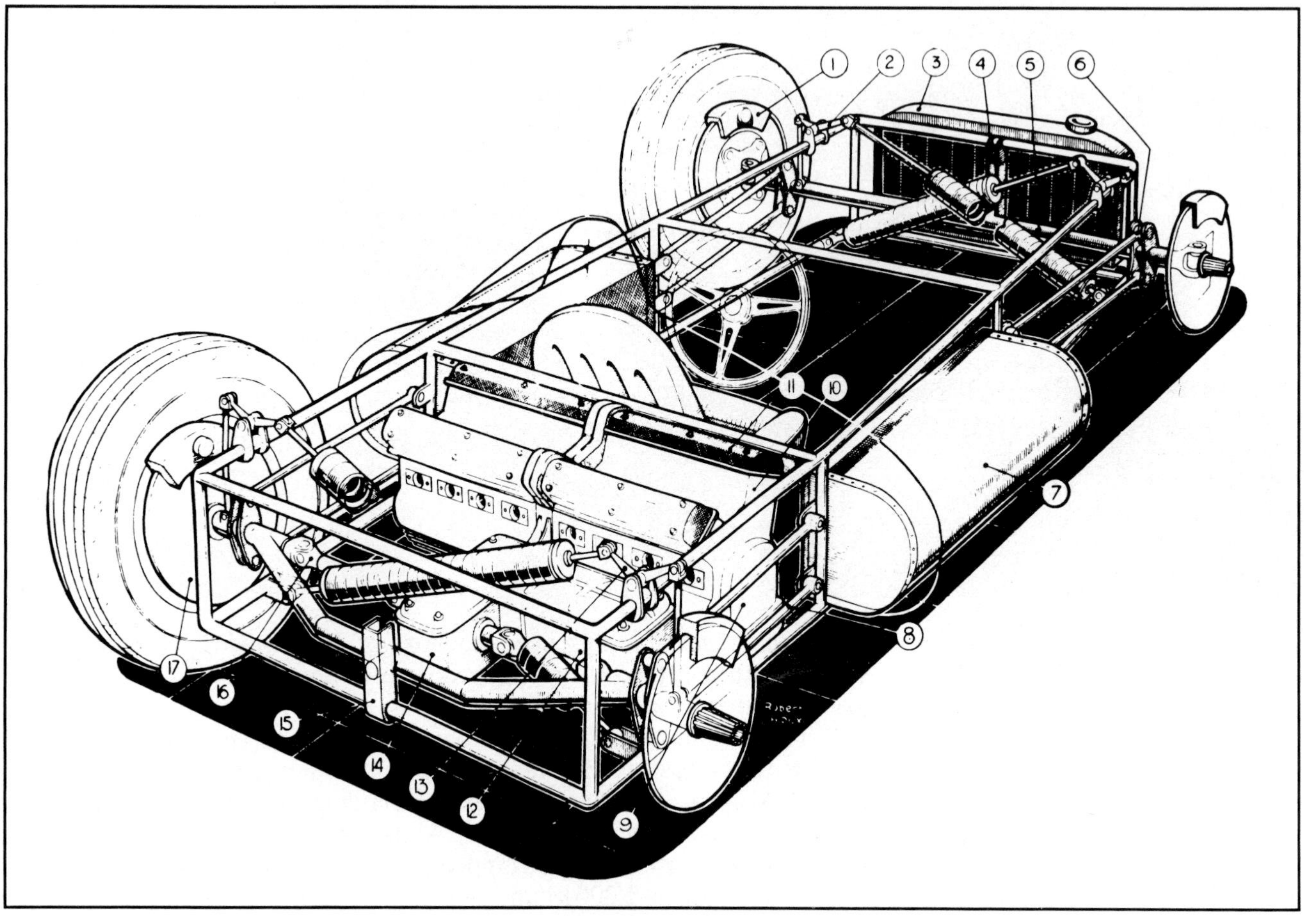

The layout of the Colombo-designed T251 racing car.

The conception of the car as a whole – tubular space frame with transverse engine – was mostly Colombo's, although the general idea of a rear engine sprang, via Roland, from the impression that the pre-war Auto-Union had created on his father Ettore. The radiator-to-engine water connection was through the tubular frame.

The main problem was the suspension. Colombo naturally wanted an up-to-date independent system. Roland would have nothing of this: a car without a rigid and hollow front axle would not be a Bugatti, he said. In the end the prototype appeared with a rigid axle, guided in the centre by a pin and slot (shades of the 1926 GP d'Alsace car); the suspension was by means of complex links and rockers and coils springs working on the ends of the axle. At the rear there was a type of De Dion system, again with a solid axle.

On test the vehicle was a disaster – it would neither hold the road nor steer. It was here that one can see the breaking point between the era when the highly competent Ettore, by intuitive skill could 'imagine'

solutions to practical problems more often than not, and a time when the younger son Roland, with little or none of his father's talent, would seek to impose his ideas when troubles arose on his much more experienced engineers. Many men, raised by circumstances above the natural level of their talents, seek to achieve authority by arbitary decision, thinking that it is wiser to decide than to seek advice. Roland seems to have been one of these. Thus it was Roland who decided to 'improve' the front suspension, by scrapping the linkage and coil springs above the axle, and replacing them with a leaf spring over it, tied to its ends by a short link (perhaps derived from the Lancia Aprilia). At the rear was a pair of coil springs.

The second car so modified appeared at Reims in 1956. Trintignant the driver did 18 laps in the Grand Prix, and brought the car into the pits, saying that he valued his life and would not continue in such a death trap (the race was won by Peter Collins in a Ferrari).

The press, excited at the prospect of a French Grand Prix car, attacked Roland! He in turn made a statement implying that the fault was Colombo's in his design conception. Colombo who overheard walked away in disgust!

The car went back to the works and never turned again. It now lies in the Museum at Mulhouse.

Type 252. There was also a project for a 1½ litre sports car using half of the 8 cylinder engine, but nothing came of it.

Type 451. The final 'fling' was a project to build a 12 cylinder GT car, perhaps to 'out-Ferrari Ferrari'! The firm was sold to Hispano-Suiza before more than a few drawings were made.

Maurice Trintignant came to Alsace to test the first T251 on the local aerodrome. Roland Bugatti is on the left.

The only outing of the T251 was in Trintignant's hands in the 1956 French Grand Prix at Rheims.

An artist's impression of the projected T252 sports car from L'Auto Journal.

BUGATTI

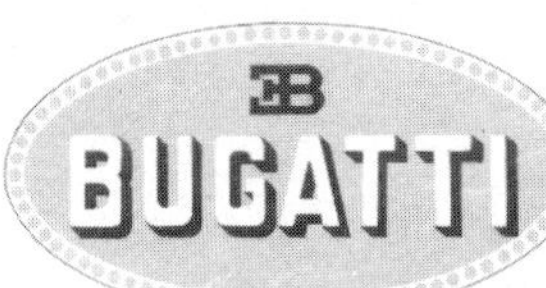

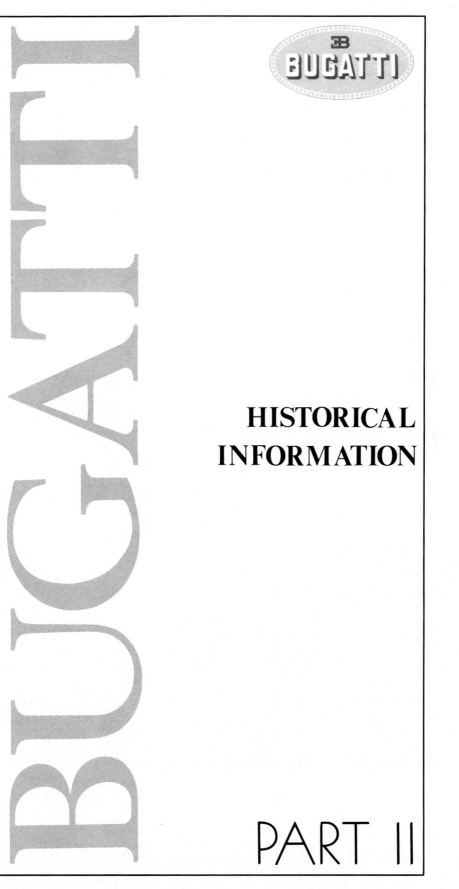

HISTORICAL INFORMATION

PART II

Early history

SINCE THE earliest days of the century when a young Italian of intriguing personality began designing cars, designs which he managed to sell to others before he was able to manufacture himself, car owners, enthusiasts, journalists and automobile engineers have been interested in his career and his productions. In spite of research begun before 1960 when the first edition of this book was being prepared, it is only in the recent period that accurate information has become available on the chronology of Bugatti's early work, particularly in one or two areas. The decisive door was opened by Mr Uwe Hucke who had acquired many early documents from Ettore's files when he took over much of Roland Bugatti's estate after his death. Willing study and debate with him over these documents has illuminated many a dark corner – although even now at least one remains.

Bugatti himself used his note paper before 1910 to remind his correspondents of what he had already achieved since 1901! In 1928 he issued a small, white illustrated brochure with a series of pictures from the past, unfortunately drawing loosely on his memory and getting some dates wrong! One caption under a photograph of the Packard-bodied Royale read, 'His Majesty King Alfonso XIII will receive this year the first example of this privileged construction'. (Nemesis intervened unfortunately, deposing the King who in the meantime had bought a Deusenberg!)

A definitive document was prepared in 1926 and it is clear from an available copy given to the author many years ago by Jules Goux, who claimed to have helped prepare it, that it formed the basis of several press publications in French journals, by Charles Faroux, André Latour and others, and indeed was certainly used in the biography of Ettore Bugatti, by W.F. Bradley (London 1948). Even this 1926 document contains a few errors, no doubt of memory.

Bugatti, born in 1881, had chosen mechanics as his direction by entering the Milan bicycle makers Prinetti & Stucchi as an apprentice in 1897 or 1898 and was soon playing with a tricycle of their manufacture fitted with a standard single-cylinder De Dion engine, then an excellent small unit readily available. He added a second engine to the tricycle and began winning local races with it.

A Prinetti & Stucchi tricycle, certainly of the type that the young Bugatti used for racing.

A Prinetti & Stucchi quadricycle; this picture from Uwe Hucke files originally from Bugatti makes it likely that it was one of these vehicles which he modified by adding another pair of engines at the rear, calling it his Type 1.

Bonneville in *Le Moteur Roi* (1949) gives details of Ettore's early successes culled from early editions of Milan journals (eg *Automobili*), the dates quoted evidently being publication not event dates.

1 March: Reference to Bugatti in Nice–Castelanne race, No. 72 on De Dion Bouton tricycle of 1·25 hp.

12 March: Verona–Mantua 161 km race; 18 tricycles start. Bugatti wins on Prinetti tricycle with De Dion Bouton engine; Count Biscaretti 2nd; Fraschini 3rd. Agnelli of Fiat won the car class.

8 May: Pignerol–Turin 90 km race; 42 entries in Tricycle class.

Bugatti wins on machine with De Dion $1\frac{3}{4}$ hp engine at record speed.

14 May: Padua–Trevise and back 175 km race. Quadricycle class, Bugatti takes 4 h 35 min and makes best time of *all* vehicles. (This may have been Car No. 1 – see below.)

11 September: Brescia–Verona and back 223 km. Bugatti 2nd in Tricycle class.

28 September: Trevise 3 km speed event. Bugatti 3rd in Handicap class.

28 September: Trevise 80 km event. Bugatti is non-finisher due to petrol blockage.

Bradley states that he entered this tricycle in the Paris–Bordeaux race on 24 May 1899 but retired half way following an accident with a dog. Bugatti did not, nor could hardly have ascribed a Type Number to this vehicle.

Type 1, 1899. What he later did claim was his first design, labelling it No. 1, P & S, was a four-wheeled machine, no doubt basically Prinetti & Stucchi, with four engines, certainly De Dion. Bradley states that there were two engines at the front and two at the rear, while Bugatti himself in the 1928 brochure stated that they were all at the rear. The anomaly arises from a misreading of the original French text from the 'release' of 1926. This states that there were two engines in front of and two behind *the rear axle*.

Bugatti later admitted that the design was not very successful, but it led him to produce his first real car!

Type 2, 1900. This car was complete and more conventional in layout. Family friends, the brothers, Counts Gulinelli, helped finance the young fanatic. It had 4 cylinders, 90 mm × 120 mm bore and stroke, 4 speeds and chain drive. This car won a gold medal at the International Breeding and Sport Exhibition, Milan, in May–June 1901 and is stated to have received an award from the Automobile Club of France in 1899; this may have been incorrect as the car seems only to have been completed in 1901.

La Gazetta dello Sport, Milan, 22 May 1901, had this to say about the exhibit:

> On the Ricordi stand there figures, by his kind permission, the sensational novelty of the Exhibition: The Bugatti–Gulinelli carriage. The engaging dare-devil of Italian motorcycling conceived the idea of producing a kind of light vehicle which was not at the time on the market. It would not be the minute and very fragile vehicle too similar to the bicycle, nor yet the complicated, useless and costly mastodon, and this first attempt made a very good job of it, a triumph in fact: a small carriage, simple and most potent with a 12 hp, 4 cylinder motor, capable of exacting daily service and of very great speed if necessary.
>
> We shall not dwell here on the most interesting characteristics of the vehicle with which we are already occupying ourselves and shall continue to do so with pleasure: on this occasion we shall only state that it rounded off the Ricordi Stand to perfection.

It is obvious that a reception such as this to a first design must have had a great effect on young Bugatti's estimation of his own abilities and must have conditioned much of his future activity.

ETTORE BUGATTI'S CAR

(Translated from *Gazzetta dello Sport,* Milan, 10 May 1901)

As a passionate follower of automobilism, this new sport which occupies more and more minds in a search for perfection, I have for some time been following the feverish development of innovation and improvements in motor construction. Yesterday was a great day for me, for I was able to observe the complete success of my good friend Ettore Bugatti, who by himself, unaided, has built a vehicle which is quite magnificent. Having followed Bugatti in his patient research for 10 months I am delighted to report his triumphant success.

In the motorcar field Bugatti is very well known; son of an artist, he is himself an artist at heart. He has served his motoring apprenticeship racing a motorcycle. He loved his machine; there were modifications every day in the workshop until his tricycle carried him victorious to the finishing line in the many road races in which he took part. But his dream was of a car, a fast car. He studied all the various types of motor, analysed them, observed their faults, thought up modifications and foresaw in his imagination a perfect car.

However, he lacked the material means to put his ideas and studies into practice. His own nature, cheerful and waggish, was little encouragement to others to take him seriously and associate themselves with him in a programme of construction, and most of them abandoned him. Then he started to make sketches of the multitude of ideas which crowded his brain. His father's studio was full of vast rolls of paper – Bugatti spent whole days designing the vehicle in pencil and crayon in all its details.

How often the worthy Bugatti took me to his studio, showing me and explaining on a score of sheets of paper the functioning of his car! His enthusiasm in describing it was such that it seemed to be already on the road at 60 km/h; indeed I feared it might turn his mind. Among his many friends, it was the brothers Count Gulinelli di Ferrara who recognized in Bugatti a hidden brilliance and helped him realize his project. It was thus that in October of last year Bugatti began to reproduce from his drawings the wooden patterns for the foundry; then the construction of the chassis, the making of the large cast parts and practically all the small delicate parts which go to make up a car.

A month ago, on my return from the Circuit of Italy trials I went to visit Bugatti in his workshop in company with Cav. Ricordi and my good friend Georges Berteaux. The car was under construction. Berteaux was most enthusiastic and told Bugatti that it would be an undoubted success even abroad. So sure was he of its success that he undertook to buy the first one of the type.

The day before yesterday Bugatti fitted the wheels, installed the provisional ignition system and drove out of the workshop for the first test. The car went superbly and can at present do 60 km/h, but the power of the engine is such that it can without any effort pull a higher gear ratio.

It is a light car not to be confused with a cycle car. The motor has four vertical cylinders with electric ignition tubes; valve housings and cylinders are contained in a single casting. Completely new is the system for closing the inlet valves, the removal of a single nut being sufficient to dismantle each pair of valves without removing any tube. The engine, the gear change and all the rest of the machinery are fixed on a double frame of rectangular steel of very great rigidity. The chassis with all the mechanical parts is completely adaptable to any type of coachwork.

Yesterday the courageous and enterprising young man received the enthusiastic compliments of the most competent automobilists. Yesterday's boy – he is only 19 – has disappeared: today he is the esteemed constructor of a model which has reached a high degree of perfection.

The car now built is the welcome result of the anxieties, the difficulties and the efforts of the past. Now Bugatti, teamed up with the brothers Count Gulinelli will start a vast establishment in Milan for the building of motorcars.

E.V.

Bugatti's first 'real' car was the car built in 1900 when he was 19, calling it later Type 2.

The car was a 4 cylinder, with overhead valves, and chain drive.

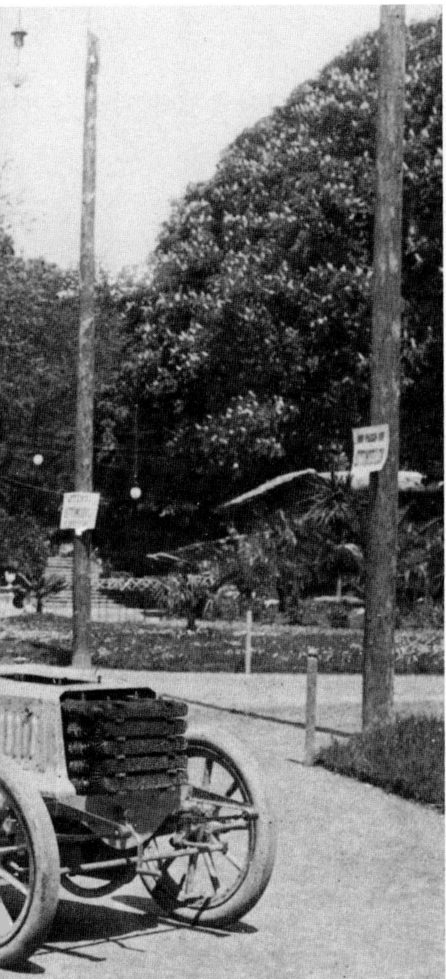

The young designer in a well-garlanded car. The third lever at the gear gate is probably an additional lever to engage reverse.

Type 3, 1902. Baron de Dietrich, Director of the large industrial concern at Niederbronn in northern Alsace, then part of Germany, visited the 1901 Milan Show, and, struck by the Bugatti design, took a licence for its production and engaged young Bugatti to design other vehicles for him, including a racing machine. Ettore being under age at the time, his father Carlo signed the licence in June 1902, but it seems certain that Ettore had started work after the Milan exhibition a year previously, since he was soon to compete in a 'de Dietrich-Bugatti' of 20 hp in the

Frankfurt races. This car had the driver sitting over the rear axle, with luggage space between him and the engine!

Possibly the first English reference to Bugatti's design is in the now defunct *Automotor Journal*, 18 April 1903, which illustrates and describes a 4 cylinder, 114 mm × 130 mm car, rated as 24 hp. This car had a 4 speed gearbox and chain rear drive. According to the description the overhead valves were operated from a pair of camshafts by what appear to be pull, as opposed to push, rods. The cylinders were cast in pairs, each pair being surrounded by a cylindrical aluminium casing acting as a water jacket.

Type 3 produced for de Dietrich; first versions had an exposed film type radiator.

The German motor journal *Der Motorwagen* refers to Ettore Bugatti in its issue of 15 September 1902, describing the Frankfurt race meeting held on 31 August. Race No. 6 was a handicap event for gentlemen drivers, the cars carrying a total of four persons, and the distance being 12·87 kilometres. Goebel won in an 8 hp Bergmann from a 3·75 km handicap, Bugatti 2nd from 250 metres, in a 20 hp de Dietrich, and Emil Mathis from scratch being 3rd in a 24 hp de Dietrich. In the next scratch race over 16 km Bugatti was again second, this time to a 40 hp Mercedes. But the journal had this to say:

> In the case of Race 7, in which a Mercedes Simplex of 40 hp was competing against a Panhard & Levassor and a de Dietrich of 16 hp and a de Dietrich of 20 hp, every spectator had the feeling that such a race was an absurdity, for here the victory was decided at the start. It must go to the Mercedes car of 40 hp,

The Type 3 and 4 engine, two pairs of cylinders, with overhead valves operated by pull-rods. (*From* The Autocar, *27 February 1904*)

providing no accident occured. But the result appears quite different, if the speeds of the four cars in this race are calculated; we then get the following:

	hp	*km/h*
Mercedes-Simplex car	40	68·48
de Dietrich-Bugatti car	20	63·83
Panhard & Levassor car	16	58·15
de Dietrich-Turcat-Méry car	16	55·16

and then the real winner is the new Dietrich-Bugatti car, with a 20 hp engine, which achieved almost the same performance as the Mercedes-Simplex with 40 hp!

Curiously enough, the spectators during the race had the right idea all along, and greeted Mr Bugatti, who proved himself to be a driver of the very first rank, every time he drove past the Grand Stand. Even the officials who were present left their places in order to get as close as possible to the bends, where one could see exactly in what masterly fashion Mr Bugatti took them every time.

This is the first reference found to Bugatti in a racing car, and indeed with a car bearing his name. He celebrated his twenty-first birthday two weeks after the races, on 15 September.

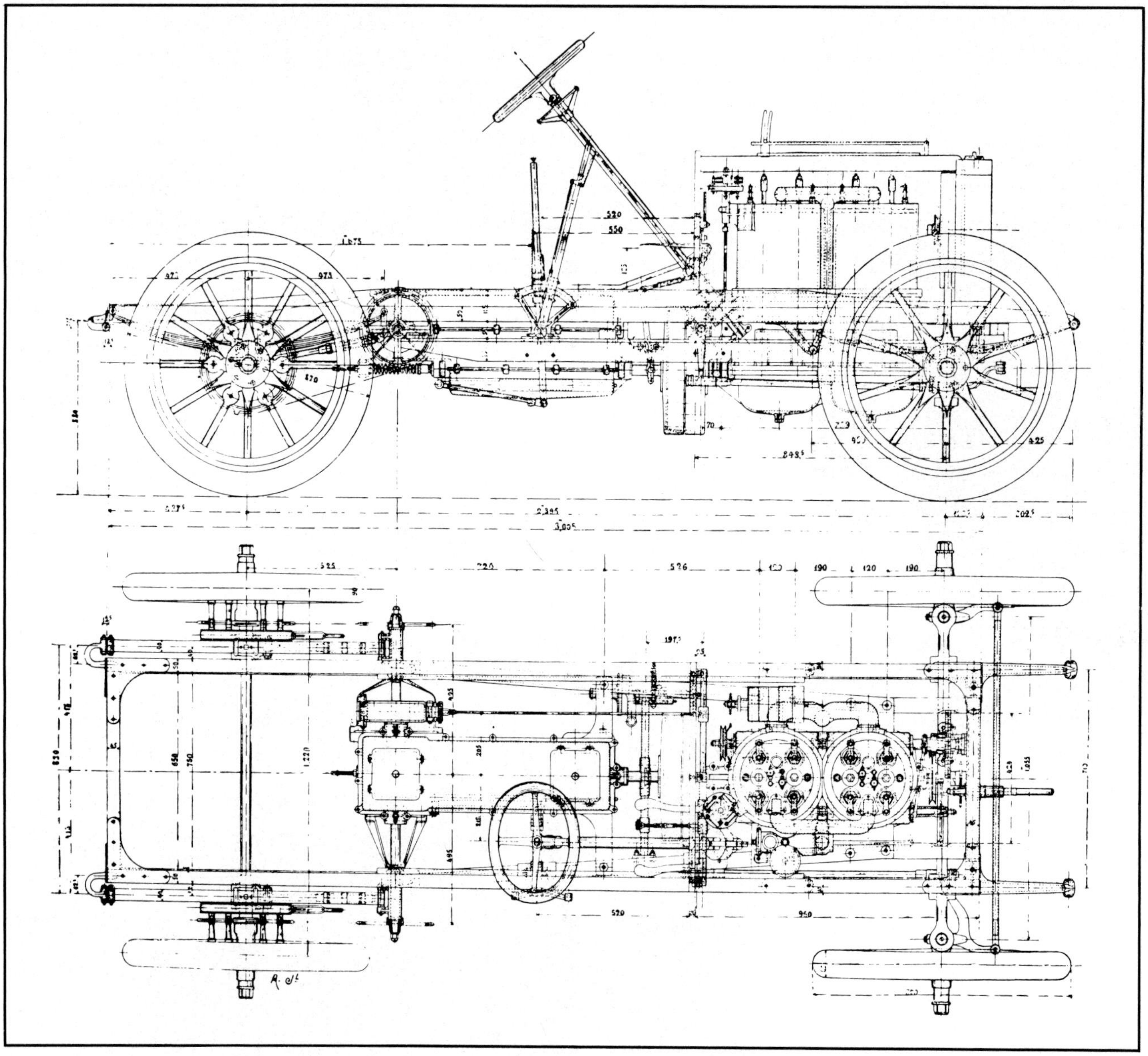

The chassis layout of the Types 3 & 4. The engine is carried on a sub-frame, and the gearbox secondary shaft is above the primary one.

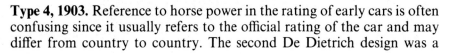

Type 4, 1903. Reference to horse power in the rating of early cars is often confusing since it usually refers to the official rating of the car and may differ from country to country. The second De Dietrich design was a

Bugatti and his friend Mathis in a racing version of the Type 3/4 chassis, a car which Bugatti drove in competition; this is similar in layout to the later Paris Madrid car (Type 5) which had a tubular frame. Later copies of this picture had Mathis touched out!

Ettore arrives from Niederbronn to attend the 1903 Vienna show, in a new car. His passenger was J. Y. von Ritsch, the de Dietrich importer.

Bugatti and Mathis in a touring version; the windscreen and top were detachable.

'24 hp', 130 mm × 140 mm 7·4 litre machine, able to carry reasonable coachwork; it still had the same layout of engine, and chain transmission.

The Show number of the *Autocar*, 6 February 1904, records a 24 to 28 hp and a 30 to 35 hp 'de Dietrich (Burgatti)' (*sic*) with 4 cylinders, 4 speeds and chain drive, and handled by the Burlington Carriage Co. These were offered in addition to the de Dietrich (Turcat-Méry) cars. The *Autocar*, 27 February 1904 describes the 24 to 28 hp car under the title Burlington, and the illustrations show that it is similar to Car No. 3, except that the latter has a proper radiator shell, while the Burlington had an exposed film-radiator. The smaller Burlington car had an engine 130 mm × 140 mm, with cylinders in pairs and again boxed in by twin copper water jackets, the 30 to 35 hp presumably being similar but larger in scale.

Type 5, 1903. *The Automotor Journal* quotes Bugatti as designing a 50 hp car for the 1903 Paris–Madrid race, and states that the frame was made from large diameter tubes, serving to carry cooling water. Bugatti himself stated that this car, as originally intended for the race, had the driver sitting over the rear axle (see upper photograph on page 305). Bugatti was refused permission to race due to the lack of visibility for the driver.

He drove it, however, in the 1903 Frankfurt races in August. Later he modified the chassis, the modified version being shown below.

Type 5 Paris–Madrid car. This is in the modified form with the driver placed normally, after the authorities would not let Bugatti drive the car in the original position at the rear, as used in the smaller racing car. The car had a tubular frame and an engine of 160 × 160 mm (12·86 litres). What became of it is not known.

Types 6 and 7. The de Dietrich arrangement terminated, probably with the firm being tired of Ettore's lack of attention to the detail and reliability of the cars he had designed, and shortly afterwards he signed an arrangement with his friend Emil Mathis (on April 1, 1904) to design for him, the car to be known as the Hermes, and to be produced at Illkirch-Graffenstaden, near Strasbourg. The car was a logical development of the earlier de Dietrich design, but now only the inlet valves were overhead, the exhaust being on the side and operated by the now normal push up from the camshaft. The gearbox had its output shaft below the engine axis to lower the seating, and now the gears were changed by selector rods to avoid going through the gears successively. The chain final drive was however retained.

Bugatti allocated Types 6 and 7 to these designs although the Mathis catalogue quotes 50, 60 and 90 hp versions. The first type seems to refer to the first two, bore 136 or 140 mm × 150 mm stroke, while the other may be the larger 160 mm × 160 mm model.

Mr L.T. Delaney arranged to import the car into Britain and raced one at Blackpool (*Autocar*, 5 August 1905) but did not manage to make any sales and turned elsewhere. Bugatti himself appears to have driven a Mathis (or Hermes) in the Herkomer Cup of August 1905. In the *Autocar*, 19 August 1905, there is a brief report of the Bleichroder Race which more or less occured at the same time as the Herkomer Cup. Entries included Mr Mathis with a Fiat and 'Mr Bugatti with a Bugatti' – perhaps the first known reference to a Bugatti car in its own unqualified right. One of these cars still exists in the National Museum at Mulhouse.

Types 6 and 7. The 1905 Mathis car designed by Bugatti and sold as the Hermes. The chassis number can be read on the chassis plate, No 15. Chassis 30 still exists.

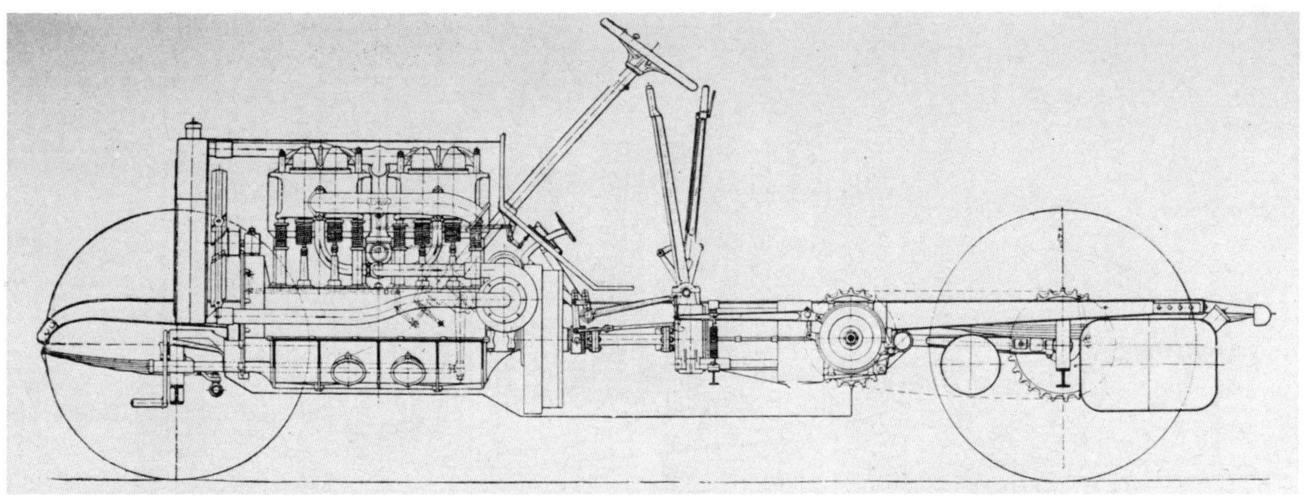

A sectional elevation of the Mathis chassis, overhead inlet valves and side exhaust.

Left: *Bugatti at the wheel of one of the Mathis cars at the Kaiserpreis, at Taunus, 13–14 June 1907. A copy of this illustration signed by Emil Mathis and sent to Ernest Friderich on 10 October 1948 had the name 'Mathis' inscribed on the radiator. This original copy from the Fiat library shows that the car originally had 'Bugatti' painted on the radiator. From left to right in the photograph: Scarfiotti, President of Fiat, Friderich, Bugatti, P. Marchal, Felice Nazarro, Vincenzo Lancia, Rembrandt Bugatti, Mathis, Louis Wagner, and G. Agnelli.*

Only a few of these cars were produced, probably not more than 15, and the contract arrangement came to an end in 1906.

Some details of the car can be culled from *La Vie Automobile*, 4 March 1905, pp. 136–7; there are illustrations of the chassis and engine and a section drawing of the inlet valve operation by means of a pull-rod. The chassis is also illustrated in the *Handbuch des Automobilbaues* by Thomas Lehmbeck, 1909. He quotes 50, 60 and 90 hp models.

Type 8, 1907. In 1907 Bugatti parted with Mathis and became an independent consulting engineer. He designed two cars for the Deutz Company at Cologne; the first was a 4 cylinder, 50 to 60 hp, 145 mm × 150 mm with overhead valves driven by curved tappets from an overhead camshaft; the construction was similar to the later Type 13 and Brescia design except that the curved tappets had rollers at their ends. The clutch was of the pure Bugatti multiplate toggle operated type and the car had a 4 speed gearbox and chain drive. The engine is illustrated in *The Motor*, 24 August 1955, but the whole chassis is well illustrated by Heller in the *Z.V.D.I*, June 1908, page 919 *et seq.*

The engine now had an overhead camshaft operating the valves by curved tappets, the cam drive being at the rear.

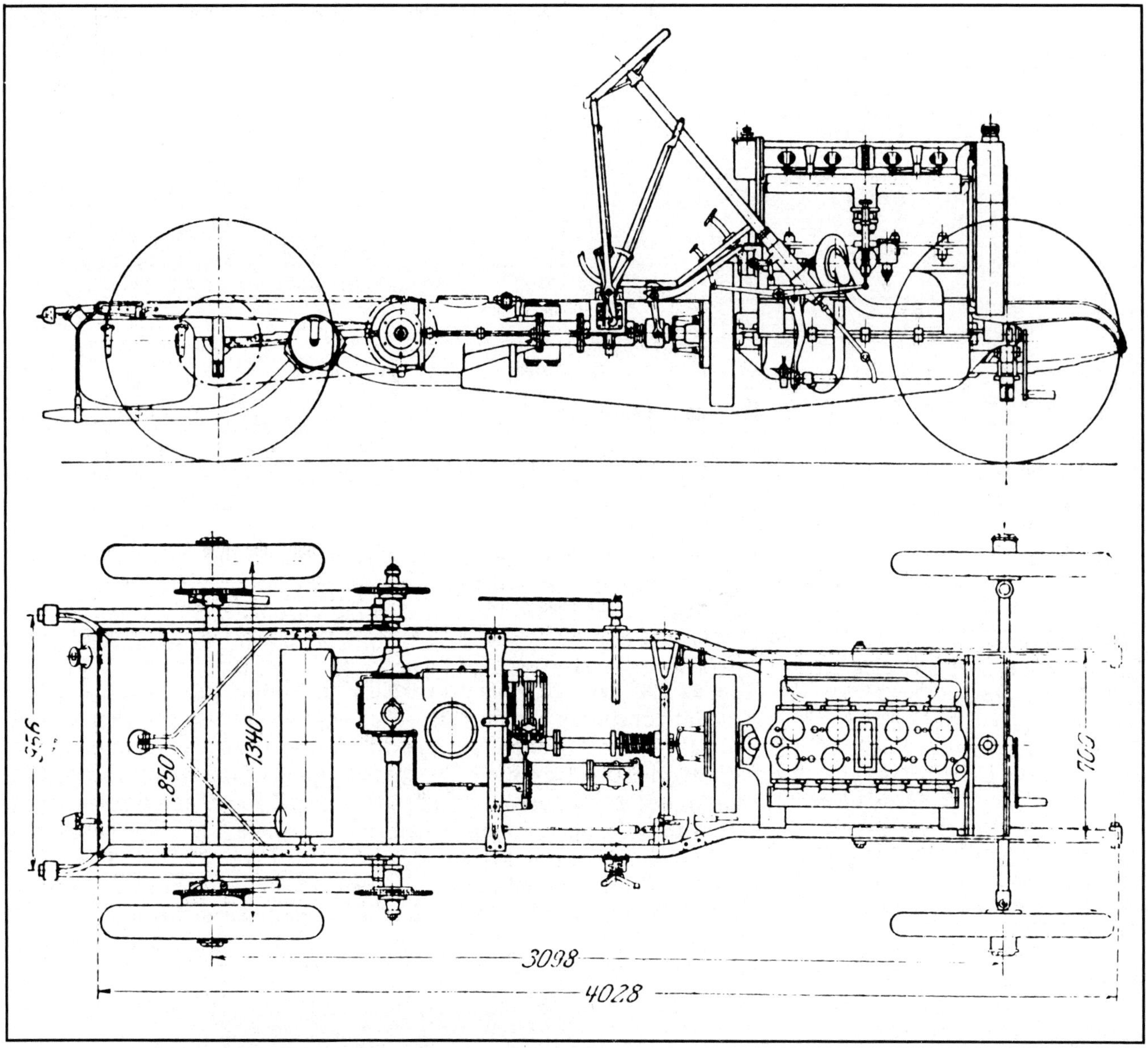

The Deutz design looked very workmanlike.

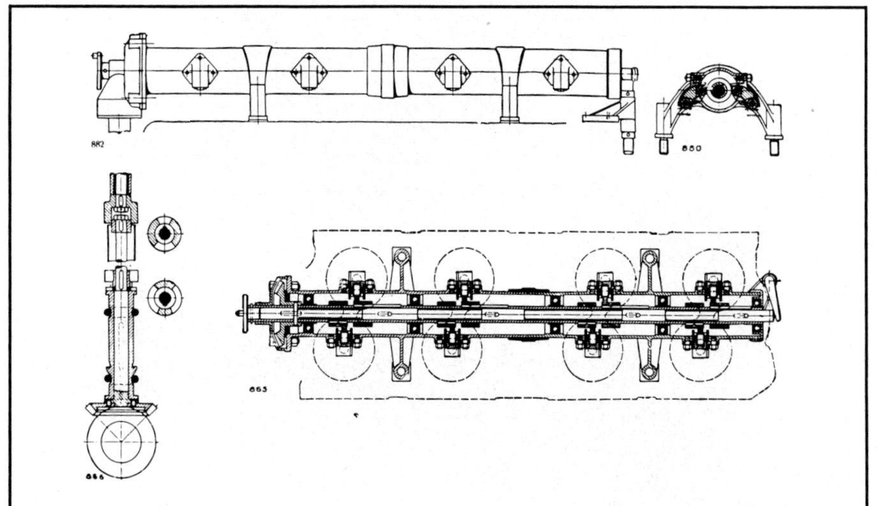

Detail of the valve operating mechanism. The arc-shaped followers had rollers at their ends.

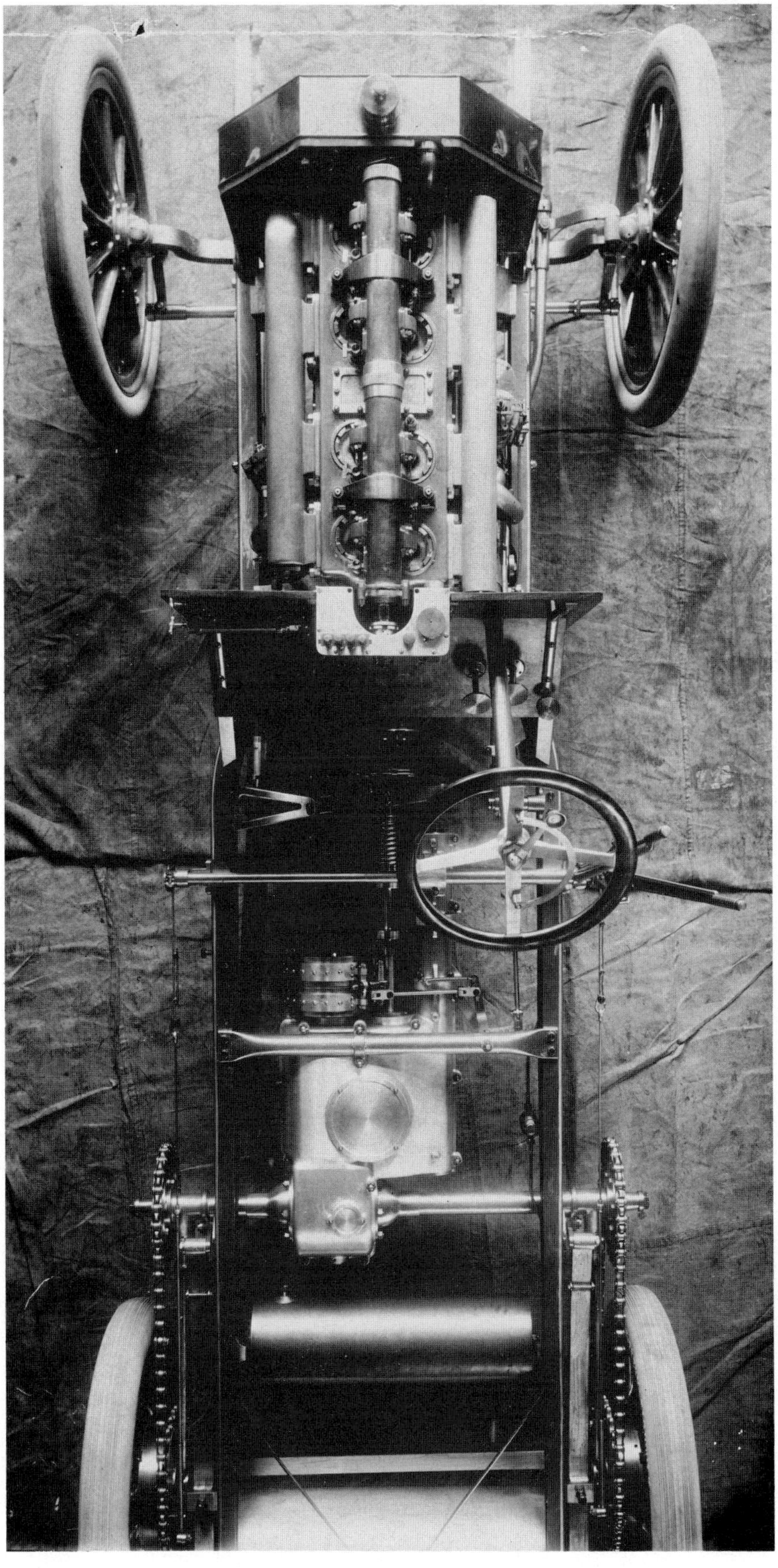

Type 8. The first Deutz design retained chain drive.

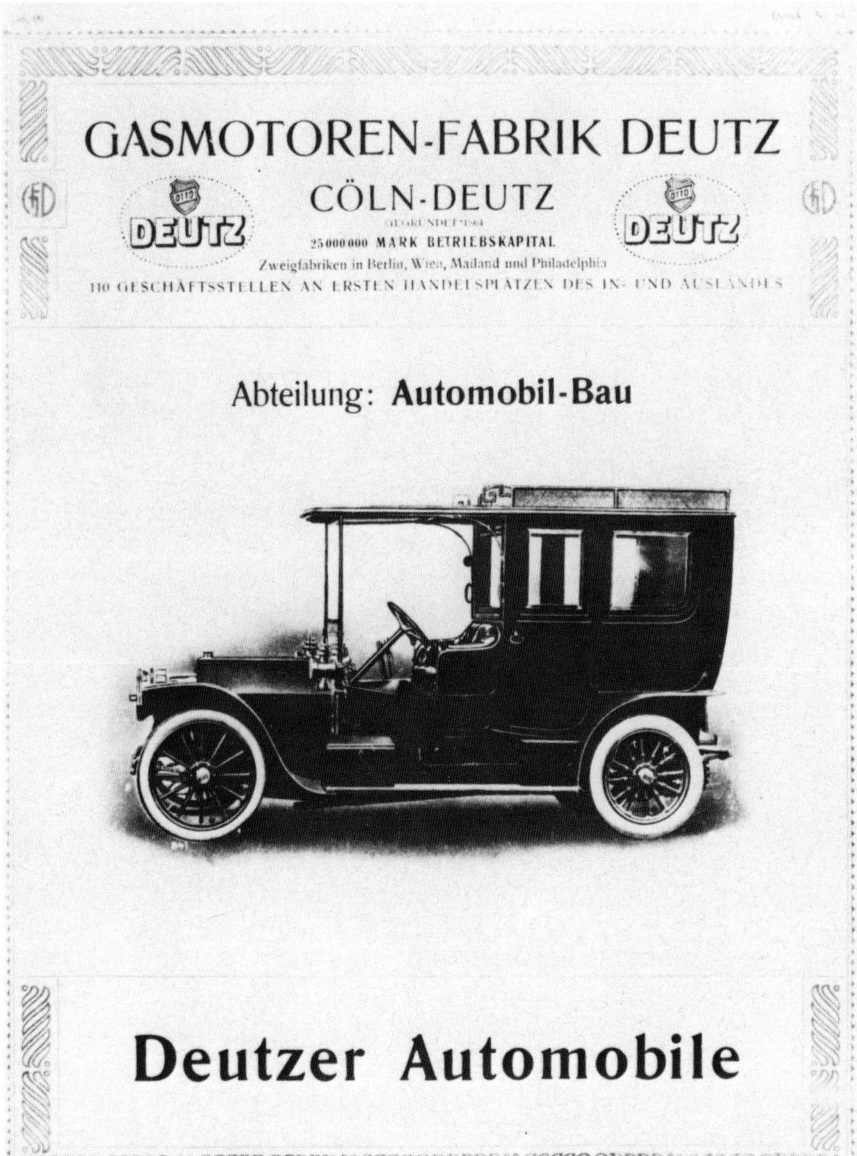

GASMOTOREN-FABRIK DEUTZ
OTTO
DEUTZ
CÖLN-DEUTZ
GEGRÜNDET 1864
25000000 MARK BETRIEBSKAPITAL
Zweigfabriken in Berlin, Wien, Mailand und Philadelphia
110 GESCHÄFTSSTELLEN AN ERSTEN HANDELSPLÄTZEN DES IN- UND AUSLANDES
Abteilung: **Automobil-Bau**
Deutzer Automobile

A page from a Deutz catalogue, proud to be able to mention the famous name Otto, the inventor of the 4-cycle engine.

Right: *Type 9. Now Bugatti for the first time designed a bevel back axle.*

Type 9, 1909. This is the second Deutz design fully described and illustrated in the *ZVDI.* 11 June 1910. This car dating from 1909, was a 4 cylinder, 95 mm × 120 mm, 3·2 litre, with 4 speed box, Bugatti clutch, propellor shaft and torque rod, normal rear axle and rear half-elliptic springs. This article does not show the engine in section, but the general layout is pure Bugatti – front cross-mounted magneto and water pump, front bevel drive to overhead camshaft, steering box mounted above engine bearer and so on.

Isotta-Fraschini. There has been much conjecture over the years which sought to connect Bugatti with Isotta-Fraschini in Milan, due to the resemblance of the excellent little car the latter company entered in the Coupe des Voiturettes at Dieppe in 1908. *The Motor* of 28 July 1908 describes and illustrates the car and shows clearly its resemblance to the later Bugatti Type 10 'Pur Sang'. It refers to Isotta-Fraschini of Milan being a subsidiary of Lorraine-de Dietrich of Luneville; later information

One Isotta came to England. It was of much heavier construction than that achieved by Bugatti in his T10.

the interests of production.

3. General change in the circulating water system, resulting in the elimination of many pipes and connections. This change has worked out in a perfectly satisfactory manner, and the cooling of the motor being correct in every way.

4. Re-design of the front end by substitution of series of Hess-Bright compound annular and radial thrust bearings in place of the very complicated double bearings used on the original French model. These re-designed parts have given perfect satisfaction, having stood up for eighty hours of heavy running without defect or appreciable wear on the bearings or the closely associated gears.

The specific design of the motor has been changed in other minor particulars, but aside from the points above enumerated is substantially the same as the original Bugatti.

The outstanding features of the design of the motor lies in the general arrangement of cylinders whereby two series of vertical cylinders arranged in parallel groups of eight on each side are each coupled to an independent crankshaft, each crank being geared to the central propellor shaft. The motor, therefore, consists substantially of two eight cylinder motors arranged side by side driving a common propellor shaft. Owing to the small size of the cylinders and the compact grouping the area of the vertical cross-section of the assembled group is exceedingly small resulting in very low head resistance when housed. The overall length of the motor is also exceedingly short, and the general bulk of the design is such that the motor as a whole in its overall dimensions lies within the dimensions of any aviation motor of 300 hp or over. Into this concentrated package is incorporated a motor conservatively rated at 420 hp and actually capable of delivering 500 hp at approximately 1,550 revolutions per minute, propellor speed.

Further advantages of this design are as follows:

1. Carburetion and ignition are arranged in groups of four cylinders thus avoiding complicated and uneven gas distribution and difficulties in ignition incident to the ordinary six and twelve cylinder grouping.

2. The use of forked or articulated connecting rods is entirely avoided, thus eliminating a source of trouble common to 'V' type motors.

3. The use of parallel crankshafts and the central propellor shaft and housing running laterally the full length of the case results in an enormously stiff crankcase and an even and divided distribution of stresses. This motor has probably the most substantial crankcase found in any aviation motor.

4. The gear drive is so arranged that the total load is absorbed at *two* points on the periphery of the driven gear. Gears are of comparatively small diameter and, because of the fact that the whole gear load is not carried at one point, gears are materially smaller and lighter than would be necessary to transmit the same amount of power through a single spur. The enormous difficulty heretofore encountered in building gear drive motors of ordinary or 'V' type construction have been entirely overcome in the Bugatti motor. Sets of these gears have been operated for eighty hours without the least trouble, and during such period have transmitted from 400 to a maximum of 500 hp.

5. The use of sixteen comparatively small cylinders results in a perfectly balanced running condition and perfect synchronization. The size of the cylinders permits operation with safety at high engine speeds, and the skilled adoption of the gear principle permits the use of these engine spees at *useful* propellor speeds. The motor at its rated horse power (420) operates at an engine speed of 1,996 revolutions and a propellor speed of 1,330. At its maximum of 500 hp it operates at an engine speed of approximately 2,300. The maximum power of the motor as developed on the stand may, therefore, be made useful in flight, which is *not* true of the non-geared type of motor which develops an unusual amount of power developed at 1,700 revolutions. This condition represents the outstanding advantage of the Bugatti motor over any motor approaching it in power, and is made possible by the successful working out of its unique gear system.

6. The unique design makes possible the introduction of a cannon mounted within the propellor shaft housing and firing through the hollow shaft and centre of the propellor hub. This arm is adapted to use 37 mm ammunition, and when used in connection with a synchronized machine gun of the same ballistic energy, can be discharged automatically six successive times as the instant range and alignments are determined by the flight of the tracer bullet fired from the synchronized machine gun, which is also attached to the motor. This peculiar advantage is of use only in connection with combat planes. It is an incident to the design of the motor increasing its usefulness in the combat field, but in no way impairing its usefulness in other types of planes.

7. The great power, compactness, flexibility and *reliability* of the motor permits its use in a variety of planes covering a range from the very high-powered combat plane to the heaviest type of bombing and sea plane.

8. The motor in weight, per hp, compares favourably with the Liberty and is much lighter per horse power than the Rolls-Royce or other reliable foreign motors. On the base of its rated horse power (420) the weight is two and one-half pounds per horse power, and upon the base of its maximum useful horse power approximately two pounds per horse power.

In conclusion, it may be stated that the Bugatti motor is to be regarded as a fully developed product subject to possible small refinements as production progresses, but at the present moment suitable for general use. It is a significant fact that in spite of the changes in design the third motor submitted to the fifty-hour endurance test went through this test successfully. It may be noted that the motor as at present built is essentially a low compression engine, and that as need develops there is every reasonable expectation of securing very much greater powers, by the increase in compression. Particular attention is again called to the fact that the power developed by this motor is a *useful* one, and that the rating of the motor at 420 hp less than the amount of real power that can be taken from it in flight.

The above is respectfully submitted.

Even allowing for the optimism of a Company anxious to be allowed to proceed further, it is to be regretted that work on this engine was not allowed to continue when the Armistice came a few days later. The now defunct US journal *Aerial Age Weekly*, 9 December 1918, refers to Bugatti engine production up to 22 November 1918 as 11 engines. By June 1918 orders had been placed for 2,000 engines, but *Automotive Industries*, 24 April 1919, quotes the production by the time the Armistice was signed as 40 engines, and illustrates a line of about this number. This same journal has a comprehensive description of the engine in the issues of 24 April and 1 May 1919.

Aerial Age Weekly also had an interesting series of articles on the construction of the engine, with full details of the changes made by Mr King. Many of the changes seem to the present Author to have been fully justified and merely underline some of the bad detail design for which Bugatti was, and continued to be, famous even if he did manage to succeed in spite of it! Quoting from *Aerial Age Weekly*:

> Because of its unique type of design the Bugatti, when it was first brought over from France, and it was determined to put it into manufacture in this country, aroused a very great deal of interest in automotive circles, the interest being second only to that evidenced in the Liberty. The Bugatti was of the geared type possessing certain features not embodied in the Liberty, and with the special feature of being able to mount a 37 millimetre cannon firing through the propeller shaft.

The engine in fact was rated at 410 hp at 2,000 rpm rather than the 500 hp originally suggested (and 520 hp sometimes mentioned), but as the

power:weight ratio seems to have been better than the famous Liberty engine, no doubt this was not a matter of consequence. Undoubtedly later engines would have been uprated as the design was developed. To quote once more:

One of the points that required special study was the pressure oiling system due to cross interference of oil in the crankcase. The non-pressure system as used in the French type of Bugatti was considered unsafe owing to the many long leads and on the uncertainty of outside temperature, and it was consequently abandoned. The pressure system developed by Mr King has worked out very satisfactorily, as was proved by the fine condition of the bearings and running parts after the fifty-hour test.

This extract underlines the basic weakness of all or at any rate of most of Bugatti engines up to 1928 or so. Bugatti insisted on relying on splash or drip lubrication of the type seen on the Types 13, Brescia, 30, 35 and early Type 40 etc, and indeed on the pre-1910 Deutz and earlier designs.

The oiling system as applied to the French Bugatti engine can be considered an open system non-pressure type, the pressure being determined by the diameters of the open orifices. In other words, with heavy or cold oil will take the path of least resistance and will not travel to the remote ends of oil leads. The small openings in bearings become clogged with sediment, waste or coagulated oil. Owing to the pressure not being sufficient to clear these passages, trouble can be expected. Such trouble has already been experienced in engines built in this country. The fundamental principle in the American Bugatti engine was to obtain a true pressure system on all bearings, including camshafts. The oil to be controlled by a relief valve. This can be regulated and the proper pressure obtained.

These remarks might be echoed as a criticism of the Type 35 GP engine; one can't help wondering whether the roller-bearing crank on the GP engine was really introduced as a means of making the Bugatti non-pressure system work! Certainly his racing car engines might have been the better for adopting the King improvements, but Bugatti was unusually conservative for all his brilliance.

In the course of a very interesting report, *Aerial Age Weekly* continues:

Mr King offers definite data concerning the specific changes made in the Bugatti design and reason therefor. Owing to the fact that the French engine which was sent over to this country had had a limited test in Paris of 37 hours and had not been in flight, all of the points in the design were very carefully considered. It was soon discovered that if the job was to be made a production one, numerous changes would have to be made.

It was evident that difficulties were experienced in cooling the valve seats of the French Bugatti, as cylinders and sample sections of used cylinders showed cracks between the exhaust and inlets. In the American design, centres of the valves were increased in both directions from centre of line. The drawing shows the deep unjacketed section of the cylinder in which the strain was set up, causing the cracked valve seats. To obviate this difficulty, the shape of the intake passage and exhaust passages were improved.

The exhaust valve stems were not properly taken care of as to heat transference to the water jacket. The depth of water around valve stem guides is shown in the diagram where the French Bugatti and American Bugatti are contrasted. Owing to poor conductivity through threaded portions of valve guides, the threading was eliminated and cast iron valve guides were pressed

King adjusts an engine on the testbed at the Duesenberg factory, Friderich second from left.

into place, thus making a much more uniformly cooled stem. The bronze guides taken from the French Bugatti showed evidence of high heat.

An astonishing snag with the original water pump is referred to:

The French Bugatti pump as mounted on the engine permits water leakage to enter the sump and mix with the lubricating oil. This will lead to difficulties in the operation of the engine. In the American model the pump was moved back, a better support added and an opening was arranged so that the leakage could pass to the outside of engine sump.

The overhead camshaft valve gear is the familiar Bugatti design, much like the later GP engines except that the cams bear on rollers on the rocker arm; the valve caps have the familiar button caps for adjustment. The exhaust valve design has the drilled hole oil mist pumping system (found later on the GP engines), as the following quotation will indicate.

The exhaust valve stem is hollow from the head to within a short distance of the necked portion at the upper end. The hole is closed at the head end by a short threaded plug screwed in below the surface of the valve, the recess then being filled level with the surface of the valve by welding. This closes the hole tightly and locks the plug in position. The lower end of the exhaust valve stem is of larger diameter than the upper end. Both the large and small diameters take a bearing in the valve guide. At the shoulder formed by the junction of the two sizes of stem three $\frac{3}{32}$ in. holes are drilled at an angle of 30 degrees with the

axis of the stem sloping towards the head of the valve and connection with the drilled hole in the stem. At the upper end of the stem just below the necked portion a $\frac{5}{32}$ in. hole is drilled through the wall of the stem. The movement of the valve up and down in the guide cause a pumping action, the transfer of air within the valve stem being thought to cool the stem to a certain extent. This drilling also lightens the valve.

The magneto driving gear has an interesting advance and retard mechanism seen later on the GP cars.

The gear has four internal spiral grooves sliding over splines on the sleeve which is keyed to the driving shaft, but may be moved along the shaft by lever. The movement of this sleeve revolves the magneto driving gear in relation to the shaft driving gear, thus advancing or retarding the magnetos.

The 8 cylinder engine

Some details have come to light on the 200 hp 8 cylinder aero-engine licenced in 1916 to Diatto at Turin (from *Motori Aero Cicli et Sports*, November 1916). This engine, which was also licenced to Delaunay-Belleville, preceded the 16 cylinder engine licenced to Duesenberg. The photographs in the article, however, show it to be of exceptionally clean appearance with a rear camshaft drive (the 16 cylinder engine had a central drive to each bank), and cross-located magnetos and water pump, all similar to the Type 13 or Black Bess. At the front is a propeller

The 8 cylinder Diatto-built Bugatti engine.

reduction gear and an oil pump in the centre appears to be driven by spur gears from a gear on the mid-point of the split crankshaft. The cylinders were in two blocks of 4 cylinders, 120 mm × 160 mm, with 4 valves per cylinder, obviously designed by Bugatti immediately after his 4 valve Type 27 engine which he had had to leave behind, buried, at Molsheim.

We do not know what happened to the engine, but evidently Bugatti, as part of his work on the 16 cylinder engine, made a few 8 cylinder versions, presumably then using its 3 valve layout. One at least was sent over to Duesenberg.

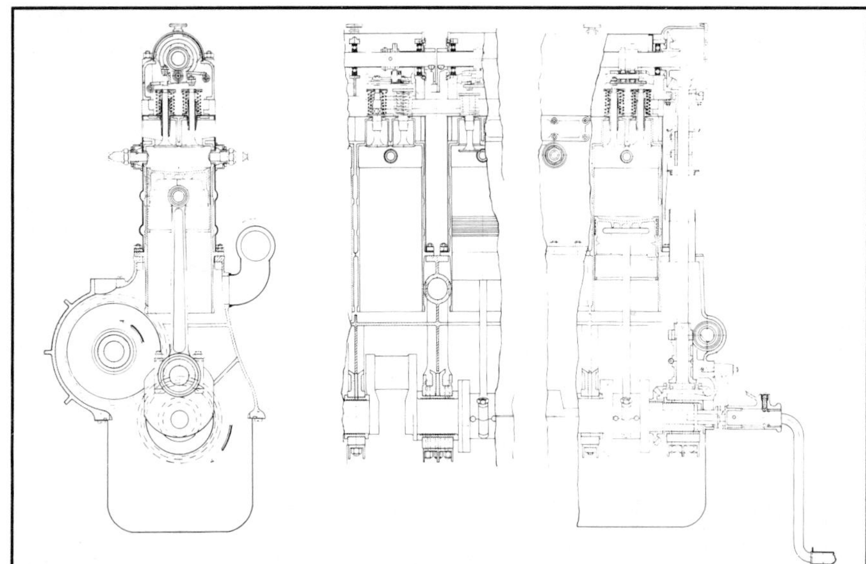

Section drawing of the Diatto engine representing the state of Bugatti's design art in 1916.

The first Breguet-Bugatti engine, 32 cylinders!

The Breguet-Bugatti

After the war the French aircraft company Breguet took up a licence of the 16 cylinder Bugatti engine in order to couple two together, initially in-line but stepped, and later in H-form, with 16 cylinders inverted. These were required to engine Breguet's plans for a large commercial transport, the Type 20 Leviathan. A few were made but evidently the aircraft itself did not proceed. To quote from an early issue of *Jane's All the World's Aircraft* (Samson Low, 1920 ed.):

Two Bugatti units are set in line, turned end for end, with the crankshafts of one unit at a lower line than the other, and all four shafts gear into a common spur wheel, which drives a single airscrew shaft carried on special bearings under the crankcase of the upper of the two units. But instead of the pinion of each crankshaft being firmly keyed to its crankshaft, an automatic clutch is interposed between each crankshaft and its gear.

The details of the clutch gear are not discoverable, but each clutch is operated by a short length of quick-thread screw on the crankshaft end, in such wise that if any one crankshaft is being driven by its cylinder at a speed less than that corresponding to the speed of the screw-shaft, the clutch is automatically withdrawn, and if it again picks-up speed unloaded in excess of that corresponding to the main shaft, it automatically re-clutches itself.

Thus the arrangement provides the equivalent of four eight-cylinder engines complete with driving gears.

As compared with the German multiple unit power plants for driving a common airscrew there is a marked saving in space, and one imagines in weight.

The unit is of 800 hp and the space occupied is about three metres long by one metre wide by 1·5 m high – including gears, clutches and starting motor.

Judging from the illustration in *Jane's* the engine was nearer 6 m long than 3 and it is no wonder that Breguet soon produced another version in the form of an H, although several of the tandem types were produced and fitted and flight tested in the Berguet Type 20 Leviathan in 1922. One of these much more compact engines is still in the Musée de l'Air in Paris, alongside two samples of the earlier one (but not at the time of writing on public display in the Museum's new site at Le Bourget). This was claimed to produce 1,000 hp and was fitted and tested to a later version of the Leviathan, Type 21. However, a 1,000 hp engine at that time was an ambitious target even for a large and experienced aero-engine maker and Breguet was probably not up to the task.

American engines

A sample American-made engine No. J46, dated 14 January 1919, is in the hands of the National Air Museum of the Smithsonian Institution in Washington D.C. (Plate 322). Another is in the USAF Museum at the Wright-Patterson A.F. Base, Fairborn, Ohio. What happened to most of the remaining engines is not known but Mr O.A. Phillips writes:

In the late 20s and early 30s, I had considerable experience with these engines, as a close friend of mine had two, which he used as wind machines for both the movies and for blowing away flames in oil-well fires. They were also used occasionally to defrost orange groves, by circulating the air over large areas. Unfortunately my friend was killed in 1937 when he lost his footing and fell into the propeller blades of one of these wind machines during a motion picture. I do not know what became of his engines, but believe they were scrapped during World War II.

Mr Phillips has recounted also how one engine was fitted to a power boat used by a bootlegger during Prohibition to run whisky from Lower California (Mexico) to the Los Angeles coast; how he kept another as an exchange engine; and how at last the US Customs managed to intercept the fast boat, which was scuttled to avoid capture; and he believes he knows where a Bugatti engine lies in the bay!

The Type 34 engine project of 1925. The engine may not have been built but the cylinder block formed the basis of the Royale engine.

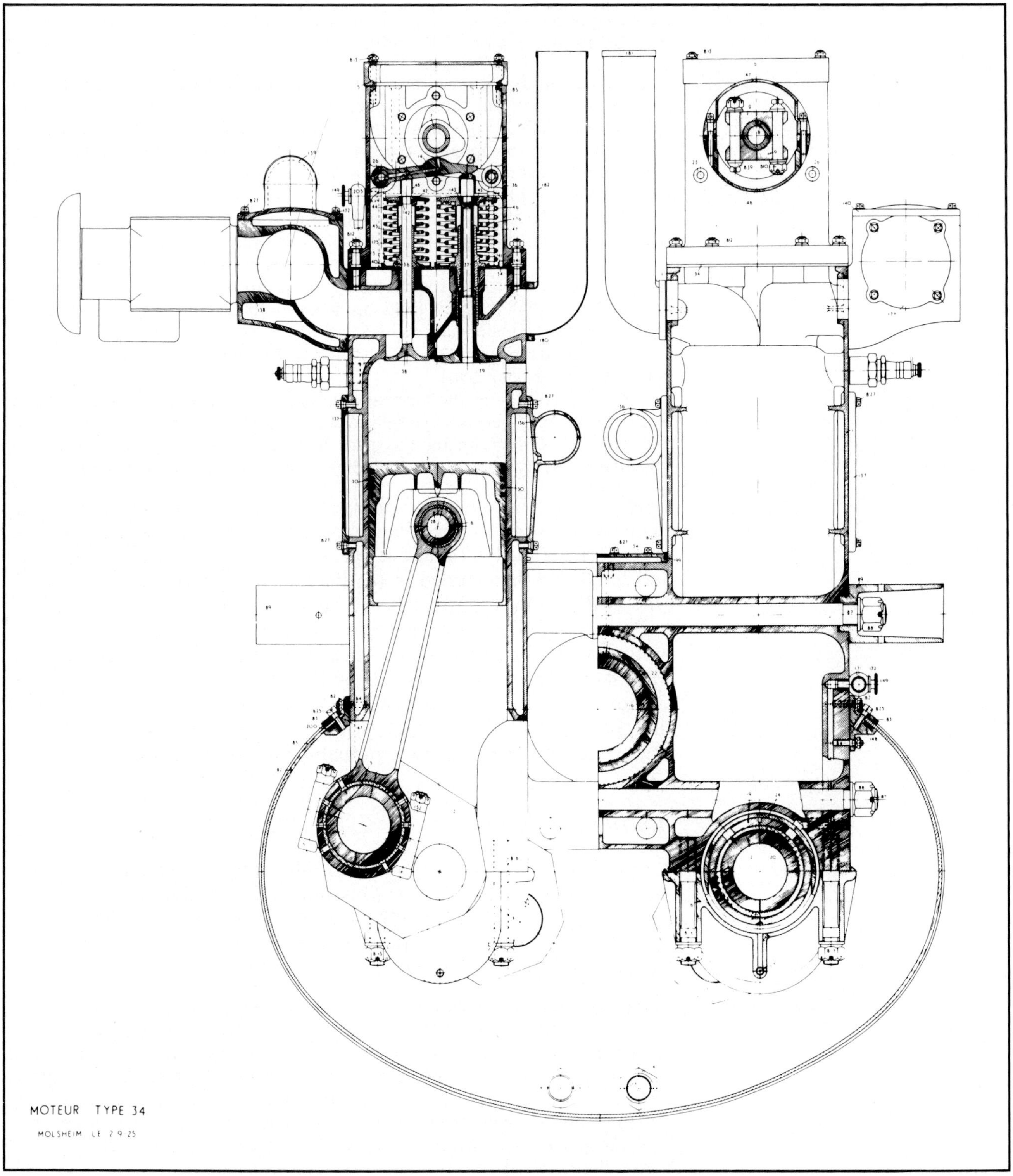

MOTEUR TYPE 34

MOLSHEIM LE 2.9.25

The Type 34 engine of 1925

No details of Bugatti's interest or activity in the aero-engine field after the war are known other than that he produced a design for a large 16 cylinder engine, 125 mm × 180 mm, very similar in general outline to the wartime unit. The original drawing is dated 2 September 1925. The design is perhaps of interest as illustrating the system of suspension of the crankshaft directly from the cylinder block, as used in the Royale, T50 etc. The main bearings also seem to be water cooled, as on the Royale. the crankshaft appears to have proper pressure lubrication at last – perhaps Ettore had decided that Mr King was right after all.

Brescia aero-engine

In 1925 Louis de Monge (see below) was experimenting with 'Flying Wing' aircraft where all passengers and crew would be housed within the wing. He built a scale model of his design, known as Type V, using two standard Bugatti Brescia engines, and extolled the virtue of using standard automobile power plants, which could be started on the handle, inside the plane, instead of requiring the dangerous practice of swinging the propeller! The aircraft flew a few times but nothing came of it.

Type 50B aero-engine

In 1938 Jean was working on the 4·9 litre 50B engine, an improved and lightened Type 50 engine for the racing car programme. Ettore evidently thought of its adaptation for aircraft use, since an announcement in the French press on October 22 of that year refers to his intentions. He must have been able to convince the French Air Ministry, since his contract for an aeroplane to beat world records in August 1938 (see below) specified the engine, and gave him orders for a number.

The engines were to be used coupled and contra-rotating in the aircraft, achieved by mirror-handing one of the pair. The engine was otherwise similar to the racing car engine which produced over 475 hp on test but was de-rated to about 400 hp, thus 800 hp for the aircraft.

The aircraft was not finished due to the invasion of France in 1940, and the engines eventually went to the USA for use in car applications.

The Bugatti aeroplane

In 1938 Bugatti set up a special design office in the rue du Debarcadère, Paris, and began to build an aeroplane under a French Air Ministry contract which offered him substantial prize money if he broke the World's speed record (at the time held by Howard Hughes with a land-based machine bearing his name at 352.5 mph, although the absolute record was held by Agello in a Macchi seaplane at 440.6 mph) and another prize if the aircraft broke the record for the 100 km closed circuit, as represented by the Coupe Deutsch de la Meurthe. He had enlisted the (essential) help of Louis de Monge, a well-known Belgian aircraft engineer living in Paris, to design the machine; there were two versions, differing in wing area, the smaller for extreme speed.

The two engines were in tandem behind the pilot, angled suitably and connected to a coupling and reduction box at the front to drive the contra-rotating Ratier propeller. Exhausts were outward, blowers central. The radiators were ingeniously housed in the tail of the aircraft, which was of 'butterfly' type with entry in the roof of the aerofoil, reverse flow through the radiators and exhausting forward. The wing had very complex flaps with automatic operation controlled by airspeed signals.

As already indicated the aircraft was not completed; it survived the war at the family chateau at Ermenonville and is now in the USA without engines. The pilot was to be Maurice Arnoux, later lost in combat flying for his country in 1940.

Bugatti boats

A model of Bugatti's transatlantic boat project was built, but the project got no further!

IN 1927 BUGATTI began to dream of building a boat that would cross the Atlantic, Brest to New York, in 50 hours. The boat was to be 35 metres long and 2·5 metres in width, with very low water drag; side elevators were to be used to assist the boat to plane. Eight engines each of 300 hp (perhaps versions of the Type 34 aero-engine) were to be used,

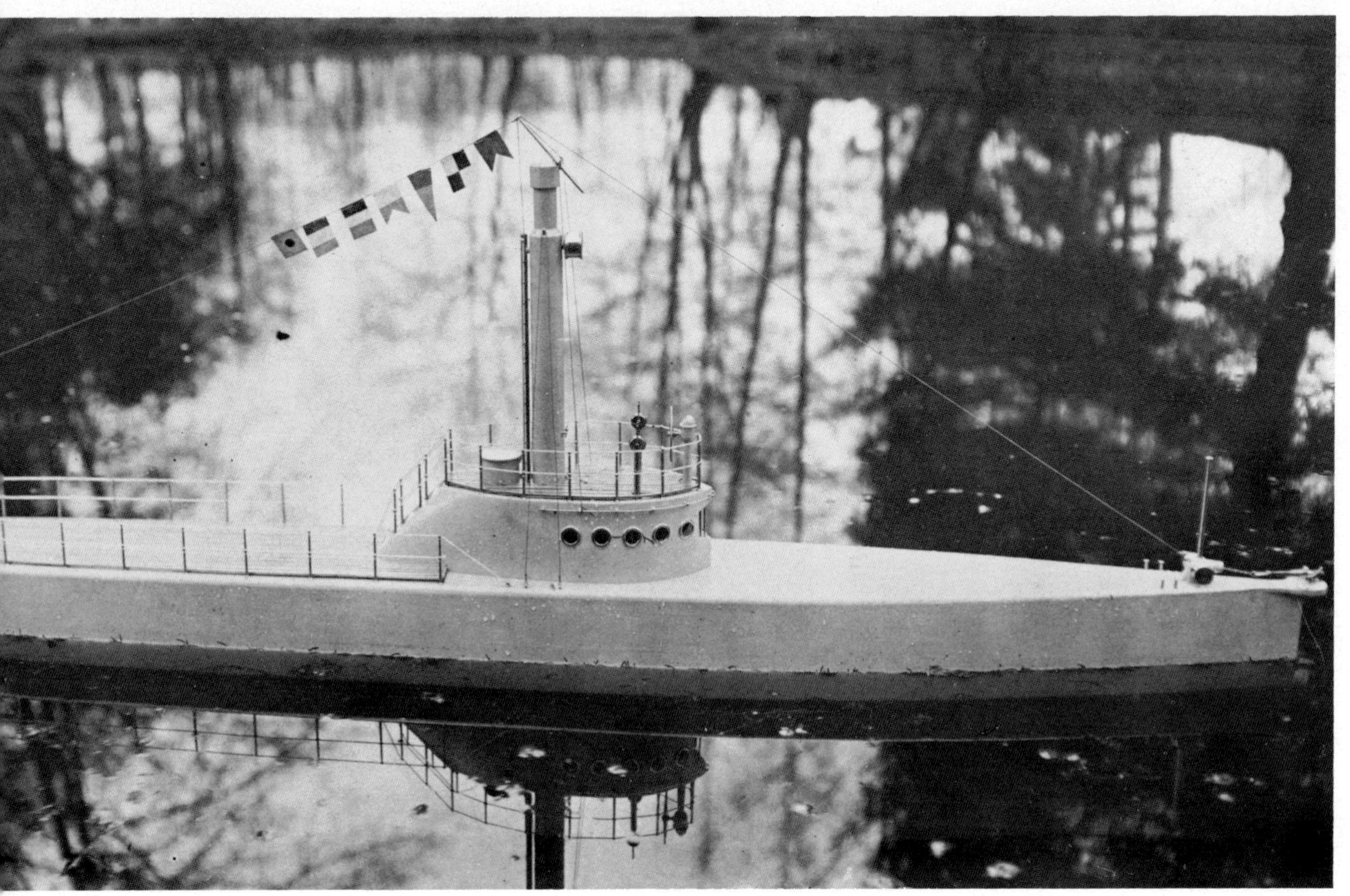

two with reverse gear. A ninth auxiliary engine looked after cooling air supply when the boat was at rest. The crew of eight could remain below deck, navigating from the bottom of the conning tower or in fine weather the captain could climb on to the bridge. The cruising speed was calculated to be 140 km/h (90 mph).

Nothing came of the design, but in 1939 Bugatti tried again with a shipyard at Deauville and when war came was designing a sailing yacht

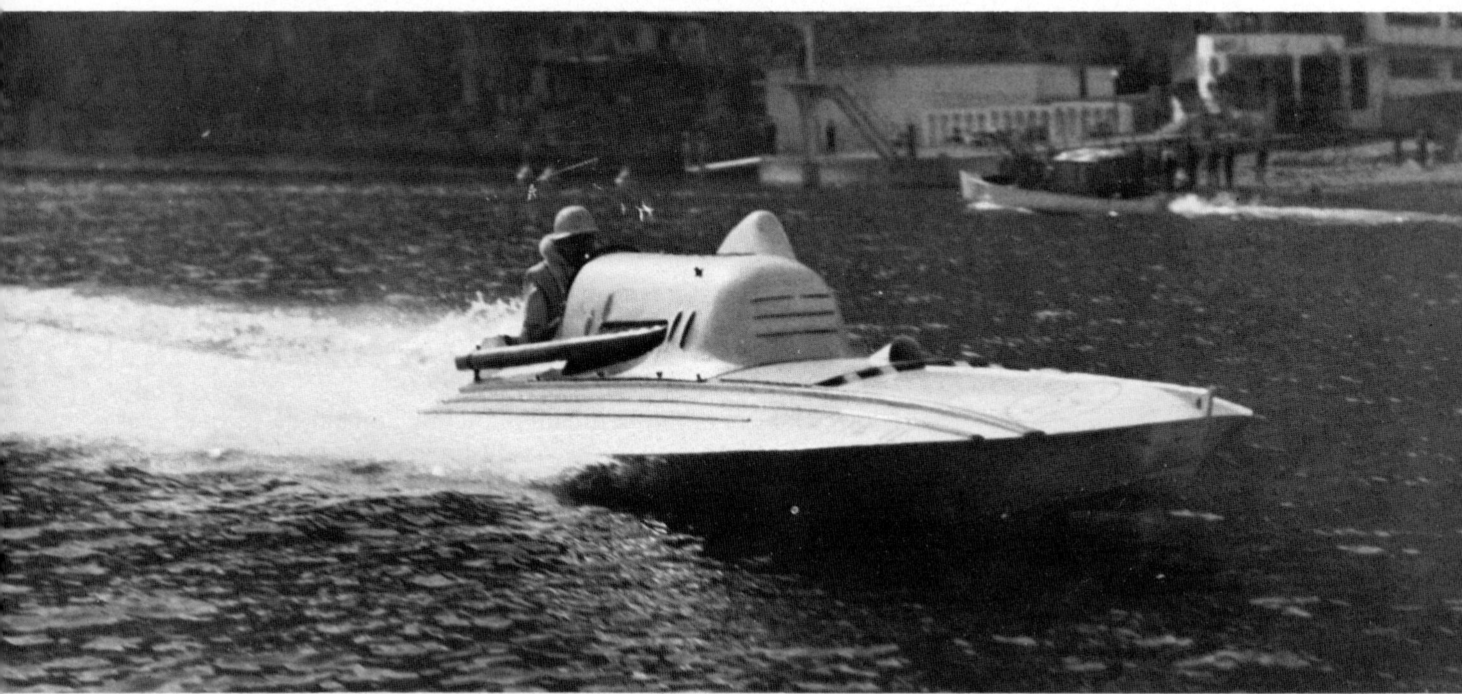

Prince Ruspoli's boat Niniette, *Bugatti engined, in 1932.*

The 'You-You' (dinghy) project of 1945, the half-sectioned show model in the Mulhouse Museum.

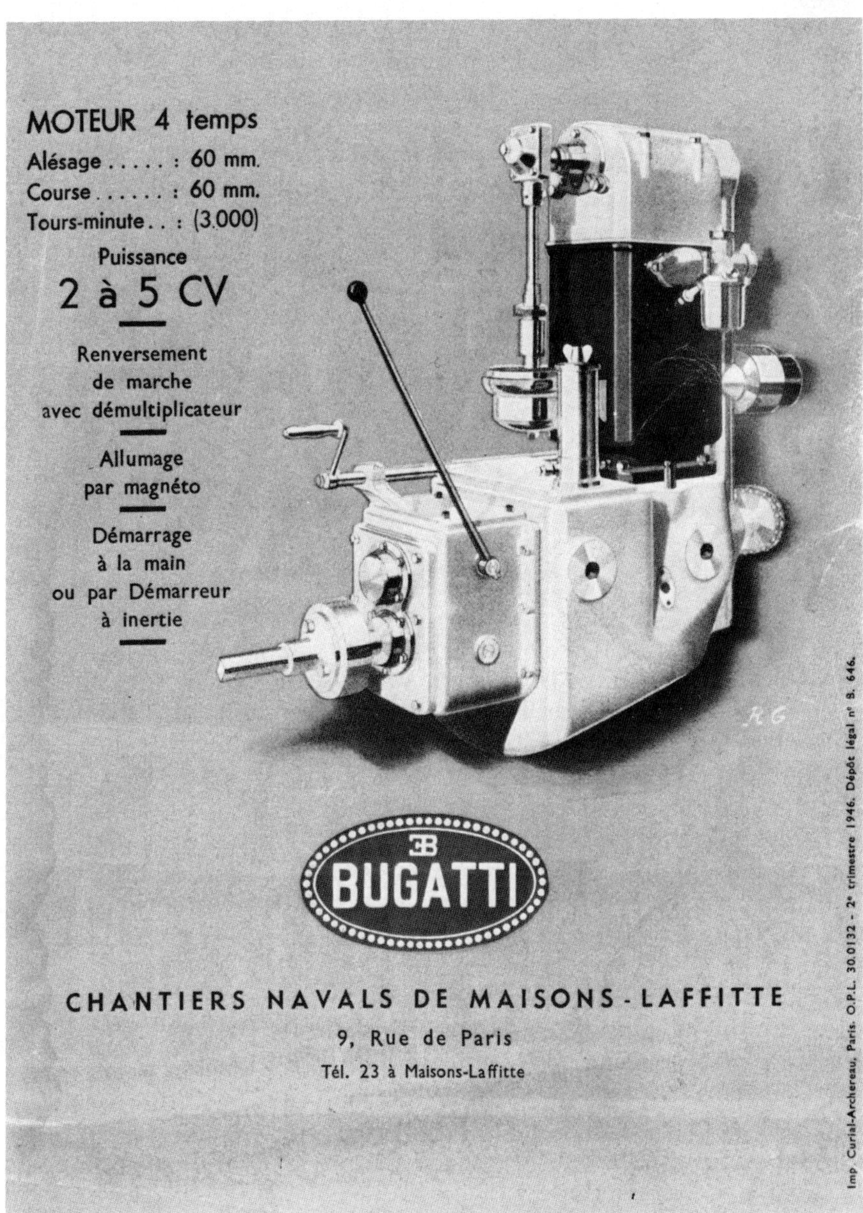

MOTEUR 4 temps
Alésage . . . . . : 60 mm.
Course . . . . . . : 60 mm.
Tours-minute . . : (3.000)
Puissance
2 à 5 CV
Renversement
de marche
avec démultiplicateur
Allumage
par magnéto
Démarrage
à la main
ou par Démarreur
à inertie
BUGATTI
CHANTIERS NAVALS DE MAISONS-LAFFITTE
9, Rue de Paris
Tél. 23 à Maisons-Laffitte
Imp. Curial-Archereau, Paris. O.P.L. 30.0132 - 2e trimestre 1946. Dépôt légal n° 8. 646.

The 1946 catalogue illustrated the single cylinder engine.

full of personal features, including a rotating reefing sail, and many of his versions of boat fittings. It was launched in 1940, taken by road to Le Havre as the Germans advanced and spent the war years in England. Although returned to France in 1945, Bugatti's death came too soon for it to be completed.

He had, prior to this, fitted engines to several racing boats and had won two world records for 6 litre boats (pilot Vasseur) and one for boats not exceeding 800 kg in weight, the latter with the boat Niniette* in the hands of the Italian Prince Ruspoli. Later Ettore purchased the shipyard Chantiers Naval de Maison-Laffitte but although he worked away during and after the war nothing became of this yard's boats. One was catalogued under the name 'You-You', which is French for dinghy, (believed to be Type 75), an open boat for 6 to 10 people, single cylinder engine forward, and available in lengths 10, 12 and 14 feet. One boat has survived with its single cylinder engine (Type 75), and a half section of another is in the National Museum at Mulhouse.

* After Lidia Bugatti's family nickname.

Bugatti railcars

BUGATTI concentrated from about 1932 on railcar design, producing three basic types, using the Royale engines as motive power. The first railcar was put into service in the summer of 1933 on the Paris–Deauville run, and ran regularly at a cruising speed of 70 mph. Later Jean Bugatti drove an autorail on the Paris–Strasbourg run of 320 miles, at an average of 90 mph and shortly afterwards gained a world record for a railway by completing 70 kilometres at an average speed of 196 km/h (122 mph). The three basic types produced were: a light type of 400 hp (two engines); a double type of 800 hp (four engines) with a single trailer; and a triple version with a trailer front and back.

The design made use of centrally-mounted engines driving the bogie wheels through hydraulic fluid-flywheel clutches, and propeller shafts. A reverse gear was included in the bevel boxes on the driving axles. The bogies themselves were fully sprung and so mounted as to give safety and an excellent ride, far removed from

The single Bugatti railcar, with the driver in the centre top.

the normal British railway bogie. The wheels were insulated from the steel tyre rims by a rubber layer. Brakes were mechanical, fully compensated and cable operated from a pneumatic cylinder.

The whole design of all types, owed little to any known railway practice and bristled with excellent and ingenious features. The main weakness was in the use of petroleum based fuel, in fact an alcohol-petrol-benzole mixture, which resulted in a high fuel consumption. At the time ethyl alcohol distilled from grain was cheap, but eventually the railways demanded Diesel which Bugatti was unable to provide.

Production at Molsheim in the 1930s was in a new shop and kept many busy.

The interior was light and elegant.

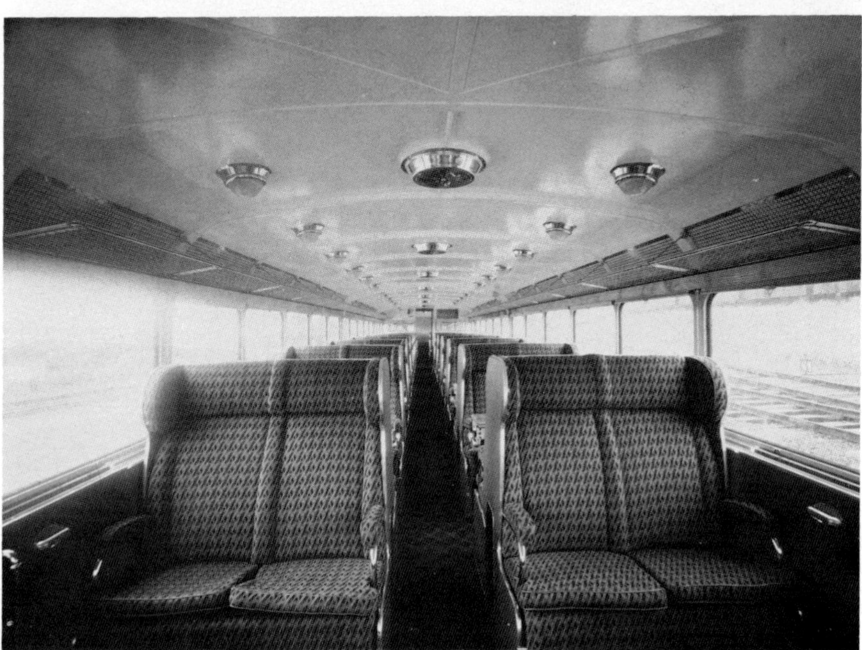

For most of the period 1932–39 it was railcar production that kept the factory going. Certainly the modern French high speed trains (TGV) seem in their appearance to have drawn much from the fine lines of the Bugattis.

The triple put the driver even further from the front. The train was most handsome, and a worthy forerunner to the modern French 'TGV'.

How fast is a Bugatti?

IF YOU DROVE a Bugatti in good and standard tune today, on a few miles of decent flat highway, how fast would it go? A Brescia would do about 70 mph; so would a Type 40. You might wind a Type 30 up to 75 mph if you have the nerve. With a Type 44 or 49 you should reach 80 mph. A good Type 43 should reach 95 mph without much trouble. At least two Type 43s can still exceed 100 mph with the screen down. The Type 50 was reputed to have reached 115 to 120 mph, but probably today 100 mph if reached would seem a bit hazardous. An ordinary Type 57 should touch 95 mph, a 57C the genuine 100 mph, and a 57S or 57SC at least 110 mph.

Racing models in all cases must have been able to exceed 100 mph. Today a typical 35B will reach 5,500 rpm in top at Silverstone (125 mph), and an unblown 2 litre 35 just over the hundred mark. The Type 59 3·3 litre was reputed to have been capable of 180 mph which may well have been true. A Type 35B belonging to Lehrfeld in Portugal (Car No. 4952) did a standing kilometre in August 1930 in 30·4 second and a flying kilometre a month later at 124·4 mph. However, if Bugattis get older, tuning methods and perhaps fuels do not: Mr P. Stubberfield's famous single-seat, Type 35B Bugatti did the kilometre at Brighton, post-war, in 26·96 sec, crossing the line with rather unsuitable hill-climb gearing at 120 mph at 6,000 rpm. Another T35B recently did the standing quarter mile in just over 14 sec. And a T51 has been timed, also recently, at the end of a standing kilometre at 140 mph. At Elvington in 1983, under proper timing conditions, a 35B did a standing kilometre in 26·64 secs, and a 51 in 24·90, well below the times achieved when the cars were new!

Some known acceleration data may be of interest. A good Type 43 (new in 1928, and at Brighton in 1959) did the standing kilometre in just under 35 sec; this is the equivalent of 0 to 60 mph in about 12 seconds. A Type 55 was timed accurately on 12 August 1932 and gave the following figures:

0– 60 mph	9·5 sec
0– 80 mph	24·55 sec
0– 90 mph	27·7 sec
0–112 mph	53·0 sec

These are as impressive for a 2·3 litre car today as in 1932.

In 1928 a T35B secured the world record for the standing start kilometre in 29·3 sec. In 1930 a T35C managed 26·9 sec for the same distance. In 1933 a T51 obtained world (Class D) records at 27·1 sec for the standing kilometre, which is rather slower than the smaller single-cam car. In 1930 Prince Lichenstein broke the world's Class E record for the standing mile in 38·29 sec (94·01 mph) in a T35C, a record which stood until 1961 when beaten by the Thompson dragster, fitted with a blown 420 bhp modified Tempest engine. Even in 1985 Bugatti still holds a few British national records! (Class F, 1·5 litres, 1 hour G. Eyston T39, 115·55 mph; 50 and 100 mile and kms, C. Staniland, T37A, circa 115 mph).

Mr W. Boddy has dug out the fastest Bugatti lap speeds at Brooklands including the following:

1914: 8 valve, Lambert, 72·7 mph
1921: (1920 Le Mans car?) 16 valve T13, Segrave, 75·69 mph
1923: Brescia, Marshall, 89·41 mph. (In the JCC 200 mile race in that year, Cushman running on alcohol came in 2nd at an incredible 91·1 mph)
1925: T30 Indianapolis single seater, Duller, 111·17 mph
1927: T35B, Eyston, 120·59 mph
1929: T37A, Staniland, 122·07 mph
1931: T35B, Penn Hughes, 127·97 mph
1934: T54, Froy, 134·97 mph
1935: T51, Staniland, 133·16 mph
1936: T59, Howe, 138·34 mph
1938: T51C, Brackenbury, 127·05 mph

These speeds will represent very nearly the maximum speeds of the cars.

'Le million'

IN 1934 THE French National Auto Club started a subscription to foster motor racing in France and to produce or subsidize a GP racing car to carry French Blue in International races. In 1937 the Government were persuaded to offer two prizes of 400,000 and 1,000,000 francs, respectively, for the fastest time achieved over 200 km of the road circuit at Montlhéry, and then for a similar contest, restricted to cars complying with the 1938–40 International formula (3 litre supercharged or 4·5 litre unsupercharged). The minimum qualifying speed was 2 per cent greater than the winning speed at Montlhéry in the 1934 French Grand Prix.

Wimille in a 3·3 litre supercharged Type 59 won the first prize in April 1937, completing the 200 km course (16 laps) at 146·65 km/h, or 4·9 sec below the maximum time. The second, million, prize was won with greater drama. The attempts had to be completed by 31 August and, as the circuit was not lighted, departures could hardly be made much after 6 p.m. On 23 August Bugatti made an attempt in a 4·5 litre unsupercharged single-seater (presumably with an unblown linered-down 50B engine). Wimille had been injured in a motor accident in the south of France and was still in hospital; the veteran Benoist drove, but failed by 9·5 seconds to achieve the set maximum time of 1 hour 21 min 54·4 sec (146·508 km/h) for the 16 laps, compared with Wimille's time which had bettered the average by 4·9 sec.

On 25 August René Dreyfus appeared on the scene with a 12 cylinder 4·5 litre unblown Delahaye single-seater, and then on the morning of 27 August he completed the 200 km at 146·65 or 4·9 sec better than the required average, and strangely enough the exact same time as Wimille had achieved in April.

On 30 August Wimille arrived once more on the scene, still scarred, but evidently fit and the battle was on! A few tests on the circuit with the Bugatti and a shaft in the gearbox broke. Back it went to Paris to be worked on all night. By 4 pm next afternoon it was again on the Track, the Delahaye team ready and waiting anxiously to start again should the Bugatti show signs of beating their time. Wimille did a few test laps and returned with a broken rear axle! '*The decision to change the unit was immediately taken*', wrote *L'Auto* of 1 September, '*and in 1 hour 10 min,*

the Bugatti mechanics had completed the operation – it was a "tour de force"'. Not a minute to be lost, as it was already late. At 6.43 pm exactly Wimille set off, followed two minutes later by Dreyfus in the Delahaye amid great excitement. Alas, on the second lap, Wimille came in to have a plug changed and set off again, but two laps later had to give up with 'cylinder trouble'. All was over – Dreyfus had deservingly won the 'million'!

Bugatti Coachwork

WHO BUILT the body on the beautiful Royale Roadster delivered in 1932 to Armand Esders? Consultation with Noel Domboy who was Technical Director at Molsheim before the war provided the answer and much data of historical importance.

Bugatti's building of bodywork, he writes, began in 1923 when he designed and built the 1923 AC de F Tours tank – the famous tank which was later to be copied by Bugatti himself and many others.

Then came the beautiful 1924 GP de Lyon Car and the classic body on the Grand Prix models. All subsequent single and two seat racing bodies were built at the works. By 1939, on the eve of war, the coachwork shops were well equipped with machine tools and equipment enabling them to make bodies for Type 57s, trimmed and finished in all respects.

This indeed had applied also to many bodies on Types 46, 46S, 49, 50, 55 and so on. The Esder Roadster was built at Molsheim in 1932. Domboy himself remembers clearly going over the works with Jean Bugatti at Easter that year, on the Saturday, and seeing the body in course of manufacture.

On the Type 57, Molsheim built:

- the Galibier coach or saloon (4 door)
- the 2 door Ventoux coach
- the coupé Atalante on 57C and 57S
- the coupé Atlantic on 57S and 57SC
- the 4 door saloon on the 1939 57C

An experimental 2 door 'Gull Wing' body was also tried out on the T64 but was abandoned as impracticable, and the Atlantic pursued instead. This anticipated by several years the Mercedes 300 SL 'Gull Wing'!

The racing tanks Type 57G which won at Le Mans in 1937 and 1939 were made in their entirety at the works, as well as the Model 64, the last creation of the pre-war period and still at the prototype stage when Jean Bugatti was killed in 1939.

The Gangloff firm at Colmar was another principal supplier of coachwork to Bugatti on several models (eg the Stelvio coupé) even after the war (on Types 101 and 101C). But as Mr Domboy points out, from the beginning of Type 57 production, the works produced the greater part of the bodywork.

It was Jean Bugatti himself who was really responsible for this works coachwork from a period which probably dated from about 1930. But in truth it is difficult to separate the role played by the two creators, Ettore Bugatti and his son Jean in the conception of these new models.

Taking over more and more the initiative, Jean Bugatti, as his father had done before him, made his own imprint on each new design, and contributed himself to the continuing success of the marque.

The conception, the design and the practical realization in the factory fell to him entirely. He instructed the preparation from his own ideas of small scale models, using drawings produced by the draughtsmen allocated to him personally; then outline drawings were made and finally when a particular model was adopted for production, the draughtsmen made outline drawings for the factory itself.

The closed coachwork (coach, coupé, berline, etc.) had a framework in wood (mainly in ash) on to which the sheet metal was nailed or screwed.

For each new model, the wood framework was first of all drawn out in full scale on a large vertical drawing board, giving:

- a vertical elevation
- a half view in plan
- longitudinal sections of the main forms of the body profile.

It is to be noted that these layout drawings, fully detailed in all aspects were used by the joiners in the body shop to determine the body lines under the orders of the Chief of the Coachworks and Jean Bugatti himself. The joiners then built the wood frames with their complex profiles as required by the layout drawings, assembling them by rebates and glue, and attaching them to the chassis by appropriate metal work.

At the same time the sheetmetal shop produced the covering sheet-work, the body sides, top, rear part, wings, bonnet (hood) and so on. These sheet parts were offered up to fit the woodwork, then welded to each other and attached as already indicated.

The coachwork joinery department was a section of the general woodwork shop, and had a considerable complement of wood working machines, as well as a large drying autoclave.

The sheet metal shop was fully equipped with all necessary machines for working sheet by the methods of contemporary sheet metal workers – shears, bending machines, presses, hammers, riveters, welding machines and so on.

Naturally this sort of hand made coachwork had no relation to the modern production methods which produce the many hundreds or even thousands of bodies a day of the modern car.

The trimming shop which had many highly skilled workmen, completed the trimming and upholstery of the bodies as well as the seats; and then finally there was the paint shop.

The Guide*

ALTHOUGH A Bugatti enthusiast of some years' standing, I am a hopeless mechanic, but when there's a job of work to be done there's no one more willing than I am to tackle it in the right and proper way, and the Guide Book is my constant companion.

Now for the benefit of those who perhaps are less gifted than I am, I will show you exactly how to set about any little job which may require attention.

In order to make sure that everything is functioning as it should I suggest that each page of the Guide Book be studied, and by carefully comparing what it says with what you know, you can tell at once whether all those little interesting processes which go on all the time inside the car are doing their job.

First of all take the Guide Book in your left hand (you will need your right to turn over the pages) and firmly open the cover. The cover only says, *E.B. Bugatti* surrounded by pearls, and 3L300 *Type 57*. This information is of so little use that you can now tear the cover off and throw it away.

The first page is completely blank on both sides, and I assume that this is intended to set your mind completely at rest in preparation for the task it is about to undertake.

We now come to page 1, and it is headed *Charactéristiques Générales*. Although, at first glance, this would appear to be something to do with Army manœuvres you will find by referring to your dictionary that it merely sets out in order all those things you can see for youself by looking at the car.

Page 2 is far more important. It says *Précautions D'usage Courant*. It is a serious warning, but do not worry unduly. I am assuming that you have already used your car, and as this merely tells you all those things which are essential before you do, as you have, things must be all right otherwise it wouldn't, if you understand.

For instance – *placer le levier de changement de vitesse au point mort*. I mean you are bound to have known if you hadn't.

And again – *s'être assuré que le frein à main est serré et des niveaux d'eau du radiateur, d'huile du carter-moteur ainsi que de la provision de combustible*, etc. You simply couldn't have motored at all if you hadn't, especially the combustible – I like that word.

Therefore both sides of this page have been dealt with and, as you know them by heart, you can tear them out and throw them away. It will save you time next time you refer to the Guide.

Page 3 has a pretty picture so you can keep this one, especially as it tells you what to do when you get back, *à la rentrée au garage*. This is far more

* *Bugantics*, 6, 6, pp. 25–6, November 1937.

important than going out, because *pour arrêter le moteur, retirer la clef de contact.*

If you fail in this important procedure little will be left of your 3L300 Type 57 when you go to the garage the next morning.

Before turning to page 4, note the heading at the foot of page 3, *Réglage du Moteur*. My dictionary tells me that this means 'Regulating the Motor', and the diagrams that follow are frightful and far beyond my limited compression – I mean comprehension. Also it tells me to *Demonter le couvercle de l'arbre à cames*, and I simply wouldn't dare, would you? Then I advise that you tear out this page and throw it away – it will only confuse you.

Page 5 is a continuation of page 4 only worse, but it goes on to tell you all about *Allumage*. This sounds very much like *Réglage*; in fact, most things in the Guide seem to end in 'age', and it is probably done to rhyme with garage.

Both pages 6 and 7 talk about *Réglage* again, its awful the amount of this that seems necessary, and in any case I would never dare tamper with a *Carburateur*, especially a thing full of *pompes*. We now come to the *Réglage* (there it is again) *des Freins*. The first line says, however *le réglage des freins est correct*. Well, they must know best so don't worry, just pass on to page 9, *Graissage*.

I find this rather puzzling. In addition to keeping one eye on the speedometer to make sure that the 30 mph limit is not being exceeded, you must also keep this same eye on the mileage department. As you go along you must indulge in mental arithmetic and as soon as you reach 187·5 miles your quick calculation will tell you that it is equivalent to 300 kilometres, and you must jump down and *nettoyer le filtre du moteur* (*fig. 9*). My dictionary translates this as to clean, to cleanse, to scour, to sweep, to wipe, to pick. This apparently could mean 'Pick 9 figs from the moving strainer', but I don't believe this is really what they mean.

And again, as soon as you reach 312·5 miles you find this is 500 kilometres, and once more you must dismount, but horrors, you must now *Graisser les articulations de la bielle du direction, les axes des jumelles des ressorts AV et les pivots de fusée* (*seringue speciale*) *voir fig. 12*. If you are like me, you must again refer to the dictionary, and it tells me to 'Dirty the allegation of the Government Rod (or should it be Whip?) the semi-detached axle of the front lock, and the hinge of the intricate business (the peculiar squirt). Examine 12 figs'. Or have I got it wrong?

Well, anyway, you probably get the hand of things now. Personally, I've thrown the Guide away. I find Brixton easier.

ELGY

A Bugatti controversy*

BUGATTI'S CARS have frequently been involved in heated controversy, due no doubt to an unusual blend of qualities leading (certainly) to endearment and (sometimes) hysterical enthusiasm, and faults which irritate or leave cold the less sensitive (or is it sensible?) of car owners. An enchanting example, probably forgotten and certainly worth recording, is contained in the *Automotor Journal*, 25, 1920. (This journal was founded by Stanley Spooner in 1896 and ceased publication about 1932.)

An excellent illustrated description of the 1920 models is given in the 8 July issue, this referring to the 4 cylinder models as Types 22 and 23 (the latter with a longer wheel-base), and shows the steering box separate from the engine bearer unlike the later models. The engine size in both models is 68 mm × 100 mm (most people consider that Type 23 is always 69 × 100).

The fun begins on 9 September when the contributor 'Omega', referring to the success of the car at the 1920 Le Mans race, was so bold as to suggest that 'sensible people know that a machine like the Bugatti is built primarily to race, although [he] was prepared to hear that a Bugatti can be a very pleasant little car for ordinary driving'. On 23 September 'Omega' had to defend himself with a whole column against numerous correspondents:

They tell me, with one accord, and almost in identical phrases, that the Bugatti is eminently a touring car. I receive their protests. I have never personally handled, nor even sat in, a car of this make. But turning up my *Auto* of 8 July last, I find that the 1920 standard model Bugatti of 12 hp nominal rating, with a cylinder-bore of 68 mm, has two inlet and two exhaust valves to each of its businesslike four cylinders, and enormously long pistons, with four rings apiece, and other signs of something more than 'touring' efficiency in the mind of the man responsible for the design.

Now it may well be that duplex valve-ing is something to which nearly all manufacturers may come in time, excepting those who go to the other extreme and do without valves (as generally so-called) altogether. But for the present I regard the mere duplication of valves as suggesting racing, or extreme, high, 'stunt' efficiency practice. This being so, I am not going to take back what I said. A machine like the Bugatti – I quote my exact words – is built primarily

* Originally published in the *Bulletin VSCC* No. 66, Spring 1960.

to race, although I am prepared to hear that a Bugatti can be a very pleasant little car for ordinary driving. My withers are unrung. I am prepared to be prepared, because my sagacious friend Lefrère, of Messrs Jarrot & Letts Ltd, tells me that if he sat me blindfolded in a Bugatti, in standard tune (which means one good for 70 to 80 mph on a straight stretch of level British road), and drove me along at from 35 to 40 miles per hour, I should never dream that I was on something which had twice the speed-potentiality tucked away under its bonnet.

This is all very well. I accept anything Lefrère tells me, about either cars or cider; and I am equally satisfied of the truth of the statements made in this matter by other friends, so many of whom have written me more or less abusively.

In the same issue was a letter from a Lt-Colonel C. Dawson in defence of the car. He was almost certainly the previous owner of the famous Peter Hampton Type 13. 'I can assure Omega', he says, 'that the Bugatti is an extraordinarily pleasant little car to drive in an ordinary way, and will go so far as to say that we have nothing to touch it here'.

On 30 September 'Omega' contributed this interesting column:

It appears that this gentleman's own Bugatti is of fairly early date (about 1912, I gather), and was originally fitted with a saloon body. It was, in fact, essentially a touring car, although possessed of ginger and running-freedom notably in excess of those of most standard cars. Thus its owner is quite justified in saying that the Bugatti is just as suitable a car for everyday touring use as for stunts of the Le Mans circuit order.

Further than this, my friend (who is also Colonel Dawson's friend, and has personally satisfied himself of the magnificent running of the Colonel's eight-year-old car only this summer) tells me something about M. Bugatti which makes interesting reading. Directly the results of the voiturette race were published, he wrote M. Bugatti, asking him if he could have one of the cars used in the Grand Prix, to run at Brooklands.

And how did the constructor reply: 'You can, possibly, but why do you specify one of the racing cars, when every Bugatti of this year will give you practically the same performance? Please understand, my dear man, that I never did and never will build two sorts of cars – one for sale and the other for demonstrations. Any performance of one Bugatti is easily repeated with another Bugatti. We do not build "special" chassis. Some seem better than others, because no two articles made even by the most skilled artificers are ever exactly alike in performance. But we have always a minimum standard of efficiency, and it is perhaps because we allow to leave the factory nothing which will not come up to this minimum standard of efficiency that our factory remains comparatively small, and modest as to its production.

'I could build six times the number of cars if I were satisfied to let anything with a Bugatti name-plate go forth on to the road as a Bugatti. But I am not. Our disposition, here, is that we will not allow to leave our gates any car which we are not perfectly satisfied will represent us with credit.

'Thus if you want a car for Brooklands you simply want a car – any car we ship you. It is idle of us even to try to "tune" it for you, there being such surprising differences in your atmosphere and ours, and your fuel and ours. Let me send you the next car I can spare, and do what you can with it. You will not be disappointed.'

Now this is a very free translation of M. Bugatti's remarks, but the 'freedom' is imported merely to make clear his exact meaning, in English English.

Is it not a magnificent working-principle? Is not that the spirit in which every constructor should regard his productions? It may well be that one Bugatti is enough for France, and that one similar product would, at present, be enough for England. But that is the spirit we want at work, on a car of the Bugatti type in this country.

'Omega' goes on to wonder if there is a market in Britain for a car of the Bugatti type, necessarily of rather high price; he remarks that Bugatti owners appear, one and all, deeply to resent a word of seeming depreciation (we still do!)

On 14 October a new contestant enters the battle in the shape of Mr G.P.H. de Freville, the designer of the Alvis car, and the sparks begin to fly; de Freville claims to have 'considerable experience of this car' and supports the views of Colonel Dawson as to its excellence. He was interested 'in "Omega's" remarks in regard to whether there is a Bugatti market in this country; this is a question which (he had) been trying to solve for a long time.' Well, well! So the Alvis sprang from Bugatti stimulus. 'Omega' in a footnote to the letter becomes petulant: 'with regard to the Alvis of which so many of us have heard so much, I will leave it to Mr de Freville the explanation of the reason that I never saw and tried his car, despite his making an appointment to do so'.

On 21 October Mr Lionel Martin, joining the fray, answers 'Omega' that he, in the Aston Martin, is trying to design a British Voiturette de luxe, having put the prototype on the road since Easter, 1915, and after 80,000 miles of development hopes shortly to put it on the market. 'While I have had in mind', he says, 'during the designing period the excellent and lively little machine which bears (Bugatti's) name, I have also used as a standard the typically English Rolls-Royce and it is a blend of these two cars which I hope to produce'. Another one for the Patron! The correspondence continues in later weeks, mostly acrimonious and quibbling back and forth on what was or was not said, or meant, and then, on 18 November, the Editor really drops a brick in the editorial description of the Bugatti at the 1920 Olympia Show – detachable head and a 3-speed gearbox included! There are 'overhead valves in extravagant profusion', and he thinks the 710–90 tyres too large.

The next week 'Omega' replies to the Colonel': 'Anyhow, now that I have seen his pet at Olympia I think it more than ever remarkable that such a fly-weight should run at all. I agree with [the] technical writers that the engine looks "hot" but the rest of the chassis is not at all what I had expected. I hope that there is more in the Colonel's 1912 chassis, otherwise when one of these days I ram him in my 1921 Horstman, his mount will be sadly crumpled.'

The correspondence ends on 23 December with a further objecting letter from Colonel Dawson to which 'Omega' added a footnote:

> I fear that I cannot follow the hon. and gallant member through his mazy intricacies. I can only pray for another war, to distract his attention, and offer my heartfelt sympathy to anybody who has ever sold him anything, or corresponded with him about anything. I have again read through his letters, and found five more points on which I should like to question him, but forbear. His announcement that a veil must descend evidently means that he has been rash enough to go for a run on his dear old Bugatti, and must now go into dock for a spell. Only one protestation – I am not a 'critic'. I leave criticism to a brutal and licentious soldiery.

After which further comment is (temporarily) impossible!

The sequel

A noticeable change however takes place in the following year (1922).

In February 'Omega' begins to weaken:

I have been learning a little more about this very special voiturette chassis. I have not yet tried it, but I have been privileged to look into the experience of a number of owners. And really to read and hear what they say about it, you would wonder that anything else had ever sold anywhere at anything but Ford price! I have seen pictures of it with two, three and four-seated bodywork, and fuel-consumption-records, and speed-stunts, and tyre-mileage, and bills for replacement-parts over five years (and 120,000 miles). Now I am sitting down awaiting with what patience I can muster the day when I can see if all that these good people say about the car is justified by the behaviour of this year's model.

We know perfectly well that a man who has decent luck with his first car swears by its manufacturers for the rest of his life, as a rule. But these Bugatti-enthusiasts are no novices, revelling in the first flush of possession, and over-looking little things which would annoy old stagers. In at least fifty per cent of cases they are people who bought Bugattis when they were using other, larger cars. They bought Bugattis to be able to flip-about speedily on errands which could be done by a two-seater; but during the doing of those jobs of work they wanted to enjoy the refinement of performance to which they were accustomed on much larger and more powerful cars. Well, they all seem to have one opinion, and that decidedly complimentary to M. Ettore Bugatti and Alsace, and – as I have hinted – if the coach-builders keep up their promised date, by about the time these words are in print I should be in a position to join the gladsome, if still small, band of Bugattini, and raise my voice to swell their chorus of praise [3 February 1921].

A few weeks later (24 February) he has to defend himself against a correspondent who wonders why people buy Bugattis at high prices when similar performance can be obtained with the British light cars. 'Omega' retorts:

There are, however, buyers for all the Bugattis Messrs Chas. Jarrott and Letts, Ltd, are likely to get, this year or next, to be recruited from among people who would not look at a car of the type and class amply satisfying [the gentleman from Leicester]. These are people who are becoming small car users by stress of circumstances, or by conviction. They have given up, or are giving up, big fast cars.... There are many of those people, wanting high efficiency at low running-cost, that they will readily absorb all the chassis M. Bugatti can produce. The British sole concessionaires are advertising the 'Bug.', I understand. But M. Bugatti has never done so. He does not think it necessary to do so now. He sells chassis today as Antonio Stradivari sold fiddles, in old Cremona; steadily, but only as he builds them (which means every one as fine as he knows how) and when he builds them (which means as soon as he can, they being as they are).

In the weeks that follow the signs of weakness continue as 'Omega' enjoys his Bugatti (a 16 valve 2 seater Type 22)! By 13 October 1921 he is fully indoctrinated:

The great delights of the Bugatti, as I find them, are its wonderful acceleration (accompanied by marvellous freedom from over-run), its suspension, its steering, and that wonderful bubbling song of the exhaust, be the cut-out opened ever so modestly. Fully open, the little beast sounds like the whole of Brooklands paddock gone mad. But only a hog would use it fully open within a mile of any houses, so we need not worry about that!

Oh! I forgot another charm – the marvellous ease and lightness and surety of the speed-changing mechanism. A finger suffices to engage any gear; two fingers suffice to shift the lever across the pretty little gate; and the merest pat of the clutch-pedal is all that is required. I double all my changes, up and down, from habit, and I don't intend to drop a good habit, because to do so would spoil me for other cars I have to drive, by way of making a living. But I have already discovered that one can get third-to-fourth or fourth-to-third changes cleanly and noiselessly without touching the clutch-pedal at all, and I can well believe that Bugatti experts, like Cushman, Blackstock, Major Lefrère and Colonel Dawson can go right through the four changes without declutching, as I am told.

L'Amende Honorable! Now to grovel! Suitably garbed in a white sheet, a halter round my neck, ashes on my head and contrition in my errant heart, I apologize to Colonel Dawson for having ever doubted any of the charming things he said about his Bugatti.

He was quite right. Before mine is run-in, I agree that it is a touring car, at will, though it is also a little terrestrial flying-maching, at will. But it can be driven, even in its first 1,000 miles, as smoothly and sweetly and economically as the woolliest, heaviest old hay-barge imaginable, if one will make full use of the gearbox (put there to be used) and watch one's spark-lever. It will dawdle along at 20 mph in the sedatest manner imaginable....

Colonel Dawson was right, and I was wrong, and I regret all the nasty, petulant things I was provoked to write, when he was justly belabouring my imprudent head. Don't shoot, Colonel! I have already 'come down'!

A surprising, but happy ending to an interesting quarrel!

Colonel Sorel

Bugatti in London

BUGATTI OPENED a branch in London in 1926 since Britain was perhaps his most important market after France, and Col. Sorel was appointed Manager. The story of the early days is best told by the late Mr M.E. Bouldin.

I joined Charles Jarrott & Letts, Westminster in 1923. They were the London concessionaires for Crossley Motors. Earlier than this Bugatti had arranged for Crossleys of Manchester to manufacture 25 cars under licence to be known as 'Crossley-Bugattis'. Charles Jarrott & Letts were agents for all these Crossley-Bugattis and followed up by becoming sole agents in England for Bugatti cars. Early in 1926 Ettore Bugatti opened a Sales and Service branch at 1–3 Brixton Road, London SW9. I was offered the post of storekeeper by Colonel Sorel the Managing Director of this London branch. The job for me lasted 14 years until the closure in 1940 due to the war; it was both interesting and varied. I dealt with customers, technical letters, was receptionist for customers bringing their cars for repairs and helped with sales. This sounds a great deal by modern standards of high pressure business but we were only a small concern consisting of a total staff of 15 or 16 for the first 5 years then reduced to about 10.

When the first consignment of chassis and spares, benches and machines, arrived at Brixton from Molsheim there also came over Messrs Marco, Mischal and Lück. Monsieur Marco, a very competent mechanic, endeavoured to practice the thoroughness of the methods used at Molsheim. He had proved himself earlier as a worthy driver of Bugatti cars in many races. After a brief stay he and Lück returned to the works leaving Mischal behind in the capacity of works foreman, a position he held until 1939 when he was compelled to join the French forces. Luckily for him he never left England, instead he was chauffeur to a high ranking official of the French Navy in London and when France capitulated he was discharged, enabling him to use his skill in an engineering works. [The British representatives of the Messier Company who now own Bugatti!] I never met him after 1940 although our association during the 14 years was close. Other mechanics joining the Brixton staff were J. Hanham, F. Blackman, L. Phyllis, each of these being previously with Charles Jarrott & Letts. The first named, J. Hanham, stayed with Bugatti London until the end and even after the war ended in 1945 he still carried on servicing the same named cars for J. Lemon Burton – a total of twenty odd years. I would describe Hanham as patient and reliable – maybe the cars he worked upon helped to fashion this attitude for in no way could hurried incompetence achieve any satisfactory

results with cars of Bugatti design; often it was necessary to dismantle far more to overhaul a unit than in other makes of cars, but then the designer did not consider this fact of major importance. One other person who was a member of the works staff was P.E. Thomas who for a time after leaving joined Leo Villa helping to service cars raced by Sir Malcolm Campbell; from there he was in the employ of Lord Howe assisting in the successes achieved with several racing models of Bugatti.

One very important omission of the Molsheim technical staff was data for the customer and even for the works at Brixton; we had to obtain information the best way possible, even a trip to Molsheim by Mischal to get timing, clearances etc for the latest model was almost a stealthy process and he in turn was reluctant to part with the information obtained. I can only believe that the purpose was to discourage unqualified mechanics even to commence overhauls.

Although I was unable to speak French and nobody at the Factory used English I managed to glean from advice notes and invoices the name and sometimes part number of parts sent, gradually building up a satisfactory spares description. Many times my orders to Molsheim showed drawings of the required part instead of their detail, and although Colonel Sorel spoke very fluent French he left this to me as my method produced the required goods. I remember on one occasion he sent a telegram ordering a special part to be sent by air and back came the wrong part, a mistake by the storekeeper at Molsheim. I mention the above details to illustrate what to me was an inexcusable failing in an organization where precision was very important. A weak link in the chain!

The arrival of new chassis from the works was always a special event, and LEP Transport used to bring them invariably on high platform lorries using skids to get them off. The men from the workshop manœuvred them whilst I sat on the tool box tied across the chassis steering; sometimes the crankcase would not clear the back of the lorry so all hands were required to lift the bottom ends of skids to clear, not exactly the method of modern car manufacturers. I probably handled 90 per cent of all Bugattis ariving at Brixton in this manner. In the early years, bodies were made for these chassis in England and very good some of them were.

A few words about Colonel Sorel, DSO. His early days were connected with cars of the pioneer era, de Dietrich being one of them, and any person who visited Brixton may remember the several drawings on the wall of his office showing racing cars during the period 1890–1904 with W. Sorel at the wheel. It was during this period that the first association with E. Bugatti was made. During the entire period I worked at Brixton I can happily say I never once knew Colonel Sorel to lose his temper and all his dealings with staff and customers were most courteous and helpful.

(H.E. Bouldin, 1978.)

And:

(from the *Automotor Journal*, 4 March 1926)

Colonel W.L. Sorel has fine premises, a good and representative stock, and for adjustments, overhauls, repairs or tuning he has a staff recruited from Molsheim – a great point, this, because of late years there have been so many selfstyled 'Bugatti specialists' who were nothing of the sort. Any car which is inclined to be 'quick' creates its own 'specialists', at times with most direful consequences, because a fastish car which has been 'improved' by such people can in quite a few seasons be reduced to a sorry wreck, so many folk knowing so much more about Bugattis even than M. Ettore Bugatti himself.

Even as late as 1921, people stared with interest at every Bugatti they met. Today Bugatti-users are no longer embarrassed by this degree of interest on the part of other road-users, and there are almost as many lady owner-drivers as those of the other persuasion, simply because, although this car is so fast, it has latterly become just as easy to maintain as anything else of comparable performance. It has always, of course, been a very economical little machine to run. When I first had one it was rather prone to oil up if one ran the engine too slowly. To use fourth speed at less than 20 mph was not good for it, because it had been designed and built for faster work. I have changed four plugs in ten miles, on my first; but the lubrication system was very drastically redesigned in 1922, and since then people who have used really good and suitable plugs, like Bosch or KLG, have been quite free from the only (or at least the main) crab even of the earlier models.

It cannot too often be said that all 'quick' cars are much better when run as their designers intended them to be run than when fitted with all sorts of weird devices intended to improve upon nature. One has to be very clever indeed to show M. Ettore Bugatti how to get better than the best out of his own motorcars, and I would counsel anybody who has anything but a perfectly satisfactory Bugatti to get in touch at once with Colonel Sorel, in Brixton Road. Very little and inexpensive things will in some cases make very large differences in the behaviour of a car, but those little things are best done by somebody who really does know what he is doing. The village blacksmith, or his modern prototype, has great virtues, but unfortunately he does not know everything, and that is where he can slip up now and again, especially in playing with mechanism of the delicacy and beauty of that inside the little box on top of a Bugatti cylinder-block!

The Molsheim spares*

WE LIKE TO think that 50 years from now Bugatti Club members will be as interested in what happened in 1978 as we are in what happened in 1928 when the first rumblings of the Bugatti owners in England started to take place, leading to the formation of our Club at the end of 1929. We can be forgiven, and maybe even thanked later, for recording for posterity exactly how it came about that the club took over the residual spares from Molsheim. I have to apologise in advance for the story being a bit personalized. It will become apparent why later.

Many of us visited Molsheim in the 1960s when François Seyfried was in charge of Bugatti spares. There was an enormous stock of bits, even cylinder blocks for pre-1914 8 valve cars, and Brescias, all from before the 1939 war, and which I believe had remained tucked away even during the Trippel days of wartime occupation. After all why not – did not spares lie in stores all over the world? Why would any occupying power bother with such stuff. Some material, especially gears and 57 parts were made in the 1950s but are still genuine Bugatti bits.

I remember many happy hours spent in the stores in the period 1956–66, literally scrounging bits from Seyfried and buying Brescia cylinder blocks for the equivalent of £20. But then the end of Bugatti as we know it came with the Hispano take over, the Schlumpf affair and the clearing out of all the historic cars in their collection, and indeed all the pre-war patterns for the various castings. The stock of spares ran down rapidly as the knowledgeable bought bits and such specialists as Raymond Jones bought large amounts of bits, evidently for his own stock.

Then about 1969–70 Schlumpf brought a court case against the works claiming that a large amount of chromium plating done by them on the restoration of many of his Bugatti collection was improperly done, since rust became apparent; he demanded that the work should be redone, entirely at the works expense – not just replating the parts but removing them from the cars and refitting them. This was clearly a bit of a disaster to the works, who if the case had been lost would have been faced with enormous costs.

In the end Schlumpf had been kicked out of France before the case was settled and as far as I know it is now in suspense. However, Surrel, the Works Director at the time – I think 1969 or 1970 – decided to stop selling the spares, thinking no doubt that this residue of bits might be a weapon in some final settlement with Schlumpf. So spares sales stopped, letters were more or less unanswered and visitors were discouraged. Then François Seyfried died, and

* from *Bugantics*, Vol 41, No. 2, 1978

the stocks were moved twice, each time getting more and more muddled. 'Tony' the storekeeper retired, and by 1975 no one had much idea of what was what.

Somewhere around the end of 1971 I went to Molsheim and found out that it was still possible for a few people whom they knew (Bart Loyens, myself and obviously others) to get into the stores and make odd purchases. In subsequent years one maintained contact out of interest and reminded Surrel and later his successor Droesch, that when Hispano-Suiza in Paris had ceased to be interested in their cars they handed over the residue of their spares, on a sale-or-return basis, to Artic-Auto in Courbevois or wherever.

Some three years ago Droesch told me that he was trying to get agreement to dispose of the spares and promised that the B.O.C. would be consulted; I confirmed our interest in writing.

I now have to digress and say that many years ago – in 1939 in fact – I joined, as No. 2 employee, a company who took a licence of the French Messier Company, the pioneer company in retractable aircraft landing gear in Europe. (c.f. Bendix in USA, and later Dowty in the UK.) I was with them for several years. By a strange trick of fate, Bugatti is now merged with Messier and Hispano, and so I am well known to the new bosses in Paris. This made certain that when the works eventually decided to unload their spares they would keep in touch with the BOC via me, and this is in fact what happened in mid-1977. I do not know exactly whom else they contacted, other than Bart Loyens – the possibilities must have been very limited – but we got a letter in June 1977 proposing that we should buy the stock for the princely sum of 450,000 FF (£55,000 or $110,000 odd!) This of course was ridiculous, but, having said that, Barry Price and I went over and spent two days going through the whole stock, 3,000 square metres of shelving, making a rough stock list of what was there. There were no store records available and in fact our list, which we sent them, is the only list available so far.

We concluded that the ultimate sale value of the stock was around £20,000 if you were lucky, mainly as there was a lot of 57 stuff. Molsheim seemed to think that the value was much higher as people would buy obsolete bits as mementos (we agreed, but not for much!)

Anyway, to cut a long story short, we had meetings in Paris, and explained our view point, and made a rough estimate of the cost of selling – stores, store keeping, cataloguing and so on, to say nothing of finance charges – and we eventually agreed that our costs over 4 years would be 100,000 francs, that we should pay down 100,000 francs and that we should then share proceeds beyond 200,000 francs (£22,000). This was agreed amicably and the club managed to find from its resources the £11,000 to make the initial payment. Some council members guaranteed about half of this sum, because to be fair it did involve a bit of a risk, notwithstanding the views of a few died-in-the-wool Bugattistes like Barry Price and myself. Some of you will know that the club has benefited by substantial legacies from several members, and this really explains where the money comes from – in any event not from members subscription income. Anyway at the moment of writing there does not seem to be much doubt that the Club will get its direct investment back; whether we ever achieve sales over £22,000 remains to be seen as a lot of the stock is unbalanced. For every new and every saleable T57 camshaft, there are boxes of bits which no one wants except as souvenirs at souvenir price. The Contract with the French Company, now called Messier-Hispano-Bugatti, is interesting and similar to what was done with another organization in Paris when they handed over the residue of Hispano diesels. The Club has a 'concession', title to the parts remaining with the French until we sell a part, when it becomes the property of the owner. The reason no doubt is to make sure that we continue to act responsibly, and to avoid them being accused of handing over property of what after all is a French nationally owned company to a mad bunch of Englishmen! And we for our part are very happy to demonstrate that we are the most capable organization to handle such an unusual deal.

So the long term problem is really what to do with the stuff which does not go quickly, where to keep it and who will look after it. But we don't have to worry about this for sometime. Meanwhile you have one last chance to stock up with genuine Molsheim parts.

We are trying to allocate parts to Bugatti owners as fairly as possible although it is up to them to ask or push a bit and not to expect bits in short supply to be available in a years time when they want them. And, as almost all work is being done by voluntary help we expect to avoid a lot of paper work, bills rendered and so on.

As for pricing, obviously we have to have a three way balance, being fair to members, fair to the Molsheim Works and fair to the Club which has taken the risk. Three of us do the judging and set price levels undoubtedly well below what it would cost you to make individual parts, but equally noting the successful Club spare parts scheme for common items, where the prices are very fair. Some parts are in such quantity that we would rather sell the lot cheaply than a few at their true replacement price. The best (or is it worst!) example is the ring of steel (bullring we call it) on the spare wheel strap on a GP car. We have a few hundred! But to make one and plate it would cost a lot of money. So get one from us for your mantelpiece at a nominal price!

H.G.C

Schlumpf

THE SAGA of the Schlumpf collection and its museum has been well documented in recent years. It remains an extraordinary story, of profit and loss, megalomania, of contented sellers and a happy buyer with a large purse, of an autocratic 'patron', of over-expansion of a textile industry killed off by an oil-crisis, and now a superb French National Museum.

The story itself is best told in:

The Schlumpf Obsession, by Denis Jenkinson and Peter Verstappen, Hamlyn 1977.
The Schlumpf Automobile Collection, edited by Halwart Schrader, (3 languages) Schrader, Munich 1977.
L'Affaire Schlumpf, by F. Lafon and Elisabeth Lambert, (in French only), Bueb & Reumaux, Mulhouse 1982.

The first two books tell the story of the crash, and formation of the Museum just before it. The later one tells much more of the inner detail leading to the crash, from much excellent research into the local events, Schlumpf's own background, and views the whole saga from a local point of view.

The brief history of the creation of the National Museum out of the Schlumpf collection can be summarized as follows:

1971	Schlumpf amalgamates most of the textile spinning factories in Alsace into a large combine.
1976	Hans and Fritz Schlumpf, the two brothers, and their firm, become bankrupt.
March 1977 – March 1979	The Museum is occupied by the workers of the bankrupt company.
April 1978	The collection classified by a French Government decree as an 'Historic Monument'.

Two views of the Schlumpf museum, shortly after occupation by the workmen in 1977, showing the extraordinary wealth of Bugatti cars therein, and the 800 lamps illuminated, copied from those on the Alexander III bridge over the Seine in Paris.

March 1981	An Association for the National Automobile Museum of Mulhouse formed, with as partners: Town of Mulhouse Dept of Upper Rhine Mulhouse Chamber of Commerce Auto Club of France Panhard Company Paris Auto Salon Committee
April 1981	Legal Authorization for the collection to be sold to the Association.
October 1981 – December 1982	Management Company set up to run the Museum. Patrons: Town of Mulhouse Dept of Upper Rhine Chamber of Commerce Local Tourist Associations Local Economic Council Mulhouse Museum Authorities President of Association: The Mayor of Mulhouse
April 1982	Director appointed
10 July 1982	Museum opens

The story of how Schlumpf came to make his collection, particularly his 120 or more Bugattis, is an extraordinary one. He had owned a 35B and driven it in the Ballon d'Alsace hill climb in the early 1930s. His name first cropped up when compiling the Bugatti Register about 1960, François Seyfried at the factory producing a list of about 20 Bugattis which Schlumpf had by then collected. Correspondence started about these, friendly enough, and it was obvious that if you were asked to help sell a Bugatti, you could in all fairness suggest an approach to Schlumpf. Indeed a friend in Dublin came into this category and wanted to dispose of a 1920 Silver Ghost (armoured car) chassis which would still start by moving the ignition advance lever, an air-cooled Franklin, a fine Isotta-Fraschini, and a rare piece, a Scott Sociable. He was more interested in selling the lot at one time and Schlumpf readily agreed prices – the R.R. chassis went for £100! Both parties were happy!

Then an owner of a 57S could not find a buyer at a sensible price (£1,200 in 1961!), and Schlumpf got another one! Now came the extraordinary transfer from the USA to Schlumpf! In 1962 Mr John Shakespeare wrote to the BOC stating that he wanted to sell his 28 Bugattis for what he had paid for them, around $105,000, The collection was at the time a very large and important one, including a Royale! No one could be found who wanted *twenty-eight* Bugatti's and the seller was not interested in individual sales. So Schlumpf was written to. A telegram came in reply. 'Collection Shakespeare interests me telegraph him to reserve letter follows'! A letter was soon received confirming the telegram and arguing that $105,000 was too much (of course!) and that $70,000 was reasonable. Then immediately following came a second letter wanting any spares and demanding full details of the cars' 'colours, leather, photographs. . . .'!

What the final price which was agreed is not known but no doubt less than $100,000, a fair and sensible figure for the period. Schlumpf now 'had the bit between his teeth'! When the BOC Bugatti Register came out, everyone in it was written to to see if the car would be sold. Two entries, two separate letters: three cars, three letters and so on! And the point can be made that a substantial number of owners, probably over 50 accepted the good prices offered.

All this took place while cars were stored in part of the wool-spinning factory at Malmerspach, and the Bugattis were being overhauled in the Repair Shop at the Bugatti factory at Molsheim.

During a visit to Schlumpf in 1971 in response to a question why did he not set up a Museum, he answered, 'I am today 65 years of age, I still have 35 years to enjoy my cars!'

Shortly afterwards, on 24 June 1971 a circular was issued by Schlumpf from his main factory, the 'Filature de Laine Peignée de Malmerspach' announcing an amalgamation with the other main Alsatian textile firm 'Gluck & Co' of Mulhouse. A final paragraph reads:

'Thus is realized a plan conceived by Fritz and Hans Schlumpf some 34 years ago, to acquire, possess and dominate the worsted spinning industry of Alsace, and the objective attained that they have mapped out, assigned and set themselves, and this by will, stubbornness, endurance, perseverance, courage, with difficulty, care and hard work.' The merger with Gluck soon brought industrial unrest from wage differentials, and active strife with the main Union involved, who were keeping a close eye on what Schlumpf was doing with his car collection.

By 1973 an oil crisis had brought financial trouble to the world and Europe's textile industry. Soon Schlumpf's factories went into recession, then bankruptcy, the workers occupied the shops and his museum, which indeed was being built but not yet completed, Schlumpf himself fleeing to Switzerland, his home country, to avoid arrest.

BUGATTI

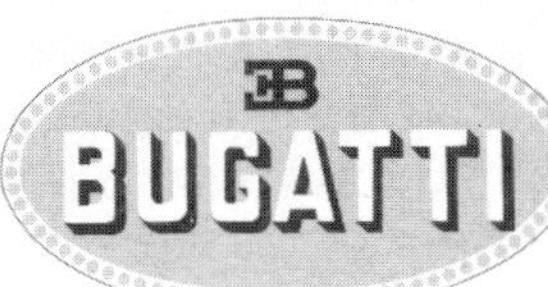

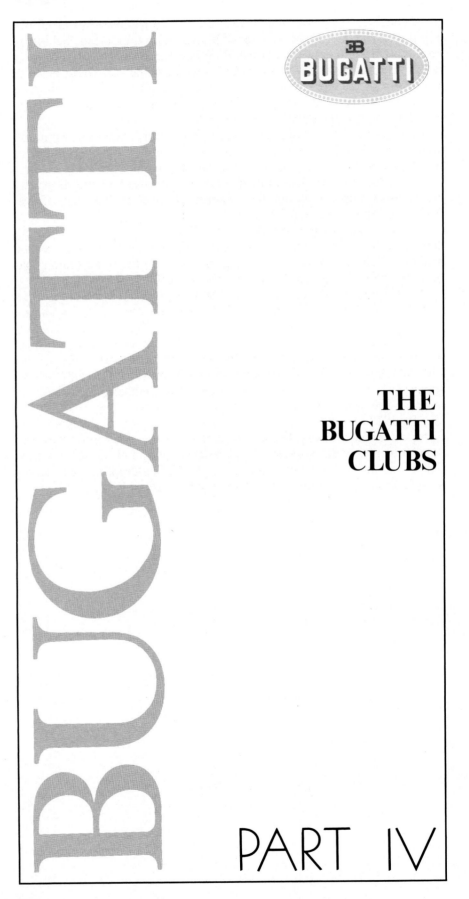

THE BUGATTI CLUBS

PART IV

The Bugatti Owners' Club

IF THE BUGATTI Owners' Club can claim to have started it all in 1929, others have followed in Holland, America and Germany – we even have one in France, two in fact now! These Clubs fan the flames of Bugatti's immortal glory, foster the enjoyment of the marque and generally provide a lot of pleasure to their many members.

Mr Eric Giles recounted the beginnings of the BOC in the Silver Jubilee issue of *Bugantics*, 17, 1 February 1954.

The credit for the idea of forming a Bugatti Club in Britain belongs to one D.B. Madeley by name. He has another claim to fame because he is the only person we have ever known or heard of who owned a Crossley-Bugatti – the early Brescia model made in this country just after the 1914–18 war by the Crossley car people under licence from Bugatti.

I believe he started his ball rolling by writing to the motor press suggesting the formation of a Club for Bugatti enthusiasts and as a result of this, one evening way back in 1929, three people met over a glass of beer – two pipe smokers and one using a cigarette holder – and, as you know from the familiar picture at the beginning of every copy of Bugantics, out of the smoke of that meeting the Club was born. The three people? One pipe, of course, belonged to Madeley, the second belonged to Colonel Giles and the cigarette holder to T. Ambrose Varley.

At that time, probably as a result of Madeley's letter to the press, another little group, headed by the late Dr Ewan, got together with the same object in view. Colonel Giles attended one of these meetings to see whether the two groups could not amalgamate, but their ideas were so different from ours that it proved impossible and we immediately registed the name 'Bugatti Owners' Club Ltd' so as to prevent anyone else using the name Bugatti.

So the Club was formed and the first meeting was held at Colonel Giles' house in Regent's Park. Varley became the first Hon. Secretary, Madeley was made Hon. Treasurer and a Committee (which we call a Council) was formed with Colonel Giles as Chairman.

Thus Madeley was No. 1 on the Club Register, Varley No. 2, Colonel Giles No. 3, I was No. 4, J.R. Crouch No. 5, J. Lemon Burton No. 6, K.W. Bear No. 7, H.J. Morris No. 8, followed by G.P. Powles, F.J. Fielding and J.D. Jevons.

Varley's tenure as Secretary was rather short-lived as he suddenly disappeared in rather curious circumstances and I remember rushing down to his

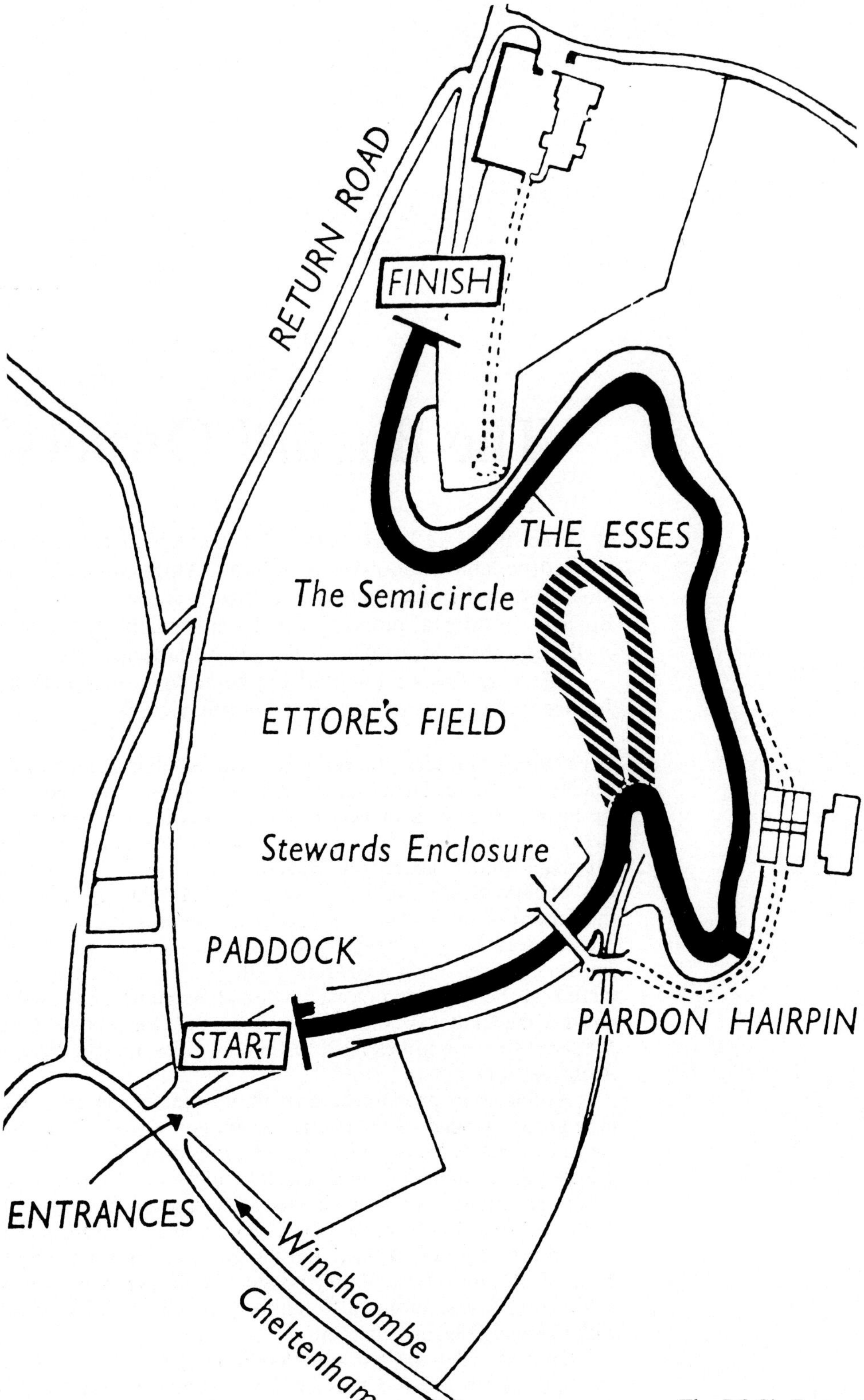

RETURN ROAD
FINISH
THE ESSES
The Semicircle
ETTORE'S FIELD
Stewards Enclosure
PADDOCK
PARDON HAIRPIN
START
ENTRANCES
Winchcombe
Cheltenham

The BOC's Prescott hill-climb course.

house to retrieve the Club's books etc, before they also vanished. Bear then took over the Hon. Secretaryship and I became Trials Secretary until Bear relinquished his job and I took over as Hon. Secretary and Treasurer on January 1932.

Early in those days Earl Howe joined us and became our first President, followed by Malcolm Campbell as Vice-President, and not long after we received official recognition from Molsheim when Ettore himself gave us his blessing by joining the Club and becoming our first Patron.

This set-up remained in being for many years during which time the only changes were in certain members of the Council.

Finally I resigned as Secretary in 1946 and was elected Chairman in place of Colonel Giles who became Vice-President, a position which I held until the AGM of 1951, when I resigned from the Council and was elected President after Earl Howe had been made Patron.

After having served on the Competitions Committee for some time, and later on the Council, our present dynamic Chairman then really came into the picture and all present-day members know full well how much he has done for the Club.

No history of the Club could possibly be complete without a reference to *Bugantics* and its various Editors because those who are lucky enough to have a complete set (and there are very few) have in their possession a complete record of the Club and its doings.

The first Editor was Madeley, who successfully launched the first issue in June 1931, and kept it going from strength to strength until J.S. Steele took over in August 1932.

Steele did a wonderful job and ran it right up to November 1935, when Colonel Giles took over, and kept it going so successfully until Peter Hampton relieved him of the burden in December 1948.

And now, with this Jubilee Number we very reluctantly say farewell to him as Editor after what has undoubtedly been the most successful period in the whole history of this famous little book.

Only those who have had anything to do with the preparation of *Bugantics* can have any conception of the terrific amount of work and thought which has been put into the production of this unique publication over the past 23 years.

In 1937 (in order to provide themselves with a hill-climb course) the Bugatti Owners' Club purchased the estate of Prescott House, which lies in the beautiful country close to Cleeve Hill. It is about five miles from Cheltenham, in Gloucestershire, and ninety miles from London. The house is a delightful one, built of Cotswold stone and owned, up to 1871, by the Earl of Ellenborough. In the grounds will be found the lovely wrought-iron gates put up in memory of the late Ettore Bugatti and his elder son, the late Jean Bugatti.

The original course was roughly 1,000 yards long with an average gradient of 1 in 20, cars attacking the hill singly and being timed electrically. The record for the original course stands to Martyn Griffiths in a Pilbeam at 32·73 sec (June 1986). The present record on the longer course of 1127 yards is held by Martin Bolsover in another Pilbeam in 38·81 sec (September 1983). The Bugatti record on this course is held by Ivan Dutton in a Type 51 in 53·20 sec (September 1985). While the course is virtually unchanged the surface has been improved, and the modern racing machine benefits enormously from the latest tyre compounds and construction. Bugatti's are raced on the original 500 × 19 in racing covers, fortunately still available from Dunlop.

Approximately 5 meetings are held each year.

The American Bugatti Club

THE BACKGROUND to the formation of this Club is best told from the following extract from the Club Journal *Pur-Sang*, 1, 1, 1960:

In the late 1920s and the early 1930s, there were approximately seven Bugattis in the Los Angeles area, and all of the owners more or less knew each other. Several picnics took place, and there was talk of forming a US Bugatti Club, but, as usual, nothing came of it except informal meetings and unorganized tours to such places as Lake Arrowhead and Muroc Dry Lake. It was a pleasure then to be able to drive a Grand Prix model on the streets without full road equipment, and if the local policia took exception, well they were only equipped with Dodge 4's and underpowered Buicks (and no radios), so it was really great sport to make a run for it.

At this time Bugattis were also being raced on the East Coast by such long-time enthusiasts as George Rand, Dick Wharton and Walter Gerner, to name but a few. The racing activities of the marque at Indianapolis and Vanderbilt speedways during this period have largely been overlooked or forgotten. Later in the 1930s, Bugatti activity in this locality almost died out, and there appeared to be little interest in these cars; to such an extent that Grand Prix models and excellent Type 38s and 57s were offered for sale for a few hundred dollars, often with no takers. From 1940 to 1950, with World War II intervening, there was no interest at all in this area.

Within the last six years, a number of ardent enthusiasts began to import Bugattis in appreciable quantities and, owing to this movement, interest began to freshen. Occasionally a Bugatti would be shown at a Concourse, and, thanks to Mr Milton Roth, a Type 35C and Type 55 were shown at the Los Angeles Auto Show in 1955. This activity, plus the kind assistance of John Bond of *Road and Track* who has featured Bugattis several times in his publication, including Bob Day's and Al Crundall's Type 51As, John Caperton's Type 50, and Lucille Phillips' Type 49, has done much to stimulate interest in the marque.

On 15 October 1958 a local group of owners organized a picnic which took place in Arroyo Seco park, in South Pasadena. This was attended by 17 Bugattis and their owners. A report and pictures of this gathering was published in the February 1959 issue of *Road and Track*. Although this event was a great success, the first picnic held at Fred Treat's estate was even more so, and we were now assured that we must form our own Club. After several informal gatherings we finally decided to 'give it a go' and on 10 February 1960 a meeting was held to select officers and set dues, and to finalize the name of the Club.

Bugatti Club Nederland*

IT WAS BACK IN OCTOBER 1955 that, during a veteran car rally organized by the now famous Pionier Automobielen Club, five Bugatti owners met each other, virtually for the first time in their lives, each of them driving a well preserved specimen of 'le pur-sang de l'automobile'. The city of Utrecht was selected as rallying place and there, before the start of a joint drive through beautiful country towards the Zandvoort-race track as a finishing point, one had the opportunity of inspecting at leisure a Type 37A, a mighty looking Type 43, two Types 40 and another Type 43 carrosserie-roadster. In the evening of that memorable day of motoring, during dinner at Zandvoort, the five Bugatti owners† spontaneously decided to form their own club which is now well known as the Bugatti Club Nederland consisting of some 40 members and totalling 36 Bugatti cars.

The Dutch are notorious individualists and especially when driving their always new looking mass-production vehicles of any European or American make on the well maintained roads of their small country most of them behave as if alone in the world. Bearing this in mind the reader will readily appreciate the fact, that, long before there was any sign of the birth of a BCN, it was quite an event when two Dutchmen driving their 'pur-sangs' met each other by chance, each of them being convinced he was driving the one and only Bugatti in the country.

The BCN brought all owners of Bugatti together and what a variety of individuals they turned out to be! A dentist, a musician, a salesman, a printer, an industrial designer, a medical student, a psychiatrist, an automobile engineer, a ship owner, an oil specialist, an importer of timber, a banker, a farmer; in short, really every conceivable profession seems to be represented in this Club. All these people had become at some stage in their lives ardent lovers of 'la marque', fascinated by the pecularities, effectiveness, simplicity and beauty of design, intent on experiencing over and over again this automobile's extreme road worthiness, the strange feeling it gives one that it has a mysterious life and a will of its own, that with a driver's skill and quick reaction it will do the impossible and perform magnificently under any road and weather conditions. Add to these qualities the symphony of mechanical sound plus that very particular exhaust note and there one has a true picture of Ettore Bugatti's automobile which united all these different people in the BCN.

In 1958 the BCN successfully organized the Grand Rally International Ermenonville – Le Mans which, amongst others, lead to the Bad Honnef Rally, so well organized by the German Bugatti Club in 1960.

* Communicated by Mr W.M. Pieters 7 April 1961

† Founders: B. Laming, W.M. Pieters, van Ramshorst, G.F.M.F. Prick, R. Andersen.

Bugatti-Club Deutschland

THE GERMAN BUGATTI Club was founded by Kurt Kieffer on the occasion of the *Grosser Pries von Deutschland* (Grand Prix of Germany) at the Nürburgring on 4 August 1956. Mr Kieffer was a Bugatti enthusist of long standing (owner of a Type 35B from 1931 until 1937 and from then up to now of a T49).

The Club consisted at first of some twenty Bugatti owners, ten former Bugatti racing motorists, another twenty enthusiasts for the car and three owners from Luxembourg, over fifty in all. There is no subscription fee to the Club; its offices are at Am Reichenberg 17 in Bad Honnef (Rhein).

The aims of the *Bugatti-Club Deutschland* are the maintenance of the Bugatti tradition, the promotion of comradeship amongst the Bugatti drivers and mutual support in all Bugatti affairs as well as the care of the Bugattis still existing. Members are under the obligation not to trade with Bugattis. Louis Chiron and Maurice Trintignant became Honorary Members.

Since 1950 the '*Bugattisten*' have met every year on the Nürburgring during the *Grosser Pries von Deutschland.* In addition the *Bugatti-Club Deutschland* have organized, at Bad Honnef in 1960 and at Diez (Lahn) in 1962, international Bugatti meetings. These were well attended and made a lasting impression on everyone attending of the pleasure and good fellowship among owners of these vintage cars.

Club Bugatti France

A CLUB FOR BUGATTI enthusiasts was founded in 1967 under the title *Club des Proprietaires de Bugatti.* The foundation date was 31 October 1967, and the original principals were Paul Badré, Pierre Bardinon, Wladimir Granoff, Jess Pourret and Philippe Vernholes, the first President being Paul Badré.

In the 1970s the Club was associated with Ferrari owners, but later the two branches split amicably.

For several years the Club, under the enthusiastic leadership of Jess Pourret and Phillipe and Marie-André Vernholes ran very successful International Bugatti rallies in several parts of France.

Recently they have maintained excellent relationship with the club *Enthousiastes Bugatti Alsace* based in Molsheim, whose mainstay is Paul Kestler, and whose President is Roland Wagner.

APPENDICES

Appendix 1

Leading particulars of Bugatti Cars

(For fuller data and engine adjustments see the Data Book published by the Bugatti Owners' Club.)

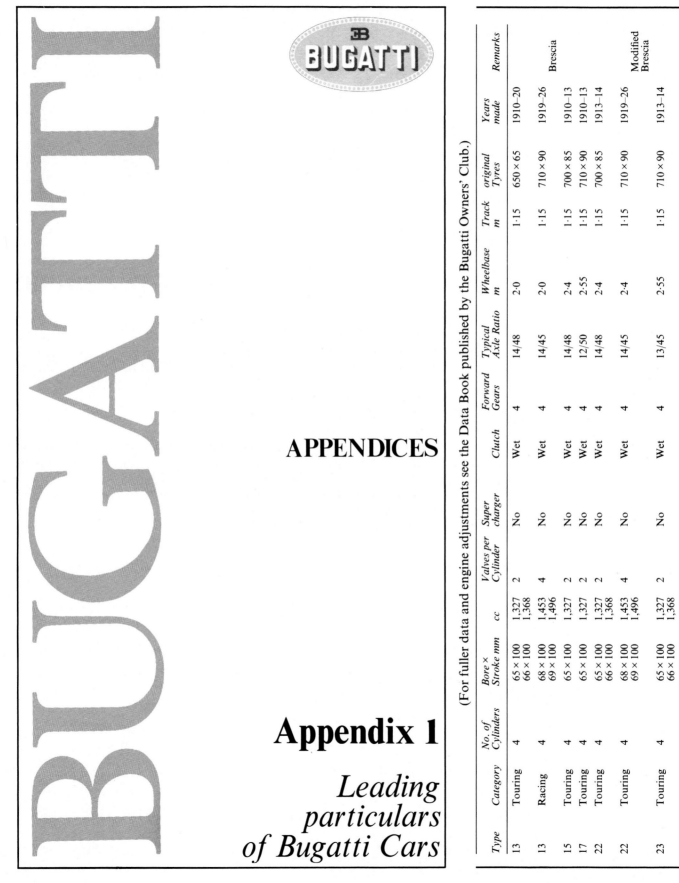

Type	*Category*	*No. of Cylinders*	*Bore × Stroke mm*	*cc*	*Valves per Cylinder*	*Super charger*	*Clutch*	*Forward Gears*	*Typical Axle Ratio*	*Wheelbase m*	*Track m*	*original Tyres*	*Years made*	*Remarks*
13	Touring	4	65 × 100 66 × 100	1,327 1,368	2	No	Wet	4	14/48	2·0	1·15	650 × 65	1910–20	
13	Racing	4	68 × 100 69 × 100	1,453 1,496	4	No	Wet	4	14/45	2·0	1·15	710 × 90	1919–26	Brescia
15	Touring	4	65 × 100	1,327	2	No	Wet	4	14/48	2·4	1·15	700 × 85	1910–13	
17	Touring	4	65 × 100	1,327	2	No	Wet	4	12/50	2·55	1·15	710 × 90	1910–13	
22	Touring	4	65 × 100 66 × 100	1,327 1,368	2	No	Wet	4	14/48	2·4	1·15	700 × 85	1913–14	
22	Touring	4	68 × 100 69 × 100	1,453 1,496	4	No	Wet	4	14/45	2·4	1·15	710 × 90	1919–26	Modified Brescia
23	Touring	4	65 × 100 66 × 100	1,327 1,368	2	No	Wet	4	13/45	2·55	1·15	710 × 90	1913–14	
23	Touring	4	68 × 100 69 × 100	1,453 1,496	4	No	Wet	4	13/45	2·55	1·15	710 × 90	1919–26	Modified

30	Touring	8	60 × 88	1,991	3	No	Wet	4	12/50	2·85	1.2	765 × 105	1922–6	
35	GP	8	60 × 88	1,991	3	No	Wet	4	14/54	2·4	1·2	710 × 90	1924–30	Rol. bgs
35A	Sport	8	60 × 88	1,991	3	No	Wet	4	13/54	2·4	1·2	710 × 90	1926–30	Plain bearings
35B	GP	8	60 × 100	2,262	3	Yes	Wet	4	14/54	2·4	1·2	28 × 4·95	1927–30	Rol. bgs
35C	GP	8	60 × 88	1,991	3	Yes	Wet	4	14/54	2·4	1·2	28 × 4·95	1927–30	Rol. bgs
35T	GP	8	60 × 100	2,262	3	No	Wet	4	14/54	2·4	1·2	28 × 4·95	1927–30	Rol. bgs
37	Sport	4	69 × 100	1,496	3	No	Wet	4	14/54	2·4	1·2	27 × 4·40	1926–30	
37A	GP	4	69 × 100	1,498	3	Yes	Wet	4	14/54	2·4	1·2	27 × 4·40	1927–30	
38	Touring	8	60 × 88	1,991	3	No	Wet	4	12/56	3·12	1·25	28 × 4·95	1926–7	
38A	Sport	8	60 × 88	1,991	3	Yes	Wet	4	12/56	3·12	1·25	28 × 4·95	1927	
39	GP	8	60 × 66	1,493	3	No	Wet	4	13/54	2·4	1·2	28 × 4·95	1926–9	Rol. bgs
39A	GP	8	60 × 66	1.493	3	Yes	Wet	4	13/54	2·4	1·2	28 × 4·95	1926–9	Rol. bgs
40	Touring	4	69 × 100	1,496	3	No	Wet	4	12/56	2·56/2·71	1·2	27 × 4·40	1926–30	
40A	Touring	4	72 × 100	1,623	3	No	Wet	4	12/56	2·71	1·2	27 × 4·40	1930	
41	Touring	8	125 × 130	12,763	3	No	Wet	3	15/54	4·3	1·6	6·75 × 36	1929–33	Royale
43/43A	Gr. Sport	8	60 × 100	2,262	3	Yes	Wet	4	13/54	2·97	1·25	28 × 4·95	1927–31	Rol. bgs
44	Touring	8	69 × 100	2,991	3	No	Wet	4	12/50	3·12	1·25	28 × 4·95	1927–30	
45	GP	16	60 × 84	3,801	3	Yes	Wet	4	15/42	2·6	1·25	28 × 4·75	1929–30	Rol. bgs
46	Touring	8	81 × 130	5,360	3	No	Wet	3	12/47	3·5	1·4	32 × 6	1929–36	
46S	Touring	8	81 × 130	5,360	3	Yes	Wet	3	12/47	3·5	1·4	32 × 6	1931–6	
47	Gr. Sport	16	60 × 66	2,986	3	Yes	Wet	4	13/54	2·75	1·25	28 × 4·75	1929–30	Rol. bgs
49	Touring	8	72 × 100	3,257	3	No	Dry	4	12/50	3·12/3·22	1·25	28 × 5·25	1930–34	
50	Sport	8	86 × 107	4,972	2	Yes	Dry	3	14/54	3·1/3·5	1·4	6·50 × 20	1930–4	
51	GP	8	60 × 100	2,262	2	Yes	Wet	4	15/54	2·4	1·2	28 × 5	1931–5	Rol. bgs
51A	GP	8	60 × 66	1,493	2	Yes	Wet	4	14/54	2·4	1·2	28 × 5	1931–5	Rol. bgs
51C	GP	8	60 × 88	1,991	2	Yes	Wet	4	15/54	2·4	1·2	28 × 5	1931–35	Rol. bgs
53	GP	8	86 × 107	4,972	2	Yes	Dry	4	14/42	2·6	1·25	28 × 5	1932	FWD
54	GP	8	86 × 107	4,972	2	Yes	Dry	3	13/45	2·75	1·35	29 × 5	1931–4	
55	Super Sport	8	60 × 100	2,262	2	Yes	Dry	4	13/54	2·75	1·25	28 × 4·75	1932–5	
57	Touring	8	72 × 100	3,257	2	No	Dry	4	11/46	3·3	1·35	5·50 × 18	1934–40	
57C	Touring	8	72 × 100	3,257	2	Yes	Dry	4	11/46	3·3	1·35	5·50 × 18	1937–40	
57S	Touring	8	72 × 100	3,257	2	No	Dry	4	11/46	2·98	1·35	5·50 × 18F 6·00 × 18R	1936–8	
57SC	Touring	8	72 × 100	3,257	2	Yes	Dry	4	11/46	2·98	1·35	5·50 × 18F 6·00 × 18R	1937–8	
57S45	Racing	8	72 × 107	3,257	2	Yes	Dry	4		2·68	1·35	5·50 × 19F 6·50 × 19R	1936–8	
59	GP	8	72 × 100	3,257	2	Yes	Dry	4		2·6	1·25	5·50 × 19	1934–6	Double reduction
64	Touring	8	84 × 100	4,432	2	No	Dry	4		3·3	1·35		1940	
68	Touring	4	48·5 × 50	369	4	Yes							1942	
73A	Sport	4	76 × 82	1,488	3	Yes				2·6	1·26	165 × 400	1947	
73C	GP	4	76 × 82	1,488	4	Yes				2·4	1·2		1947	
101	Touring	8	72 × 100	3.257	2	No	Dry	4	11/46	3·3	1·35	6·00 × 17	1951	
101C		8	72 × 100	3,257	2	Yes	Dry	4	11/46	3·3	1·35	6·00 × 17	1951	

Appendix 2

Restorations and its problems

WHEN THIS book first came out in 1963 it followed a period of intense debate on the 'correct' method of restoring a Bugatti. What most considered to be over-restoration had occurred in the USA and occasionally in Britain, all steel and bronze parts being chrome plated, wire wheels chromed, and racing bodies polished bright.

Many, indeed most, owners abhorred such practice, especially the use of chrome plating, the ultimate sin being to plate the beautiful nickel-silver of the radiator shell of pre-T57 cars, to avoid the continual polishing that they demand (after every rain storm in the case of smog-laden atmospheres in modern cities!)

In 1963 it was still possible to obtain spare parts from Molsheim, thus 'original' ones. Modern equivalents had to be accepted for such items as tyres, but 19 in. were still being produced.

As Molsheim stock dwindled, so production of replica parts began. By about 1970 the Bugatti Owners Club began to produce parts to original drawings and others were able to supply particular items such as gears. A major development by the Club was the production of replacement cylinder blocks, when Molsheim stock was depleted, culminating in the Club taking over the patterns for the T57 block.

While this production of spare parts has undoubtedly kept many a car on the road, and several T35s and 51s still racing, it has inevitably encouraged the re-creation of cars, some legitimately around incomplete Molsheim-built frames, and unfortunately some as replica frames, even a few with effectively no original parts in them.

No one would begrudge someone building up a 'new' Bugatti, indeed Ettore might take it as a compliment were he with us, if it were done properly *and did not purport to be other than it was.*

Today we may be able to expand a few 'rules' or words of advice to the new Bugatti owner!

1. Quality of workmanship at Molsheim was the tradition: do the job right with the right tools, and a clean bench.
2. You will get more pleasure from a car more nearly as it was when it left the factory, than in 'improving' it, with wider tyres,

multiple carburettors, telescopic shock absorbers, and so on: the cars are now out-classed and it is not worth trying to squeeze the lost ounce of performance from a car at the risk of expensive noise. On the other hand a Bugatti was built to be driven, not pottered about in nervously!

3. Some parts, especially electrical items, are virtually unobtainable and it has to be accepted that substitutions must be made.
4. Some modifications for road safety reasons may be obligatory, but this should not extend to hydraulic brake conversion on models not so originally fitted. Original lamps can be adapted for twin beam dipping.
5. As to finish: Bugatti cars of the Brescia or earlier types left the factory with the engines painted and comparatively poorly finished. The correct polish standard on T30 and later cars, as produced at Molsheim, was mottling or fine hand scraping on the visible parts of the dash, plain polishing on manifolds and such things as blower drive casings and blowers, an as-cast finish on parts not showing (eg lower crankcase, gearbox etc) and wavy scraper finish as on a lathe bed on camboxes and visible parts of the crankcase. Mottling on camboxes is definitely wrong. GP wheels were plain polished. All circular axles on early cars were polished and oiled, on later cars being nickel plated.

Index